DAILY JOY

DAILY JOY

A DEVOTIONAL FOR WOMEN

CROSSWAY®

WHEATON, ILLINOIS

Daily Joy: A Devotional for Women

Copyright © 2022 by Crossway

Published by Crossway
        1300 Crescent Street
        Wheaton, Illinois 60187

Cover design: Dan Farrell and Jordan Singer

First printing 2022

The daily devotionals were first published as part of the *ESV Women's Devotional Bible* (Crossway, 2014) and are reprinted by permission.

Printed in China

Hardcover ISBN: 978-1-4335-7986-8
ePub ISBN: 978-1-4335-8192-2
PDF ISBN: 978-1-4335-8190-8
Mobipocket ISBN: 978-1-4335-8191-5

Library of Congress Cataloging-in-Publication Data

Title: Daily joy : a devotional for women.
Description: Wheaton, Illinois : Crossway, 2022. | Includes bibliographical references and index.
Identifiers: LCCN 2021028876 (print) | LCCN 2021028877 (ebook) | ISBN 9781433579868 (hardcover) | ISBN 9781433581908 (pdf) | ISBN 9781433581915 (mobi) | ISBN 9781433581922 (epub)
Subjects: LCSH: Christian women—Religious life. | Devotional calendars.
Classification: LCC BV4527 .D2438 2022 (print) | LCC BV4527 (ebook) | DDC 242/.643—dc23
LC record available at https://lccn.loc.gov/2021028876
LC ebook record available at https://lccn.loc.gov/2021028877

Crossway is a publishing ministry of Good News Publishers.

RRDS		30	29	28	27	26	25	24	23	22
15	14	13	12	11	10	9	8	7	6	5	4	3	2	1

Contents

Introduction

THE READINGS IN *Daily Joy: A Devotional for Women* are carefully designed to connect important passages in the Bible with the heart and life of the reader in a gospel-rich, biblically responsible, and warmly accessible way. Simply put, these readings, which appeared earlier in the *ESV Women's Devotional Bible*, are intended to help God's people understand and apply his word in their everyday lives.

Every day of the year supplies a devotion written by a thoughtful voice in today's church on a given passage of Scripture. More than fifty women and men who have proven themselves to be faithful leaders and servants in the church have contributed readings. A complete list of the contributors appears following this introduction.

The devotional readings are not arranged topically or thematically, but rather are tied closely to the biblical texts on which they are based. At least one reading is drawn from every book of the Bible, and all are connected with the passages that most clearly capture the key themes in the various biblical books. If the 365 devotions are read consecutively throughout the year, along with the passages on which they are based, beginning in Genesis and ending in Revelation, by the end of the year the reader will have gained an extensive overview of Scripture and the history of salvation.

Whether read sequentially, occasionally, or as a supplement to the study of a particular book, the devotionals are designed to enhance your study of God's word by helping you reflect deeply on the biblical text and its meaning for us today.

Our prayer is that *Daily Joy* will nurture women in their relationship with the Lord by guiding them in daily, prayerful reading of the Bible and by deepening their understanding of Scripture through theologically rich devotional content that inspires heart-engaging application of God's word to all of life.

The Publisher

Contributors

ERIKA ALLEN
Director of Bible Editorial, Crossway

GEOFF ALLEN
Freelance writer

KRISTIE ANYABWILE
Pastor's wife, mom, speaker

CAROLYN ARENDS
Recording artist, author, speaker (www.carolynarends.com)

W. BRIAN AUCKER
Professor of Old Testament, Covenant Theological Seminary

MARY PATTON BAKER
Author, teacher

BRIAN BORGMAN
Founding Pastor, Grace Community Church, Minden, Nevada; author, *Feelings and Faith*

LYDIA BROWNBACK
Author, Bible teacher

MIKE BULLMORE
Senior Pastor, CrossWay Community Church, Bristol, Wisconsin

LAUREN CHANDLER
Musician, songwriter, author

BRYAN CHAPELL
Pastor Emeritus, Grace Presbyterian Church, Peoria, Illinois; President Emeritus, Covenant Theological Seminary; President, Unlimited Grace Media; leader, administrative committee of the Presbyterian Church in America

KATHLEEN CHAPELL
Wife and mother, musician, women's conference speaker

TASHA D. CHAPMAN
Professor of Educational Ministries, Covenant Theological Seminary

CAROL CORNISH
Bible teacher, author

DAN DORIANI
Professor of Biblical and Systematic Theology, Vice President at Large, Covenant Theological Seminary

ZACK ESWINE
Pastor, Riverside Church, Webster Groves, Missouri

ELYSE FITZPATRICK
Author and lecturer

KERI FOLMAR
Bible study author; teacher, United Christian Church of Dubai

GLORIA FURMAN
Author, *Glimpses of Grace* and *Treasuring Christ When Your Hands Are Full*

KRISTYN GETTY
Songwriter, recording artist

ELIZABETH W. D. GROVES
Lecturer, Westminster Theological Seminary; author

NANCY GUTHRIE
Bible teacher, author

MARY WILLSON HANNAH
Bible teacher; Director of Women in Ministry, Second Presbyterian Church, Memphis, Tennessee

HEATHER HOUSE
Freelance editor, writer

SUSAN HUNT
Author, former Director of Women's Ministry for the Presbyterian Church in America

BETHANY L. JENKINS
Vice president of media at the Veritas Forum, a contributor at the Gospel Coalition, and a senior fellow at The King's College

MARY A. KASSIAN
Author, conference speaker

KAREN S. LORITTS
Bible teacher, speaker

GLENNA MARSHALL
Pastor's wife; author, *The Promise Is His Presence* and *Everyday Faithfulness*

CAROLYN MCCULLEY
Author; speaker; founder, Citygate Films

COLLEEN J. MCFADDEN
Director of Women's Workshops, Charles Simeon Trust

MARY BETH MCGREEVY
Speaker, author

STARR MEADE
Author, teacher

JOSEPH P. MURPHY
Adjunct Professor, Indianapolis Theological Seminary

TRILLIA NEWBELL
Wife and mother; author, *United: Captured by God's Vision for Diversity* (www.trillianewbell.com)

KATHLEEN B. NIELSON
Author and speaker; advisor and editor for the Gospel Coalition; member, board of directors of the Charles Simeon Trust

DANE C. ORTLUND
Senior Pastor, Naperville Presbyterian Church, Naperville, Illinois

JANI ORTLUND
Renewal Ministries, Nashville, Tennessee

ROBERT A. PETERSON
Retired professor, Covenant Theological Seminary

ELISABETH MAXWELL (LISA) RYKEN
Homemaker

JENNY SALT
Dean of Students, Sydney (Australia) Missionary and Bible College

CLAIRE SMITH
Bible teacher, author

LEEANN STILES
Women's Ministry, Redeemer Church of Dubai

SAM STORMS
Lead Pastor of Preaching and Vision, Bridgeway Church, Oklahoma City

JONI EARECKSON TADA
Author, disability advocate

LEE TANKERSLEY

Pastor, Cornerstone Community Church, Jackson, Tennessee

DONNA THOENNES

Adjunct Professor, Torrey Honors College, Biola University

JESSICA THOMPSON

Author, speaker

ANN VOSKAMP

Author of New York Times bestsellers *One Thousand Gifts* and *The Greatest Gift*

MICHELE BENNETT WALTON

Publisher, SeeJesus Press

KRISTEN WETHERELL

Author, speaker, pastor's wife, mother

JEN WILKIN

Author, speaker, Bible teacher

A Helper Fit for Him

SAM STORMS

I'VE HAD NO GREATER joy in life than witnessing the wedding celebrations of my two daughters. One thing that contributed greatly to the happiness of that experience is that I, their father, performed the ceremonies. In doing so I reflected at length on Genesis 2, where we find profound teaching on what it means to be a woman.

After God created Adam from the dust of the ground and breathed into him the breath of life, he placed him in the garden of Eden. There, in the splendor and beauty of that garden, as yet unstained by sin, one might think that Adam could ask for little more. With dominion over the creation and access to all the glory of God's handiwork, it seemed as if "paradise" was the only word fit to describe the life that was his.

But something wasn't quite right. There was something incomplete and unfinished about Adam's existence. For we read that the Lord God of heaven and earth looked down upon the pinnacle of his creative efforts and said, "It is not good that the man should be alone; I will make him a helper fit for him" (Gen. 2:18). On the one hand, a woman is made in the image of God, whether married or not. At the same time, a husband and wife are made for one another. They are to be lifelong companions, best friends, united in covenant relationship.

But there is an even greater message in marriage. When God created the universe, he had one all-consuming purpose in his heart. Whatever else God would do or say, it would all serve to achieve this single, consummate design—namely, to glorify himself by securing a bride for his Son, our Lord Jesus Christ. All of biblical history, from the creation of Adam and Eve in Genesis to the descent of the new heavens and new earth in Revelation, is the story of the Father's loving redemption and relentless pursuit of a bride, the church, for the bridegroom, Jesus Christ. Marriage is the glorious opportunity for a man and a woman to embody, express, and illustrate this love relationship between Jesus Christ and his bride.

This is not to say that marriage is required for a fulfilling life. Jesus himself, after all, was single. As meaningful as marriage is, what brings supreme fulfillment in life is not knowing and being loved by any other human being, but knowing and being loved by God. While it may be painful to lack the companionship of marriage, all God's people, married or single, are called to trust in him alone for their joy and comfort. He will never leave us or forsake us.

JANUARY 2 · GENESIS 3

The Fall of Man and the Grace of God

ERIKA ALLEN

CREATED IN THE IMAGE of God and placed in a garden of serene beauty, Adam and Eve had nothing to fear or be anxious about. They enjoyed beauty and goodness and unhindered fellowship with one another and their Creator. But with one act of disobedience, everything changed. In a moment, death and evil were introduced into the world, devastating both creation (Rom. 8:20–22) and humankind (Rom. 5:12–15). When we read this passage, we feel the gravity of what was lost in the fall.

At the same time, the evidences of God's grace in Genesis 3 are astounding. God would have been completely just had he immediately returned Adam to the dust from which he came and been done with humanity. Instead, he showed mercy and compassion. Reason for hope, in spite of sin, is evident in at least four ways in this passage.

The first is seen in God's curse upon the serpent: "I will put enmity between you and the woman, and between your offspring and her offspring; he shall bruise your head, and you shall bruise his heel" (Gen. 3:15). Theologians call this the *Protoevangelium*—the first announcement of the gospel. Immediately after sin enters the world, God initiates a plan to deal with it. This plan to reconcile people to himself becomes a unifying theme throughout the Bible, culminating in the person of Jesus Christ, the second Adam (Rom. 5:18–21), whose death and resurrection defeated sin, death, and the devil (Heb. 2:14–15).

The second place we see God's grace is in Genesis 3:20, when Adam gives his wife a name. The verse almost seems out of place. Why mention this here? The name Eve means "life-giver." Although it will be in pain that she will bring forth children (v. 16), God is not done with humanity. Despite her sin, Eve will have the distinction of being "the mother of all living."

Third, verse 21 says, "the LORD God made for Adam and for his wife garments of skins and clothed them." That these garments were made of skins implies that an animal had to die. This hints at the sacrificial system as well as the eventual work of Christ, through which we are clothed with his righteousness. It also shows the fatherly love of God toward his children. He did not leave us naked and ashamed.

Fourth, even God's driving Adam and Eve from Eden was an act of grace. The tree of life apparently served in some way to confirm a person in his or her moral condition (vv. 22–23). God refuses to allow Adam and Eve to eat from this tree of life and thus remain forever in their sinful state. He bars access to the tree until Jesus returns, at which time those of us who belong to him will once again be able to enjoy its fruit (Rev. 22:14).

JANUARY 3 • GENESIS 12:1–9

The Call of Abraham

MIKE BULLMORE

ABRAM (LATER RENAMED ABRAHAM) is the exemplary man of faith. The apostle Paul makes much of this in Romans 4 and Galatians 3, even speaking of Abraham as the "father" of all who have faith in Jesus Christ. Abraham is also featured as the leading member in the great "Hall of Fame" of faith in Hebrews 11 (vv. 8–19). Without question, Abraham emerges in the New Testament as the model of faith for us. And it all gets started here in Genesis 12.

So what are the words God speaks to Abram in this passage that beget such a powerful trajectory of faith? God begins by directing Abram to leave his country, kindred, and familiar home. This represents everything in which Abram would have found security, comfort, and enjoyment—everything he held dear. By anyone's measure, this was going to mean a monumental and comprehensive change in his life. But it is in what God said next that the great significance is found: "And I will make of you a great nation, and I will bless you and make your name great, so that you will be a blessing" (Gen. 12:2).

We see here that God's intention to make Abram a great nation is not an end in itself. It is "so that" blessing might be poured out, and not just in some local or even national way. Through Abram God intended to bring blessing to "all the families of the earth" (v. 3). This comprehensive change in the life of one man was, in God's grand plan, to result in a much larger and more comprehensive blessing. By the time we arrive at the New Testament, we are able to see clearly that line of blessing and where it leads. The Gospel of Matthew sets it forth for us in a simple but profound genealogy—from Abraham to Jesus (Matt. 1:1–16).

Verses 4–9 of Genesis 12—in fact, the next several chapters of Genesis—recount for us Abram's faith in action. It isn't always perfect, but it is exemplary. God directed Abram to "Go" (Gen. 12:1). "Abram went" (v. 4). He trusts and he obeys. And he continues in a journey marked by trusting obedience, regularly pausing to acknowledge his dependence on God (see vv. 7–8).

Is this not what God calls for from us? The Christian life is a walk of faith. Someday we will be able to set aside this inferior faith for glorious sight (2 Cor. 5:7). But until then, faith-filled obedience is what God calls us to, and Abraham gives us a picture of what that looks like. And the larger story tells us how God weaves our faith into the unfolding of his grand redemptive plan.

The City . . . Whose Designer and Builder Is God

ROBERT A. PETERSON

EVEN THOUGH ABRAM and Sarai are unable to have children, God assures Abram that his "very own son" will be his heir. Taking him outside to look at the stars, God promises Abram that his offspring will be equal to their number. The New Testament quotes Abram's reply four times: "And he believed the LORD, and he counted it to him as righteousness" (Gen. 15:6). This verse reveals a key scriptural pattern. In grace God regards Abram as righteous, accepting him because of his faith. Paul agrees: "For by grace you have been saved through faith" (Eph. 2:8).

In the next two verses in Ephesians, Paul says God did not save us *because of* our works but so that we would perform good works. And again, Abram sets the pattern. First, God counts him righteous based on faith apart from deeds. Then Abram (by then renamed Abraham) demonstrates his righteousness *by* his deeds (see Gen. 22:12). It is the same for everyone everywhere. No one earns God's favor. Right relationship with God is due only to his good will received by faith in the crucified and risen Christ, who loved us and gave himself for us. And those justified by grace through faith are to "be careful to devote themselves to good works" (Titus 3:8).

Abram is also concerned about God's promise to give him a land. Again God assures him: "I am the LORD who brought you out from Ur of the Chaldeans to give you this land to possess" (Gen. 15:7). And God graciously makes a promise and performs a ritual to assure Abram. God predicts something that would occur at least six hundred years later: the Israelites' oppression in Egypt and the mighty exodus from there to inherit the land of Canaan. Then, while Abram sleeps, the Lord, symbolized by a smoking fire pot and flaming torch, passes between pieces of animals to assure Abram that he will fulfill his promise to give the land to Abram's descendants.

Although some Christians may be expecting an eternal existence as disembodied spirits in heaven, the Bible teaches something different and much better. Scripture portrays final salvation as a resurrected existence on a new earth underneath a new heaven. The land of Canaan, which the Lord promised Abram, was a token or foreshadowing of the new earth. And in fact, that is what Abraham anticipated, for "he was looking forward to the city that has foundations, whose designer and builder is God" (Heb. 11:10). By God's grace, through faith, we do the same!

JANUARY 5 • GENESIS 17:15–18:15

Is Anything Too Hard for the Lord?

NANCY GUTHRIE

WHEN WE MEET SARAI in the Scriptures, she seems to be defined by her emptiness and failure. We read, "Sarai was barren; she had no child" (Gen. 11:30). Her situation becomes even more poignant when we read that God has promised to give her husband descendants as numerous as the stars of heaven (15:5). How will this happen? The promise appears impossible to fulfill.

Abram and Sarai sought to solve the problem of this seemingly impossible promise through their own ingenuity and effort. Sarai gave her maidservant to Abram, and Ishmael was born. For thirteen years Abram nursed his hopes that Ishmael would be the son through whom all of God's promises would become a reality.

That's when the Lord visited Abraham and made it clear that his wife, Sarah, would bear him a son who would be the heir of the covenant promises. But this was just laughable to Abraham and Sarah. At their age and stage, continuing to hope for even one child, let alone descendants as numerous as the stars in the sky, seemed ridiculously beyond reason. Sarah knew her own body—that it was worn out and dried up. The idea that she could ever have children was absurd. Hearing Sarah's laughter of unbelief, God asked, "Is anything too hard for the LORD?" (18:14).

Sarah had been focused on whether or not it was too hard for her and Abraham, and there was no question it was. But the Lord turned to her with the more important question, which was, *"Can I do it?"* And of course he could. He is God Almighty.

We read in Genesis 21, "The Lord visited Sarah as he had said, and the Lord did to Sarah as he had promised. And Sarah conceived and bore Abraham a son" (21:1–2). By a miraculous work of God, "from one man, and him as good as dead, were born descendants as many as the stars of heaven and as many as the innumerable grains of sand by the seashore" (Heb. 11:12).

What is impossible in human terms is not too hard for God. For the God who spoke the world into being out of nothing, it is not difficult to fill the barren womb of Sarah with life and to fill her life with laughter. In fact, God still accomplishes the impossible, creating life out of death apart from human effort. "God . . . when we were dead in our trespasses, made us alive together with Christ. . . . And this is not your own doing; it is the gift of God" (Eph. 2:4–5, 8).

JANUARY 6 • GENESIS 22

The Sacrifice of Isaac

JOSEPH P. MURPHY

THIS STORY OF ABRAHAM and Isaac brims with whole-Bible significance. It foreshadows God's redemption of the world through the substitutionary death of Jesus Christ, his only Son, and it portrays human reception of that redemption by faith, resulting in transformed human relations.

But isn't this really a story of a monstrous God who deals out death to those he supposedly loves? Abraham *did* ask that question; it is his answer that differs from that of so many who pose it today.

First, the God who commanded the sacrifice *did not* allow Abraham to kill Isaac. The command to sacrifice Isaac was never about Isaac. Rather, it addressed the human fear, rooted in sin and guilt, that instead of loving us God seeks to do us harm. Yet God seeks our good through a change in us, separating us from our sin. Father and son shared life together before and after, but this occasion changed them.

Second, Abraham answered the question by obeying. This child meant *everything* to Abraham: God's promises, past, present, and future. To truly intend to put the boy to death for God's sake meant death to Abraham—nothing less. Yet Abraham moved toward full obedience, knowing that the Lord would "provide for himself the lamb" (Gen. 22:8). Fully conscious of God's power to keep his promise, "[Abraham] considered that God was able even to raise [Isaac] from the dead, from which, figuratively speaking, he did receive him back" (Heb. 11:19).

To obey, Abraham had to die to himself. Trusting that God was truly good, just, and all-powerful was the key. Despite lacking any understanding of what exactly God was doing, Abraham obeyed, not with intent to do evil, but in confidence that God would do good. And God did!

Isaac was also changed, because, as the horror of the event became clear to him, he had to realize that God was his true Father, to be trusted over Abraham. Yet God *had* provided the sacrifice, and it meant nothing less than life for Isaac. Family life is transformed through this event: God is to be trusted above all others. Social relations, with God and humans, were put in right proportion for both father and son: love God first and foremost, *and then* love all others.

JANUARY 7 · GENESIS 24

The Everyday Sacred

ANN VOSKAMP

THE WAY THIS CHAPTER begins is the way to begin a day, a lens to rightly see life: "The LORD had blessed Abraham in all things" (Gen. 24:1). The Lord had graced Abraham with blessings *in all things*—amid fading dreams (ch. 15), amid family tensions (ch. 16), even amid Abraham's sinful choices (12:10–20; 20:1–18).

Now Abraham is old and widowed and wants a godly wife for his son. He sends his servant, a faithful disciple not afraid to do hard things. The servant travels with a dowry, asking God for discernment to know his will. Only to find one very faithful woman, Rebekah, who, in four short verses, is the subject of eleven action verbs. Rebekah came and went and filled and gave and emptied and gave again. The woman is a steady dance of giving grace.

And there it is, the way to finish any task: the servant stands before the potential bride with bowed head, blessing God with his thanks, for our God "who has not forsaken his steadfast love and his faithfulness" (24:27). John Calvin looks at the response of Abraham's servant to God and suggests that we should respond in the same way: "Giving thanks is a more acceptable service than all sacrifices. God is continually heaping innumerable benefits. . . . Ingratitude, therefore, is intolerable."[1]

The servant pours out his prayer of thanks: "As for me, the LORD has led me . . ." (v. 27). Elsewhere, "led" or "lead" (*nahah*) refers to guidance in the wilderness, well-being in a time of stress. The best-known use of *nahah* is in Psalm 23: "He leads me in paths of righteousness for his name's sake." *God leads.* Throughout the entire journey, God has led.

Yet nowhere in this story has God spoken, made visitations, or blazingly directed. In this story, God is not about obvious intervention but about ordinary orchestration. This story, the single longest narrative in the entire book of Genesis, is a story of attention to details, to an ordinary woman doing daily things, to all these everyday moments. Why all the focus?

Because God is in the details. God is in the moments. *"As for me, the Lord has led me in the way . . ."*

Because this is always reality: God may not seem to be doing anything—when he's actually directing everything. Because what seems like the everyday secular is actually the everyday sacred.

Because God isn't only in the spectacular, he is in the small. God leads (*nahah*) amid the pots and pans and pitchers of water. So we bow our heads and bless our God with our thanks. He has led us in the way.

Our Sin Does Not Stop God

HEATHER HOUSE

SIN HARMS FAMILIES. This was true for the families in the Bible, just as it is for us today. In Genesis 27, Isaac's family sins terribly against one another and against God's word. Yet this is the family through whom God has promised to fulfill his promises to Abraham (Gen. 12:1–3). Eventually, God transforms each individual's sinful behavior and culturally shaped inclinations into results that glorify him (Rom. 8:28).

The family's sin cannot stop what God wants to accomplish. Deceived into blessing his younger son, Jacob, rather than the older son, Esau, Isaac unwittingly fulfills God's word to Rebekah in Genesis 25:23. Rebekah manipulates her husband and pits her sons against each other, yet the men eventually reunite and bury their father together (Gen. 35:29). Jacob lies to his father to get the blessing of land and family; his actions cause him to be sent far from home (28:1–5). But in the end God gives him a large family and brings him back to the land (35:11–12). Esau hates Jacob for his trickery and plans to kill him—but later God enables Esau to forgive (33:1–11). Every act of faithlessness, selfishness, and bitterness is remade into something that benefits later generations, including us today. Believers should be encouraged by these examples of how God changes sinful attitudes and behaviors in his people and how he redeems what is intended for evil (50:20).

Just as God is not ultimately hindered by his people's sins, he is also not confined by cultural traditions. In biblical times, when the father was about to die, it was typical to call the family together so that the patriarch could give a blessing. The oldest son generally received the bulk of the family's resources and responsibilities. For example, Isaac intends to bless Esau with abundantly producing land, with rule over the family and other nations, and with destruction of his enemies. But here God does something different. He chooses the younger son to carry on the promises that he had made to Abraham (see Gen. 48:13–20; 49:1–4 for other times this happens in Jacob's family). God expects his followers to trust him, even when what he asks them to do is not what the culture expects.

The fact that God chooses Jacob instead of Esau to lead the family does not mean that Jacob was inherently superior in some way. Jacob does nothing to win God's favor, and Esau does nothing to lose it. God loves both. These brothers are wonderful reminders that God's grace is undeserved and unearned.

JANUARY 9 · GENESIS 29

Even the Weak and Unworthy

KATHLEEN CHAPELL

IN THIS CHAPTER of Jacob's life, he seems to be on the brink of a fresh start. He has fled from his angry brother, his manipulative mother, and his easily deceived father. He is heading to his uncle's land and safekeeping, with instructions to marry into that family. *And* he has just had an extraordinary dream, in which he has been given a prophetic vision of what God will do to restore humanity to himself: he will provide a way for sinful people to be admitted once again into the presence of a holy God—he will provide the "ladder" between earth and heaven.

Jacob must have felt encouraged! In the dream, God actually said to him, "Behold, I am with you and will keep you wherever you go" (Gen. 28:15). But Jacob's past deceitfulness and selfishness must also have threatened to haunt him.

Jacob is such an unlikely hero—a liar, a cheat, and a coward. As the story progresses, it is clear that not all that happens is as Jacob would have hoped. He works for years to win the hand of the woman he loves, only to find that he also has been duped—the deceiver gets deceived! And the following chapters reveal ongoing lies, deception, and trickery.

Still, God will continue to use this broken man and his family to bring about an eternal plan of salvation and restoration. What can we learn from this story? In the revealed history of his redemptive plan, God used Jacob to teach us that even the weakest and most unworthy are not beyond his mercy. I, too, am weak and unworthy. The Scriptures tell me that even my best efforts are "like a polluted garment" (Isa. 64:6). There is no earthly reason that God should love me. And yet he does—even sending his own Son to suffer and die in my place.

The story of Jacob is not only a story about one of the patriarchs in the Bible—it is the story of how God walks with his people as they stumble and wander from his way, make mistakes, choose badly, and sin greatly. And yet he still walks with us! He still loves his broken, sinful people; he still works his amazing providence through his fallen creatures. And the conclusion of this story has already been written: God has made a way for us to get to him!

JANUARY 10 • GENESIS 35:1–15

The One Who Answers Me

ELIZABETH W. D. GROVES

GOD KEEPS HIS promises. This passage tells of God calling someone to stop, stand still, and remember that.

The last time Jacob was in Bethel, twenty years earlier, he was fleeing from his brother Esau (Genesis 29). At that time God promised Jacob that he would be with him, protect him, and return him to the Promised Land; that Jacob would inherit that land; and that his offspring would be as plentiful as the dust and would be a blessing to all the peoples of the earth (ch. 28). Now Jacob has a dozen sons, and the Lord has returned him safely to the land, even through the hazardous reencounter with Esau in chapter 33. God changed Jacob's name and sent him back to Bethel, the place where the promises had been made, where he could remember them and reflect on God's faithfulness.

Jacob could look back over his life and see how God had been faithful at all points. In Genesis 35:3, Jacob describes God as "the God who *answers me*" (the Hebrew verb has the sense of ongoing action). As he stopped and reflected on that, it would have helped Jacob to trust God to be faithful to the parts of the promises that had not yet come to fulfillment, including a new promise God made to him: that kings would be among his descendants.

God's faithfulness to Jacob also demonstrated his faithfulness to his larger promises to Jacob's family line (e.g., land, descendants) and to his plan for history to bless all nations through them (Genesis 12; 15; 17; 22). The promise of royal descendants, originally given to Abraham (17:6) and Sarah (v. 16), was fulfilled not only in David and the kings of Judah but preeminently in Jesus. He is the King through whom God's blessing to Abraham and Jacob would come to all nations. As Jacob trusted the Lord to keep his promise of kingly descendants, he was looking ahead to Christ, the ultimate fulfillment of that promise.

Today we, like Jacob, can look back on God's faithfulness. We have the advantage of seeing it displayed so much more clearly and gloriously in the life, death, and resurrection of Jesus. As we stop and reflect on it, our faith is strengthened to trust God in the present as well as for the future. We look ahead to Jesus coming again, as a triumphant king.

Stop and reflect on specific details of God's past faithfulness to you, maybe even difficult things God has brought you through, as he did Jacob. Reflect on his faithfulness to his plan of salvation accomplished by Jesus. And gain confidence to trust him in the present and the future. *Remember* and *hope*, because God keeps his promises!

JANUARY 11 · GENESIS 39

God's Presence and Blessing in Adversity

GLORIA FURMAN

WHEN WE SUFFER adversity and our circumstances are bleak, we might wonder, "Where is God?" Has the Lord turned his back on us? Has he forgotten us? Is God mindful of his promise to be with his covenant people and bless them (Gen. 12:2–3)?

Joseph may have asked these questions when he was thrown into the pit and sold into slavery by his brothers. And when he was accused of committing sins against the Lord and against Potiphar's house. And when he was left in the king's prison for many years. Did God forsake or forget the promises he had made? The evidence in the life of Joseph is abundantly clear: God's hand was present amid this adversity, and he meant it for good (50:20). The Lord never left Joseph (39:2–3, 21, 23), and he blessed him and made him a blessing.

The Lord was fulfilling his promise to bless the nations as he "blessed the Egyptian's house for Joseph's sake" (39:5). But even as Potiphar's wife enjoyed abundant provision at the hand of God, she sought the destruction of God's servant through tempting him to sin and accusing him of evil. Again, like years earlier when his brothers threw him into the pit (37:23–24), Joseph's garment was stolen for the purpose of deceiving others (39:12; compare 37:31–33). Yet God had ordained that all the nations would be blessed through his covenant people (12:1–3; 18:18; 22:17–18; 30:27). His purposes could not be thwarted by this woman's accusations and lies.

God's covenant people are still accused today. But the accusations of Satan, the one who tempts and deceives, hold no weight in God's holy throne room. The blood of Jesus, who is "the mediator of a new covenant," speaks on our behalf (Heb. 12:24). Even if we have given in to temptation and seduction, the blood of Jesus cleanses those whose faith is in him (1 John 1:7). Through repentance and faith in Christ Jesus, those "who once were far off" have been "brought near" to God by his blood (Eph. 2:13).

The Lord was committed to Joseph, and Joseph was committed to the Lord. God's word leaves no room for doubt that "the LORD was with Joseph" (Gen. 39:21; see also Acts 7:9). Believers in Jesus have this rock-steady assurance. As Christ dwells in our hearts through faith, we are rooted and grounded in his love (Eph. 3:17). As we are grounded in the love of God, he enables us to persevere through adverse circumstances and resist temptation—to the praise of his name in all the earth. God is with us in our trials, and he causes us to prosper in them as he shows us his steadfast love.

From Tribulation to Glory

CAROLYN ARENDS

BETRAYED BY HIS brothers and framed by his boss's wife, Joseph spends thirteen years in slavery and imprisonment before the plot finally twists in his favor. And yet his long-awaited "rags to riches" transformation in Genesis 41 confirms something that's been clear all along—"The LORD was with Joseph" (Gen. 39:2). In good times and bad, God has been active and alive, providentially weaving together the trajectory of Joseph's life and the unfolding story of salvation.

Joseph is living an incredible adventure set within an even greater story. Recall that Yahweh promised to bless all the nations through the descendants of Abraham (12:3). Joseph, Abraham's great-grandson, is now second-in-command over Egypt, blessed with the spiritual insight and administrative skills necessary to guide the region safely through famine. Yahweh's promise to Abraham reverberates in the chapter's conclusion, when the narrator observes that, "all the earth came to Egypt to Joseph to buy grain" (41:57).

So Joseph's story reveals that God is present and active, even in difficult and mysterious circumstances. It affirms that God keeps his promises, and that the unfolding of his plan of salvation will not be thwarted. But Joseph's life also inaugurates a pattern of what biblical scholar Bruce Waltke calls "tribulation to glory because of God's presence."

For Joseph, it's a journey through a pit to a palace. For the later Israelites, it will be an exodus from slavery to the Promised Land. For Mary, it will be an implausible transformation from pregnant teen to mother of the Messiah. The author of Hebrews brings this connection between humility and greatness into sharp focus when he asks us to look to Jesus, "the founder and perfecter of our faith, who for the joy that was set before him endured the cross, despising the shame, and is seated at the right hand of the throne of God" (Heb. 12:2).

There are as many variations on this "tribulation to glory" theme as there are people. In some cases, tribulations are clearly discipline or the natural consequence of sin. In other situations (like Joseph's), the trials seem unjust. In every case, however, we can trust that "all things work together for good" for those who love God and are called according to his very good purposes (Rom. 8:28). For Jesus went through the ultimate tribulation to glory, so that all our tribulation can only result in our glory and radiance. "Humble yourselves, therefore, under the mighty hand of God so that at the proper time he may exalt you" (1 Pet. 5:6).

Identity Revealed, Forgiveness Bestowed

JESSICA THOMPSON

IN THIS PASSAGE, Joseph reveals his identity to his brothers. He can no longer contain the secret that he is the one they had sold into slavery. This revelation must have brought great fear into his brothers' hearts—for now Joseph is in a position of power, and they are his servants. They are at his mercy, begging for food. But Joseph offers them all that is at his disposal to give.

The account is interestingly similar to the story of Joseph's father, Jacob, receiving forgiveness from Esau, the brother he had wronged (Genesis 33). Joseph was there for that reconciliation and benefited from it. Forgiveness begets forgiveness; now it was Joseph's turn. He tenderly assures his brothers of his forgiveness and his continued love for the family.

But who treats those who hate him as his brothers? Who showers overwhelming grace upon those who have despised him? Who gives abundantly to his enemies? Who kisses the very ones who betrayed him out of jealousy? The supreme instance of this is our lovely Savior, Jesus Christ, who himself said that the first books of the Bible were about him (John 5:39, 46).

Though we look at the story of Joseph and can scarcely believe that a man would extend such love to his betrayers, we can look at the history of redemption and see Jesus doing this very thing a thousand times over. His extravagant forgiveness of our sin should motivate us to forgive others.

Genesis 45:5–8 reveals what gave Joseph the ability to overlook past wrongs and to give generously to his family: "God sent me before you to preserve life. . . . And God sent me before you to preserve for you a remnant on earth, and to keep alive for you many survivors. So it was not you who sent me here, but God." The knowledge of a heavenly Father who cares for every need, and who has everlasting power and wisdom, gave Joseph the ability to trust him. God sustained Joseph through years of injustice. Christ's faith in God's love sustained him through the greatest suffering any human has ever known.

We can be certain that our Father will sustain us. Though we may not see an answer to all of our questions here, and our situation might not have a tidy ending, we will one day with clear eyes see the absolute majesty and loving kindness of a God who works all things together for our good. He is on our side (Rom. 8:31) and makes every situation in our lives conform to his glorious will (Rom. 8:28).

JANUARY 14 · GENESIS 49:1-27

The Plan and Promise of God

LEE TANKERSLEY

THE GREAT PREDICAMENT in the biblical storyline, after Genesis 3, is how a sinful people might dwell in the presence of a holy God. There has never been a greater dilemma in all of world history. While mankind would have to wait thousands of years to hear John say, "Behold, the Lamb of God" (John 1:29), identifying Jesus as the Christ, the answer to this great problem was in the plan of God from eternity past. He would send his Son to take on flesh, live, die, and be raised for his people. And because this was God's eternal plan, we find clues to the identity of the Savior all along the Bible's unfolding storyline. One of the earliest places the Lord provides a clue as to who the Messiah would be is in Genesis 49.

As Jacob addresses his sons, his strongest word of blessing comes to Judah. To him Jacob declares, "Judah, your brothers shall praise you; . . . your father's sons shall bow down before you. . . . The scepter shall not depart from Judah, nor the ruler's staff from between his feet, until tribute comes to him" (Gen. 49:8, 10).

Centuries later, John would have a view of this "tribute" as he had a vision of the throne room of heaven. Weeping because none was found worthy to take and open the scroll, enacting God's work of judgment and salvation, John was told, "Weep no more; behold, the Lion of the tribe of Judah . . . has conquered, so that he can open the scroll and its seven seals" (Rev. 5:5). Then, as John turned and saw the Lamb, taking the scroll from the right hand of him who was seated on the throne, "every creature in heaven and on earth and under the earth and in the sea, and all that is in them" worshiped. Jacob's promise was fulfilled. Our salvation was secure.

As we walk through life, our struggles and the dilemmas we face can be overwhelming. We may well be tempted to question God's plan. But in these times we can remember that the God in whom we trust is the One who promised thousands of years before Christ came that he would raise up a Lion from the tribe of Judah. And we can look back at the Lamb who was slain for us and see that God kept his promise. Therefore, as we consider that this faithful God had every one of our days written out in his book before we ever lived them (Ps. 139:16), how could we ever doubt him? Let us rest in his plan for us today.

JANUARY 15 · GENESIS 50:15–21

When God Turns Evil into Good

SAM STORMS

JOSEPH'S BROTHERS not only sold him into slavery and lied to cover their tracks; they also failed horribly in their assessment of his character. They couldn't bring themselves to believe that Joseph's kindness and long-suffering were heartfelt and sincere, the fruit of a genuine love for them and concern for their welfare. Surely his treatment of them must be due to some external pressure, constraint, or fear? Perhaps his kindness was due solely to the influence of Jacob, their father. "Might it be that Joseph is good to us," they wondered, "because he doesn't want to break our father's heart?" Once Jacob died, they feared that Joseph would no longer treat them with compassion. So they compounded their earlier sin by fabricating a story that Jacob, just before his death, had requested that Joseph forgive them for their transgressions.

But Joseph had a far more expansive view of God and his purposes than his brothers could imagine. Without for a moment excusing the gravity of their sin in betraying him and selling him into slavery, Joseph set it within the larger providential purposes of God. Their evil deed was itself part of God's greater goal of making provision for his people in Egypt. This isn't to say that his brothers wouldn't be held morally accountable for their treachery. Their wicked deeds were not suddenly transformed into righteous acts simply because God is capable of orchestrating all things for a greater good. Evil is evil.

What we learn, then, is that everything we encounter in life, whether a tragedy or a triumph, falls within the framework of God's overarching, always loving, and ever wise eternal plan. It is natural for us to see tragic events only in terms of their immediate impact. When life hurts or people fail us, we tend to conclude that God cannot be trusted. We fail to grasp how painful and inconvenient circumstances are either intended or turned by God for his glory and our good.

Joseph's view on life was shaped by the greatness and all-encompassing providential power of God. Nothing catches God by surprise. God was not caught off guard, as if the evil actions of Joseph's brothers forced him to scrap his original design and revert to plan B. Nothing is too random or wicked to escape God's goals for us or to thwart his purpose. Joseph's response instructs us on how important it is always to take the long view in life. We may be confused and disheartened by some awkward and irksome turn of events, but God is always in control, working "all things according to the counsel of his will" (Eph. 1:11).

He Was a Fine Child

JANI ORTLUND

ISRAEL WAS IN CRISIS, as God had predicted in Genesis 15:13. They were slaves to the greatest superpower in the ancient world, and their lives were "bitter with hard service" (Ex. 1:14). Despite this oppression, they were multiplying, and Pharaoh was determined to stop their growth. When Pharaoh's secret plot involving the Hebrew midwives failed, he enlisted every Egyptian to carry out his new plan of infanticide (1:22). The Nile, Egypt's source of life-sustaining water, was now to become a place of death for helpless Hebrew baby boys.

But there was a King more powerful than this puny pharaoh, a King who brings life out of death. The Lord had made a covenant promise to Abraham (Gen. 15:14), and the time had come to fulfill it. God always keeps his promises, and in Exodus 2 he begins a thrilling rescue story for all to see.

The Nile was the scene of many baby murders as Egyptian masters obeyed their king's command to cast into it every Hebrew baby boy. Amid this madness, we find a mother refusing to submit to the horror of her infant son being drowned. We can only imagine the tension in that little family—mother trying to quiet all baby sounds that could be heard beyond their living quarters; older siblings sworn to secrecy; father wondering what he would find at home after serving his ruthless taskmaster all day. Perhaps Jochebed was required to return to her slave work. Maybe the baby was just growing too big and noisy. Whatever the reason, she could hide him no longer (Ex. 2:3). But she determined to give him every possible chance for survival. She fashioned a baby-sized ark, took the basket down to the river's edge, and, rather than casting her boy into the river as Pharaoh had commanded, she gently placed him among the reeds by the bank, leaving his big sister to spy at a distance.

Any mother who has ever had to part with a child can see her trudging back home, pleading with God to protect her baby boy. Imagine her fear when she heard Miriam shouting, "Mother, come quickly! Pharaoh's daughter wants you!" Had she been discovered? Was this to be the end of her family? Ponder her amazement when, through young Miriam's bold intervention, she found her beautiful baby boy placed back in her arms, and in an incredible turn of events, she would be paid to nurse her own son (v. 9)!

God hadn't forgotten his promise to Abraham. He was continuing his great redemption story, and he used a slave-mother and her infant son. God keeps his promises—to Israel, and to you.

JANUARY 17 • EXODUS 3

A Close Encounter of the Glorious Kind

JENNY SALT

HAVE YOU EVER looked at the circumstances of your life and wondered, "How did that happen?" Life does not always go the way we expect or even hope. The world is unpredictable, and we can feel unsafe and insecure. So how do we live by faith, as we follow Jesus?

In Exodus we read about the people of Israel and their relationship with the Lord God Almighty. The book opens with the Israelites in Egypt four hundred years after their forefathers had settled there. What started as a good relationship and arrangement between the tribes of Israel and Pharaoh had become a painful, desperate situation. The children of Israel were slaves, suffering under Egyptian oppression (Ex. 1:8–11). Despite this, they had multiplied and grown strong (1:20)—another reason the Egyptians "were in dread of the people of Israel" (1:12).

Into this time of oppression, Moses was born. In God's providence, Moses was kept safe as a baby and raised in Pharaoh's household. A series of events took him into the wilderness as a young man, where he settled with a family of his own. Meanwhile, the people of Israel cried out under their oppression and the Lord heard their groaning. This brings us to chapter 3.

While Moses was tending his flock in the wilderness of Midian, the angel of the Lord appeared to him in the burning bush—he had a close encounter with the Holy God of Israel, a close encounter of the glorious kind. He met the One who is holy, faithful to his promises, and mighty to save: "I am the God of your father, the God of Abraham, the God of Isaac, and the God of Jacob" (v. 6). This chapter records God's calling of Moses to lead Israel out of slavery. "Come, I will send you to Pharaoh that you may bring my people, the children of Israel, out of Egypt" (v. 10). "Say this to the people of Israel: 'I AM has sent me to you'" (v. 14).

Exodus 3 reveals the Lord's character and his purposes for his people. He is mighty to save and faithful to his promises. The rescue from Egypt points forward to an even more amazing rescue—rescue from sin and death through Jesus's work at the cross. "He has delivered us from the domain of darkness and transferred us to the kingdom of his beloved Son, in whom we have redemption, the forgiveness of sins" (Col. 1:13–14).

How do we live by faith, as women who follow Jesus, especially when life doesn't go the way we want? Look to the One who is faithful, who has given his Son to die for you, so that you may live for him, not for yourself. Trust and obey, commit your ways to him, with full assurance that the Lord, who knows our needs, will always do what is right.

JANUARY 18 · EXODUS 7:14-25

God Makes Himself Known through the Plagues

STARR MEADE

MIRACLES EXPLODE across the pages of Exodus. The Bible records more miracles through Moses than through any other individual except Jesus. The miracles, however, are not the greatest wonder in the book of Exodus. The wonder of Exodus is this: God makes himself known to his people. God needs nothing from us—not our companionship, not our service, not our praise. Yet he reveals himself to us and invites us to bring him those things for our good and his glory. In Exodus, God revealed to his people his name (Ex. 3:13–15), his power and faithfulness (6:6–8), his character and his covenant (34:27–28), and his very presence to dwell among them in the tabernacle (25:8).

In the plagues of Exodus, too, God acted in order to be known. When Moses first approached Pharaoh with God's message to let his people go, Pharaoh only scoffed. He didn't care if Moses had come from the Lord. "Who is the LORD, that I should obey his voice?" he replied. "I do not know the LORD." (5:2). So God set out to make himself known to Pharaoh. "The Egyptians shall know that I am the LORD," God told Moses—ominous words, as it turned out, for the nation and its ruler (7:5). As the Israelites watched judgment after judgment fall on a hard-hearted Pharaoh, they too would come to know who God was. Through mighty acts, God would take them to be his people. As a result, God promised them, "you shall know that I am the LORD your God" (6:7). Watch for this language of someone coming to know that God is the Lord, or coming to understand something about him through the plagues. It recurs often.

At first, the Hebrews could not see what God was doing. They only saw Pharaoh's harsh response, making their lives even grimmer than they had been (5:1–23). God had a plan, however, and his plan is always to reveal his glory. In the ten plagues on Egypt, as in all of Exodus, God was out to make himself known. God had told Moses that he saw his people's sufferings and was coming to deliver them. This he would surely do. But along the way, he would make Pharaoh, Egypt, and the Israelites themselves know who he was.

When, like the Hebrew slaves, we cannot see why God allows difficulties and why they keep increasing, we must remember this: his ultimate goal is not to make us comfortable. His ultimate goal is that we would know him.

Our Passover Lamb

MARY BETH MCGREEVY

GOD HAS ANNOUNCED to Moses the tenth and final plague upon Pharaoh and the Egyptians: death to every firstborn in the land. However, unlike the previous plagues, in which the Israelites were spared because they were God's covenant people, this plague will fall on *everyone* unless they appropriate God's provided means of escape: the blood of a male, year-old, unblemished lamb, applied to the doorposts and lintels of their homes. When the Lord sees the blood, he will pass over that house and their firstborn will be spared (Ex. 12:13).

The Israelites are to roast the lamb and eat it with unleavened bread and bitter herbs, dressed for the journey ahead (v. 11). For God has warned that when the Egyptians see the death of their firstborn, they will drive away the Israelites completely (11:1), and so they must leave in haste. The meal will provide the strength they need for the exodus.

God institutes the Passover and the Feast of Unleavened Bread to be celebrated by Israel in the Promised Land (12:14–27). Like the original meal, it will be a communal event with an emphasis on family. It will distinguish God's covenant people from all others. They will participate in the sacrifice and eating of the lamb, remembering as they do God's great act of redemption. Their reenactment of that first Passover will illustrate the fact that the benefits of God's redemption of them as his people are ongoing.

It was at a Passover feast that the Lord Jesus Christ revealed a greater redemption of which the Exodus was only a foreshadowing. At that meal with his disciples, Jesus took bread, blessed and broke it, and gave it to them, saying, "Take, eat; this is my body" (Matt. 26:26). He also took the cup, gave thanks, and gave it to them, saying, "Drink of it, all of you, for this is my blood of the [new] covenant, which is poured out for many for the forgiveness of sins" (Matt. 26:27–28). He instituted the Lord's Supper so that we, like the Israelites, may celebrate God's provision of the perfect Passover Lamb sacrificed for all who trust in his blood to turn away God's wrath and spare them from eternal death. In the communion meal, Christ offers us the ongoing benefits of his redemption.

When you have opportunity to participate in this marvelous means of grace, enter into it fully. Reflect on your Passover Lamb's blood, which gives you forgiveness and life. Celebrate his resurrected life, through which you have strength for your journey. And look forward to that ultimate meal, the Marriage Supper of the Lamb, which you will one day celebrate in his presence (Rev. 19:9).

JANUARY 20 · EXODUS 14

Footprints Unseen

ZACK ESWINE

EVEN THE FAITHFUL can be fearful. Here we see faithful women, children, and men standing trapped by the Red Sea, bone deep with fright (Ex. 14:10). Creation itself conspires against them: "the wilderness has shut them in" (v. 3). Nothing they do can stop what threatens them. God's people must bear with neighbors-turned-enemies, helpless, at their mercy.

Moreover, hoofbeat and chariot wheel crush celebrations. Crowds of God's people panic like agitated horses caught in stalls. They begin to quit on God's promise. Who wants God, if attaining his promise requires this kind of faith and peril (vv. 10–12)?

Why does God permit them the wild taste of freedom, only to turn around and allow them to be imperiled again? What good is getting a balloon at the fair only to see it popped? After all, prior to this moment multitudes of God's people suffered and died at the hands of Pharaohs. Israel cried out. Heaven was silent. Year after year, justice was postponed for the oppressed, and God himself seemed like myth. Why? Here is why: so that "the Egyptians shall know that I am the LORD" (vv. 4, 18). God intends to fulfill his promises for Israel without abandoning his purposes for the nations.

God's deliverance for us is never separated from his purpose for our neighbors. Even our enemies' misdeeds serve God's purpose for reaching their hearts. God told Abraham that, through him, the nations would find blessing (Gen. 22:18). God is bringing about this larger covenantal promise for the nations through this particular promise of deliverance for Israel. Likewise, when he works marvelously and personally to deliver you, it is not for you alone.

Also, like those who died before the sea miracle came, we may not see the fulfillment of God's plans. But this does not mean that our children's children won't see it. The God who hears our prayers now, might choose to answer them for us and for them, then (Heb. 11:39–40).

The psalmist takes us here too: "Your way was through the sea, your path through the great waters; *yet your footprints were unseen.* You led your people like a flock by the hand of Moses and Aaron" (Ps. 77:19–20). God's footprints were unseen but present, because *he* was.

God delivered the people of Israel. He delivers us too. "When the fullness of time had come, God sent forth his Son" (Gal. 4:4). Justice and mercy meet. Dividing walls between nations crumble. Forgiveness and deliverance exult! Enemies can be saved. No more judgment by the sea. The cross of Christ stands now. The glory of the Lord reveals itself over the earth.

JANUARY 21 · EXODUS 16

Grumbling and Grace in the Wilderness

NANCY GUTHRIE

GOD HAD HEARD the cries of his people and sent a deliverer to bring them out of slavery in Egypt. He had held back a wall of water so they could cross through the Red Sea on dry ground, and then released it to drown their enemies. Most recently, he had brought them to an Eden-like oasis and sweetened the bitter water there to satisfy their thirst. They should have been overflowing with gratitude. But instead, they grumbled, accusing God of bringing them out into the wilderness to die of hunger.

God would have been just to let them starve right there in the desert. But God's grace is greater than his people's grumbling. His gracious response to their grumbling was to provide for them supernaturally. He had made his intentions clear before bringing them out of Egypt, telling them, "I will take you to be my people, and I will be your God" (Ex. 6:7). Here in the wilderness, he intended to teach them that this covenant relationship is a dependent relationship. He provides; his people receive. So that day and every day to follow for forty years, God's people awoke to find that bread from heaven had rained down on them so that all they needed to do was take and eat. Every day, as they faithfully refused to store up the manna and went to bed expecting it to rain down again the next morning, they were learning what it means to live by faith, learning to trust the one who said, "I will be your God."

Centuries later, when Jesus fed five thousand people with a few loaves and fish, the people remembered the miracle of the manna and wanted Jesus to do it again. When Jesus responded, saying, "I am the bread of life; whoever comes to me shall not hunger" (John 6:35), they did just what their ancestors did in the wilderness: they "grumbled" (John 6:41). "Your fathers ate the manna in the wilderness, and they died," Jesus said. "I am the living bread that came down from heaven. If anyone eats of this bread, he will live forever. And the bread that I will give for the life of the world is my flesh" (John 6:49, 51). Jesus, in his righteous life and atoning death, is God's provision that nourishes and satisfies the human soul.

As we live by faith in the wilderness of this world, Jesus, the true and living bread from heaven, continues to offer himself to us. Eating the true bread means savoring his sacrificial death as our life. It means nourishing our souls with the benefits of his atoning death, confident that we will be fed in this way day by day until we cross over into the Promised Land.

Whoever Touches the Mountain Shall Be Put to Death

ROBERT A. PETERSON

FEAR AND TREMBLING. These words describe the emotions of Israel at the foot of Mount Sinai. Why? Because they, a sinful people, are approaching the presence of the holy God. The people have come and encamped at the foot of Mount Sinai. God speaks through Moses, the covenant mediator, and reminds them of God's great judgment on the Egyptians and his great deliverance of the Israelites from Egyptian bondage: "I bore you on eagles' wings and brought you to myself" (Ex. 19:4).

Now the Lord encourages the people to obey him faithfully. Though all the earth belongs to him, he promises to make Israel his treasured possession among all peoples, as they trust and obey him. Indeed, God will make them "a kingdom of priests and a holy nation," his representatives to other nations (v. 6). The people quickly agree to obey all the Lord's commands.

So, why the fear and trembling? One reason is God's warning that any person or animal that touches Mount Sinai will die by stoning. God's holy presence makes the mountain holy. He tells the people to consecrate themselves and wash their clothes in preparation for receiving the Ten Commandments. A second reason for the people's fear is the awesome sound-and-light-show the Lord produces. He appears in a thick cloud and fire with thunder, lightning, loud trumpet blasts, and smoke. Even "the whole mountain trembled greatly" at the presence of the holy God (v. 18)! No wonder "all the people in the camp trembled" (v. 16).

All of this is good preparation for the tabernacle worship that follows. Then, as now, it is easy for us to forget the awesome holiness of God. He commands us today to conduct ourselves with proper fear and reverence toward him (1 Pet. 1:17). Should we then tremble before God's holiness, as Israel did before receiving the law? The New Testament answers this question: "For you have not come to . . . a blazing fire and darkness and gloom and a tempest and the sound of a trumpet. . . . But you have come

to Mount Zion and to the city of the living God, the heavenly Jerusalem
. . . and to Jesus, the mediator of a new covenant, and to the sprinkled
blood that speaks a better word than the blood of Abel" (Heb. 12:18–19,
22, 24). Praise God that all believers belong to Jesus, the Mediator of the
new covenant, whose blood cleanses us of all sins!

JANUARY 23 · EXODUS 25:10-22

Place of Meeting

MARY A. KASSIAN

INTERIOR DESIGNERS often choose a feature piece as the foundation of their
design. The feature piece of the tabernacle was the ark of the covenant,
which was kept behind a veil in the innermost room, the Most Holy Place.
It was the central and most important item, for it was where God "met with"
the high priest, the representative of his people. That's why the tabernacle
was also called "the tent of meeting" (Ex. 40:34).

The ark was a small but very elegant gilded chest that measured 45
inches long and 27 inches high and wide. The chest contained the "testimony," the two tablets of the Ten Commandments written by God, one
copy being his and one copy being Israel's, stored together as a symbol of
their covenant agreement. The lid of the chest was made of a solid slab
of pure gold that probably weighed about two hundred pounds, the current value of which would be well over four million dollars. The gold was
shaped, at either end, into the form of cherubim, who marked off through
their positioning, posture, and outstretched wings a sacred space just
above the ark's cover.

Unlike other angels, cherubim are not messengers. These intelligent,
powerful beings remain in God's presence as throne attendants and palace
guards, denying access to anything unholy (Gen. 3:24; 2 Sam. 22:11; Ezek.
28:14, 16; Ps. 18:10). The Bible tells us that the Lord "sits enthroned upon
the cherubim" (Ps. 99:1). This means that the cover of the ark of the covenant was an earthly symbol of a heavenly reality—a three-dimensional
image that represented the burning angels beneath God's throne.

The lid was called the "mercy seat." The Hebrew word carries the meaning of "covering over" in the sense of covering over sins. It contains the concept of atonement and reconciliation, the process that turns enemies into friends. On the Day of Atonement, the high priest sprinkled blood on and in front of the mercy seat (Lev. 16:14–15).

The symbolism is powerful. God, in all his holiness, sits enthroned above the cherubim. The blood of a pure, spotless lamb on the mercy seat atones for and covers up people's failure to live up to the law's holy requirements, making it possible for sinners to approach God. The ark of the covenant symbolized for Israel what was later accomplished by Christ, who as the Lamb of God made atonement for sin by his shed blood, thereby tearing the veil that guarded the ark, so that everyone who believes in him can freely meet with God (Matt. 27:50–51; Rom. 3:25; Heb. 4:14–16; 9:11–14).

JANUARY 24 · EXODUS 30:1–10

The Altar of Incense

DAN DORIANI

TWO ALTARS, both located in the tabernacle, were essential to Israel's worship. The most well-known is the altar of burnt offering, where priests offered sacrifices to atone for the sins of the people. The altar of incense was smaller, but Exodus 30:10 still calls it "most holy to the LORD." It stood by the Most Holy Place, near the curtain that separated the Holy Place from the Most Holy Place (Ex. 30:6; 40:26). God commanded priests to burn incense on it daily, in the morning and at twilight (30:7–8). Priests would offer incense on the altar of incense at the same time that other priests were offering blood sacrifices on the altar of burnt offering. The incense burned continually, filling the Holy Place with a sweet aroma and a cloud of incense.

In Psalm 141, David compares prayer to incense: "Let my prayer be counted as incense before you, and the lifting up of my hands as the evening sacrifice!" (Ps. 141:2). Revelation 8:3 also links the altar of incense to prayer: the smoke rising from the golden altar before God's throne symbolizes the prayers of the suffering church.

Ultimately, Jesus's atoning sacrifice takes the place of the burnt offerings. It is his sacrifice that lets us approach God in prayer. If we know Jesus as Savior, God receives us with pleasure and our prayers are like incense before him.

Exodus 30 specifies how the altar of incense must be built. It was made of acacia wood and overlaid with pure gold. A horn protruded from each of the altar's four corners. Its base was square, eighteen inches to a side, and stood three feet high (vv. 2–3). Two golden rings were mounted on each side, and the priests moved it by slipping poles through the rings (vv. 4–5).

The instructions are very specific, down to the formula for the incense (vv. 34–38). This teaches us that we must worship, not however we please, but as God directs. That is why our worship today features prayers, confessions of sin, words and songs of praise, gifts and tithes, the reading and proclamation of God's word, and—above all—a focus on the work of Christ. We no longer need altars, however, because Jesus offered the sacrifice that permanently opens the way to the Father: "For by a single offering he has perfected for all time those who are being sanctified" (Heb. 10:14).

JANUARY 25 · EXODUS 33:12-23

He Knows Us by Name

BRIAN BORGMAN

MOSES IS UNIQUE in the history of redemption. God spoke directly and intimately with him (Ex. 33:11). He was a prophet and an intercessor, speaking God's words to the nation and speaking to God on behalf of the nation. Moses was the covenant mediator. He also played a special role in pointing to the coming One, who would be a prophet like himself (Deut. 18:15–19).

In this passage, Moses continues to intercede for the wayward Israelites. His intercession had spared them previously, and now Moses intercedes once more. Although stubborn, this people belongs to the Lord. They need more than deliverance from judgment. Moses knows that God himself must accompany the people. God's covenant presence must be what distinguishes them from all other people on the face of the earth. Moses appeals to the favor he has with the Lord; he appeals to God's character, to God's previously spoken words, and to the fact that the people are actually God's own possession. God grants his petition: "This very thing that you have spoken I will do, for you have found favor in my sight, *and I know you by name*" (Ex. 33:17).

In response to God's gracious answer, Moses declares that he wants to see God's glory (v. 18). But even Moses needs *mediated* glory. No one can see God's face and live. Moses, the covenant mediator, has persuasively interceded with God, and yet even this great mediator needs to be shielded from the glory of God. He is hidden in the cleft of the rock and covered by God's hand (v. 22).

Moses points us to our supreme covenant mediator, God's Son, Jesus Christ. Like Moses, Jesus also prays for his people (John 17). His intercession preserves us and secures us all the way to the end (Heb. 7:25). Jesus's prayers are better than the prayers of Moses because Jesus is the Son who is over God's house. Jesus is a better mediator than Moses because Jesus not only had no need to be shielded from God's glory; he was the manifestation of God's glory (John 1:14; Heb. 1:3).

Moses points us to Christ, our intercessor and mediator. Through Jesus Christ we can confidently enter into God's presence, safe in the cleft of the true Rock. As we come to the Father, through the Son, in the Spirit (Eph. 2:18), we can pray with confidence, appealing to God's character, appealing to God's own words. We can know that we have found favor in God's sight because of Christ, and *he knows us by name* (Isa. 43:1; John 10:3, 27).

Second Chances

MARY PATTON BAKER

HAVE YOU EVER been brought back from disobedience or moral failure to the realization of the wonder of God's forgiveness? How did you demonstrate your gratitude for his grace? Such is the situation presented to the Israelites when Moses came down the mountain the second time to deliver the Ten Commandments and to request contributions for the building of the tabernacle.

Before the debacle of the golden calf, the Lord had already described in great detail to Moses the requirements for building the place where he was to dwell with his people (Exodus 25–31). We also read there the list of contributions needed, which would come from the Israelites' plunder carried out from Egypt: their most precious metals, gemstones, and wood; their finest threads and linens; their most fragrant spices; and their richest hides (Ex. 25:1–9).

How difficult it must have been for Moses when he came down the mountain that first time—after spending forty days and nights enveloped in the presence of God—only to find that the Israelites had already offered up their golden jewelry to fashion an idol, a golden calf. In casting the calf, the people demonstrated their distrust of the Lord and of Moses, which gave way to disobedience and carnal desires.

While the instructions given by Moses in this passage may seem repetitive after reading Exodus 25:1–9, the repetition itself is the message. Despite Israel's apostasy, God did not abandon his promise to come and dwell among them in his tabernacle. He is giving them another chance to demonstrate their faithfulness. What we treasure reveals our hearts (Matt. 6:21). Therefore, the Lord is asking his people to love him above any other by giving from their hearts. God offers all Israelites, both male and female, the chance to give their finest possessions and talents in the construction of his dwelling. Everyone is given the opportunity to express gratitude and love to the Lord for his forgiveness.

Happily, the Israelites take this second chance and succeed. We are told that the Israelites' hearts and spirits were "stirred" (Ex. 35:21–26) to give and to do everything the Lord commanded. Riches that previously would have been offered for the building of the golden calf were now offered for the worship of the Lord. They gave willingly and generously.

There is forgiveness for those who sin. God does not abandon his plans for us when we fail. And true giving can come only from a heart softened and stirred by God's forgiveness, love, and grace.

JANUARY 27 · EXODUS 40:34–38

He Is with Us

KATHLEEN CHAPELL

OUR SON COLIN was three years old when he asked Jesus into his heart. Literally. After we prayed with him, Colin opened his eyes, pulled the neck of his T-shirt away from his chest, looked down into his shirt, and said cheerfully, "Are you in there, Jesus?"

We had talked with Colin many times about how much Jesus loved him, how Jesus died and rose again, and that when we ask Jesus to be our Savior, Jesus will live in our hearts forever. Colin wanted to make sure that Jesus was, indeed, *in* his heart—that Jesus was actually *with* him.

For the Israelites, the tabernacle indicated the very presence of God with them. "For the cloud of the LORD was on the tabernacle by day, and fire was in it by night, in the sight of all the house of Israel throughout all their journeys" (Ex. 40:38). The visible sign of the cloud and fire represented God's presence to his people.

The design and contents of the tabernacle also spoke to the people. The ark contained the rod of Aaron—representing the delivering grace of God. God's sustaining grace to his people was represented by manna. The tablets of the Ten Commandments showed the law, which reveals God's character and also reveals our failure to fulfill that law in our own strength. The cover of the ark—the mercy seat—was the place where sin was covered, sprinkled by the blood of a sacrificial and spotless lamb.

These physical articles, combined with the very design of the tabernacle—its colors, the courts, the veil—all served as powerful symbols. They were visual means by which the Israelites were to recognize their need of God, their inability to approach him on their own merit, and the means by which they could know his presence—through sacrifice and priestly intercession.

And yet, this presence would not be completely fulfilled by this tent and its furnishings, nor by the beautiful temple later built by Solomon. God's presence with his people would not be fully realized until the true Immanuel—"God with us"—appeared. The full manifestation of the glory cloud of Exodus is Jesus, Immanuel, who comes to "tabernacle" with us, first in the form of a man, and now through the work of the Holy Spirit (John 1:14; 14:17).

We want to *know* that Jesus is in our hearts. We long to feel his presence. "Are you in there, Jesus? Are you *still* in there, Jesus?" The testimony of all of Scripture points to God's relentless love for his children—his faithfulness, his compassion, his provision, his presence! He is with us. He is "in there"! He will never leave us.

JANUARY 28 • LEVITICUS 8

God Provides Priests

MARY WILLSON

LIKE A GOOD SCHOOLTEACHER, God illustrates profound truths for his children in ways we can grasp. He demonstrated fundamental aspects of his character when he instructed Moses to ordain Aaron and his sons for the priesthood. Bringing them before the people, Moses washed (Lev. 8:6), robed (vv. 7–9), and anointed them along with the sacrificial instruments (vv. 10–13). Moses then made atonement for these new priests by offering sacrifices and placing elements of these purification offerings upon them to identify them with the altar (vv. 14–29). After completing the priests' consecration (v. 30), he sealed their ordination with a covenant meal (v. 31). While we may be tempted to view these rituals as meaningless tedium,

God skillfully engaged his people's senses to reveal essential attributes of his character and theirs.

First, God's instructions confirmed his desire to dwell with his people in a relationship of covenant love. While the Israelites lived in tents in the wilderness, God also lived in a tent in the center of their camp. He provided everything necessary for his dwelling place, including priests. God's passion to "tabernacle" with his people culminated in his Son, who took on flesh (in John 1:14, the word translated "dwelt among" could be rendered "pitched his tent").

Second, these rituals displayed God's holiness. God's presence required atonement and sanctification for every element of the tabernacle, including the priests. In their role as covenant mediators, Aaron and his sons received a dangerous ministry (Lev. 8:34–35). The very day the Lord accepted Aaron's high priestly offering (ch. 9), two of Aaron's sons transgressed their priestly orders and died (10:1–3). In contrast, Jesus Christ is the perfect high priest who never had to make atonement for himself to appear before God (Heb. 9:6–14).

Third, these special ceremonies showcased God's mercy. In the sequence of Israel's unfolding story, Aaron's most recent official action had been his construction of the golden calf. Aaron's idolatry led to thousands of deaths and severe division among the Hebrews. Yet in this passage, God clothed this chief of sinners with beautiful robes to commission him as his servant. In full view of the congregation, God indisputably restored Aaron's ministry and graciously crowned an egregious sinner.

These consecration rituals prepared God's people for the gospel, when God would ordain his own Son as the perfect high priest. Jesus atoned for the guilt of his people by becoming sin in our place and shedding his own blood so that he might crown us with salvation, clothe us in robes of righteousness, and bind himself to us in covenant love. By his blood, Christ consecrates even the vilest offender as part of his royal priesthood (1 Pet. 2:4–12). In light of such a gospel, fly for refuge to this holy God who goes the distance to dwell with sinners like us, and joyfully proclaim his excellencies in this world.

Sin Cleansed and Carried Away

NANCY GUTHRIE

THROUGHOUT THE YEAR, the Israelites brought the prescribed sacrifices for sin and presented them to the priests. The priests would sprinkle the blood of the animals against the veil of the tabernacle and upon the horns of the altar of incense, symbolically transferring the sins of the people into the sanctuary. Once a year, on the Day of Atonement, the sanctuary was ceremonially cleansed of the accumulated sins.

On that day, as he represented the people in the Most Holy Place, the high priest exchanged his usual royal robes for the garments of a servant. To enter into God's holy presence, he had to be ceremonially cleansed of his own sin, so after washing, he offered the blood of a bull as a sin offering for himself. Then two goats were brought to him.

When the people saw the high priest slit the throat of the first goat and carry its blood behind the veil they should have thought, "That should be my blood. Death is what my sin deserves. But God has allowed the death sentence I deserve to be passed onto this animal instead of me." As the priest sprinkled the blood over the mercy seat and on the horns of the altar, it became a cleansing agent, washing away the collected sins of the people.

Then the high priest put his hands on the second goat's head and began to confess the sins of the people, ceremonially transferring their guilt to the goat. As the priest worked his way through their specific sins—their lack of love for God, their cruelty toward each other, their coveting, their lying, their adultery—the people would have heard their own sins spoken by the priest. Then they would have watched as the goat was led away through the sea of tents, out of the camp, and into the wilderness, never to be seen again, and they would have felt relief that their sin-guilt had been carried far away.

But perhaps they also longed for a priest who did not need to offer a sacrifice for his own sin, a priest who had no sin. Perhaps they longed for a sacrifice that would be of such perfection and worth that they wouldn't have to offer animal sacrifices day after day and year after year. Jesus was that great high priest who had no sin. He became both the sacrifice whose blood cleanses away sin as well as the one who carries away sin. At the cross, "the Lord has laid on him the iniquity of us all" (Isa. 53:6), so that we might know, "as far as the east is from the west, so far does he remove our transgressions from us" (Ps. 103:12).

Love Your Neighbor as Yourself

GLENNA MARSHALL

IN GIVING HIS LAW to Israel, God calls his people to holy living. Now that he has rescued them from slavery in Egypt, they belong to him and can live as his people in the Promised Land that he will one day give them. Holy living reflects the holy God Israel now serves.

In Leviticus 19 God commands Israel to be generous, fair, and honest in its treatment of others. Every Israelite is to exercise kindness toward his neighbors, caring for their needs just as he cares for his own.

Who qualifies as a neighbor? While the command certainly includes fellow Israelites, verse 10 extends the command to the sojourner—a foreigner, an exile, or an outsider passing through the land. In verse 34 God commands the Israelites to love sojourners as their own people, remembering that they themselves had been sojourners in Egypt until God delivered them. Loving one's neighbor as oneself means extending care for people beyond ethnic Israel. We see a specific demonstration of this kind of care for sojourners in the book of Ruth.

Underscoring each command in Leviticus 19 is a statement about God himself: "I am the Lord your God." Written into his laws for Israel are reminders of what God has done for his people in rescuing them from slavery, splitting the Red Sea for their dry passage, and caring for them as they began their trek toward the Promised Land. He is their rescuer, their deliverer, their God.

The command found in Leviticus 19:18 extends to believers in Christ. We are commanded by Jesus to love our neighbors and pray for our enemies (Matt. 5:44), just as Christ did (Luke 23:34). Jesus explains that all the Law and the Prophets can be summarized in the two commands to love God and to love one's neighbor (Matt. 22:37–40). The apostle Paul echoes Jesus: "Love does no wrong to a neighbor; therefore love is the fulfilling of the law" (Rom. 13:10).

Israel was to love her neighbors in a way that reflected the love she had been shown by God. Likewise, we as believers love and care for others because we recognize and are grateful for the love our Savior has lavished on us. Jesus laid down his own life for us, his enemies (Rom. 5:8), putting flesh and bone to the command to love one's neighbor as oneself. When we were outsiders, he loved us and gave himself for us, bringing us into the family of God (Eph. 2:13).

JANUARY 31 · LEVITICUS 22:17–31

What Is Your Currency?

CAROLYN ARENDS

THERE IS A POPULAR notion in parenting that, in order to effect change in a child, parents must discover that child's "currency." When parents control the access to whatever matters to a kid (be that toys or computer privileges or whatever), they have the ability to capture her attention and encourage desirable attitudes and behaviors. In a healthy household, the goal is not so much manipulation as motivation; the idea is to use a child's currency to promote the conduct that will allow both the individual and the family as a whole to flourish.

Here in Leviticus, God captures his children's attention by quite literally controlling their currency. Livestock both feeds and funds the Israelites, and unblemished animals fetch the best prices. In insisting that only perfect livestock be used for sacrifices, God teaches that flourishing can take place only when they make *him* the ultimate priority.

The prophet Malachi will bring this point home later in Israel's history, pointing out that if blemished animals aren't sufficient for the payment of taxes, they certainly aren't worthy of the living God (Mal. 1:6–9). And

Jesus will cover this principle succinctly when he observes, "Where your treasure is, there your heart will be also" (Matt. 6:21). When God asks the Israelites to place their most valuable livestock on the altar, he's really asking for their hearts.

There's more to the story, of course. The extensive regulations given in Leviticus are not an arbitrary accumulation of religious red tape. Rather, they are a means of grace, an ongoing way to deal with the people's guilt and shame so that the holy God can live among them. They reveal the extent of humanity's "sin problem," the seriousness of the measures needed to remedy it, and the radical restructuring of priorities required in order to be God's people. The cost to the Israelites will include their best animals. The cost to God will be immeasurable.

In demanding perfect sacrifices, God is not only teaching the Israelites to prioritize their relationship with him. More deeply, he is beginning to reveal the ultimate cost of that relationship—the sacrifice of his own perfect Son. Centuries later, the apostle Peter will remind us that we have been ransomed "with the precious blood of Christ, like that of a lamb without blemish or spot" (1 Pet. 1:19).

How should we respond to such sacrifice? What is our "currency"? How can we lay it on the altar? In Jesus, the sacrifice of atonement has been made once and for all. Let's make our lives an offering of thanksgiving.

FEBRUARY 1 · LEVITICUS 26

The Motivation for Obedience

MIKE BULLMORE

THERE ARE TWO great lessons to learn from Leviticus 26. The first has to do with what motivates our obedience; the second has to do with God's seriousness about our obedience.

Too often we can think of our obedience to God only in terms of his authority. He's in charge, and that's why we have to obey. But mature obedience first sees, and then responds to, the manifold character of God—his wisdom, his goodness, his justice, and his fatherly eagerness to bless.

The refrain "I am the LORD your God" appears repeatedly in this chapter (Lev. 26:1, 2, 13, 44, 45). What is significant is not just how often it appears but *where* it appears, very noticeably at both beginning and end. Clearly, God is emphasizing something here. When God says to his people, "I am the LORD," he is assuming some prior knowledge on their part. He is reminding them of how he has cared for them, been faithful to them, and poured out blessing on them. So when we hear that God's people should obey "*for* I am the LORD your God" (v. 1), we should hear God saying not just "Obey, because I'm in charge" but also "Obey, because I desire you to continue to experience goodness from my hand." Obedience is fundamentally a matter of trust, and trusting God takes all of God into consideration. A growing knowledge of God is what should, and will, rightly motivate our obedience.

But there is also something for us to learn here about God's seriousness regarding our obedience. What strikes us as we read this chapter is that the description of God's punishment for disobedience is considerably more extensive and graphic than the description of his blessing for obedience. This is to be understood not as some study in God's cruelty but as an indication of his absolute commitment to turn his people from their sin. Why? Because sin is destructive.

Yes, there will come a point where God will turn away from those who persist in sin. He himself will be against them (v. 28) and even "abhor" them (v. 30). And yet notice this: "If they confess their iniquity" (v. 40) and their "heart is humbled" (v. 41), "I will not spurn them, neither will I abhor them so as to destroy them utterly" (v. 44). Instead, God says, "I will remember my covenant with them, for I am the LORD their God" (see vv. 44–45).

In the end, Leviticus 26 reminds us that it is God's heart of love we hear in his call to obedience. As Paul tells us, "Note then both the kindness and the severity of God" (Rom. 11:22).

Time to Move

MARY A. KASSIAN

ISRAEL WAS ON the verge of a change. God's people had been camped at Mount Sinai for almost a year. There God gave them his commandments. He provided detailed instructions for building the ark of the covenant and the tabernacle. He taught them about the priesthood and the sacrificial system. He instructed them about commemorating the Passover. He appointed tribal leaders and instituted statutes to govern the nation. Their preparation was complete. It was time for them to tear down camp, step out into the wilderness, and move on.

It must have been unsettling to leave the familiarity of Mount Sinai and head out into the unknown. But there was one thing they could be sure of: they wouldn't be alone. The Lord was going with them. He would be their protector and guide. He had been with them ever since the day they left Egypt. On their three-month trek to Mount Sinai, "the LORD went before them by day in a pillar of cloud to lead them along the way, and by night in a pillar of fire to give them light" (Ex. 13:21). Then, when the tabernacle was finished, the glory of the Lord settled over it, in a cloud by day and "like the appearance of fire by night" (Ex. 40:34–35; Num. 9:15). If there was one lesson the Israelites should have learned, it was that the presence of God was always there. This new journey into the wilderness would be no different. Just as God had guided them out of Egypt, so he would continue to guide them on their journey to the Promised Land.

The cloud was the manifestation of the Lord's very person and presence (Ex. 40:34–38). When the cloud lifted, it represented the movement and leading of God. When the cloud settled over the tabernacle, it represented his stopping and settling. Sometimes the time of rest was long (Num. 9:19); at other times the cloud remained only for a few days or a night (vv. 20–21). In every circumstance, the people were prepared to respond to divine direction (v. 23). When God moved, they moved. When he stopped, they stopped. It would have been foolish and dangerous for the camp or any part of it to move without God's leading. He not only showed them where to go but also showed them the right timing. What an amazing picture of his guidance!

Under the terms of the new covenant, you have something infinitely better than a fiery cloud to lead you. The Lord gives you the indwelling presence of his Holy Spirit to be your personal counselor and guide. As you rely on the word of God, the Spirit will lead you always—by day and by night. So, when you're on the verge of a change, and it's time to move on, be assured that you will never be alone.

FEBRUARY 3 · NUMBERS 13:1–14:38

How Faith Changes Everything

SAM STORMS

MANY MISTAKENLY think that, if they could only witness a miracle, some sign or wonder, their faith would forever remain strong. While signs, wonders, and miracles are wonderful expressions of divine power and provision, they often do not accomplish what we hoped they might. The fault is not with the supernatural, of course, but with us.

Consider Israel. No people at any time in history witnessed the power of the supernatural as often as did the nation of Israel. The ten plagues in Egypt, deliverance at the Red Sea, the daily guiding presence of the pillars of cloud and fire, manna falling from heaven, water flowing from a rock, the giving of the Ten Commandments, and the stunning defeat of Israel's enemies, to name a few, would seem to be sufficient to sustain and deepen their faith in God and their confidence in the leadership of Moses. But such was not the case.

The Lord commanded Moses to send twelve spies into the land of Canaan to investigate the people who inhabited it. Upon their return, all but two responded in fear, doubt, and hesitation. God quite simply never factored into their assessment. They saw only the problem and proceeded to shrink. Caleb and Joshua, on the other hand, looked upon the situation in the land from the perspective of God and his power and promises. They were looking at the same group of Canaanites as were the ten, but their conclusion was altogether different. God's discipline against the spies was severe, as only Caleb and Joshua were allowed to enter the Promised Land.

We learn from this sad tale that how we perceive and think about God will inform and shape how we perceive and think about everything else. Our concept of God will govern how we think about politics, relationships, suffering and hardship, marriage, sex, the economy, and everything else.

We often act as though the reverse is true. How often do we experience success or failure, pleasure or pain, hope or despair, joy or frustration, and then from that draw conclusions about who God is and whether or not he can be trusted or believed? Like so many of the Israelites, we invest in our circumstances the authority to dictate our concept of God. We see him in light of the circumstances, rather than the reverse.

Joshua and Caleb did not reason from the bottom up, as if life and its mysteries and struggles determine who God is. Rather, they reasoned from the top down. They saw everything in life in the light of who God is. It wasn't that Caleb and Joshua were "positive thinkers" or overly optimistic whereas the other ten were pessimists. The issue was one of faith versus unbelief.

FEBRUARY 4 · NUMBERS 16

Pride and Rebellion

LEEANN STILES

KORAH SHOULD HAVE known better. After all, he was first cousin to Moses (Ex. 6:18–21). His clan guarded the most holy things of the tabernacle (Num. 4:1–20). He crossed the Red Sea, followed the cloud, and listened to God's commandments. He saw God ban his generation from the Promised Land for believing the bad report of the spies (14:28–35). He watched Aaron's sons, Nadab and Abihu, die when they offered unauthorized fire before the Lord (Lev. 10:1–3). And as if this were not enough, the Lord gave one final warning: his glory appeared as Korah and his men approached the tent of meeting (Num. 16:19).

But Korah didn't act on what he knew. Pride blinded him. The Lord expected his people to remember and obey all of his commandments, and he set aside Aaron for the holiest of duties. So how could Korah claim to be pure while coveting the high priest's position? Korah manipulated God's words to suit his own desires, and persuaded no less than 250 leading men to rebel along with him.

Others revolted, too: Korah opposed Aaron; Dathan, Abiram, and On opposed Moses. They mocked the leadership of the men God chose.

It shouldn't surprise us that the Lord's judgment came against these rebels quickly and irrevocably. He acted according to his character and his covenant with Israel. He upheld his holiness in the destruction of the defiant. But amid the judgment we see his mercy: Aaron's censer stilled the plague (16:47).

Yes, Korah should have known better. But what about me? I receive God's blessings and understand much more than Korah about his character and ways. I listen to teaching on biblical leadership and my responsibility to respect and follow. Yet a Korah lurks in my heart. I'm a rebel. Pride too often motivates me. I think I deserve bigger and better things. I want my way, and so I balk at godly leadership. I'm careless about God's holiness. My complaining poisons others' thoughts and actions.

These sins and many more merit God's judgment. My only hope is foreshadowed in Aaron's life-saving run through the dying camp (v. 47). It's a beautiful picture of the One who interceded for our sin on the cross, offering salvation from the punishment we deserve. "For the wages of sin is death, but the free gift of God is eternal life in Christ Jesus" (Rom. 6:23).

FEBRUARY 5 · NUMBERS 21:4-9

The Bronze Serpent and the Son of Man

BRYAN CHAPELL

THE VENOM OF the serpents that came upon the people of God was symbolic of the poison of ingratitude that was coming from their mouths. The consequences of sin often echo its nature—if we tell lies, people think we are a liar; if we are unfaithful to our spouse, our family cohesiveness unravels; if we walk away from God, he seems distant to us.

Jesus uses the symbolic nature of the bronze serpent to describe his own ministry. Jesus said, "as Moses lifted up the serpent in the wilderness, so must the Son of Man be lifted up, that whoever believes in him may have eternal life" (John 3:14–15). In order for the people of Moses's time to be saved from the consequences of their sin, they had to look at the bronze serpent. However, the serpent did not look like a deliverer—not like God, nor even like Moses. Instead, the serpent looked like (represented) the sin of the people that they had to face in order to be rescued by God.

When Jesus says that just as the serpent was "lifted up," so also would the Son of Man be lifted up, he is reminding us that our rescue requires looking toward him in his suffering on the cross. But when we turn to him there, with the nails in his hands and the thorns on his brow, what we are seeing represents the consequence of our sin. His suffering was caused by our sin and its penalty resting on him. And, as we look at him "lifted up" on the cross with the belief that our sin is upon him, God delights to grant eternal life by his grace.

Spiritual rescue from our sin is not about being good enough to merit God's love; it is a result of believing that our sin was put upon Jesus at the cross. When we face his suffering, with the belief that the sin represented and punished there is ours, then God promises that we shall *live*—both now and eternally without the condemnation of our sin. He who was perfectly righteous became sin for us so that, as we look to him for our salvation, his healing righteousness is ours (2 Cor. 5:21).

FEBRUARY 6 • NUMBERS 24

If God Is for Us

KRISTIE ANYABWILE

THE BOOK OF NUMBERS focuses on Israel's journey from Sinai to Canaan. A primary theme of the book is the unfolding of God's promise that Abraham's descendants would be his special people and occupy the Land of Promise. This passage highlights God's faithfulness and his power, clearly showing that if God is for Israel, nothing and no one can prevail against them.

Numbers 24 continues the saga of Balak, a man gripped with fear by the approaching Israelites, one who would stop at nothing to destroy them before they reached his country of Moab. Out of desperation, Balak had petitioned a sorcerer, Balaam, to curse the people of Israel, in the hope that Balak would then be able to defeat them. God spoke to Balaam directly, specifically, and clearly, commanding him to refuse Balak's request. But when Balak upped his offer (Num. 22:15–17), Balaam faltered. Clearly, he feared Balak and the potential loss of a sizable fortune more than he feared God's anger over his disobedience.

Balaam's first two attempts to curse the Israelites had been laughable. With no choice but to speak God's truth, he ironically ended up proclaiming oracles of blessing upon God's people! (ch. 23). In Numbers 24, God continues to speak through Balaam—*in spite of Balaam*. In his final oracles, Balaam prophesies about the rise of the Davidic dynasty and the fall of Moab: "a star shall come out of Jacob, and a scepter shall rise out of Israel; it shall crush the forehead of Moab" (24:17).

Man's efforts cannot thwart God's plans for his people. Indeed, out of Balaam's mouth came this final oracle that would ultimately be fulfilled in Jesus: "a star shall come out of Jacob, and a scepter shall rise out of Israel." This future King would usher in peace and blessing for all of God's people who would turn from trusting in their own power and wisdom. This King would establish a kingdom that will never end.

FEBRUARY 7 · DEUTERONOMY 4:1–40

The Power of Remembrance

SAM STORMS

FORGETFULNESS IS the fuel for idolatry (Deut. 4:23). Spiritual amnesia often leads to faithlessness. This is the most important lesson of Deuteronomy 4. God's concern is that his people might "forget the things" that they had seen, and that the memory of their gracious deliverance might "depart" from their hearts (v. 9). Thus we read here of the crucial importance of remembrance, of calling to mind again and again the history of God's dealings with us and his faithfulness at every turn.

The Bible has much to say about remembering the past. But we do not remember or reminisce out of some romanticized nostalgia or desire to return to days gone by. We don't remember just to complain that things now are worse than they were then. The purpose of biblical remembering is to remind us that the God who acted in the past is the same God who acts in the present. Remembering is not meant to transport us back in history but to prepare and equip and encourage us for the future.

This passage also teaches the importance of passing on a godly heritage to our children and grandchildren, who in turn can pass that heritage on to *their* children and grandchildren. What will your children remember as having mattered most to you? Will they grow old thinking of you parked in front of the TV, or glued to the Internet, or playing with your smart phone rather than engaging them in meaningful conversation? Mothers, will they think most of the many excuses you had for not showing up at their dance recital or ball game? Will they remember angry outbursts at their father and constant verbal criticism? Will they think only of the countless reasons for not taking them to church on Sunday, or the many nights you weren't there to read to them and pray for them as they went to bed?

What are you doing to preserve and sustain the knowledge of God in your heart and in the hearts of your children? What are you doing to keep both yourself and them mindful of his faithfulness? How are you teaching them a reverence for God and confidence in his word?

We must remember in order to fuel our worship of and love for God, and our gratitude for all he has done (see Psalm 103). Remembrance also brings power to overcome despondency, hopelessness, and doubt (Psalm 77). "I will remember the deeds of the LORD," declared the psalmist; "yes, I will remember your wonders of old. I will ponder all your work, and meditate on your mighty deeds. Your way, O God, is holy. What god is great like our God? You are the God who works wonders; you have made known your might among the peoples. You with your arm redeemed your people, the children of Jacob and Joseph" (Ps. 77:11–15).

Because I Love You

MARY BETH MCGREEVY

"WHY DO I HAVE TO go to bed now?" "Why do I have to eat my vegetables?" "Why can't I play in the street?" Parents hear questions like this every day. And the answer? "Because I love you and want what's best for you."

Moses anticipates this kind of question from the children of Israel: "What is the meaning of the testimonies and the statutes and the rules that the LORD our God has commanded you?" (Deut. 6:20). And God the Father's answer is much the same as an earthly parent's: "That your days may be long" (v. 2); "that it may go well with you, and that you may multiply greatly . . . in a land flowing with milk and honey" (v. 3); "because I love you with a jealous love" (see v. 15); "because I redeemed you" (see vv. 21–23); "for your good always, that I might preserve you" (see v. 24).

Some parents might give a different answer, such as, "Because I said so." Certainly, the Lord God has the right to say that. He could say, "Because I'm God, and you're not." But God does not base the motivation for obeying his commands to the Israelites on the fact that he is God, but on the fact that he is *their* God: "I am the LORD your God, who brought you out of the land of Egypt, out of the house of slavery" (5:6). Because he has set his love on them, he gives them his commandments (5:7–21). His commands flow out of his gracious love; the love comes before the commands and is not dependent upon obedience. God sets his love on sinners.

How can a just God do this? Because one day Someone would obey the commandments perfectly on behalf of God's people. Through his righteous life, substitutionary death, and glorious resurrection, the Lord Jesus Christ has fulfilled all the commands for everyone who will put their faith and trust in him. The Israelites looked forward in faith to his coming (Gen. 3:15; 12:3; Rom. 4:3). And just as with the redemption of the Israelites, the initiative is with God, who "shows his love for us in that while we were still sinners, Christ died for us" (Rom. 5:8).

The response of God's people in the Old Testament as well as the New is to be the same: "You shall love the Lord your God with all your heart and with all your soul and with all your might" (Deut. 6:5; Matt. 22:37). Our love is demonstrated in trusting obedience: "If you love me, you will keep my commandments" (John 14:15). How? By his enabling grace (2 Cor. 9:8; 12:9; Heb. 4:16). Why? "Because I love you" (1 John 4:19).

FEBRUARY 9 · DEUTERONOMY 7

Devoted to Destruction

NANCY GUTHRIE

WHEN GOD CALLED Abraham to go to Canaan, God told him that his descendants would be servants in a land that was not theirs for four hundred years but that they would eventually come back to Canaan, "for the iniquity of the Amorites is not yet complete" (Gen. 15:16). Evidently the evil of the various peoples living in Canaan at that time had not yet reached the point of deserving an obliterating judgment. But one day it would.

As the people of God prepared to cross over into Canaan, that day had come. Moses gave the Israelites clear instructions to devote the peoples living in the land to complete destruction. They were squatters and interlopers on land that belonged to God, land that had been promised by God to his people, where he intended to dwell among them. If the Israelites simply settled among them, the Canaanites' worship of false gods would threaten the purity of the Israelites' love for God alone. God had chosen the Israelites for the very purpose that they would belong exclusively to him, that they would be his "treasured possession," a special instrument of his purposes in the world. God was establishing what he intended to be his kingdom on earth.

The land of Canaan, however, was really just the launching place for God's plan to bring his people into his true holy land, the new heavens and new earth. And the physical descendants of Abraham who inherited the Promised Land of Canaan were just the beginning of the people from every tribe, language, people, and nation whom God has chosen to live in his holy land with him forever. "He chose us in him before the foundation of the world, that we should be holy and blameless before him. In love he predestined us for adoption . . . as sons through Jesus Christ" (Eph. 1:4–5). Israel was chosen in spite of her unworthiness. So are we. Israel was made holy by God's choosing. So are we.

The day will come when all who live in rebellion against God will be eternally evicted from God's holy land, the new heavens and new earth. On that day there will be no compromise with evil, no accommodation. Everything evil will be devoted to destruction so that nothing will pollute God's new creation. Finally, God's people will be everything he intended them to be. Forever they will enjoy the love of the God who chose them to be his treasured possession.

FEBRUARY 10 · DEUTERONOMY 9:1–12

Don't Forget: It's the Lord's Victory

JENNY SALT

AN ADVERTISEMENT that aired on Australian television several years ago boasted the slogan, "For the most important person in the world: you!" This attitude takes us back to Adam and Eve and the desire to "do it my way." Unfortunately, even some within God's church have contributed to this flawed way of thinking—that God will act for me because I deserve his goodness.

But the Bible teaches a different message—a message of grace and a warning of judgment in the context of God's holiness and glory. How then shall we live, in the context of God's grace and holiness?

In Deuteronomy, Moses addressed the children of Israel, the second generation of those he had rescued out of slavery in Egypt. The journey to the Promised Land that should have taken eleven days had taken nearly forty years because the first generation refused to take the Lord at his word and trust and obey. They were not permitted to enter. Now, forty years later, Israel was on the verge of entering the land, and Moses addressed them, reminding them of the appropriate response to God's covenant, and preparing them for what lay ahead.

Deuteronomy 9:1–12 is part of Moses's second and longest speech to the Israelites. Here the point is, the Lord will act with power and in judgment, and will defeat the Canaanites: "Know therefore today that he who goes over before you as a consuming fire is the LORD your God" (Deut. 9:3). The Lord will do what he says he will do. Why? Not because of his people's righteousness but because of the wickedness of the Canaanites, and because the Lord is faithful to his promises to Abraham, Isaac, and Jacob (v. 5). It was not because Israel deserved it or earned it, or because of their innate goodness. "Know, therefore, that the LORD your God is not giving you this good land to possess because of your righteousness, for you are a stubborn people" (v. 6). In other words, don't forget, Israelites, you have a history . . . and it is not a good one! "They have turned aside quickly out of the way that I commanded them" (v. 12).

God's help and deliverance are by grace alone. We cannot earn it, and we don't deserve it. To truly understand what we have in Christ, we need to understand the consequences of our sin and God's wrath. That is why Christ went to the cross. How should we respond in the light of his grace? "Therefore let us be grateful for receiving a kingdom that cannot be shaken, and thus let us offer to God acceptable worship, with reverence and awe, for our God is a consuming fire" (Heb. 12:28–29).

FEBRUARY 11 · DEUTERONOMY 11

The Choice between Blessing and Curse

DONNA THOENNES

WE ALL WANT God's blessing. The Israelites had waited four hundred years for the blessing of the Promised Land. After that long journey, Moses prepared them to cross the Jordan and finally enter the land. Earlier in Deuteronomy, Moses rehearsed God's blessings, but in chapter 11 his "pregame speech" recalls God's disciplinary actions. He reminds the people that they had personally witnessed God's actions: "your eyes have seen all the great work of the LORD that he did" (Deut. 11:7). Israel's personal experience should bolster their trust in God and result in future obedience.

Moses tells Israel plainly and simply, if you want to possess the land and remain in it, you must trust God enough to keep his commandments. After waiting so long for the Promised Land, the threat of exile must have been sobering. Moses reminds them how much they need God's protection and provision. In Egypt, irrigation watered the crops, but now God alone provides rain. Even the rainfall will be dependent on their obedience to God. If they turn from God, he will provide no rain, and they will perish. Lest the Israelites think they might be able to withstand a short-term curse, Moses reminds them there are long-term consequences as well. But with obedience, even the days of their children will be multiplied in the land.

Crossing into the Promised Land brings freedom for Israel: freedom to choose between blessing and curse. Moses desires deeply that they will make the right choice. He seems to plead with them to remember that God has acted on their behalf and has proven himself to them; why would they go after gods that they have not known, gods who had done nothing for them? It seems so foolish yet so familiar as we read Scripture and observe our own inclinations.

Moses instructs the people that, after they cross the Jordan, they are to reaffirm their covenant commitment publicly between two mountains (v. 29). God knows how forgetful his people are! There is power in reaffirming our commitments to God and to one another, mindful of his grace to us. Each time the Israelites would look up at those two mountains, they would be reminded of their choice between obedience and disobedience.

Thankfully, Jesus kept the law perfectly for us and took on himself the curse for our disobedience. Ultimately, our future includes only blessing for obedience. Yet in the day-to-day, God's warns us to obey his word and not depart from what we have learned. We obey not to remain in the land or to keep our end of the covenant, but with gratitude for Jesus's saving work on our behalf and eager expectation that we will one day see him face-to-face.

Godly Giving

MARY BETH MCGREEVY

AS MOSES ENDS his discourse of specific stipulations, he gives a splendid pattern for prayer and praise, knowing that these things will build the Israelites' faith and are the proper response to everything that God has done. After they enter the Promised Land and it produces a harvest, they are to remember all that the Lord their God has given (Deut. 26:1, 2, 9, 10, 11, 15) and respond in kind.

The Israelites were to take the first of all the fruit to the place that God would choose for the tabernacle (and later, the temple), and offer it before the altar (vv. 2–4). Then they were to recite a creed of what God had done— from Jacob and his family going to Egypt and becoming a great nation, to the Lord's mighty deliverance from slavery there, to his bringing them into the land flowing with milk and honey (vv. 5–9). They were to rejoice in *all* the good that the Lord their God had given to them, to their families, to the Levites, and even to the foreigners living among them. The greatest joy of all was that God had declared them "a people for his treasured possession, . . . a people holy to the LORD" their God, as he had promised that they would be (vv. 18–19). This glorious truth was to motivate them to love him and to obey all of his commands. "You shall therefore be careful to do them with all your heart and with all your soul" (v. 16).

Believers are blessed by following this pattern today. As the Lord our God prospers us, we are to take a portion of our material blessings to our place of worship on the first day of the week (1 Cor. 16:2) and give cheerfully (2 Cor. 9:7). When we are asked, "O Christian, what do you believe?" we respond with the Apostles' Creed, reciting what God has done through the Lord Jesus Christ—from his mighty deliverance from our slavery to sin, to the certainty of the resurrection of our bodies. We are to rejoice in *all* the good that the Lord our God has given to us in Christ. The greatest joy of all is that, in union with Christ, God has made us "a chosen race, a royal priesthood, a holy nation, a people for his own possession" (1 Pet.

2:9). As with the Israelites, this glorious truth ignites love for God and a desire to obey him, not *so that we might be* his treasured possession, but because *we already are.*

As you enter the worship service at your church this week, remember that prayer and praise for what God has given builds your faith and leads to loving obedience.

FEBRUARY 13 · DEUTERONOMY 30:11–20

Life or Death

ELISABETH MAXWELL (LISA) RYKEN

AS MOSES REACHES the end of his life—and the end of his faithful service in leading God's people—he preaches his final sermon, which he ends with one very practical exhortation: choose life, not death. It is a brilliant sermon, as he lays before the Israelites a brief history of God's work among them over the previous forty years (Deut. 29:2–8). He reminds them of the wonders they had witnessed in Egypt (29:2–3). He draws their attention to God's generous provision during their many years of wandering in the wilderness (29:5–9). And he calls them to renew their faithfulness to God's covenant (29:12).

Now, as the great prophet comes to the end of his sermon, he lays out the practical application: choose life. Unfortunately, having led these people for forty years, Moses knows all too well what they are like. He can anticipate their objections: "Moses, what you are asking is too difficult. We cannot possibly do it. How do we know what God requires?"

But Moses tells the people that what God demands is "not too hard for you, neither is it far off" (30:11). Moses has spent the better part of four decades teaching the people what God expects. Moses makes it simple for the people by giving them an either/or choice (v. 15). Choose life *or* death. Choose good *or* evil. Choose blessing *or* curse. Choose the living God *or* dead idols.

In presenting these options, Moses is calling the people to obedience, knowing that the alternative will bring only misery and death. Finally, he pleads with them to love "the LORD your God, obeying his voice and holding fast to him, for he is your life and length of days, that you may dwell in the land that the LORD swore to your fathers, to Abraham, to Isaac, and to Jacob, to give them" (v. 20).

Each of us is given the same choice: whom will I serve? We must decide. We are called to walk faithfully with our God, to obey his voice, to turn away from idols, and to hold fast to God. And we have even more reason to make these choices than the Israelites did. They knew about God's faithfulness to their fathers: Abraham, Isaac, and Jacob. They had witnessed the wonders that God had performed in Egypt, and the provision he had made for them in the wilderness. How much more provision we have in the finished work of Christ Jesus! Jesus has brought us out of the Egypt of our sins. He has offered himself as the Passover Lamb for our salvation. He gives himself to us as living bread. Now he calls us to follow him. What choice will you make?

FEBRUARY 14 • DEUTERONOMY 32

Singing the Faith

KRISTYN GETTY

IN BIBLICAL TIMES, people did not have history books the way we do today. So one way they learned about their past was in the singing of songs passed down to them. This song of Moses is a memory device to remind the children of Israel who God is and who they are in relation to him. Composed in the key of God's unfolding melody of judgment and redemption, it is a warning to Israel to keep themselves from the mistakes their ancestors made. At the same time, it is also a beautiful reminder of God's faithfulness to restore his wayward people. Moses tells Israel to take his words to heart, for they are not empty but are "your very life" (Deut. 32:47).

What we sing as the family of God is of critical importance. The songs of a generation shape minds and hearts more profoundly than we could imagine. The songs of the church today should build our understanding and enrich our celebration of the whole story of faith that has been passed down to us. "Remember the days of old; consider the years of many generations" (v. 7). We are not the first to follow this God; no, like rings growing in the same tree, each generation of God's people are adding their lives to the same great heritage of divine redemption that holds us all together. At the center of this heritage is the saving work of Christ, the song of mercy that covers every page of time.

The songs of the church should reach to us over time and circumstance, into our present moment. If our words are based in God's word, they will be like rain on the thirsty ground of this world and speak with timeless, undiminished strength (v. 2). This song remained in Israel's songbook to be sung while experiencing national freedom, in foreign occupation, and in long exile. What an incredible thing it is to see multiple generations singing together songs old and new—songs that bear truths that have been celebrated in the best and worst of times. Songs that become testimonies of failure and grace, encouraging us to persevere despite our circumstances.

The songs of the church must ring with our future hope. God promises that "he avenges the blood of his children. . . . and cleanses his people's land" (v. 43). At the cross our enemy, sin, was defeated, and when Christ returns our final enemy of death will be defeated forever. There will be judgment, and there will be restoration. This hope should shape the rhythm of our lives.

May the music of our mouths and our lives be as deep rushing rivers flowing from the ocean of his grace to our families, our congregations, and all those who listen, that we might remember over and over again what should never be forgotten: God's great work of grace in Christ on our behalf.

Be Strong and Very Courageous

ZACK ESWINE

WHAT SCARES YOU? Joshua has shown his courage valiantly (Num. 14:5–10). But even warriors grieve and fear. A grief-stricken leader and people must rouse themselves to responsibilities that did not die when Moses did. Promise waits, but frightens.

It is strange, isn't it, to feel frightened by promise? But promise often takes longer and comes harder than we imagined. Overcome by sorrows, hardships, and fears, we can give up, settle into the gloom, and sing dirges together about what might have been. No wonder, then, that God looks with kind strength into the eyes of this community. In nine verses, he calls for courage three times (Josh. 1:6, 7, 9). When fears haunt us, when circumstances do not turn out as planned, when tombs take their places in our memories, how do we "arise" and "go" forward?

First, God gives us himself. Joshua and the people have the same provision that Adam and Eve possessed, the same provision that Jesus would fulfill through the Spirit. "I will be with you," God says. "I will not leave you or forsake you" (v. 5). Every moment of providence—triumphant, tragic, or fearful—becomes a sanctuary from which we can learn to detect God's presence.

Second, God gives us each other (v. 2). Israel will look after each other—the aged, the children, the sick, and the weak along with the seasoned and strong. They will cross into the Promised Land, not alone but together.

Third, God gives his word. With God's help, Israel will look to the written word (v. 8). This will rearrange how they inhabit time, day and night. In contrast to the nations around them, they will find success, not in their wealth, power, or position, but in their God-shaped moments.

God's promises do not include an immunity pass from fear. We wish they did. And, like these spiritual ancestors of ours, we too can disbelieve his presence, disregard the neighbors he gives us, and try to do our days by meditating on words other than his. But this fearful community also gathers to remember the Passover (5:10). They recount the lamb's blood spread on doorposts. The death spared people, as they looked to a forgiveness based on a spotless offering that was not their own but was provided on their behalf. Likewise, you fearful ones, look to the spotless Lamb. Jesus takes your faltering and failing upon himself. He gives you his courage, his recognition of the Father in every circumstance, his neighbor love, his meditation on God's words. He did this and is with you. Be strong and very courageous.

A Heroine by Faith

CAROLYN ARENDS

JOSHUA 2 has all the elements of a blockbuster movie—espionage, impending warfare, and an unlikely but courageous heroine. Percolating beneath the action is an even bigger story: Yahweh is keeping the promises he made to Abraham (Genesis 15). He's already grown Israel into a great nation; now it's time to give his people their long-awaited land.

Joshua secretly sends two spies into Jericho. He hasn't forgotten what happened the last time the Israelites stood poised to enter the Promised Land. Moses had sent in twelve spies, and the terrifying reports delivered by ten of the men had turned the people fearful and rebellious (Numbers 13–14). Only Joshua and Caleb had believed God could do what he had promised; only Joshua and Caleb have survived to see that they were right.

This time, the spies have good news. The Canaanites have seen what Israel's God can do, and their hearts are melting with fear. But Jericho has its own reconnaissance, and the king knows that spies are afoot. The fate of the Israelite agents rests on Rahab, a Canaanite prostitute.

Rahab's house is situated within the city wall. It's an ideal lookout, and the spies are lodging there. Rahab knows who they are. Surprisingly, she also knows who their God is. "He is God in the heavens above and on the earth beneath," she declares (Josh. 2:11). Pagan Rahab demonstrates a faith greater than that of many of the Israelites when she decides to cast her lot with God's people. She presumes their impending victory, and agrees to aid the spies if they promise to spare her and her family.

There's nothing in Rahab's resume that should qualify her for a leading role in Israel's story. And yet, her faith is a matter of historical and theological significance. In the fast-paced account of the conquest of Jericho in chapter 6, the narrator pauses to note that Rahab is spared and is included as a member of the Israelite community (vv. 22–25). The author of Hebrews lists Rahab in his Hall of Fame (Heb. 11:31), and James cites her actions as examples of the works that accompany faith (James 2:25). Best of all, Rahab becomes a direct ancestor not only of King David, but of Christ (Matt. 1:5–6).

In Rahab, we see God beginning to accomplish yet another of his promises to Abraham—the pledge to expand his blessing to all nations. We also detect him continuing a pattern that should give us great hope. Repeatedly, God does his best work with the least likely people. For those who believe, human weakness becomes the perfect opening for divine strength (2 Cor. 12:9). When it comes to God's story, you cannot be disqualified!

Proofs of His Presence

KATHLEEN CHAPELL

MY FRIEND SARA has a three-year-old nephew. One afternoon little Nathan brought her a picture he had drawn. "Oh, Nathan," Sara said, looking at the drawing of a round circle containing two eyes, a dot for a nose, and a crooked little mouth, "This is wonderful! And who is it?"

"It's God," replied Nathan proudly.

"Oh," said Sara—and then, "How is this God?"

"Well," said Nathan, "I learned in Sunday school that God is a spirit, and has *no body* like man."

And there you see the cognitive difference between a three-year-old child and the scholars he was quoting: the child was thinking in pictures, the scholars in propositions. Of course, we all need our word pictures, parables, and illustrations to understand spiritual truths. We remain God's children in many ways. The Israelites were no different—they needed to be shown concrete illustrations of God in order to understand him.

In Joshua 3, God told Joshua that just as he was with Moses, he would be with Joshua and the Israelites in their journey. And then God provided concrete, visible proofs of his presence. The ark of the covenant represented the purity and power of God as well as the direction and safety he provided them. As the ark went before the people through the desert and across the Jordan, they were instructed to follow at a distance to acknowledge the holiness of God. The people were also told to follow the ark as an acknowledgment of their need for God's leading. "You have not passed this way before" (Josh. 3:4), they were reminded.

The distance kept the crowd from dishonoring the holiness of God and from choosing their own path. The distance was a visual lesson: God will provide all you need—the holiness you require and direction you need. When Jesus comes, God closes the distance, but the message has not changed: he provides the holiness we require and the direction we need. Jesus is Immanuel, God with us, purifying and guiding us as the perfect illustration of God's heart.

As the Lord made a way through the Red Sea in Exodus, and here across the Jordan, the people passed on dry ground. The destination was earthly for them. But in Jesus, God provides a way eternally—not through a sea or a river, but through his own Son, one who himself walked on the sea as if it were dry land.

"God is a spirit, and has no body like man." And yet he chose to put on a body, to suffer and die as a man, to provide for us a way to eternal rest.

FEBRUARY 18 · JOSHUA 6

The Fall of Jericho

ELIZABETH W. D. GROVES

THIS PASSAGE SHOUTS of God's might! The Lord God can destroy a mighty walled city simply by decreeing that it will happen. A word from his mouth—and a shout from his people—can knock down an enemy stronghold. This God, who created the world in seven days simply by saying, "Let there be . . . ," can send his people on a seven-day march around strong walls and make them fall down without so much as a touch. Forty years earlier, the Israelites had been awed by the impressive strength and prosperity of ancient Canaan and had doubted that the Lord could give them victory over it (Numbers 14). God's dazzling display of might in this episode is a resounding rebuke to their lack of faith.

God had promised the patriarchs the land of Canaan once the sin of the Amorites was "complete" (Gen. 15:16), and that time had now come. Sitting where it does in the flow of redemptive history—right at the outset of the conquest of Canaan—the fall of Jericho has a place of prominence and uniqueness. God overthrew Jericho in a way that demonstrated that nothing was impossible for him, the Divine Warrior, and that he was entirely capable of delivering the land into his people's hands. What a boost to their faith!

The response to such a mighty God should be faith and obedience. The Israelites needed to obey in precise detail, marching around Jericho for seven days, even if that felt ridiculous—just because the Lord said so. And they had to march in over the tumbled walls and fight the inhabitants of Jericho. In the next chapter we will see an Israelite who did *not* trust and obey God, and who was put to death because of it. But here we see God spare Rahab and all her family because of her faith that led to action. She was a Gentile *and a woman* (!), not a power broker even in her own society and certainly not in Israel. Yet because she had faith in the God of Israel and demonstrated it by risking her life to aid the Israelites, she saved her whole family, joined God's people, and even became an ancestor of Jesus!

Jericho was left a perpetual ruin, both because it was the firstfruits of war, holy to the Lord, and as a constant testimony and visual reminder of the Lord's might and faithfulness. Today we can look back at the cross and see an even greater thing the Lord has done for his people: dying for us and rising from the dead! May we be women who have faith in him and follow him, no matter the cost.

FEBRUARY 19 • JOSHUA 10:1–15

How Big Is Your God?

ELISABETH MAXWELL (LISA) RYKEN

HOW BIG IS YOUR GOD? Donald Grey Barnhouse, who preached in Philadelphia and traveled around the world as an evangelist, once described a conversation he had with a former professor who asked him if he was a "big-Godder" or a "little-godder." The professor explained that a "big-

Godder" believes in a God who is omnipotent and can do amazing miracles, whereas a "little-godder" believes in a limited god who can only do ordinary things.

You can only believe Joshua 10:1–15 if you have a great, big, omnipotent God. Cynics, skeptics, and other "little-godders" have a hard time with this passage. They do not believe that God is capable of killing with hailstones (Josh. 10:11) or preventing the sun from setting (v. 13). They want to know how God could have sent such deadly hailstones or could have made the sun stand still. Did he perform some optical illusion? Did he slow down the rotation of the earth?

We do not know exactly how these things happened, and it is unlikely that this passage will ever be explained well enough to satisfy the skeptics' questions. But if we believe in a big God, who created the universe, then it is certainly possible that he could create hailstones large enough to kill a man, or could cause the sun to stand still.

In the short time that they had been in the Promised Land, the people of Israel had already seen how big God is. They had watched him work powerfully on their behalf. They had witnessed the walls of Jericho crumbling to the ground (ch. 6). They knew that God had helped Joshua conquer the city of Ai (ch. 8). Now they were being called upon to help the Gibeonites, who had deceived them into signing an ungodly treaty. When they were called to fight, Joshua and his army did not hesitate. They believed that God was big enough to fulfill his promises.

Back in Joshua 1, when God commanded Joshua to take his people across the Jordan River and into the Promised Land, he promised to be with Joshua and to "cause this people to inherit the land that I swore to their fathers to give them" (1:6). Thus Joshua believed that God was big enough to take the mess they had made with the Gibeonite treaty and use it for good. He had the courage to believe that God would fight for his people against the armies of the Canaanites.

How big is your God? If he is big enough to conquer death and accomplish our salvation, then he is big enough to fight and win the little skirmishes of our daily lives. Believe that God is big enough to make the sun stand still—and you will know that God is big enough to deliver you. In Christ, he already has given you the biggest deliverance.

Be Very Careful, Therefore, to Love the Lord Your God

ROBERT A. PETERSON

ABOUT TWENTY-FIVE YEARS after Israel crossed the Jordan River into the Promised Land, Joshua makes a farewell speech to the leaders of the people. He reminds them of God's mighty deeds: "And you have seen all that the LORD your God has done to all these nations for your sake, for it is the LORD your God who has fought for you" (Josh. 23:3). God has enabled Israel to defeat the Canaanites and possess their land.

What does the Lord desire from his covenant people, as he addresses them through Joshua? He wants them to obey him from the heart: "Therefore, be very strong to keep and to do all that is written in the Book of the Law of Moses" (v. 6). In the historical context, the main thing this means is that God's people should not marry Canaanites. Why? Because this would lead them to follow false gods and turn away from the Lord. They are not to serve and bow down to idols. They are to cling to the Lord their God and worship him alone (v. 8).

It is not difficult to summarize what the Lord desires from his people then and now: "Be very careful, therefore, to love the LORD your God" (v. 11). He wants us to love him because he first loved us (see John 13:34). And he wants us to obey him out of hearts overflowing with love for him, out of a sense of his love for us. If Israel does this, they will completely occupy the land the Lord has given them. However, if they marry the Canaanites, they will go astray into idolatry, God will judge them, and they will lose the land.

As Joshua prepares to die, he is eager for the people to remember "that not one word has failed of all the good things that the LORD your God promised concerning you. All have come to pass for you" (v. 14). But the truth and firmness of God's holy word is a double-edged sword. For, even as he keeps his promises to bless his people, so he keeps his promises to judge them if they are unfaithful and break covenant with him by going after other gods.

Some Christians may think, "This message is obsolete. We are not tempted to bow down before idols." It would be good for such people to examine their hearts, for the temptation of the heart is the same for us today. That is why John warns his first-century readers, "Little children, keep yourselves from idols" (1 John 5:21). An idol is anything we put in God's place. Idolatry is loving even good things more than God.

Praise God that he sent his Son for idolaters like us. This is where we see supremely God's great love for us, which ignites our love for him.

Choose Whom You Will Serve

DAN DORIANI

AFTER DECADES OF faithful service, first under Moses, then as leader of the conquest of Canaan, Joshua's work is almost done. But like Moses, David, and Jesus, he has final words before he departs. He addresses Israel's leaders in chapter 23 and the nation in chapter 24. He reminds them of God's redemptive acts and covenants, and of his gifts, which include even the vineyards and orchards they enjoy (Josh. 24:1–13, 17–18). Then Joshua pivots to the present and future. He begins with the command to "fear the LORD and serve him." By "fear" he means the fear of a son, not the fear of a slave or foe (v. 14).

Joshua knows Israel is childlike and addresses them accordingly, giving commands and choices. "Put away the gods that your fathers served" (v. 14). They are free to choose the gods of Egypt or Canaan—gods the Lord has just defeated!—if they reject the Lord. But Joshua makes it very clear where he stands: "As for me and my house, we will serve the LORD" (v. 15).

Almost all ancient peoples were polytheists, meaning they worshiped a number of gods and goddesses. They thought each god had its territory and powers. This notion infected the Israelites, who repeatedly tried to serve both the God of Israel and the "gods" of fertility and prosperity. Thus Scripture must often say, "You cannot serve both God and . . ." We still need this message. Like Israel, we tend to think, "Why not both?" We try to serve God and family, or career, or health, or reputation. But no one can serve two masters, and good *things* make wretched *gods*.

Mindful of God's redemption, the people promise to "serve the LORD, for he is our God" (v. 18). Joshua insists that this is harder than they think. The Lord is holy and jealous—he tolerates no rivals. Joshua warns the people that if they forsake God, "he will turn and do you harm and consume you, after having done you good" (v. 20). The people insist, so Joshua commands again, "put away the foreign gods . . . and incline your heart to the LORD." When they again promise to serve and obey God, Joshua renews the covenant with them (vv. 21–25).

Because Israel was so prone to unfaithfulness, Joshua sets up a stone "as a witness against [them]," lest they become disloyal (v. 27). Sadly, such stones would testify against Israel all too often. But through Jesus there is another testimony—his atoning sacrifice. He forgives when we repent. By grace, through faith, we are declared righteous and are called his beloved children, despite our many sins.

FEBRUARY 22 · JUDGES 2

Judge, Deliverer, and King

ELIZABETH W. D. GROVES

GOD'S PLAN FROM the beginning was to bless all the nations of the earth through Abraham's descendants. Israel was to be a restored Eden—a community that demonstrated to the world the holiness, compassion, integrity, mercy, kindness, and peace of their heavenly Father. At the end of Joshua, that looked hopeful.

But the book of Judges is the tale of the repeated, ongoing faithlessness and inability of God's people. This passage describes the cycle that repeats throughout the book: Israel would run after other gods, abandoning the Lord and failing to teach their children about him (ponder Judg. 2:10); the Lord would sell them into the hands of a neighboring nation, who would plunder and oppress them; they would cry out for help, and the Lord would raise up a deliverer. Then the cycle would start all over again, tumbling in a downward spiral until the Israelites were more corrupt than the Canaanites whom they had replaced. They did not reflect their heavenly Father.

But the Lord had a plan that would not be thwarted. *He* was faithful—faithful to his plan and faithful to his people. In Deuteronomy he had promised that he would bless the people's obedience and judge their disobedience. So, he was faithful to judge them. But he did so in a way designed to purify their hearts, to drive them back to him, to help them become a people who would reflect him.

The book of Judges is an anguished cry for help, because we as humans are incapable of keeping covenant with a holy God. It cries out for a king (21:25)—a godly, covenant keeping king (Deut. 17:14–20)—who would help God's people to be faithful. But the Davidic kings were not the answer. The answer finally came in Jesus. He was the faithful judge and deliverer who broke the power of the enemy and placed his Spirit in his people's hearts so that, at last, they could obey him from the heart and model his character to the world (Deut. 30:6; Jer. 31:33–34).

Even in this age of the Spirit, we struggle to love the Lord wholeheartedly and to help our children to do so. The penalty for our sin has been paid in full by Jesus, but the Lord still wants our hearts, and he still wants us to show the world what he is like—as individuals, as families, as the church. Sometimes he walks us through difficult times in that process. Let's open ourselves up to his sanctifying grace so that we can become more like him and have the privilege of reflecting his character to the world.

FEBRUARY 23 · JUDGES 4

An Unlikely Leader

DONNA THOENNES

EVEN WITH GOD'S gracious provision of judges to lead Israel, the nation seemed intent on Canaanization. A predictable pattern emerges in the book of Judges: God blesses his people, they fall into sin and idolatry, God disciplines them, they repent, God introduces a new judge; and so the pattern continues.

Following the death of Ehud, the third judge, the people again "did what was evil in the sight of the LORD" (Judg. 4:1). Because of their sin, God "sold them into the hand of Jabin king of Canaan" (v. 2). For twenty years, the commander of Jabin's army, Sisera, cruelly oppressed them. When the people cried out to God, he provided an unlikely judge: a woman named Deborah.

Of the twelve judges God used to deliver Israel, Deborah was the only woman. Her humility also set her apart: she was intent on making *God* the hero. Deborah answered Israel's plea for help by challenging a man named Barak to lead a military strike against Sisera. God had provided a specific strategy for the attack and promised that Israel would be victorious. Nonetheless, Barak hesitated to lead, agreeing to do so only if Deborah accompanied him. She agreed, but cautioned Barak that the glory for the battle would go to a woman.

Rather than deploying Barak's troops in her own power, Deborah affirms that Yahweh himself goes before the army (v. 14). (How our own ministry efforts would be enhanced if we gave others the confidence that God is with us!)

During the battle, Sisera escapes on foot and Barak kills all of his troops (v. 16). Meanwhile a woman, Jael, acts independently and ruthlessly, breaking all social customs of hospitality and marital roles. She doesn't appear motivated by a concern for Israel; she simply hates Sisera. She woos him into her home and brutally murders him with a tent peg. Barak comes in pursuit of Sisera, only to realize that Jael has had the honor of killing him. Barak must have been surprised at how Deborah's prediction had been fulfilled!

Throughout the narrative, Deborah preserves God's glory, speaking for him and assuring Israel of his power. She was not a perfect judge, but even powerful Barak recognized God's presence with her and responded to God's message through her. Ultimately, she reminds us of Jesus, who would also bring a message from the Father and seek to glorify him. In the power of the Holy Spirit, God often gives us the honor of being his spokesperson; let's do it with humble confidence that he is with us and has secured the final victory.

God's Honor and His Steadfast Love

LEE TANKERSLEY

FEW TEXTS WEAVE together God's commitment to honor his name and his love for his people as clearly as Judges 7. To this point in the book, we are given no reason to pity the Israelites. Though they find themselves repeatedly falling into the hands of oppressive enemies, it is only because they continually "did what was evil in the sight of the LORD" (Judg. 2:11; 3:7, 12; 4:1; 6:1). Just as diligently as Israel pursues sin, however, so the Lord pursues his people. But why does God relentlessly pursue them? This chapter answers by showing that God's commitment to honor his name is displayed in his steadfast love for his people.

Because Israel profaned the Lord's name by their rebellion, their deliverance reveals God's commitment to honor his name. This is shown in the opening declaration that Gideon's thirty-two thousand men are too many. How can this be, when the people against whom they would do battle were "like locusts in abundance" (7:12)? The Lord answers, "The people with you are too many for me to give the Midianites into their hand, lest Israel boast over me, saying, 'My own hand has saved me'" (v. 2). God wanted to make it clear that this military victory would come by his might alone. He was seeking to honor his holy name, which Israel had profaned.

But it is equally true that the Lord delivered his people because of his love for them. God's gentle love is first revealed as he addresses Gideon's fears prior to battle (vv. 9–14). Then his relentless love is displayed as he conquers the Midianites so that he might free his people, who had been oppressed for seven years (6:1).

Sometimes we can be tempted to think that God's commitment to honor his name somehow lessens his love for us. However, Judges 7 shows us that God's commitment to his name is actually *manifested* by his love for us. Israel had no claim to deserve God's love. But because God had bound himself to them in covenant and was committed to honor his name, which they had profaned, his pursuit of his honor could not be separated from his love for his people.

Because God has bound himself to all believers from the foundation of the world, we too can rest in God's commitment to honor his name by loving us. And since our Lord is unchanging, we should never doubt God's loving devotion to us. When we do doubt, however, we can fix our eyes on the cross, where the One "who loves us and has freed us from our sins" (Rev. 1:5) glorified his name (John 17:4) by shedding his blood for us.

FEBRUARY 25 · JUDGES 16:23–31

A Squandered Life

MARY PATTON BAKER

THE STORY OF Samson is the story of Israel. Like the Israelites, he was called out by God to live a life separate from the Canaanites, as exemplified by his special Nazirite vows. The Lord gave Samson superhuman strength to rescue his people from the Canaanite world with its false gods, exploitation of women, and violent cycles of vengeance. Despite God's special calling upon his life, Samson appears oblivious to the oppression of his people by the Philistines. Instead, he consorts with the enemy, is enticed by their women, and engages in pagan debauchery. By doing so, he breaks not only his Nazirite vows but also the basic requirements of the Mosaic law.

Today's passage opens with Samson's pagan captors celebrating his defeat by offering a sacrifice to their god Dagon. The Philistines have brought this drama to a new level by declaring that it was their god who delivered them from Samson (Judg. 16:23–24). They fail to comprehend that it was the Lord who had delivered Samson to them for his disobedience. As Samson is brought out to entertain them, he remains preoccupied with his own honor and once again seeks vengeance (v. 28)—this time for the loss of his eyes, which had gotten him into so much trouble with the Philistine women. True, in faith he calls upon the name of the Lord. But there is no indication that he seeks to reclaim the Lord's honor through victory. Rather, his final cry of "let me die with the Philistines" (v. 30) displays his ultimate self-absorption.

Yet the Lord's special plan for Samson to "begin to save Israel from the hand of the Philistines" (13:5) was not thwarted by Samson's sins. The Philistines' laughter and amusement was abruptly terminated as their temple came thundering to the ground, killing thousands and demonstrating God's power over the Canaanite god Dagon. But regarding Samson himself, the narration ends on a pathetic note: only in death does he fulfill the will of the Lord; his twenty-year rule of Israel only furthers its downward spiral into apostasy.

This tragic story prompts self-reflection. Are we standing against the evils of our own culture, or are we preoccupied with its temptations? The Scriptures exhort us to take up the armor of God to withstand evil (Eph. 6:10–17). We are not to rely on our own strength. Rather, taking up the shield of faith and calling upon the Holy Spirit as our strength, we can fulfill our calling and advance God's kingdom.

A Return in Ruin

TASHA D. CHAPMAN

THE BOOK OF Ruth is a beautiful story of redeeming love in one family during the war-torn period of the judges, when the Israelites were rebellious against God and his law (Judg. 2:6–23; 21:25). The story begins with the ruin of Naomi. When she left Bethlehem to find more prosperous living in Moab, she had a husband and two sons. Now they were dead, leaving her destitute in a foreign land of idol worship.

Naomi thought she had no means of support, security, or hope. However, she had two significant blessings. First, she still believed in Yahweh, the God of power and personal care. She knew that he rescued his people from famine (Ruth 1:6); that he blessed foreigners (vv. 8, 9); and that he was sovereign (vv. 13, 20–21).

Naomi also had the blessing of faithful family. Ruth and Boaz prove to be loyal and loving to her and to God. Ruth's pledge to Naomi is boundless (vv. 16–17). She promises to stay with Naomi until death, using an oath in Yahweh's name. Ruth will worship Naomi's God. In reckless abandon, she leaves her homeland—and seemingly her possibilities for remarriage and security—in order to be with Naomi and the people who worship Yahweh.

Naomi seems to have no faith in God's grace. Does she not know Yahweh's compassion for widows (Ex. 22:22–24; Deut. 10:17–18)? She knows his law concerning them (Ruth 1:11–13; Deut. 25:5–10). Does she not remember God's love and covenant faithfulness to his people (Ex. 15:1–21)? In bitterness, she thinks her destitution is God's punishment (Ruth 1:13, 20–21). She seems to have a legalistic misunderstanding of God: "May the Lord deal kindly with you, as you have dealt with the dead and with me" (v. 8).

In his endless grace, God brings bitter Naomi out from ruin and returns her joy (contrast vv. 13, 20 with 4:14–17). God blesses her with renewed faith, family, and security as Boaz redeems Ruth to be his wife. And in God's unfolding plan of redemption, this story of Ruth's simple faithfulness and piety becomes part of the ancestry and story of the ultimate redemptive work of Christ in redeeming the church to be his bride (Matt. 1:5–6; Eph. 5:25–33).

When we suffer loss and feel hopeless, we may worry that God is punishing us. We may become bitter. It would help us greatly to remember the blessings Naomi forgot: God's promises, his gracious covenant love, and the fellowship of his faithful people. These can revive our faith and hope as we trust that God is working out his redemption of the world in ways we cannot imagine. He is able to use even our most desperate crises to bring about great things.

Trust We Must

MARY BETH MCGREEVY

LIVING WELL REQUIRES a measure of trust. To whom would you trust your life and reputation?

In her desperate position as a young Moabite widow of a Jewish husband, Ruth first places her trust in Naomi's God, pledging her love and loyalty to him as well as to Naomi. After they arrive in Bethlehem, she trusts Naomi's plan to approach Boaz with a marriage proposal to be her "levirate" husband and to redeem the property of her late husband's family. We know that Boaz is "a worthy man" (Ruth 2:1) who has already been Ruth's generous protector (2:8–16). He is a close relative of Ruth and Naomi, one of their redeemers. He is not bound by law to take on either of the responsibilities that Ruth requests, yet she comes to him in trust that he will do right by her.

Boaz lives up to his description as one who is worthy. He feels honored to be the recipient of Ruth's kindness, considering that she chose to approach him rather than a younger man (3:10). Boaz calls her a "worthy woman" (3:11) and agrees to do everything she asks. Although he is not the nearest kinsman-redeemer, he assures Ruth that he will make her redemption sure—for if the nearer relative is unwilling or unable, Boaz is willing and able to do what she needs.

Boaz is one of the few people in the Bible about whom only positive things are written, yet he was a mere man who had his flaws as we all do. Even so, we must trust some people if we are going to have families, friendships, and societies that function well. Boaz had demonstrated to Ruth by words, deeds, and fulfilled promises that he was worthy of her trust.

The sovereign God who is so beautifully orchestrating this story of Ruth and Boaz has provided the ultimate Kinsman-Redeemer in whom all people must trust if they are to be saved from their desperate position as sinners before him. He is the flawless One who will never disappoint, as every human will. Jesus Christ, David's greater Son (and a descendant of Boaz; 4:21–22; Matt. 1:1; Rev. 22:16), is the only one with the ability and willingness to do the work of redemption on behalf of sinners. This he accomplished, as the perfect God-Man, when he paid the price of his own blood on the cross for the forgiveness of all who will trust in him (Eph. 1:7; Heb. 9:12), although he was under no obligation to do so. By his words, deeds, and fulfilled promises, Jesus has demonstrated that he is worthy of our trust.

Redemption's Story

KATHLEEN B. NIELSON

WHAT IS GOD DOING HERE? This is a good question to ask at any point in any of our own stories! It's a question Ruth's final chapter encourages us to ask. So . . . what is God doing here, in this last, joyful portrait in the book?

God is first of all *overseeing the story.* How did this baby come into being? Ruth and Boaz obviously had a role—but what does the text say? "The LORD gave her conception" (Ruth 4:13). Conception is God's gift to give, in his own timing. Ruth had been married to her first husband (now deceased) for ten years and was not given this gift. Now God gives it. He's in charge of it. What is God doing at any joyful or sorrowful point in my life? He is overseeing the story.

God is also *resolving the story*—and not just for Ruth and Boaz. There's a bigger story going on. The book begins with Naomi far from her home in Bethlehem (1:6), empty and bitter toward the Lord (1:20–21). It ends with Naomi's story resolved: she has come home with Ruth to the place of God's provision for his people, pictured richly by Boaz's generous care. In this final scene, Naomi's lap is full of her new grandchild, and all the women's voices are full of praise to the Lord. The book ends with praise to God who abundantly provides for his needy people, generation after generation. What is God doing, at any blessed or bitter point in my life? He is offering the resolution of his abundant provision, to be received by his people with praise in our mouths.

What is the ultimate nature of God's provision? It is not just physical, as in a child, or needed food—although in God's providence all these things are his gifts. What is God doing here, finally? He is *accomplishing redemption's story*. That's the biggest story taking place here: the story of a God who accomplishes his promises to redeem a people for himself from all nations. Ruth the Moabite shows us God's redeeming love for the nations. She becomes part of God's family and also part of the ancestral line of King David (4:17–22)—the line of the promised Christ. The child born here is called a "redeemer," one whose name is to be "renowned in Israel," "a restorer of life" (vv. 14–15)—celebratory names for the baby born to Ruth, but glorious names for the Christ child finally born in Bethlehem.

What is God doing, at any point in any of our stories? He is accomplishing redemption's story, through the gift of his own Son. And so, along with the women here in Ruth, we can bless the Lord, who has not left us without a Redeemer (v. 14).

MARCH 1 · 1 SAMUEL 1:1–2:11

The Petition and the Praise

JESSICA THOMPSON

THE BOOK OF 1 SAMUEL opens with the plight of Hannah, a young woman who is childless. Understandably, Hannah is heartbroken over her inability to conceive. Her husband's other wife has many children, adding to Hannah's anguish and causing great contention between the two women. Hannah is distraught to the point of not eating or drinking. Her husband tries in vain to comfort her with gifts and the assurance of his love. But Hannah knows that if she is to find comfort, it will come only from God. She cries out to him: "O LORD of hosts, if you will indeed look on the affliction of your servant and remember me and not forget your servant, but will give to your servant a son, then I will give him to the LORD all the days of his life, and no razor shall touch his head" (1 Sam. 1:11).

Weeping bitterly, Hannah falls before her Father and pleads for a son. She vows that if her prayers are answered, she will give the child back to God to be a servant in the temple. He will be a Nazirite, his entire life completely poured out in service to the people of God.

God grants Hannah's desire, and Hannah turns back to God in praise. Her prayer of thanksgiving in 1 Samuel 2:1–10 is remarkable, because she mentions having a child only once (2:5). Her focus is more on the Giver than on the gift. With a heart of gratitude, she willingly and cheerfully gives her son, Samuel, to a life of service in the temple. Oh, for the grace to have the heart of this mother, who freely gave her son!

Hannah's song of praise resembles Mary's hymn—the Magnificat—recorded in Luke 1:46–55. Both of these songs of praise are in response to the gift of a son. Two mothers give their sons to complete consecration. The agony these two must have felt as they released their boys is known most deeply by our heavenly Father, who gave his Son to us, his enemies!

Hannah prayed that God would look on her affliction and remember her and give her a son. He graciously answered that prayer through the birth of Samuel—and Hannah would have additional sons and daughters as well (1 Sam. 2:21). God has given his own Son to us. He has not forgotten us or left us in our spiritual barrenness. He "raises up the poor from the dust; he lifts the needy from the ash heap" (2:8). Because of his great kindness in giving his Son, we, like Hannah, can exult in the Lord and rejoice in his salvation (2:1).

The Lord Calls Samuel

GLENNA MARSHALL

SAMUEL WAS THE ANSWER to barren Hannah's prayers, but she did not keep him for herself. Desiring that Samuel would serve the Lord all his life, Hannah brought him to the temple, where she had so fervently prayed for the Lord to open her womb. Samuel grew up in the temple, ministering alongside the high priest, Eli, who was advanced in years and troubled by poor eyesight.

In those days a word from the Lord was rare, as no prophets were receiving visions. At other times in Israel's history, God's silence was part of his judgment for the people's disobedience (see Amos 8:11–12). Although Samuel was serving the Lord alongside Eli in the temple, he apparently did not yet know God himself, for he had never heard God's voice. Unlike Eli's evil sons, who did not know God and were wicked and abusive in their roles as priests, Samuel did not know God *yet*. One night, however, that changed.

During the night, God called Samuel's name. Samuel ran to Eli, certain that the priest had called him. This happened twice more before Eli realized the Lord was calling Samuel. Eli instructed Samuel to respond to the Lord when he heard his voice again. When Samuel lay down once more, the Lord came and stood before him (1 Sam. 3:10), calling his name a fourth time. This time Samuel was ready for the Lord to speak to him, but he might not have felt ready for the message: it was a message of judgment on Eli's family—against his sons for their blasphemy (see 1 Sam. 2:12–17, 22–25) and against Eli for failing to restrain them in their wickedness. Samuel's very first message as a prophet would be a difficult one to impart.

Samuel grew up in the presence of the Lord, and his messages from God always proved true, validating his role as a prophet of God (see Deut. 18:21–22). He also served as a priest and as the last judge of Israel. He anointed Israel's first two kings, an integral part of God's plan one day to send his Son, Jesus, through King David's line.

Although he was a child when he first began listening to the voice of God, Samuel learned to recognize God's voice and obey it, thus setting the stage for that later and greater prophet and priest, Jesus Christ, who would listen to the word of his heavenly Father and obey it (John 5:30; 8:29; 14:31). Today, as we follow in the footsteps of our Savior with the help of the Holy Spirit, we can hear the voice of the Lord every time we open the Bible. The more we listen to Christ the great prophet through regular intake of his word, the more readily we will recognize his voice and learn to obey him.

But It's Only a Box

SAM STORMS

LIKE MOST OF YOU, my family owns numerous boxes that serve a variety of purposes. My wife has a jewelry box, multiple shoe boxes, a cedar chest, and a box that contains some of our family's important documents. But none of them are regarded by our family as anything more than containers. So what could possibly have been so special and powerful about the ark of the covenant? It was, after all, only a box, and not a very big one at that: 47 inches long, 27 inches wide and high. Granted, it was overlaid with gold and overshadowed by two angelic figures, and it contained the golden jar of manna, Aaron's rod, and the tablets of the Ten Commandments. But it was still only a box.

After defeating the Israelites in battle (1 Sam. 4:1–2), the Philistines took the ark to the city of Ashdod and placed it in the temple of the pagan deity Dagon. What happened next, recorded for us in 1 Samuel 5:1–5, is both tragic and funny. Beyond the mutilation of the pagan idol, God inflicted the people of Ashdod with tumors (5:6). Some argue that this was an outbreak of bubonic plague, while others suggest they were hemorrhoids. The people of Gath and Ekron likewise suffered because of their desecration of this unusual box.

What was it about this box that could possibly justify all this? The answer is found in several texts of Scripture. According to Exodus 25:21–22, it was at this box that God would speak to his people. According to 1 Samuel 4:4, God was "enthroned" above the box. It was in and around the box that the glory of God resided (see 4:19–22). The ark, the box, was the place of God's personal, powerful, manifest presence with his people! The majestic glory and power of God Almighty lived in the box! It is where he would meet with his people and speak to them. Thus, when the tabernacle was constructed, and eventually the temple built by Solomon, the ark of the old covenant was placed in the Most Holy Place, behind the veil.

But how does this relate to us today? There is a sense in which we, the church, are the ark of the new covenant! The glory of God's presence no longer dwells in a box, but in us (Eph. 2:22). The law of God is no longer found on tablets of stone but has been written by the Spirit on our hearts (2 Cor. 3:3; Heb. 8:10). And the true manna from heaven, Jesus Christ (John 6:32–35), now dwells within each believer (Col. 1:27). What we do with our bodies is therefore of no small significance (1 Cor. 6:15–20). How we view the church is of utmost importance (1 Cor. 3:10–17). And our approach to worship and the proclamation of God's excellencies has been eternally transformed (1 Pet. 2:4–10).

MARCH 4 · 1 SAMUEL 8

Israel Demands a King

BRYAN CHAPELL

SAMUEL'S SONS "did not walk in his ways" and, as a consequence, the people of Israel said, "Now appoint for us a king to judge us like all the nations" (1 Sam. 8:3–5). These words come as a shock on the heels of the declaration of the previous chapter: "Till now the LORD has helped us" (7:12). From such full dependence upon God, the people quickly turn to hope in a human king. God tells Samuel what their request really means: "They have rejected me from being king over them" (8:7).

The Old Testament prepares us for the ministry of Christ by both positive and negative examples. We see many positive expressions of God's grace in the ways that release from slavery, provision of temple practices, and deliverance from enemies displayed God's mercy to a sinful people. But negative examples (dead ends of human effort) also demonstrate why the ministry of Jesus Christ would be needed. In this one chapter we see the failure of one of Israel's greatest prophets, Samuel (whose sons turned from God), and the mistaken notion that the nation's rescue could come through human ability, by a mighty king.

God would ultimately allow his people to pick the tallest, most attractive man among them as their king, to demonstrate that even the best of human efforts cannot rescue us from the consequences of our sin. In fact, if we depend on human solutions to fix all of our problems, then our "solutions" will ultimately lead only to greater problems. Israel's kings eventually used their power to enrich themselves and enslave their people (vv. 11–18).

Ultimately, the message of the Old Testament is that we need a greater prophet and king than human effort can provide to rescue us. The New Testament gospel is that Jesus is that greater prophet (providing us the word of God without compromise) and king (providing us the rule of God without selfishness). Jesus's word and rule are from a heart of infinite care demonstrated upon the cross, where he also acted as our greatest priest by providing the ultimate sacrifice to take away the guilt and power of our sin.

The message to each of us today is not to trust human wisdom, sacrifice, or power to solve the inevitable problems of our life, but to trust in the perfect prophet, priest, and king—Jesus Christ. He alone gives us the word of truth upon which we can depend, the forgiveness for sin our heart requires, and the power of hope that our family, friends, community, and soul need.

The Lord Will Not Forsake His People

COLLEEN J. MCFADDEN

THE LORD OF GRACE will never forsake his people. He cannot. He will not forsake us even amid heinous sin. Instead, the Lord pursues us. He pursues us for his pleasure, to be a people for himself.

As a prophet who spoke on behalf of the Lord, Samuel had three messages for the Israelites. First, Samuel reminds the people of God's past faithfulness, which they have witnessed despite their tendency to forget "all the righteous deeds of the LORD" (1 Sam. 12:7). Time and again in Israel's history, they have followed after other gods (v. 10), and as a result, God has given them over to their enemies (v. 9). But as the people cry out to the Lord, he rescues them. Through Moses and Aaron, and through other leaders such as Jerubbaal and Barak (vv. 6, 11), God always sends an intermediary to rescue his people. God is faithful.

Samuel's second message confronts the people with their present sin. Once again the people have forsaken the Lord. This time they sin by requesting a human king, even though, as Samuel reminds them, "the LORD your God was your King" (v. 12). The request came in the face of the enemy's approach: Nahash, king of the Ammonites, threatened their nation (see 11:1–11). Israel figured that if a foreign king was against them, then they wanted their own king to fight for them. But their true King did not need "sword and spear" (17:47). If only they had remembered that the commander of the heavenly army was their King, they would not have craved an earthly king.

Even amid their rejection of him, God promises never to forsake his people. This is Samuel's third message. The Lord has every right to hand his people over to enemy hands for rejecting him. But instead, he pursues them. When the people recognize their wickedness (12:19), they are rightly afraid (v. 18). How are they to reconcile themselves to the King they themselves have rejected? Samuel's response is beautiful: "Do not be afraid. . . . For the LORD will not forsake his people, for his great name's sake, because it has pleased the LORD to make you a people for himself" (vv. 20, 22).

The frightened people are reassured by God's promise that he will not forsake them. That promise extends to us today. God does not leave us dead in our sins but reconciles us through the blood of Jesus Christ. We are united as brothers and sisters who trust that reconciliation to the Father comes through his intermediary, his Son. This calls for a response of fearing the Lord and serving him faithfully (v. 14). It calls for guarding against sin lest we be swept away (vv. 15, 21, 25). May we always "consider what great things he has done" for us in Christ Jesus, his Son (v. 24)!

Nothing Can Hinder the Lord

CAROLYN MCCULLEY

THIS STORY IS set in the context of an ongoing battle with the Philistines in the central hill country of Israel. If you read a little before this account for context, you might think the story is about metal technology, for at that time the Philistines had the ability to forge metal and the Hebrews did not. Their weapons had been confiscated, and they did not have a blacksmith among them. Apparently, the Philistines reasoned that if the Hebrews could not make swords or spears, they would have the advantage over them in battle.

In reality, Jonathan and his father, Saul, still had some weapons. But this story is about which of them relied on the right weapon.

This passage opens with Jonathan deciding to pay a visit to the Philistine garrison with only his armor-bearer by his side. "It may be that the LORD will work for us, for nothing can hinder the LORD from saving by many or by few," he said to his armor-bearer (1 Sam. 14:6). His armor-bearer agreed: "Do all that is in your heart. Do as you wish. Behold, I am with you heart and soul" (v. 7).

Jonathan's faith was rewarded as the Lord created a panic among the Philistines. There was an earthquake, which would have been understood by both sides as a sign of divine intervention. The Philistines scattered, and the rest of the Hebrews pursued them in battle. Verse 23 closes this story with a simple declaration: "So the LORD saved Israel that day."

It didn't matter if the Hebrews had all the latest technology or not. The battle was the Lord's, and he was able to save his people. He still does. So often we look at our own resources and decide that it's not possible to enter the battle, so to speak—to struggle for the provision we need, to stand our ground against spiritual opposition or temptation, to risk the comfort we have to take new ground for the kingdom of God. It seems better to wait in our caves until the trouble passes. But it doesn't matter what difficulties we are looking at. The battle is still the Lord's. "Nothing can hinder the LORD from saving by many or by few." He doesn't need our puny contributions, but he is delighted to work through weak people like us to build our faith toward him and bring praise to his name.

Today, as you consider the battles that surround you, may you have the same response toward the Lord that Jonathan's armor-bearer had: "Behold, I am with you heart and soul." He is fully worthy of that trust and will not let you down.

MARCH 7 · 1 SAMUEL 16:1–13

Matters of the Heart

MARY WILLSON

AGAINST THE DEPRESSING backdrop of Saul's failure and God's rejection of him as king, God took the initiative to restore his people. He mercifully provided a new king and called Samuel to anoint him. Saul's radical sinfulness could not compromise our Redeemer's commitment to bless his people with a king "after his own heart" (1 Sam. 13:14). Imagine how this must have comforted God's people, who had suffered on account of Saul's foolish leadership!

Yet God provided the new king in a surprising way. Rather than revealing the new king's name, God instructed his prophet to journey to Jesse's household in Bethlehem and promised to guide him in anointing the new king. Samuel had to depend entirely upon God's counsel. Had Samuel relied on his own intuition or others' expectations, he would have wrongly anointed a man who seemed more "kingly" by the world's standards. Instead, God shocked both Samuel and Jesse's family by choosing the shepherd boy, David, whom Jesse had not even called from the field to meet Samuel. The least likely candidate was God's best, and the way God orchestrated David's anointing reinforced his initiative, his sovereign wisdom, and his personal investment in his redemptive plan.

God does not see as we see. Often we base our decisions on the shifting sand of temporary circumstances, but God bases his decisions on the solid ground of everlasting truth. God does not make snap judgments. While

Samuel's assumptions centered on outward appearance, God focuses on the seat of our core commitments and desires: the heart.

Is God's focus on the heart good news or bad news for you? The answer to this question depends entirely upon your relationship with Jesus Christ. Apart from the Father's gift of cleansing through Jesus, your heart is far from beautiful, and you are fully exposed before God, who sees everything (Heb. 4:13). King David knew this well (Ps. 51:3–5). God's knowledge of human hearts underscores our desperate need for his mercy. We receive this life-giving mercy from David's greater Son, Jesus Christ ("Christ" means "anointed one"), whom God commissioned by his Spirit as the ultimate King after his own heart. Though Jesus was scorned by the world as having "no form or majesty that we should look at him" (Isa. 53:2), he is God's sovereign choice and reigns eternally.

What does God see when he looks on your heart? Though you may be the least likely of saints (1 Cor. 1:26–31), if you are united to God's anointed Son by faith, your Father sees a purified, redeemed, and adopted child. Take heart!

MARCH 8 · 1 SAMUEL 17

Victory through Weakness

BRIAN BORGMAN

THE STORY OF DAVID and Goliath is one of the most famous Bible stories of all time. David is the underdog. Goliath is the Philistine giant and their undisputed champion. Goliath stands at 9 feet 9 inches tall. His armor weighs 126 pounds; the head of his spear, 16 pounds. He is a killing machine. This is the stuff that makes for exciting Sunday school lessons—lessons that typically convey such applications as, "Be brave like David! Face your Goliaths! Slay the giants in your life!" Unfortunately, if that is how we read this captivating story, we miss the real hero and the real point.

Goliath was not merely a military marvel; he was a blasphemer against the true God of Israel. As the formidable and seemingly invincible giant mocked the armies of Israel and slandered the Lord, Saul and his men were afraid. In God's providence, young David (not yet twenty years old, otherwise he would have been in military service) appears on the scene. On one particular morning, David heard Goliath's blasphemy. While the men trembled, David processed the scene through the grid of his own theology. Although there were many obstacles, David as a shepherd had a track record with God. God had delivered predators like lions and bears into David's hands (1 Sam. 17:34–35). David reasoned that God was also able to deliver "this uncircumcised Philistine" (v. 36) into his hands. David gathered the appropriate weapons for a blasphemer: stones.

As the giant mocked the young shepherd, the very embodiment of weakness, David made it crystal clear that he was there "in the name of the Lord of hosts," and he would no longer tolerate such blasphemous defiance. David's final words before the deadly contest pointed Israel's enemy to the true hero of this battle: the Lord. "The battle is the Lord's": he will give the victory and get the glory, and "all the earth [will] know that there is a God in Israel" (vv. 45–47). Through David, the Lord gave Israel a great deliverance and a glorious victory over her enemies.

David points us to his greater Son, Jesus Christ, who came in weakness and defeated all of God's enemies and ours. "Behold, the Lion of the tribe of Judah, the Root of David, has conquered" (Rev. 5:5). Jesus too was driven by a concern for his father's honor and glory (John 17:4) and won the ultimate victory over sin and death and the devil. We can now live for Christ in confidence and faith, knowing that he has delivered us through his victory on the cross—which is a guarantee of his faithfulness to us both now and forever.

Align Yourself with God's Anointed King

W. BRIAN AUCKER

SURPRISE MEETINGS in our lives occur for reasons that are not always clear to us. Through a divine appointment with Abigail in 1 Samuel 25, the Lord protects David, his anointed king. By seeking mercy from David, the messianic king, Abigail brings peace to all her house, even to the "harsh and badly behaved" Nabal (vv. 3, 35). This chapter shows God's people the blessings that result when they align themselves with the Lord's anointed.

David previously had refused to lift his hand against Saul, the Lord's anointed king at the time (24:10–11; see also 26:23–24). Although David is destined to be king, a fact that Saul recognizes, David commits his life to the Lord's protection. He refuses to take vengeance into his own hands. However, in his forceful response to Nabal's insult, David reverses this pattern, seeking reprisal for a wrong done him (25:21–22). Abigail's decisiveness is reflected in the key word "made haste"/"hurried," showing that the Lord sovereignly directs these events (vv. 18, 23, 42, especially v. 34).

Abigail is a woman of discretion and wisdom (vv. 3, 33; see also Prov. 11:16–31), and we find here the longest speech by a woman in the Old Testament (1 Sam. 25:24–31). Confessing her initial failure to see Nabal's folly, Abigail interprets for David what God is doing through her: the Lord is preventing David from doing evil or "saving" with his own hand (vv. 26, 33, 34, 39). Second, she shows that the enemies of David are actually "fools," like her husband, Nabal, whose name means "fool" (vv. 25–26). In this way, Abigail hopes for the demise of all those who lift their hand against the king. Finally, she grounds her hope of mercy in the fact that God promised David "a sure house," prophetically looking forward to the promise of the Davidic covenant (vv. 28–29).

Concerning the Lord's anointed, Nabal asks, "Who is David? Who is the son of Jesse?" (v. 10). Jesus, David's greater Son, will ask a similar question: "Who do you say that I am?" (Matt. 16:15). How we answer that question is all-important. Jesus is *the* King and *the* Messiah, who committed his life to the will of his heavenly Father and trusted God as his protector. Although submission to God's reign makes us fools to the world (1 Cor. 1:25–31), true folly rejects both Jesus's reign and his good news (2 Thess. 1:5–10; Titus 3:3). Like Abigail aligning herself with David, we commit ourselves to Jesus Christ and seek his mercy. As we do so, he makes us part of his bride, the church, and servants of his people. In his sure house we will dwell forever.

When Life Implodes

JEN WILKIN

THE STORY OF DAVID at Ziklag is a story about the faithfulness of God. God's complete restoration of the families and possessions taken by the Amalekites lends this scene an almost cinematic quality: it is the happy ending we want for all our stories. Indeed, there will be a happy ending for every story the believer inhabits, though we do not presently see how this could be. What makes the happy ending of Ziklag so remarkable is that God restores what was lost when life looked utterly hopeless.

Exhausted by Saul's relentless persecution, David had sought relief by sheltering among the Philistines. Yet even there he was rejected! Although David had earned the confidence of the Philistine king, Achish, the Philistine generals did not trust him. He was sent away, despite being, as Achish put it, "as blameless in my sight as an angel of God" (1 Sam. 29:9).

It would only get worse. Returning dejectedly to his camp at Ziklag, David discovered that the camp had been destroyed and all the women and children captured (30:1–3). Staring at the ashes of Ziklag, he must have wondered how his life could go from bad to worse so thoroughly and quickly. Not only this, but his own people now turned against him, wanting to stone him (v. 6).

What was left to do? Only one thing: "But David strengthened himself in the LORD his God" (v. 6). With every human source of solace taken out from under him, there was nothing left for him to do but turn to the Lord. It is clear that David did indeed trust in the Lord in that moment, for when he had successfully rescued the wives and children, while some of his comrades spoke of "the spoil that we have recovered" (v. 22), David corrected them. He spoke of what "*the Lord* has given us. *He* has preserved us and given into our hand the band that came against us" (v. 23).

When life implodes, we have a choice. Two paths lie open before us. We can crumple in defeat and despair, wallowing in self-pity. Or we can strengthen ourselves in the Lord, banking everything on what we say we believe—what we now, perhaps for the first time, are being forced to truly believe.

Yet we today have far more abundant reason to trust in the Lord than David had. For we see David's greater Son, Jesus Christ, crucified and raised. We know with utter certainty that when life falls apart, it is not a punishment for our sin. Jesus took care of that. Our adversity can only be for our ultimate good, sent from a loving Father.

MARCH 11 · 2 SAMUEL 7

The Covenant Keeping God

JENNY SALT

THE SAYING "it seemed like a good idea at the time" introduces a scenario that began with good intentions but in the end wasn't really a good idea after all. This saying could be applied to King David's plan to build a "house" for the Lord (2 Sam. 7:2). David, settled in his palace in Jerusalem, was enjoying rest from all his enemies. What could be more fitting than to build a house for God? It seemed like a good idea, but he was wrong. The Lord told David that *he*, the Lord, would be the builder of a "house"—that is, a dynasty that would endure forever. As always, God is the initiator, the provider, and the sustainer of the future, and *David was his servant.*

With promises like, "your house and your kingdom shall be made sure forever before me" (v. 16), it would be easy to think that everything would be smooth sailing for the Davidic kingship. But the reigns of the kings that followed David, starting with Solomon, were marked with sin, failure, and disappointment. Even when they returned to Jerusalem after the exile, sin was sadly still evident in the leadership of God's people. How does this reality fit with God's promises in 2 Samuel 7? Isaiah gives a clue:

> For to us a child is born,
>> to us a son is given. . . .
> Of the increase of his government and of peace
>> there will be no end,
> on the throne of David and over his kingdom,
>> to establish it and to uphold it
> with justice and with righteousness
>> from this time forth and forevermore. (Isa. 9:6–7)

God's people needed a king untainted by the sin of the people. Second Samuel 7:1–29 is a major landmark on the map of salvation history. It speaks of God's plan of salvation, pointing back to promises made to Abraham (v. 23), and pointing forward to promises fulfilled, most wonderfully and finally in God's Son, Jesus, the Messiah, who sits at God's right hand and rules forever. But this chapter also shines a light on the covenant-keeping God who is faithful to his promises, with a love that is steadfast.

What is the appropriate response to these promises? David responded by marveling at God's amazing grace and by praying that God would "do as you have spoken" (v. 25). This is what we are to do as well. We are to take God's promises and pray for his will to be done, marveling in his amazing grace.

What Kind of King May Rule God's People?

W. BRIAN AUCKER

GOD MADE A COVENANT with David, promising him a perpetual kingdom (2 Sam. 7:16–17). In David, the "anointed one" or "messiah," we find a prototype of the future Messiah, Jesus Christ. With these truths in mind, reading 2 Samuel 9 raises and answers a question: what kind of king may rule over God's people?

The king models covenantal faithfulness by keeping his promises. The anointed David inaugurated his reign in Jerusalem and gained victory over all his enemies (5:3; 8:1–14). He previously had sworn "steadfast love" to his friend Jonathan and even spared the life of his enemy, Saul. Here, twice in 2 Samuel 9, David keeps that promise by asking if any are left of Saul's house to whom he may show kindness (9:1, 3). The king who has received the kingdom now shows kindness to Mephibosheth. How remarkable that a grandson of Saul, who could potentially lead a new rebellion, becomes the recipient of restoration (vv. 7, 9). The king who rules God's people keeps his promises.

The king also models covenantal faithfulness as an agent of mercy to those in need. Twice in the chapter, once at the beginning (v. 3) and once at the end (v. 13), the text emphasizes the weakness of Mephibosheth's feet (see 4:4). Why are we told this? After the capture of Jerusalem, "the blind and the lame" became a descriptive phrase for those resistant to Davidic rule. It was said that the "blind and the lame" would never enter into the presence of the king by entering his house (5:8). How striking that Mephibosheth, a rival to the throne yet one who has difficultly with his feet, is not merely allowed into the king's house but is invited to dine at the very table of the king—always (9:7, 10, 13).

What kind of king rules God's people? Jesus Christ, the heir of David and the anointed of the Lord, is welcomed as king in Jerusalem. Indeed, upon his entry into Jerusalem, the New Testament explicitly links the healing of the blind and the lame with the cry, "Hosanna to the Son of David!" (Matt. 21:14–15). Yet he does so much more. He promises to prepare a place for us where we may dwell with him. Without him, we are broken wells in need of restoration (Jer. 2:13). Jesus Christ, the true and final King, keeps his promises and pours out mercy to those in need. We, the restored "blind and lame," now receive invitations to the great banquet of the King. He makes us acceptable to enter his holy city (Rev. 21:27; 22:14–15). Rejoice! Hear the invitation and dine at the very table of the king—always.

MARCH 13 · 2 SAMUEL 12:1-25

How Tender Is Your Conscience?

JONI EARECKSON TADA

REMEMBER BACK WHEN David was being pursued by King Saul? The tables almost turned when David's men urged him, "There's Saul, resting alone here in our cave. Kill him now! It's your day, David! Seize it!" Instead, David snuck up on Saul and simply cut off the edge of his robe. But even that minor assault deeply troubled him, for we read in 1 Samuel 24:5–6, "Afterward David's heart struck him. . . . He said to his men, 'The LORD forbid that I should do this thing to my lord, the LORD's anointed.'" This man's heart was so tender that taking a knife to Saul's garment was like taking a knife to Saul's throat.

In today's passage, we move from that desert cave to the palace in Jerusalem. Saul is history and David is now king. A bathing woman catches his eye during an evening stroll. He sends for her, sleeps with her, tries to cover up his sin and the pregnancy that results, and eventually has Bathsheba's husband killed. Where is David's conscience now? It does absolutely nothing to keep him from committing adultery and plotting murder. Even when Nathan, God's prophet, confronts David with his story about a rich guy who callously steals a poor man's one little lamb, David still doesn't get it. His conscience has been deadened.

It's almost hard to believe that the David of 1 Samuel is the same as this one in 2 Samuel. I say "almost," because the painful truth is that I understand very well. I have seen my own conscience protect me from a small sin one day, only to succumb to a major transgression a few days later. Oh, to have a tender conscience at all times!

So what is the difference between Cave-David and Palace-David? Back in the cave, David was a fugitive, on the run, and desperate for God's help. Every day, he woke up urgently depending on the Lord. Palace-David was successful, prosperous, and respected. He had people to cook for him, fight for him, and bring women to him. He had lost the sense of desperate dependence upon God's presence and strength. David was living in the pitfall of prosperity and, in return, got a weak and ineffective conscience.

In this remarkable passage, though, David's conscience does a complete about-face. Once confronted by the word of God delivered through Nathan, David humbly replies, "I have sinned against the LORD" (2 Sam. 12:13). Today, learn from David. Stay hungry for God and welcome his word when it confronts your thinking. After all, you definitely want to have an edge-of-the-robe conscience.

MARCH 14 • 2 SAMUEL 22

Telling the Story of God's Faithfulness

HEATHER HOUSE

AT THE END of a difficult time in life, it is appropriate to praise God by telling others how he provided during that time. Second Samuel 22 records a poem that David wrote to express his wonder and gratitude after God saved him from those who wanted to harm him. This personal testimony, adapted for use in public worship in Psalm 18, shows believers how they can acknowledge the ways God has acted for them, too.

When enemies threatened David, God was his defender (2 Sam. 22:1–4). God sheltered and rescued him. Here David describes God with words that emphasize his trustworthiness and protection. David needed defending because his enemies were more than capable of killing him (vv. 5–6). He thus called out to God, and God heard him (v. 7). By praying, David acknowledged his weakness and God's capability. Using images of a volcano, an earthquake, and a storm, David shows how God reacted to his plea for help (vv. 8–20). God went on the offensive to protect David. He also equipped David to fight his enemies and gave him the circumstances that would enable him to succeed in his fight (vv. 29–43).

God honored David's righteousness and obedience (vv. 21–25). David was not a sinless man, but he was righteous because he believed in God (Ps. 32:1–2; Rom. 4:1–25). And because he trusted God, he obeyed him and sought to live in a way that reflected God's character (James 2:17–18). For instance, David treated Saul with the respect that he deserved as the king God had appointed, despite the fact that Saul was attacking him (1 Samuel 24). Trusting obedience results in life and blessing (Lev. 26:1–13; Deut. 28:1–14). In defeating David's enemies, God vindicated David's choice to live in a way that honored him.

David knows that the peace he now enjoys is all because of God (2 Sam. 22:44–51). The very fact that he is king is possible only because God chose him (1 Sam. 16:12) and protected him. David wants the nations to know that God has saved him. He is awestruck that God cares for him personally, that God is active in the world, and that God keeps his promises.

Like David, we need to be aware of how God responds to needs in our lives; we must praise him for his actions on our behalf and tell others of his faithfulness. This encourages other Christians and reveals the true and living God to the rest of the world.

MARCH 15 · 1 KINGS 3–4

Stewardship Requires Wisdom

TASHA D. CHAPMAN

SOLOMON PUT TO DEATH men who challenged his rule and that of his father, King David, in an attempt to secure his reign over Israel and Judah (1 Kings 2:13–46). With political savvy, he made a powerful alliance by marrying Pharaoh's daughter (3:1). Then, in a show of great wealth and religious devotion, Solomon made huge sacrificial offerings "at the high places" (3:3–4). In this way, he demonstrated his new power and authority as king just as other ancient, pagan Near Eastern rulers did. Though Solomon "loved the Lᴏʀᴅ" (3:3), he loved power and wealth as well and was not keeping the law of Moses in his pursuits (see Deut. 7:3–4; 12:1–4; 17:16).

In the Lord's presence, however, Solomon's power and pride disappear. In his dream, Solomon responds to God with humility. He remembers who God is—a covenant keeping God of "great and steadfast love" (1 Kings 3:6) who demands that his people pursue holiness in response to his love. He is a sovereign and powerful God who establishes rulers and wealth. He is a jealous and redeeming God who calls people to be his own. In the presence of this God, Solomon knows his military might, foreign alliances, and abundant offerings are nothing. He rightly sees himself as a "servant" (3:7). The people and the kingdom belong to the Lord, not to him.

What could Solomon ask for that he doesn't already have? With new perspective that comes from humility, Solomon is overwhelmed by the responsibility of governing the people. He feels too young and naive, and there are too many people in his care (3:7–9).

What are the vocational callings and responsibilities in our lives? How are we pursuing success both in the home and out of it? It is easy to think that gaining power and wealth will help us secure our children's obedience and their future. Or that currying favor with the boss will help us win the office conflict. Or that looking youthful will help us gain friends and finances. Or that spending more resources will draw people to our churches.

What will we ask God for? We can take a lesson from Solomon by beginning our prayers with remembrance of who God is and what he has done for us. All that we have is from the Lord, and our calling is to serve him as stewards of his world, working with him to redeem it. The responsibility is huge for such broken, sinful people. Yet, in love, God delights to work through us and to answer our prayers. Solomon pleased God by asking for understanding and discernment. He prayed for wisdom in order to govern God's people justly. Perhaps godly wisdom is what we need most.

The Purpose of the Temple

KRISTIE ANYABWILE

A BEAUTIFUL WEDDING DRESS takes time and skill to perfect: just the right length, with hand-stitched sequins and buttons and sachets, all created to reflect the style and personality of the bride. On that special day, as she walks down the aisle, everyone will ooh and aah and marvel at her one-of-a-kind gown. They will say, "That dress makes her look so beautiful."

But not the groom. No matter how ornate and beautiful the dress, he will be infinitely less impressed with it than he is with the one wearing it. He will say, "She makes that dress look so beautiful." It's not the dress he's enthralled with. It's his bride.

Moses had built a portable, temporary tabernacle, according to God's specifications, to house the ark of God. Now, nearly 480 years later, Solomon built a large, beautifully ornate temple that was to serve as a more permanent dwelling for the ark. He commissioned King Hiram of Tyre to gather the best lumber from Lebanon. He hired thirty thousand men for the work. And he overlaid the entire interior with gold. Every detail was attended to. But unlike the instructions that God gave Moses in detailing the tabernacle, no similar instruction was given to Solomon, so he did what he thought would be worthy of God.

As stunningly gorgeous as the temple was, its purpose was never to draw attention to the building, just as a wedding dress is intended to draw attention not to the dress itself but rather to the bride who wears it. Solomon's temple was like a shack in comparison to the One it was made for. The temple was to point to the One who would dwell there among his people—God himself.

Right now, our body is the temple of God, and he lives in us by his Spirit. When people look at us, our lives should point them to our Savior. And on the day when Christ comes to gather his bride, the church, and ushers her into her heavenly home, it will be in a city that has no temple, because God and the Lamb, Christ Jesus, will be the temple.

How awful it would be to see the bride's train, her veil, her crown, the buttons and detailing on her dress, and miss seeing her joyful countenance as she makes her way down the aisle to meet her groom. As we await that day, we are left with pale but powerful symbols of the true temple. Let's not get so drawn to the symbols that we miss *him* altogether. What are you most captured by? Is it those elements of the Christian life that point us to God—music, spiritual disciplines, the natural world, service—or is it God himself? Ask God to help you see beyond the symbols so that you might be drawn to him and worship him for who he is.

MARCH 17 • 1 KINGS 9:1–9

Warning to a King

LEEANN STILES

IT'S THE SECOND time the Lord appears to Solomon. The first, recorded in 1 Kings 3:5–14, occurred when Solomon was young and inexperienced and sincerely sought God's help. God was pleased with Solomon's humility, and the next five chapters in 1 Kings tell of a remarkable time when Solomon reigns with great wisdom. The borders of Israel expand. The people enjoy peace. Solomon becomes wealthy, powerful, and well known.

Solomon spends seven years constructing the temple exactly as prescribed, and he devotes thirteen years to completing a magnificent royal palace. He succeeds in building everything he desires (9:1). At this point the Lord appears to Solomon again, at the height of his reign, and delivers a vital message.

First, the Lord responds to the king's earnest prayer at the dedication of the temple (this prayer is recorded in the previous chapter). God assures Solomon that he will be present there in a unique way (v. 3). But then he calls Solomon to live up to his covenant responsibilities (v. 4). Solomon must walk in the ways of the Lord. God promises great blessing if his commandments are obeyed (v. 5). He warns of severe consequences if they're not obeyed (vv. 6–9).

Why such a stern message at this point? Things seem to be going well. Still, God thinks it necessary to warn Solomon to follow him alone. He will not tolerate devotion to other gods. It's also a reminder to the king (and to us) that wholehearted obedience demonstrates sincere worship; the two always go hand in hand.

The Lord cautions Solomon amid his greatest achievements because he knows the temptations of the human heart. Will the king continue to follow the Lord, or will he give in to pride? So much hangs on his response. Sadly, in chapter 11, we read of Solomon's fall into idolatry. Israel divides into two nations after his death, and eventually the Israelites are carried into exile and the temple is destroyed—just as the Lord had warned.

Perhaps it's in moments of success that we, like Solomon, are most tempted to turn from faith in God and pursue worldly desires. When we do well, it's easy to think we're clever enough to make our own way. This passage calls us to obey the Lord, especially in those times. But it also reminds us that earthly kings can, and eventually do, fail. We do, too. The only fully wise and true King is Jesus. He perfectly kept God's statutes and rules, doing all he was commanded, even to dying on a cross. Therefore God has established his throne forever. When we repent and put our trust in Jesus, we become citizens of his eternal kingdom.

MARCH 18 · 1 KINGS 11

A Stolen Heart

KAREN S. LORITTS

"THE INIQUITIES OF the wicked ensnare him, and he is held fast in the cords of his sin. He dies for lack of discipline, and because of his great folly he is led astray" (Prov. 5:22–23). King Solomon, a man with God-given wisdom, probably wrote these words in Proverbs to challenge anyone tempted to stray from the Lord. Early in his reign, Solomon had made one request of the Lord: wisdom. And God gave him wisdom in abundance (1 Kings 3:9–12). Nevertheless, Solomon began to drift spiritually.

In Solomon's day, it was common for royals to enter into arranged marriages with royalty from other nations to forge alliances with those nations. However, as God's chosen people, the Israelites were warned repeatedly against such practices: "You shall not enter into marriage with them, neither shall they with you, for surely they will turn away your heart after their gods" (11:2).

Despite this clear command from God, Solomon had foreign wives and concubines in the hundreds. And "Solomon clung to these in love" (v. 2). His resolve to love and serve the one true God having been weakened by the physical beauty of these women, Solomon "built a high place" for each of the false gods worshiped by his wives (vv. 7–8). Because "his wives turned away his heart" (v. 3), Solomon did not follow in the steps of his father, David, whose heart was "wholly true" to God (v. 4). The once-wise king had allowed his heart to be stolen, and he walked away from truth.

When Solomon trusted in God above all, the Lord blessed him so that Solomon was able to say, "the LORD my God has given me rest on every side. There is neither adversary nor misfortune" (5:4). But sadly, as a result of his sin, the latter part of Solomon's rule was plagued by adversaries who "loathed Israel" (11:25). Most tragically, the Lord told Solomon, "I will surely tear the kingdom from you" (v. 11). God's judgment was severe, but the Lord's faithfulness to his covenant promises never wavered: "However, I will not tear away all the kingdom, but I will give one tribe to your son, for the sake of David my servant and for the sake of Jerusalem that I have chosen" (v. 13). It was from this one tribe that the Messiah, Israel's perfect King, would come (Matt. 1:1–16).

Sin is deceptive and subtle. The tragic story of Solomon's apostasy is sobering and should serve as a warning when we are tempted to serve God with anything less than our whole heart. Solomon did not turn from God overnight. We, too, must be aware that incremental compromise eventually allows other things to take God's place in our hearts.

Rehoboam Reigns in Judah

GEOFF ALLEN

WHEN WE FIRST meet Rehoboam at his coronation, we know little about him. We know his name means "he who enlarges the people," a telling piece of information, as it offers an intimate glimpse into Solomon's early life as a father and the noble expectations he had for his son. But that's really all we know about Rehoboam. In the first nine chapters of 1 Kings, we get a good idea of what kind of man Solomon is—at least at the start of his reign. We see wisdom, obedience to the Lord, and political savvy. But we see nothing about his role as father or how Rehoboam may have been influenced by him. Until the fateful day of Rehoboam's coronation.

On that day we see what forty years of being groomed under Israel's most successful and wealthiest king looks like—and the results are disheartening. Instead of seeing the father's wisdom in the son, we see his folly. Instead of obedience, we see unrepented arrogance. Even in terms of political savvy, Rehoboam receives failing marks by not listening to the elder advisers, who suggest that he end the heavy taxation (1 Kings 12:1–15). Despite all the advantages afforded to him, Rehoboam did not have what it took to be a good king because, like his father, he refused to obey the Lord's commandments. As a result, instead of enlarging the people, Rehoboam diminished them; the majority of his subjects said "enough" and left the kingdom to form their own (12:16–24).

"When Solomon was old his wives turned away his heart after other gods," so that "his heart was not wholly true to the LORD his God" (11:4). With the shrines to these other gods still firmly in place as Rehoboam exercised his rule, Judah continued its downward spiral into idolatry. Verse 22 of chapter 14 provides a devastating summary of Rehoboam's seventeen-year reign: "And Judah did what was evil in the sight of the LORD, and they provoked him to jealousy with their sins that they committed, more than all that their fathers had done" (14:22).

For those of us who are parents, this passage is a sobering reminder that our behavior and witness has profound implications for our children. It is our sacred duty to point our children to our heavenly Father; we must model for them a heart wholly committed to the Lord alone. And for those of us who are not parents, but who may have been wounded by our own, we take comfort knowing that in Jesus we are children of God (John 1:12; Gal. 4:6), and our heavenly Father never fails us, even when our earthly parents do (Ps. 68:5). "Predestined to be conformed to the image of his Son" (Rom. 8:29), we rejoice knowing that when Jesus returns and we see our Father face-to-face, we too at long last "shall be like him" (1 John 3:2).

MARCH 20 • 1 KINGS 18

Limping between Two Opinions

CAROLYN MCCULLEY

THIS CHAPTER in the Bible would make a great action film. It reads like a script, with threatening dialogue, treachery, intrigue, and an incredible fade-to-black scene of the prophet Elijah running ahead of the brewing storm. But don't be distracted by the tense plot. This is a story we live each and every day.

Consider Obadiah, who was a royal steward of King Ahab and a man of bold faith (but not the author of the book by that name). Because he "feared the LORD greatly," he hid a hundred prophets of the Lord, protecting them from the bloodthirsty queen Jezebel (1 Kings 18:3–4). But when Obadiah encounters Elijah after enduring the three years of drought that the prophet had pronounced, he is frightened. He assumes that Elijah is there to pronounce judgment for his own sin, and he frets aloud that if he tells King Ahab that Elijah has come forward, Elijah will disappear again and Obadiah will be slain for it. So certain is he of his impending death that he says it three times in their short dialogue. But when he assumes the worst, Obadiah is wrong.

Elijah does not disappear. Instead, he initiates a showdown at Mount Carmel, inviting 850 prophets of Baal and Asherah. But his message is not for that group. His message is to the people of Israel. When they arrive at Mount Carmel, Elijah draws near to them and says, "How long will you go limping between two different opinions? If the LORD is God, follow him; but if Baal, then follow him" (v. 21). The irony here was that Baal was worshiped as a weather god, and Elijah was saying this during a drought that he had foretold would happen. Elijah had already shown Baal to be an impotent deity.

Elijah's prayer on Mount Carmel reveals his desire to vindicate the Lord's reputation before his people. Elijah asks the Lord to make it known that he is God in Israel and that all these things have been done at his word. Then he concludes his prayer with this request: "Answer me, O LORD, answer me, that this people may know that you, O LORD, are God, and that you have turned their hearts back" (v. 37). His prayer was answered most definitively, inciting the people to fall on their faces in worship.

When we attribute power to sources other than God, we, like these people at Mount Carmel, are guilty of "limping between two opinions." But there is much hope in this passage. As we pray earnestly for God's glory to be revealed, he will answer that prayer. We may need to pray for an extended season, but we will receive an answer when we want to show the watching world that we, too, are God's servants.

MARCH 21 · 2 KINGS 2

Where Now Is the Lord?

GLORIA FURMAN

JESUS AFFIRMED THAT "Man shall not live by bread alone, but by every word that comes from the mouth of God" (Matt. 4:4; see Deut. 8:3). In Elijah and Elisha's day, God's people depended on his prophets to give them his word. Thousands of years later, our day is much the same. We still live by God's word. And yet our vitality is bound up in Christ, God's final Prophet, who *is* the Word (John 1:1). More than this, today we have the written word of God, the final and definitive witness to Christ and divine truth.

The transition of ministry from Elijah to Elisha would have raised many questions for the Israelites. Elisha was already appointed to be Elijah's successor (1 Kings 19:19–21). *But was he really?* Repeating the miracle of parting the Jordan demonstrated that the same spirit that controlled Elijah was Elisha's also (2 Kings 2:13–15). *Was Elijah's ministry really over?* Elijah had previously disappeared (and reappeared) suddenly (1 Kings 18:12), but this time he was really gone (2 Kings 2:16–18). *How would Elisha use his newly given power?* The miraculous power that Elisha wielded was for the joy of others, as the Lord mercifully cleansed the water at Jericho through his prophet (vv. 19–22).

Would the Lord approve of Elisha's ministry as he did Elijah's? The opposition Elisha faced in Bethel is significant (vv. 23–24). According to the law, the act of mocking a prophet, God's representative, is akin to insulting the Lord himself (Deut. 7:10; 18:19; Lev. 24:10–16). The curse Elisha issued "in the name of the LORD" (2 Kings 2:24) was the divine retribution that corresponded to the law. Because forty-two boys were torn by the bears, it is clear that there were enough youths to pose a physical threat to Elisha. In times when we ask, as Elisha did, "Where is the LORD?" (v. 14), we receive comfort from the testimony of the indwelling Holy Spirit. God is with us. Elisha's request for a "double portion" (v. 9) was for the eldest son's share (Deut. 21:17), a request that only God could grant. Now, through faith in Jesus and because of his work on the cross, God has given his Spirit "without measure" (John 3:34) to his beloved children.

Jesus spoke of the great things his followers would do when they received the Spirit (John 14:12), and assured them of his ongoing presence (Matt. 28:20). The Lord has equipped us to go into the whole world preaching the gospel. Perhaps we, like Jesus's disciples, might still be standing around staring at the sky had we not been given this gracious reminder that "This Jesus, who was taken up from you into heaven, will come in the same way as you saw him go into heaven" (Acts 1:11). Jesus, the final Prophet, is certainly returning.

Become Like Little Children

W. BRIAN AUCKER

JESUS INAUGURATES his ministry in Luke 4 by standing up in a synagogue and reading from Isaiah 61:1–2. He does this to highlight both the gospel and the healing that will characterize his ministry. Jesus then says, "And there were many lepers in Israel in the time of the prophet Elisha, and none of them was cleansed, but only Naaman the Syrian" (Luke 4:27). So, why did Jesus use the story of Naaman's healing to introduce his own ministry?

The chapter opens with a series of contrasts. Naaman, a great Syrian commander, must struggle with leprosy. An unnamed little Israelite girl, captured in a Syrian raid, must serve Naaman's wife. However, this child locates the source of healing with the prophet of Samaria. The God who gave Naaman victory also controls his destiny. Entering God's kingdom will require a humbled Naaman to recognize his need and the reality that there is a prophet in Israel (2 Kings 5:8).

Naaman's pride complicates the process of his healing. Like some today, he believes that healing comes through political connections or shows of lavish prosperity (vv. 5–7). When this fails, he goes to Elisha, who issues a simple command to perform a ritual healing. An important man, Naaman expects an audience and display of power from Elisha. The fact that the prophet sends a command by messenger is not satisfactory. Experiencing God's transformation will require Naaman to learn that divine grace comes not through powerful kings or material wealth but through obeying humble servants (vv. 3, 13).

The great Syrian commander comes to the end of himself. He descends into the Jordan. In a beautiful Old Testament wordplay, his flesh turns (*wayyashob*, v. 14), and he turns (*wayyashob*, v. 15) toward Elisha. The restored "little boy" flesh of his physical healing now reflects a deeper spiritual return. He humbles himself. Repentance in God's kingdom requires humble submission to God's word. The way up is down.

And yet Naaman's healing serves a greater purpose. His confession that "there is no God in all the earth but in Israel" (v. 15) ultimately issues in peaceful blessing from Elisha. This answers Solomon's prayer in 1 Kings 8:41–43 concerning foreigners, demonstrating that the blessings of Abraham overflow Israel's borders. This prayer would be more fully answered in Jesus, whose earthly ministry also encompassed healing lepers and proclaiming the good news (Matt. 11:5). Jesus said, "Unless you turn and become like children, you will never enter the kingdom of heaven" (Matt. 18:3).

MARCH 23 · 2 KINGS 17:6-23

God's Anger against a Wicked People

COLLEEN J. MCFADDEN

WHEN HAS GOD had enough? At what point does he get fed up? There is a point where God will say, "Enough is enough," and Israel surely heard him say it. But why exile? Why not forgiveness?

Second Kings 17:6–23 contains a laundry list of sins against God. It is a catalogue of wickedness. Since the beginning of the northern kingdom, Israel has done evil (vv. 21–22). But this passage is also filled with the things God did. Notice how the two characters play together, how God acts and Israel responds.

Israel sinned against the Lord—the very one "who had brought them up out of the land of Egypt from under the hand of Pharaoh" (v. 7). God had driven out nations before Israel, but Israel wanted, instead, to be like those nations (vv. 8, 11, 15). The Lord told them not to serve idols, but they did anyway (v. 12). He warned Israel repeatedly, but they would not listen (vv. 13–14). The Lord gave commandments and statutes, but Israel despised and abandoned them (vv. 15–16). Israel provoked the Lord to anger (vv. 11, 17).

This reality should leave us feeling dark, sad, depressed, dismal. We should feel the gravity and depth of the situation. Israel was not merely sinning. They were actively, deliberately turning away from the God who had protected them. They were stubborn after his repeated attempts of warning and reprimand. And God was angry—so much so that he couldn't bear looking at them anymore (v. 20). Enough was enough. And so they were carried away (v. 6).

In a seemingly dead-end situation, there is a glimmer of hope: Judah remains. Even though Judah is listed along with Israel for committing sin (vv. 13, 19), they remain (v. 18), and Israel alone is removed from the Lord's sight (v. 23). The Lord preserves a remnant; he preserves a people for his own glory.

We know that our great Savior is from the line of Judah. God preserved a line so that a King much greater and much better than Jeroboam could reign. At the climax of Jesus's time on earth, he hung on a cross. He was, like Israel, torn from God's sight for a time. Jesus took on the sin of God's people—the deepest, darkest, most abundant sin—and was forsaken and cast out of God's presence. He did this so we never would be. The end of the story promises complete restoration for those of us who believe in Jesus. Trust in the One who preserves us through the life of his Son.

MARCH 24 · 2 KINGS 18:1–12

The Joy of Obedience

SAM STORMS

I CAN'T IMAGINE anything more wonderful being said of a believer than that he or she "did what was right in the eyes of the LORD" (2 Kings 18:3). What others may think of us matters little if our hearts are attuned to God's. The criticisms that come our way, the judgments passed against our behavior, our standing in the community or where we work—all come to nothing as long as in God's eyes we have done what is right.

Hezekiah was just such a man. His doing right in God's sight is not difficult to grasp once we hear that he also "trusted in the LORD, the God of Israel" (v. 5) and "held fast to the LORD" and "did not depart from following him" (v. 6). What makes this even more remarkable is that Hezekiah was king of Judah (v. 1). He had all the power and authority imaginable and could have exploited it for personal gain and sinful satisfaction. But he persisted in doing what was right in the eyes of God. We must also take note of his age. This was not an elderly and experienced man who had matured spiritually, following a long life of facing challenges and temptations. Hezekiah was only twenty-five years old when he ascended the throne. Youthful impulses and fleshly fantasies that so often captivate men of that age clearly did not keep him in their grip.

Someone might wonder, "So what's in it for Hezekiah? More important, what's in it for me? Why should I bother to trust in God and do what is right in his eyes?" For Hezekiah, the only meaningful reward was the presence of God himself: "And the LORD was with him" (v. 7). Enjoying God's nearness was enough incentive for this young king. The deep satisfaction that comes from intimacy with the Most High God stirred him to persevere in his obedience. Hezekiah must have known and trusted the truth of Psalm 16:11, that it is in God's presence that fullness of joy is found and at God's right hand that never-ending pleasures are known.

God is all about transforming lives—not just Old Testament saints like Hezekiah, but you and me as well. He delights in transforming those with addictions into people who know the depths of freedom. He rejoices in transforming those in bondage into people who walk in liberty. He is passionate about changing self-centered souls into God-centered ones. He desires to take wounded people and heal them, guilty people and forgive them. He loves to take cynical people and infuse them with faith. He delights in taking depressed people and giving them hope.

You and I, unlike Hezekiah, will never be a king or a queen. But we can know the unparalleled delight of walking with God, trusting God, and holding fast to God. And to those who do, like Hezekiah, God's presence is an unbreakable promise.

Forgetting the God Who Does Not Forget His People

NANCY GUTHRIE

MOSES REPEATEDLY WARNED the people of Israel not to forget the Lord when they settled in the Promised Land, saying, "Take care, lest you forget the covenant of the LORD your God, which he made with you, and make a carved image, the form of anything that the LORD your God has forbidden you" (Deut. 4:23). But they did forget. Their forgetfulness reached its zenith in the days when Manasseh—a man whose name meant "forgetfulness"—reigned over Judah as king. While numerous idolatrous kings preceded him, Manasseh uniquely "made Judah also to sin with his idols" (2 Kings 21:11; see also v. 16). The king over God's people was supposed to rule in righteousness, leading them in loving the Lord exclusively. But Manasseh led them in worshiping idols and forgetting the Lord. The king over God's people was also supposed to listen to what God had to say to him through the prophets, but Manasseh killed the prophets who pointed out his sin.

Because Judah, along with her king, forgot God, God did something they would never forget: "The LORD brought upon them the commanders of the army of the king of Assyria, who captured Manasseh with hooks and bound him with chains of bronze and brought him to Babylon" (2 Chron. 33:11). Judah watched as her king was led away like an animal. But in that distant land, God reminded this forgetful king of his steadfast love so that Manasseh "entreated the favor of the LORD his God and humbled himself greatly before the God of his fathers. He prayed to him, and God was moved by his entreaty and heard his plea and brought him again to Jerusalem into his kingdom. Then Manasseh knew that the LORD was God" (2 Chron. 33:12–13). Manasseh, someone who deserved God's judgment, discovered God's mercy. His forgetfulness gave way to faith.

But still his people experienced the consequences of their sin of idolatry. When they read the history of the kings over Israel and Judah, they were reminded that their misery had been brought upon them "for the sins of Manasseh" (2 Kings 24:3). They must have determined never to forget God's hatred of idolatry because when they returned from exile, the worship of false idols never again pervaded the land to the same degree.

The great evil in Manasseh's life and the great mercy shown by God to Manasseh is something we should never forget. There is no evil we can do that is so great that God will not show us mercy when we call out to him in repentance. His promised judgment is meant to lead us to repentance, where we are sure to experience his mercy.

MARCH 26 · 2 KINGS 23:1–27

Repentance in Action

CAROLYN ARENDS

IN 2 KINGS 22, King Josiah's high priest discovers a long lost Book of the Law (likely portions of Deuteronomy) hidden in the temple. Josiah reads it and is overcome with grief at how far his people have strayed from their covenant obligations.

Josiah knows the idolatry besetting Judah can be largely attributed to the evil reigns of his grandfather Manasseh and father Amon. Faced with such widespread and deeply entrenched pagan practice, a lesser king might succumb to despair. But Josiah trusts the Lord. Here in chapter 23, he leads a reform.

Josiah decreed a sixfold response to besetting sin. First, he identifies sin as sin in the light of Scripture (22:10). Second, he allows the gravity of the transgression to break his heart, and he repents (v. 11). Third, he gathers his community to consult, repent collectively, and renew the covenant (23:1–3). Fourth, he systematically eliminates sinful practices, purging the temple (vv. 4–7) and destroying all illegitimate altars throughout the land (vv. 10–12).

The fifth facet of Josiah's approach involves trying to eliminate the *sources* of the sin. Compromised priests are deposed (and in some cases executed). Josiah goes farther than any other reforming king in not only destroying pagan worship sites but also forever desecrating them by putting human remains (often from nearby graveyards) on the altars (vv. 13–20).

Josiah's sixth tactic is a positive one. He reinstates the Passover, offering the people of Judah the opportunity to fill the void left by the purging of their false worship with a feast celebrating the goodness of Yahweh (v. 22).

Today, our pagan practices may be more subtle, but whether we worship wealth, security, sex, acceptance, power, or any other number of false gods, idolatry still exists. We can find in Josiah a template for proactively resisting sin's power. Perhaps the shopaholic must destroy her credit cards, while the pornography addict must restrict her Internet use. We must all find ways to desecrate our illegitimate altars. Even more, we must embrace the rituals and disciplines of our faith—prayer, confession, communion, celebration—as life-giving opportunities to grow in obedience.

We live in compromised cultures; we are the products of generations of sin. But we need not despair. Josiah was the direct descendent of evil rulers, living in an evil land. And yet, he was known as someone "who turned to the LORD with all his heart and with all his soul and with all his might" (v. 25). May the same be true of us.

MARCH 27 • 1 CHRONICLES 16

Worship Together

LAUREN CHANDLER

THE ARK OF THE COVENANT, the very presence of God with man, was a golden representation of a sure promise: he would never forsake his people; he would keep his steadfast love toward them from generation to generation.

Lost to the Philistines in a moment marked with fear and presumption (1 Samuel 4), the ark was suddenly gone. What mourning there must have been in the hearts of the people! Would they ever enjoy God's presence again? Were they now destined to sing only laments, rather than songs of praise and thanksgiving as they had once before?

But here is a sight so wonderfully odd: their fearless leader making a fool of himself, dancing like a child—uninhibited, fantastically delighted (1 Chron. 15:28–29; see also 2 Sam. 6:16). This kind of worship was something David could not keep to himself. He gathers the people to celebrate and receive back the ark of the covenant. What they once took for granted—what they had wielded as a weapon rather than holding in holy reverence—they now receive with gratitude.

This is the beginning of what we know now as a praise and worship service. David institutes worship before the ark as the primary symbol of God's presence and power. Ministers are appointed to invoke, thank, and praise the Lord (1 Chron. 16:4).

The content of their songs focuses on what Yahweh has accomplished on their behalf. God's people preach the faithfulness of God to each other: "Remember the wondrous works that he has done. . . . Declare his glory among the nations. . . . Ascribe to the Lord the glory due his name. . . . Worship the Lord in the splendor of holiness; tremble before him, all the earth" (vv. 12–30). Eyes are encouraged to look up and out. Hearts are to recount the innumerable evidences of grace. When voices are lifted, souls are also lifted. To forsake this practice would be to sabotage our strength.

Our human tendency is to look inward, to isolate, worry, and forget. Corporate worship invites us to set aside what is natural and press into the supernatural. In spirit and in truth, we recall God's character: his holiness, goodness, and faithfulness, seen in shadows in the ark but in living color through Christ's life, death, and resurrection. When we have become weary of the flesh that still remains in us, and the groaning of a creation waiting to be redeemed, we can call on the God who has never failed nor ever will fail. His steadfast love and presence have sustained his people for thousands of years and will continue to strengthen those who call upon his name.

Faithful in a Supporting Role

DAN DORIANI

THE BIBLE USES a remarkable phrase to describe David: he was "a man after [God's] own heart" (1 Sam. 13:14). David's godly character was on display as he courageously fought Israel's mortal enemies, bringing Israel peace from all foes on every side. Whereas Saul had neglected proper worship practices, David longed to restore true worship to Israel. His first act as king of Israel was to bring to Jerusalem the ark of the covenant, which was central to Israel's worship (1 Chronicles 13–15).

Seeking to honor God, the king now decides to build a permanent home—a temple—for the ark of the covenant and for public worship. David tells Nathan the prophet, who (without stopping to pray) gives his approval (17:1–3). But God has another plan. The Lord has purposes for everyone, and David's included war and bloodshed. That is not criticism; David fought just wars. But in the temple, God's people seek peace with him, and thus the Lord wanted Solomon, a man of peace, to build it (22:8–10).

David again shows his godliness by accepting God's will. But he does better than step to the sidelines. He fervently supports Solomon in his calling. First, he charges Solomon "to build a house for the LORD" (v. 6). Second, he tells his son the remarkable promise God had made concerning him: "I will be his father, and I will establish his royal throne in Israel forever" (v. 10). This is the promise that ultimately leads to Christ himself. Solomon died eventually; his own line would falter and fail. But Jesus is the true Son of David, and God established his throne forever.

Third, David blesses Solomon with repeated assurance of God's presence (vv. 11, 16, 18). Offering what is a model prayer of father for son and leader for successor, David petitions for Solomon's success as he builds, for understanding to lead the project, for obedience to God's commands, and for strength and courage for the work (vv. 11–13).

Fourth, David does everything possible to make the project succeed. He donates vast sums of gold, silver, timber, and stone (v. 14). Finally, David commands the leaders of Israel to support Solomon in every way (v. 19).

This passage teaches us (1) to accept our God-given roles, even if they are not our first thought; (2) to support God's leaders however we can; (3) to use our peace and prosperity to give to God's work; and (4) that we have a great King who reigns over our lives and all the world, who will never fail us, even though we often fail him.

MARCH 29 • 1 CHRONICLES 29:1–22

A Healthy Heart

KRISTYN GETTY

SURROUNDED WITH the grandeur of a gathering of Israel's leaders, and sensing the magnitude of the task ahead, David is drawn to something deeper as he pauses to recognize God's sovereign hand. "Both riches and honor come from you," David says in verse 12, "and you rule over all."

In this David reveals the inner workings of his heart, which led him to extravagantly sacrifice his own possessions. He knows that it is God who is the one true King and Lord of all the universe; everything in it belonging to him. He knows that it is God who has placed him on the throne and who will preserve his line forever. David delights in pleasing his Maker. These are the heart attitudes God longs to discover in us.

The Israelites also demonstrate a heart attuned to God's provision and purposes. In verse 9, "the people rejoiced because they had given willingly, for with a whole heart they had offered freely to the LORD." A healthy heart rejoices to give fully to God. In verse 22, the people "ate and drank before the LORD on that day with great gladness." A healthy heart rejoices in the community of God worshiping together. In verse 18, David prays for his people and for his son, asking God to "keep forever such purposes and thoughts in the hearts of your people, and direct their hearts toward you." A healthy heart prays for others to remain completely steadfast in the Lord.

Proverbs 4:23 instructs, "Keep your heart with all vigilance, for from it flow the springs of life." What is the condition of your heart? Are you bringing joy and life to others? Are you nurturing and praying for the hearts of your children and others around you? Once built, the temple would become the place for the Israelites to find God's forgiveness and restoration, a shadow of the cleansing ultimately found in Christ through his sacrifice on the cross. Paul referenced this sacrifice when he taught the early church about giving. In 2 Corinthians 8:9 he wrote, "For you know the grace of our Lord Jesus Christ, that though he was rich, yet for your sake he became poor, so that you by his poverty might become rich."

Having poured out his life for us, Christ restores the heart so it can function as a life-giving stream. This is where we begin if we want to put our hearts and homes in order, pouring ourselves out in daily living for his eternal kingdom—so that when by grace we reach our final days as David did, we will have stored up a treasure that will not rust.

MARCH 30 · 2 CHRONICLES 6:1–7:3

He Will Dwell with Us

MIKE BULLMORE

GOD'S PEOPLE, when they are thinking and feeling rightly, have a deep desire for God to dwell with them. God, for his part, delights to dwell with his people and make his presence known among them. This will be perfectly fulfilled someday in the new heaven and new earth, when we will experience the full presence of God. On that day it will be said, "Behold, the dwelling place of God is with man. He will dwell with them, and they will be his people, and God himself will be with them as their God" (Rev. 21:3).

Our current experience of God's presence is limited. Yet God still calls his people to draw near to him and to seek his face, and he gives them instruction on how to do so. For Solomon and the people of his time, this included building a "house" where God would dwell among them (2 Chron. 6:2; compare Ps. 132:13–14). God has made it clear that he "does not dwell in houses made by hands" (Acts 7:48; compare Isa. 66:1), and

Solomon acknowledges this openly in his prayer (2 Chron. 6:18). Still, knowing God's heart toward his people, Solomon appeals to God that "this house" that he has made might be a place where God's listening to and active presence among his people would be experienced. "O my God," he prays, "let your eyes be open and your ears attentive to the prayer of this place" (6:40). Wonderfully, "as soon as Solomon finished his prayer" (7:1), God came and made his presence known. He would indeed dwell among his people.

As dramatic as this was, it was all provisional and pointed to something far greater yet to come. In the second chapter of John's Gospel, we read that as Jesus came to the temple and drove out the merchants and money-changers, the Jewish leaders challenged his authority to do so. "What sign," they said, "do you show us for doing these things?" Jesus said, "Destroy this temple, and in three days I will raise it up." They had no idea what he meant, but John tells us clearly that Jesus "was speaking about the temple of his body" (John 2:18–21).

Jesus is the greater temple. "In him," Paul writes, "all the fullness of God was pleased to dwell" (Col. 1:19). He was Immanuel, which means, "God with us" (Matt. 1:23). And it is through him and by his blood of the new covenant that all who are in him by faith will one day know the perfect fullness of dwelling immediately with God. For this sure promise of enjoying God's presence forever, we too should bow down in worship and give thanks to the Lord (see 2 Chron. 7:3). "O LORD God . . . let your saints rejoice in your goodness" (6:41).

MARCH 31 · 2 CHRONICLES 10

Kings and Citizens

MARY BETH MCGREEVY

TO BE GOVERNED by someone who appears unwise and even foolish can be disturbing, especially when that person is a king with great power.

Solomon's son, Rehoboam, went to Shechem to be crowned ruler of Israel after succeeding his father in Judah (2 Chron. 9:31–10:1). But Rehoboam could reign there only if he was confirmed by the people (10:4, 7). Jeroboam and the people of Israel told him what they required—that Rehoboam lighten the heavy yoke that had resulted from Solomon's extravagances at their expense. Rather than heeding the advice of the elders to be a servant of the people (1 Kings 12:7), Rehoboam displayed great folly in listening to his boyhood friends who counseled him to increase the hard service imposed by his father. In a somewhat understandable rebellion, the ten northern tribes formed the nation of Israel, with Jeroboam as their king. But what of those left in Judah under Rehoboam's rule? What comfort is there for citizens who find themselves under questionable leadership?

Although the folly was Rehoboam's, the outcome was God's. Some years before, Jeroboam had been divinely anointed to be king over ten of the twelve tribes of Israel (1 Kings 11:26–40). That is why he was in Egypt when he heard the news about Rehoboam; he had fled there from King Solomon (2 Chron. 10:2). Rehoboam could have won the Israelites' allegiance, but his pride was known by God, whose hands turned affairs to fulfill his word (v. 15). So the citizens of both kingdoms could be assured that, although men were ruling, God was overruling in all human affairs.

Today, we can be comforted with the same knowledge. Like the Israelites, we must do all we can to ensure a just and good government. (Ironically, starting with Jeroboam I, the northern kingdom would have only evil rulers.) We must be active and responsible citizens. But if—after voting as responsibly as we can, and serving our communities as best we can—we find ourselves disagreeing with our government officials, we can know this: the sovereign and good God is still overruling human affairs.

For believers, our citizenship is in heaven (Phil. 3:20), where David's greater Son, the Lord Jesus Christ, is "seated at the right hand of the throne of the Majesty" (Heb. 8:1), as "King of kings and Lord of lords" (1 Tim. 6:15). One day he will return to establish his visible kingdom on earth (Revelation 21–22). Until that time, we can rejoice that, despite the foolish decisions that we or our politicians might make, Jesus, our sovereign and good King, rules over all.

Seek the Lord

CAROL CORNISH

LIVING IN THIS WORLD presents many challenges, some of which threaten to overwhelm us. Jehoshaphat, king of Judah, faced a particularly daunting trial as several enemy nations formed a coalition against him. Jehoshaphat knew that his army was no match for them. In his fear for his country, he went to the right place—to the temple, to seek direction from the Lord. It was a desperate time for the king and his people, but turning to God for help was exactly what was needed.

Jehoshaphat's prayer demonstrated the faith of the king and of his people—and God's response to that prayer was a stunning demonstration of his great power and covenant faithfulness.

Trusting in God's promises in the face of fear is one of the lessons we can learn from this story. We need to ask ourselves, Is this how I respond when my physical and spiritual well-being are threatened? Do I run to the Lord, seeking his face and asking for his direction? Do I trust in his covenant love for me and call upon him for guidance and protection? Or do I give in to fear and anxiety, shake myself loose from the anchor of my soul, and dishonor God by acting as if I have no heavenly Father to care for me?

King Jehoshaphat prayed, "We do not know what to do, but our eyes are on you" (2 Chron. 20:12). If you have been a Christian for some time, you are aware that the Christian life is marked by trials. When one trial abates, another seems to take its place.

By following the example of King Jehoshaphat and seeking God with all of our being—heart, soul, mind, and strength—we can have full assurance that he is with us and will fight with and for us in the battles of life. He does not ask much. He simply invites us to trust him.

God is faithful. No matter what he sends into our lives, God provides all we need to face our circumstances in ways that will bring glory to his name and conform us to be more like his Son, Jesus Christ. Despite what you are facing—even if today is a very dark day—seek the Lord, and you will find him. He will provide every needed grace, every comfort and encouragement, every bit of wisdom to help you through it. As you keep your eyes on him, he will surprise you with joy even amid severe trials.

APRIL 2 · 2 CHRONICLES 28

A Sinful People and a Redeeming God

KATHLEEN B. NIELSON

WHAT DO WE SEE in this chapter? Close up: *sin*. But in the big picture: *God*. Second Chronicles 28 is full of sinful people, Ahaz being the prime example. Verse 1 sums up his reign: "He did not do what was right in the eyes of the LORD." The chapter's overview highlights his idol making, his false worship, and even his sacrifice of his own sons. Ahaz was "very unfaithful" (v. 19), and "yet more faithless" to the end (v. 22).

This chapter shows sinful people in relation to a holy God. Sin here is, specifically, unfaithfulness to the Lord (vv. 1, 13, 19, 22). The narrative's events occur because of God's wrath against idolatry: "Therefore" in verse 5 highlights the logical connection. Reading on, we see not just a holy, but a sovereign, God. Human beings act, but God is directing all the action: giving Ahaz into the hand of Syria's king (v. 5), humbling Judah (v. 19), and responding with anger to faithless Ahaz (v. 25).

The more we look, the more we see of God. The chapter is encased with the story of unrepentant Ahaz, but at its center comes the intriguing little story of some Israelites who repent (vv. 8–15). When the Lord's prophet and the Ephraimite chiefs bring the message of God's wrath against sin and a call to turn from that sin, these Israelites who are taking the Judeans captive actually listen! For a moment in the middle we watch God's word breaking in and God's people not only turning from evil but also offering poignant acts of mercy: clothing the captives, feeding the hungry, anointing the weary, carrying the feeble home—all vivid glimpses of mercy in action.

We learn here that repentance of sin is necessary, possible, and beautiful. It is necessary because God is holy. It is possible because God forgives. It is beautiful because all acts of mercy ultimately reflect a merciful God who sent his Son to pay for our sin and make repentance and forgiveness possible.

Most importantly, this chapter reveals a God who is working his plan of redemption. We watch here the very people through whom God promised to accomplish this plan. The sin of Ahaz is magnified because he is king in the line of "his father David" (v. 1)—which is the line of the promised Christ. The Israelites' sin is magnified because they are part of God's chosen people, though now divided into a separate kingdom from "their relatives" (v. 8).

Through this people the promised King Jesus came to redeem us. Here in a time of great sin shines the certain hope of a holy, sovereign, and redeeming God.

APRIL 3 · EZRA 1

Seeing God's Hand

KATHLEEN B. NIELSON

MOST OFTEN, we don't get to see God's hand directly at work. We know he is there, sovereignly overseeing history, but the veil of ordinary experience is not often pulled back.

The whole Bible is God's revelation, or *unveiling*, of himself and his redemptive plan. God inspired Ezra in particular to unveil events surrounding postexilic history. Ezra pulls off the veil in a wonderful way. He wants us to see God's hand. As he begins to tell about Persian King Cyrus's release of the Jewish exiles, he addresses two questions: *why* and *how*. Both answers show us God's sovereign, saving hand at work.

Why did Cyrus decree that the Jews should return to Jerusalem and rebuild their temple? Cyrus may not have fully understood his own claim that he was charged to do so by Yahweh, the God of heaven (Ezra 1:2). This ruler issued many proclamations to gain favor from the gods of all the places in his empire. But Ezra, with full understanding, announces that this happened "that the word of the LORD by the mouth of Jeremiah might be fulfilled" (v. 1). Both Isaiah and Jeremiah had given specific prophecies about the exile and release; Jeremiah even specified a period of seventy years (Jer. 25:11–14). Why did Cyrus release the Jews? Because God decreed it.

How was the return from exile accomplished? A repeated phrase stands out, telling us that God "stirred up the spirit" first of King Cyrus and then of the Jews who "rose up" to return (Ezra 1:1, 5). Yes, all these people chose and carried out their actions. But it was God who stirred their hearts. God was in charge. God was directing history according to his word. He was then, and he is now.

What's this history all about? In Ezra we are watching the people whom God promised to bless and through whom he promised to bless all the nations of the world. They have rebelled, lost their kingdom, and suffered exile. But God's promises to them would not fail—neither the promise of return from exile, nor all the promises of blessing that would climax in the coming of an eternal King in the line of David. Just as surely as these people would return to Jerusalem to rebuild their temple, along with all their restored temple treasures, so surely would come an even greater restoration and an even greater temple—in the person of Jesus Christ.

Ezra reminds us that behind every *why* and *how* of history is God's hand—directing it all according to his word and his redemptive promises. This is true for kings and nations, and it is true for every one of us.

APRIL 4 · EZRA 3:8-13

Restoring What Was Lost

MARY WILLSON

THE COMPLETION OF the new temple's foundations brought a critical moment for the returned exiles. The foundations were being laid on the site of Solomon's temple and according to its exact pattern. Consider how poignant this would have been for those who had long been exiled in distant lands, far away from God's special dwelling place.

The priests and Levites led the people in celebratory praise upon the freshly repaired foundations. They echoed portions of the song David had composed when God brought the ark to Jerusalem (1 Chron. 16:4–36) and which the next generation of Levites also sang to dedicate Solomon's temple (2 Chron. 5:13): "He is good, for his steadfast love endures forever toward Israel" (Ezra 3:11).

God's people responded with boisterous acclaim (vv. 10–13). The noises billowing forth must have overwhelmed all those present: blowing trumpets, clanging cymbals, responsive singing, and great shouts. Yet amid such jubilation, many older Israelites who had seen the first temple wept with grief. These foundation stones reminded them of what had been lost on account of their sinfulness. Ezra records no visible indication of God's presence filling this temple, as it so powerfully had upon the completion of the tabernacle (Ex. 40:34–38) and Solomon's temple (2 Chron. 5:11–14). Though mighty sounds ascended, the heavens remained silent.

God's visible presence would not return to this temple until hundreds of years later, when Simeon held the infant Jesus in his arms (Luke 2:22–35). This child was the living temple, the fullness of God's glory, the true substance of all that the Jerusalem temple represented (Col. 1:15–20).

Jesus came to this earth to reconcile us to God. He endured alienation from his Father on the cross to restore God's dwelling place among us. Paul announced the gospel in these terms: "So then you are no longer strangers and aliens, but you are fellow citizens with the saints and members of the household of God, . . . Christ Jesus himself being the cornerstone. . . . In him you also are being built together into a dwelling place for God by the Spirit" (Eph. 2:19–22).

As those who have been redeemed from the captivity of sin and death, we loudly exult in God's workmanship to build us into his living temple. Standing upon your glorious Cornerstone, praise him, for he is good!

Rejoicing in the Sovereignty of God

MARY PATTON BAKER

THE RETURNING EXILES had to overcome many obstacles to build their second temple. Not the least of these were the bureaucrats in the province Beyond the River, who now required proof of the building permit that Cyrus had given them. But Governor Tattenai probably regretted having filed his complaint. Not only was he ordered to stop interfering with the completion of the temple; he was ordered to actually finance the temple project with provincial funds! As with the tabernacle in the wilderness, provision for the temple came from an unlikely source: the treasuries of Israel's enemies! God also spoke encouragement to his people through the prophecies of Haggai and Zechariah—so much so that the Jews *prospered* through the hearing of God's word (Ezra 6:14).

Exactly seventy years after their exile, in fulfillment of Jeremiah's prophecy (Jer. 29:10), God's people celebrated the dedication of their temple with great joy (Ezra 6:16). This kind of joy arises from knowing God's presence. The same Hebrew noun is used in Psalm 21 to describe the "joy of [God's] presence" (Ps. 21:6). In joyous response, the people offered sacrifices of atonement according to the prescriptions of the Mosaic law, in recognition that while sin had led to their exile, God's mercy had returned them to their land (Ezra 6:17–18).

It is especially significant that the first festival celebrated in their new temple was the Passover, the festival that commemorated the Israelites' deliverance from the Egyptians. As the Israelites consumed the paschal lamb in the newly constructed temple, they celebrated once again the Lord's rescue from exile.

In the final benediction, the Israelites proclaim that God has made them joyful through the fulfillment of his purposes for them—accomplished not only through Darius's beneficent decree, but also by the strength the Lord has provided them. Here, mysteriously at work, is the wonderful union of divine and human action (v. 22).

Do you look for God's sovereign hand in your life? It may come from unexpected places. A life of faith is one marked by looking for the ways God aids us in *our* work for him. But ultimately, as with the Israelites, it is God himself who must strengthen and motivate us in all our actions. As we respond faithfully to what God asks of us, we will be met with the joy of the Holy Spirit, who dwells within us and makes us glad.

The Call to Prayerful Action

JONI EARECKSON TADA

NEHEMIAH'S WORK is centered on serving and pleasing Artaxerxes, king of Persia. But when news about the desperate plight of his country and fellow Jews reaches Nehemiah, his thoughts turn homeward. His beautiful Jerusalem is in shambles and, who knows? Perhaps many of his family and friends have been killed. So we are not surprised to see what he does in verse 4: "I sat down and wept and mourned for days."

His response is one that many of us can relate to. Perhaps a terrible crime has ripped apart our community, or a drug raid has exposed the underworld of a local college campus, or an adult bookstore has opened up just down the street, putting your town's zoning laws to the test. We weep and mourn over our quiet, shaded neighborhoods, pining for the "good old days," for beautiful memories of "what once was."

But how many of us do what Nehemiah does next? Because along with his weeping and mourning, he fasts, prays, and then takes action. It is one thing to leave a prayer in the sovereign hands of God and think, *God will use my intercessions to motivate community leaders into action; he'll set things right when he is good and ready.* It's quite another to become actively engaged in God's sovereign plan, yielding *yourself* as his agent of change!

As Nehemiah interacts with King Artaxerxes, we observe a humble yet confident man who regards God as sovereign yet happy to assist human action. We know this from the last sentence in his prayer: "Give success to your servant today, and grant him mercy in the sight of [the king]"

(Neh. 1:11). We are led to assume that Nehemiah is presenting *himself* as God's man for the job of rebuilding, even though he has no history as a community organizer, no skill in petitioning municipal powers or filing building permits.

Look around you. For want of prayer, fasting, and social action, our nation is crumbling under corruption, materialism, and moral sleaze. Society no longer rallies around a moral consensus comprised of healthy social norms. It is a day not unlike Nehemiah's. Our sovereign God obviously hears our deep prayers for our country and its people, but will you take the next step? Will you pray *and* fast? Then, like Nehemiah, will you get actively engaged in God's plan to bring about spiritual and social reformation? When it comes to practicing faith with your sleeves rolled up, God isn't just looking for people with advanced degrees in theology—he's looking for anyone who is ready to trust in him and take action.

APRIL 7 · NEHEMIAH 4

God's People at Work

KATHLEEN B. NIELSON

THIS IS A WORKING CHAPTER! These Jewish exiles have returned to Jerusalem to rebuild the wall—and they're working night and day. "The people had a mind to work" (Neh. 4:6). We can be challenged by Nehemiah's portrayal of what it means to work hard and well in service to God.

First, it means we don't work alone. Every person plays a key role—as chapter 3 vividly shows. But the book's overall picture, shining beautifully here in chapter 4, is of a people working together: "So *we* built the wall" (v. 6). God calls out not just individuals but a people—first the descendants of Abraham but finally all those who by faith are redeemed through Abraham's promised Seed, the Lord Jesus Christ. My identity in Christ is as a member of his body, the church, and any work I do for Christ I do as a member of that body (1 Cor. 12:12–26). It both humbles and exalts my work to understand it as part of the work of God's called-out people.

To work as God's people also means we will face scorn and opposition. The picture of the surrounding nations jeering at these Jews rebuilding their broken-down wall might well picture believers' continuing dilemma, for the wisdom of God will always look like foolishness to unbelievers (1 Cor. 1:17–25). Indeed, until Christ comes again believers will be under attack—no longer as a nation but now as Christians from all nations. The apostle Paul makes clear against whom we Christians wrestle: not flesh and blood, but "spiritual forces of evil" (Eph. 6:10–12). Rather than the swords and spears and bows of Nehemiah 4, we now take up the "whole armor of God"—the very power of the gospel of Jesus Christ working in and through us (Eph. 6:13–17).

To work as God's people means to trust completely in him. In all our work we know this: "Our God will fight for us" (Neh. 4:20). The outcome does not depend on our work; it depends on God. And so Nehemiah and his people not only work; they pray: "We prayed to our God and set a guard" (v. 9).

God promised to multiply and bless this people. His promises did not fail. Through this remnant of Abraham's seed came the promised Seed. In Jesus Christ, God fought for his people finally, on the cross, where death and sin were defeated. Only because of that work of salvation accomplished for us can we, his people, serve God courageously and wholeheartedly with work that is acceptable to him (Eph. 2:8–10; 2 Tim. 2:15, 21).

APRIL 8 · NEHEMIAH 8

Responding to God's Word

HEATHER HOUSE

IN NEHEMIAH 8, the Israelites wanted to hear from the Book of the Law, the first five books of our Old Testament. The people had been restored to the land of Israel after being exiled because of their sin. Now they needed to be reminded of the words of Scripture and learn again how to serve and follow God. Every child and adult who could understand was there to listen as Ezra the priest read the Law. They stood for a long time, paying careful attention (Neh. 8:3). Other priests were placed throughout the crowd, explaining what listeners did not understand.

The people responded to hearing God's word by worshiping him: "And all the people answered, 'Amen, Amen,' lifting up their hands. And they bowed their heads and worshiped the LORD with their faces to the ground" (v. 6).

They also mourned and wept, for they now understood just how far they had strayed from their God (v. 9). But the very fact that they recognized their sin and had a renewed relationship with the Lord was a cause for joyful celebration! The people now understood that God was faithful to them and that they should be faithful to him. Ezra, Nehemiah, and the priests calm the people and tell them not to mourn: "do not be grieved, for the joy of the LORD is your strength" (v. 10). Israel could go forward, making decisions that conformed to God's instructions.

The next day, the heads of the Israelite households gathered to hear more. They learned about the Feast of Booths, which they had not been observing as the Law described. The Feast of Booths was a reminder of how God had provided for the Israelites when they left Egypt for the Promised Land. The people responded by celebrating the feast as God had told them to do. These times of teaching and worship prepared the people to confess their sin and pledge to obey God (chs. 9–10).

The Israelites here model how we as believers should respond to God's word. They were eager to know what God had to say. They exerted themselves to hear the word. They took advantage of the resources available to help them understand. They worshiped God as Scripture revealed his character. They grieved as Scripture pointed out the sin that they had chosen over God, but rejoiced as Scripture assured them that God would forgive their sin and they could be rightly related to him. The people obeyed God's word because they believed it was true and unchanging. As believers, we should value God's word and be eager to follow what it teaches.

What Does Confession Look Like?

KATHLEEN B. NIELSON

WHAT AN INSTRUCTIVE scene we find in Nehemiah 9, as these returned Jewish exiles confess together before the Lord. We can learn at least four lessons here about confession of sin.

1. *Confession grows from conviction by God's word.* We cannot read chapter 9 apart from chapter 8, in which these people at the start of this same month gathered in Jerusalem to be read and taught the Book of the Law (the Pentateuch). This chapter also begins with reading of the Law (Neh. 9:3). In this part of Nehemiah, the word goes in, does its work by the Spirit, and comes out again in the people's prayers: this long prayer in chapter 9 basically follows events throughout the history of Israel. They have heard the word, and it has convicted them. God's word will do that.

2. *Confession is made by God's people.* It can and must also be made individually. But this scene of corporate confession in Nehemiah 9 is significant, as "the people of Israel were assembled with fasting and in sackcloth" before the Lord (v. 1). Our sins are part of a big story of a people needing God's cleansing and forgiveness. Our sins affect others in the body of Christ. When we make corporate confession together regularly in worship, we present ourselves before God as his repentant and forgiven people, cleansed by the blood of Christ. We help each other to confess, to turn from sin, and to trust God's forgiveness.

3. *Confession depends not on us but on the character and work of God.* This prayer begins by praising God for who he is (vv. 5–6). It repeatedly affirms his mercy and grace (vv. 17, 19, 28, 31). It recalls his acts of provision and deliverance—from slavery in Egypt, through the Red Sea, with manna and water in the wilderness, from surrounding enemies, and on and on. All this gracious deliverance points ahead to the promised deliverer, Jesus Christ, and the final deliverance from sin and death accomplished on the cross and in the resurrection. The confession of God's people depends finally on that grace and that deliverance—provided for us by God himself.

4. *Confession involves saying what we turn from and what we turn toward.* It's not just a feeling of regret. These people say clearly, "We have acted wickedly" (v. 33), and they enumerate the ways. They end by making a covenant with God (v. 38; see also ch. 10), committing themselves to obey his Law. Of course, these people were not perfect after this scene—far from it! They needed the promised perfect deliverer—and so do we. Praise God for his merciful forgiveness and deliverance of us, through his Son.

For Such a Time as This

ELIZABETH W. D. GROVES

THE BOOK OF ESTHER shows us two things about the Lord: something important, and something even more important.

The important thing is that although the Lord is great beyond our comprehension, he is also present and involved in the tiniest details of our lives. The Lord used the wounded pride of Ahasuerus to remove Vashti and to clear the way for Esther to be crowned. He used the king's vanity to approve the gathering of virgins for the king. He made Esther stunningly beautiful. He gave her favor with Hegai the eunuch. He had Mordecai in exactly the right place at the right time to become aware of the assassination plot against Ahasuerus. His orchestration of events will become even clearer as the book goes along.

God is present even when we don't notice him. God is never once mentioned in the book of Esther, yet he was clearly present and involved. This is still true, even when we don't like the way he is arranging things. It is sad that Esther was an orphan, yet perhaps it was essential that she live with Mordecai at that particular time. God is in each detail!

The even more important thing about the Lord is that he has a plan, and *he will bring it to pass.* He planned from the beginning that Abraham's family would be a blessing to all nations, ultimately in Jesus, who would save mankind from sin and death. If Haman had succeeded in exterminating the Jews, there would have been no Jesus and no salvation. But the

Lord would not let that happen. From the vast scope of eternity, the Lord knew what Haman would attempt, and long before Haman hatched his plot, God began to arrange for Esther to be in the right place "for such a time as this" (Est. 4:14). *Nothing*—not even the emperor of the known world—could stand in the way of God's plans.

What a blessing to belong to such a God! Our responsibility is to do what he calls us to do, whenever and wherever he places us. Esther and Mordecai did the right thing in reporting the assassination plot. In chapter 4, Esther will risk her life to speak up for the Jews. Esther was a nobody. It's hard for us in modern society to grasp that, even after she became queen, she, as a woman, had no power in Persian society; she was no more than the king's plaything. Yet the Lord used her to save the entire Jewish people.

The Lord is present with his people, *always*. And he *will* move history to its glorious conclusion in Christ. Trust, worship, and serve our great, omniscient, omnipotent, omnipresent God!

APRIL 11 · ESTHER 4

Accepting Your Assignment

MARY A. KASSIAN

THE BOOK OF ESTHER is a fascinating story that involves power, sexuality, corruption, competition, racial tension, jealousy, resentments, conspiracy, and political scheming. The plot has intriguing twists and turns, rivaling any Hollywood movie. Mordecai the Jew refuses to pay homage to Haman, an arrogant man who clawed his way up the pecking order to become the king's top official. Incensed that Mordecai refuses to bow down and worship him, Haman hatches a crafty political scheme to exterminate the Jews. Haman doesn't know that the king's beautiful new wife, Esther, is secretly a Jew. Not only that, she's Mordecai's cousin.

Mordecai instructs Esther to appeal to the king. Initially, she's reluctant. Her predecessor, Queen Vashti, was banished when she didn't follow protocol. But Mordecai convinces Esther that God had put her in the palace "for such a time as this" (Est. 4:14). Winning the royal beauty pageant was no accident.

God wanted to use the king's penchant for beautiful women to fulfill a greater purpose—both for Esther and for the Jews. Mordecai challenges her to step up and accept her assignment. She agrees, and intervenes on behalf of her people, knowing that it might cost her position, perhaps even her life (v. 16).

God uses all sorts of people and circumstances to accomplish his purposes. Esther was an orphan who lived with the Jewish exiles in Persia with her cousin, Mordecai, a minor government official. We don't know why she entered the king's pageant; perhaps it was to guarantee food and shelter for the rest of her life. In any case, Esther became one in a long line of women who slept with the king and managed to enamor him with her beauty and sensuality. This is obviously not God's ideal for marriage. Even so, he used the situation to bring about good. He used the orphan girl. He used the beauty pageant. He used the playboy king. God's purposes touch the lives of rich and poor, rulers and commoners, the godly and the wicked. There's nothing in this world outside the influence and sovereign purpose of God.

We also learn that each of us has an assignment. Esther's assignment of petitioning the king was risky and frightening. The outcome was uncertain. Mordecai emphasized that God would accomplish his purpose even if she refused to cooperate. But if God got someone else to do the job, she would lose the blessing, joy, and reward of faithful obedience. God provided Esther the strength and wisdom to do what he asked her to do, and the outcome was beyond what she could have imagined. Her story challenges us to look beyond our circumstances, limitations, and fears, and ask the Lord, "What is your assignment for me?"

APRIL 12 · ESTHER 6-7

Tragedies Transformed into Victories

MARY WILLSON

GOD IS THE ULTIMATE hero in the great drama of redemption. While we celebrate Esther's courage and shrewdness in these chapters, ultimately it was God who outmaneuvered wicked Haman and saved the day for his people. His providence brought the king's sleepless night, his investigation of the book of memorable deeds, and his desire for counsel at the very moment Haman lurked within his court. The timing and dramatic irony confirm God's authority over human history.

Throughout Scripture, God's enemies who set themselves against him and against his chosen servants ultimately fail; they may rage for an allotted period of time, but God will bring his full justice upon them and vindicate his people (Ps. 2:1–2). The serpent bruised the heel of the woman's offspring, but God's own Son, born of a woman, bruised the serpent's head (Genesis 3). Balak schemed wickedness against God's people in the wilderness, but God transformed his curse into blessing (Numbers 22–24). Nebuchadnezzar demanded that God's people worship his golden image, but God shielded his covenant keepers from the fiery furnace (Daniel 3). Herod killed and imprisoned apostles to oppress the church, but God multiplied his gospel through their suffering and struck Herod with worms (Acts 12).

Above all, God's victory at Calvary showcased his supreme wisdom to outflank his enemies. As Paul wrote to the Colossians, God "disarmed the rulers and authorities and put them to open shame, by triumphing over them" through Christ's death and resurrection (Col. 2:15).

Like the seventy-five-foot wooden gallows Haman had built outside his home to destroy and shame Mordecai, the tree upon which Satan intended to destroy and shame Jesus Christ became the very place where Jesus openly triumphed over him. God turns the ultimate evils into the ultimate redemptions. The triumph of the cross and the empty tomb stripped God's enemies naked and exposed their ultimate impotence before him. Though they will continue to rage until that day when Jesus uses them as his footstool (Luke 20:43), he has dealt their decisive deathblow. All glory and honor to our King!

Does your life's story ever feel like a tragedy? Do you ever wonder about the outcome? Christian sister, God has redeemed you from the hands of the bitterest enemies and reversed your fortunes in Christ. Amid your momentary sufferings, remember his sovereign rule, and rest confidently in your Hero's commitment to transform your tragedies into his grand triumph.

The Agony of a Blameless Man

ZACK ESWINE

IMAGINE IF YOUR weekly Bible study decided to meet at the psych ward, the hospital emergency room, the funeral parlor, or the county jail. As the damaged inhabitants of these places encountered what ails them, you and the group would drink coffee, open the Bible, and continue with the week's passage. Such an atmosphere would deter trite talk regarding God and superficial application of the Bible to our lives.

When we open the doors and enter the rooms of Job chapter 1, God introduces us to himself and to his words by engulfing us with the agony and misery of a good man. If Proverbs tells us that "The house of the wicked will be destroyed, but the tent of the upright will flourish" (Prov. 14:11), the book of Job reminds us to resist the facile applications of such sayings. Think for a moment about the faithful people whom you know who nonetheless experience difficult and even tragic situations. Job is a good man whom God highly favors. Yet Job's life howls with anguish. By this paradox, God brings a truth, a question, a reminder, and a discovery to our attention.

First, a truth. God reminds us that he, not appearances, determines who is blessed. This mourning man, stripped of everything in the world, has the blessing of God upon his life. No other well-dressed and successful man in town is more godly than Job (Job 1:1–3). What does this picture of blessing show you?

Second, God sets before us an unsettling question: Will we still serve him when things go badly for us? The devil accuses Job to God: "Stretch out your hand and touch all that [Job] has, and he will curse you to your face" (v. 11).

Third, this chapter reminds us that Satan is not God (v. 12). Satan is a creature who can act only by permission of God. The Lord of heaven rules.

Fourth, we discover in Job our true identity: "naked from our mother's womb" (see v. 21). To whom else can we turn but to the One for whom we were made? Satan's cynicism is proved invalid. The question is answered. When things go badly, Job turns not from God to curse, as his wife encouraged, but toward God to worship. Worship sometimes looks like a broken man shaving his head, wailing upon the ground (vv. 20–21).

Paul the apostle writes about how he had to learn this truth in his own life (Phil. 4:11–13). Whatever comes, God will not leave us. Through Christ, we see more clearly than ever that he is our portion and strength.

APRIL 14 · JOB 16

Miserable Comforters

ROBERT A. PETERSON

JOB'S THREE FRIENDS Eliphaz, Bildad, and Zophar have failed terribly in their task. Despite their original intention to "show him sympathy and comfort him" (Job 2:11), they have been "miserable comforters" (16:2) to Job. Suffering acute, unrelenting pain, Job has little sense of dignity or self-worth. He wants his friends to switch places with him—mentally—to see that their words have brought him nothing but additional pain.

Job feels exhausted and alone. "Surely now God has worn me out; he has made desolate all my company" (v. 7). Job laments his situation. He is unaware of God's granting permission to Satan to strike him— yet he knows that God is in control, even of his present plight. "I was at ease, and he broke me apart; he seized me by the neck and dashed me to pieces" (v. 12). But his friends misinterpret the very situation God has put Job in as a sign of God's judgment on Job for wrongdoing. Job knows he is not perfect, but he contests their view that his pain is punishment for sin: "My face is red with weeping, and on my eyelids is deep darkness, although there is no violence in my hands, and my prayer is pure" (vv. 16–17).

Despite his sad situation, Job trusts God to bear witness on his behalf and vindicate him before his well-meaning but hurtful friends. "Even now, behold, my witness is in heaven, and he who testifies for me is on high" (v. 19). Job understands neither his situation nor why God has permitted it. But he refuses to curse his Maker. Instead, during intense suffering and frustration he trusts God.

Job cannot look to his friends for help, but only to the God who has smitten him. He longs for God to plead his case in the heavenly court: "My friends scorn me; my eye pours out tears to God, that he would argue the case of a man with God, as a son of man does with his neighbor" (vv. 20–21). Job expects to die soon, lacks an explanation for his suffering, and resolves to trust God to the end, "For when a few years have come I shall go the way from which I shall not return" (v. 22).

It is no wonder, then, that in its only reference to Job, the New Testament commends him for his steadfastness, which is held up as an example for believers: "Behold, we consider those blessed who remained steadfast. You have heard of the steadfastness of Job, and you have seen the purpose of the Lord, how the Lord is compassionate and merciful" (James 5:11). Trust this God. Even amid pain, he is with us, and for us, and he loves us.

APRIL 15 · JOB 19

Hope in the Midst of Despair

LYDIA BROWNBACK

WHAT IS GOD up to in seasons of suffering? When trials befall us, we can be tempted to question God's goodness or power, and because we want an end to our pain, we often try to figure out why God has allowed a particular trial into our life. We reason that if we can just understand what God is doing, we can begin to work toward a way out of our difficulty. That's what Job's friends tried to do when great tragedy befell Job, insisting that Job's suffering was surely the result of his sin. The friends' efforts to help provided no relief and served only to torment the suffering Job.

We learn from this a key aspect of suffering: we cannot know God's specific purposes in the trials that he allows into our lives. Scripture does, however, provide us with God's big-picture purpose, which is to test and strengthen our faith. Will we worship and love him even when he does not shield us from tragedy, grief, and disappointment?

Of one thing we can be sure: nothing can harm, including the powers of evil, apart from the sovereign, ruling hand of God. Job was unaware of Satan's involvement in his devastation, but Scripture reveals it to us so that we can learn that it is often a factor even when we cannot see it. Nevertheless, Satan could do nothing to Job that God did not first permit him to do (Job 1:6–12; 2:1–6). We see the same thing in the New Testament: Satan could not "sift" the disciples apart from God's permission (Luke 22:31–32).

One of the most painful aspects of suffering is how alone we feel. Job recounts that his friends and those of his household became uncomfortable around him because they could not handle his suffering (Job 19:13–19). Even worse, in times of suffering God can seem distant. Job felt as if God had abandoned him: "He has kindled his wrath against me and counts me as his adversary" (v. 11), and this caused Job to lose all hope (v. 10).

But Job's loss of hope was fleeting, as it will be for all who belong to God through Christ. Joyful hope is possible even in the worst kinds of suffering because God's commitment to care for us and his ability to raise us up from all the damaging effects of the fall have already been eternally established. The truth of that enabled Job to proclaim, "I know that my Redeemer lives, and at the last he will stand upon the earth" (v. 25). The ultimate explanation for all the suffering on this earth is sin, yet that is the very thing from which, through the gospel, we have been redeemed.

Remember to Extol His Work

JOSEPH P. MURPHY

WHAT ARE WE to make of Elihu? Though not one of Job's three friends, and though he was much younger than they, Elihu speaks more than anyone except Job. More importantly, in contrast to the three friends, Elihu is not corrected by the Lord, who has the last word in this intense discussion of human suffering. Despite the fact that Elihu, like Job's friends, fails in assessing Job's character, God does not treat Elihu as an arrogant young man.

If Job 36:4 represents a way for a young man to gain a hearing from his elders, citing God's perfection of knowledge (Job 37:16) as his source, then Elihu is an ancient example of the New Testament's Timothy: wisdom comes not with age but with attention and obedience to God. Youth can be wise, while the accumulation of many years does not in itself guarantee wisdom. Wisdom comes from God, and just as he is impartial, so wisdom favors those of any age who love and seek it (Proverbs 2–4).

Elihu's view is that God uses suffering to speak to us (as he does also with dreams; Job 33:15–18). Nevertheless, Elihu thinks incorrectly that what God is saying to Job concerns his sin (36:8–9), and that suffering is appropriate only as punishment for the wicked (v. 17).

Still, Elihu's focus is on God's majesty, specifically as seen in the wonders of nature, the theme that the Lord himself will powerfully reinforce in chapters 38–41. Here Elihu shows his wisdom by pointing to God. No matter how much we might get wrong in life, all true answers rest with God himself. Solutions to the conundrum of suffering can come only from God. In face-to-face, personal relationship with the God who speaks, the reality of our complex and often confusing selves and circumstances emerges into clarity. Simplistic assumptions about the reason for suffering, whether our own or that of others, are not paths to truth. Such truth comes from God alone—from the God who, in the person of God the Son, Jesus Christ, endured himself the greatest suffering of all.

For Elihu, as for us when we merely contemplate these issues, this pointing to God is an understanding that God will bless, as he does by bringing Job's suffering to resolution. When we suffer, like Job, God will also meet us as we look to the living God himself—and specifically to the Son of God, who suffered for us so that we can know that any suffering we endure can only be for our final joy and beauty.

Trusting God in the Midst of Misery

KRISTIE ANYABWILE

JOB WAS A RIGHTEOUS MAN. God called him blameless and said that there was no one else like him on the planet (Job 1:8). Then God offered Job as a test case for Satan. Job showed remarkable faith throughout his subsequent affliction. And yet, he also questioned God's ways—specifically the way his justice is carried out. Job was determined that God would hear his defense: "Though he slay me, I will hope in him; yet I will argue my ways to his face" (13:15).

What was in Job's heart that caused him to question God in such a manner? A little self-righteousness mixed with righteousness? A little pride mixed with blamelessness? A little ignorance mixed with divine insight and knowledge? The best of who we are and who we hope to be is still stained and darkened with sin. There is none righteous, not even one. No one seeks after God (Rom. 3:10–11), but God seeks us out and gives us the righteousness of Christ. Job was righteous but not perfect. His righteousness came by faith, just as it does for everyone whom God has saved.

In this chapter, the Lord proclaims his power in creation. God knows all and sees all, because he made all. He commands nature. He sees the unseen and knows the unknowable. He walks "in the recesses of the deep" (Job 38:16). By his power, he does the undoable, creating and controlling all things. He binds, loosens, brings forth, and leads out all the heavenly hosts (vv. 31–33). He controls the stars and the heavens, the skies and the weather, the light and the darkness. Even the animals trust God to provide for and protect them (vv. 39–41).

Job rightly defended himself against his friends' accusations, and he understood that his circumstances were ordained by God. But in his misery, he drew conclusions about the meaning of his suffering that did not fully take into account the fact that God's ways are infinitely higher than ours (Isa. 55:9). Thus, God graciously points Job back to the truth of his sovereignty, power, love, and faithfulness. And Job responds rightly, with confession and repentance: "Therefore I have uttered what I did not understand, things too wonderful for me, which I did not know" (Job 42:3).

As far as we know from Scripture, God never revealed to Job that he had given Satan permission to torment him. God's behind-the-scenes activity is always much grander and more important than what we're allowed to know. When we're tempted to think that no one knows what we're going through, or that our struggles and suffering are for nothing, we should consider Job and remember that God does the knowing, seeing, caring, and working. We do the trusting.

Beholding God

MARY WILLSON

THOUGH JOB NEVER rejected God, he questioned God's ways (Job 19:5–7), defended his own righteousness (29:14), and demanded God's action (ch. 31). God answered by telling Job to "man up" and defend himself, and by revealing a vision of his grandeur as Creator and Judge (chs. 38–41). With a mighty storm and a whirlwind of questions, God leveled Job, and Job felt his small stature in God's presence (40:4).

Job then humbly acknowledged God's sovereign power and confessed that he had spoken foolishly (42:1–6). Though he had heard of God, believed in him, and followed his commands, now he *saw* God.

At the point of Job's confession, his fortune had not been returned, nor his family restored, nor his boils removed. Yet he submitted to God's purposes. Job's confession resembles Isaiah's, who cried out when he saw the Lord in glory: "Woe is me! . . . For my eyes have seen the King, the LORD of hosts!" (Isa. 6:5). Similarly, when we behold Jesus through the gospel, we realize our sinfulness and foolishness. In this critical moment, we dare not commend ourselves to God by standing upon our own goodness. We cling to his mercy by acknowledging his righteousness and confessing our own unrighteousness.

God accepted Job's repentance and fully restored his health and fortune (Job 42:7–17). When God judged Job's friends for their evil words, he provided atonement for them in a way that vindicated Job. Contrary to his friends' accusations, God loved Job and had not brought calamity against him to punish him. Job demonstrated his uprightness by extending mercy to the three friends as their advocate, just as God had extended mercy to Job as his advocate. The extent to which we forgive others reveals our grasp of how God has forgiven us.

After Job confirmed his repentance by showing mercy, God rained upon him prosperity and honor. Job died a blessed and vindicated man. While we do not always receive such clarity or prosperity from the Lord this side of heaven, even when we suffer terribly we anticipate lavish blessing from our God that exceeds even the goodness described in Job 42. When Jesus returns, we will see our advocate face-to-face, and we will know fully, even as we are fully known (1 Cor. 13:12). As we behold him in truth, our God will purify us completely by his grace, wipe away every tear from our eyes, and invite us to dwell with him in his land of bounty. Because our advocate suffered on our behalf (Isa. 53:10–12), our suffering in this life, which Paul describes as "this light momentary affliction," is "preparing for us an eternal weight of glory beyond all comparison" (2 Cor. 4:17).

APRIL 19 · PSALM 1

The Pursuit of Happiness

SAM STORMS

PEOPLE ARE OBSESSED with happiness and will pursue it at all costs. Whether in the form of sexual satisfaction or material wealth or the rush that comes from exerting power over others, the relentless pursuit of pleasure is in our world to stay. This isn't to say that Christians shouldn't want to be happy or should repent if they do. It is to say that the meaning of happiness as defined by God's word differs greatly from that of society at large.

This is nowhere better seen than in Psalm 1. The psalmist celebrates the experience of being "blessed" (Ps. 1:1). He endorses "delight" as a legitimate human sensation and wants all of God's people to "prosper" (v. 3). But the way this is attained is not by hoarding financial resources. Rather, it comes by avoiding the way of the unbeliever and refusing to follow his counsel. True happiness, the sort of soul-satisfying joy that God wants for his people, is found in the revealed word, what the psalmist calls "the law of the LORD."

We aren't being told that emotional stability and physical health and a nice home with a two-car garage are sinful. We should be grateful for such blessings. But we can still be happy, truly satisfied, without them. When the psalmist holds before us the prospect of being "blessed," he has in view that state of soul in which we have come to know and enjoy God—a deep and abiding sense of satisfaction and joy in having encountered the beauty and majesty of the God who has Genesis 1 on his resume!

Some struggle to grasp how this blessed and joyful experience can be found in the "law" of God. But we need to remember what another psalmist, David, said about God's word. "The precepts of the LORD are right, rejoicing the heart." Indeed, "more to be desired are they than gold, even much fine gold; sweeter also than honey and drippings of the honeycomb" (19:8, 10).

When the "wicked" of Psalm 1:1 counsel us, and "sinners" offer their advice, we must remember that they are "like chaff that the wind drives away" (1:4). In God's law we find joy and truth and encouragement and hope and the knowledge that brings life and liberty.

The psalmist is not suggesting that we cease to engage the wicked in conversation. Nor is he saying that we should not labor and pray for their conversion. His warning is that we should beware of too close an association, of lingering too long in their presence. But merely refusing to walk in their ways or to believe their lies is not enough. We must meditate on God's revealed will and find a deeper and more lasting delight in his law. There alone will we find the happiness that truly satisfies.

God's Majesty and Our Smallness

LEEANN STILES

SEARCHING THE HEAVENS, David praises God. The Lord created everything David sees. God made everything out of nothing, even putting the moon and stars in their place. David senses his smallness in the universe; he wonders why God would single out mankind for a special relationship and position. Yet he's confident that the Lord has done just that. And in case there is any doubt, David declares that this God is *our* Lord, the one he knows as the God of Israel. Only the Lord of Israel's name is majestic.

Have you ever looked at the sky on a starry night and wondered what's out there? Have you thought about God and what he might be like? Have you questioned why you're alive, and if anyone really cares? Scripture tells us that God reveals his divine nature and eternal power in the things he has made. We can know these things about him just from considering what's around us in nature. Yet Romans 1:18–23 also tells us that people have rejected this knowledge and have become enemies of the truth.

So David's question in Psalm 8:4 is a good one to ask: Why would God be concerned about us? Why should he care about us? We've turned away from him just like Adam and Eve in the garden. We're a far cry from a close relationship with him. We are distant from God and wonder how we can possibly be significant to him.

The Bible speaks to our dilemma. Hebrews 2:5–9 quotes this same psalm and explains what David knew only in part. It's Jesus, ultimately, who became "a little lower than the heavenly beings" (Ps. 8:5) for a time—and God "crowned [him] with glory and honor because of his suffering of death, so that by the grace of God he might taste death for everyone" (Heb. 2:9). Because of Christ's death, we can turn to God in repentance and faith, and our relationship with him is restored. Jesus is the true Adam. He did what Adam failed to do.

Furthermore, Jesus was raised from the dead and has been given dominion and power over everything in creation. Psalm 8 speaks of the time when we'll fully understand this. Everything will be put under Jesus's feet, including sheep, oxen, beasts, birds, fish, and whatever else "passes along the paths of the seas" (Ps. 8:6–8). Jesus reigns now, though not obviously; one day he will come again and his reign will burst out over all creation for everyone to see.

No wonder David sings God's praises. When we see the works of his hands through creation, for our salvation, and in revealing his coming reign, we can joyfully join in. "O LORD, *our* Lord, how majestic is your name in all the earth!" (v. 9).

APRIL 21 · PSALM 15

The Presence of the Lord

JEN WILKIN

WHO CAN DWELL in your presence, Lord? This simple, profound question speaks to the deepest longing of the human heart—to enter into and remain in the presence of God. It is not a question of "which person can be with" the Lord, but a question of "what kind of person?" The psalmist poses and answers the question every believer has asked at some point in his or her life: What must I do to be saved?

It is the question posed to Jesus by the rich young ruler (Luke 18:18–30). It is the question posed to Paul and Silas by the jailer (Acts 16:25–34). In both stories the answer given is essentially the same: turn from what you love most to what you need most. How we respond to this answer determines whether we depart downcast, as the rich young ruler did, or whether, like the jailer, we repent and rejoice.

"What must I do to be saved?" The answer given by the psalmist invites repentance at every level: walk blamelessly; speak truth from your heart and with your tongue; do no evil to your neighbor; love at great personal cost. It is a call to complete denial of self, to an abandoning of our most cherished sins, much like the call to the rich young ruler to give up all his wealth. This is the kind of list that leaves us shaking our heads like the disciples, wondering, "Then who can be saved?" (Luke 18:26).

It is an impossible list. But what is impossible with man is possible with God. Because Christ himself walked blamelessly and did what was right, we have been granted entrance into Mount Zion, the holy hill. The impossible has become possible through the atonement, and those who believe in the Lord Jesus now find themselves both eager and able to attempt what was once impossible—to fulfill the description of godliness found in Psalm 15. Rather than standing judged by it, we find sweet guidance in it. We delight to do what it asks, because it speaks of the blessed obedience of our Savior.

An assurance is given to the one who delights to imitate Christ in upright living: he who does these things shall never be moved (Ps. 15:5). What more comforting words could the believer hear? Like those in a prison cell shaken to rubble, we understand the instability of this life. But as those grounded in the finished work of the cross, stability of soul is our reward. Practice blamelessness and selflessness in thought, word, and deed. The one who does these things, like Mount Zion itself, shall never be moved (Ps. 125:1).

APRIL 22 · PSALM 19

Creator, Redeemer, Friend

TRILLIA NEWBELL

AS THE SUNSET fades behind the clouds, leaving a red hue lighting the sky, there is no question: God is the transcendent Creator of the universe. Paul tells us that God's invisible attributes, namely his eternal power and divine nature, have been clearly perceived ever since the creation of the world (Rom. 1:20). We are without excuse. No one can truly deny the existence of God, for creation itself sings of God's majesty and his mighty works. It shouts his glory—a reminder that he is set apart, holy, and magnificent.

God also reveals himself through his word. In Psalm 19, God's people celebrate the law as God's supreme revelation of himself. The Lord's word is perfect, refreshing, and it revives the soul. It stands forever. Paul reminds us that the whole of Scripture is useful and perfect: "All Scripture is breathed out by God and profitable for teaching, for reproof, for correction, and for training in righteousness, that the man of God may be complete, equipped for every good work" (2 Tim. 3:16–17).

The writer to the Hebrews likewise tells us that the word is living, active, sharp, piercing, and discerning. It reveals the intentions of our heart (Heb. 4:12). Christians experience this revelation of our heart and an awareness of our depravity when we come to faith, and throughout our Christian walk. As we understand the holiness and majesty of God, and the commands of his perfect law, we can't help but recognize our moral failures (Ps. 19:12–13). Like Isaiah, we humble ourselves and cry out, "Woe is me! For I am lost; for I am a man of unclean lips" (Isa. 6:5).

At the end of Psalm 19, David offers up a sacrifice of acceptable words and meditations. We often try to offer up our sacrifices of good works, trying ever harder to earn God's favor. But we must no longer offer up such sacrifices, for the ultimate Sacrifice has paid the price. Jesus is the friend of sinners. Jesus, the Son of God, died, fulfilling the law and the promises of his coming. We can now receive his grace and sing Psalm 19 in celebration of his perfection and redemption.

APRIL 23 · PSALM 22

Why Have You Forsaken Me?

CAROL CORNISH

WHEN WE SUFFER, Satan tempts us to believe that God has abandoned us. If you are in a situation of great distress, prepare yourself to fight in the power of the Holy Spirit against this evil notion. Ready your mind by focusing on how God sustained King David through ongoing trials, as we see evidenced in this psalm.

This psalm speaks of the trials of David and, prophetically, of the greatest suffering ever endured—that of Christ on the cross. Jesus was truly and ultimately forsaken by God on the cross so that those he died for never would be: "the LORD has laid on him the iniquity of us all" (Isa. 53:6). If you are his, God is with you and will never leave you. His most emphatic promise in this regard is found in Hebrews 13:5: "I will never leave you nor forsake you"—never, ever. No, not ever.

Suffering is often a gift given to us by God so that we will take a serious look at our lives and realize our need of him. It is in our nature to want the problem or the difficult circumstances to simply go away. Our goal is relief rather than godliness. While it is normal and understandable to desire suffering to cease, if that is *all* we want, then we are wasting the pain. Jesus warned us that in this life we will have trouble. The good news? "But take heart; I have overcome the world" (John 16:33). We can endure suffering—even rejoice in it—knowing that our loving Savior endured the greatest suffering in our place. And he uses grief and sorrow to make us more like him: "We are afflicted in every way, but not crushed; perplexed, but not driven to despair; persecuted, but not forsaken; struck down, but not destroyed; always carrying in the body the death of Jesus, so that the life of Jesus may also be manifested in our bodies" (2 Cor. 4:8–10).

At the time when it happened, the crucifixion of Christ appeared to his followers to be the end of all their hopes. But their expectations were flawed. Not until the resurrection did they see the glorious hope. How about you? Can you step back from your circumstances and look at your suffering from the mountaintop of God's perfect plan, or are you sinking in the valley of ruined hopes? Are all your plans shattered and the pieces beyond retrieval? Look again at the cross of Christ. Trust the One who triumphed over death, suffering in our place. He is alive! He is the Redeemer! He makes all things new.

Illuminating Light

LAUREN CHANDLER

C. S. LEWIS ONCE WROTE, "I believe in Christianity as I believe that the Sun has risen, not only because I see it but because by it, I see everything else."[2] By calling the Lord his light, David is, in a sense, saying the same thing: not only is the Lord someone to behold; he is also the lens through which we see all of life, especially as we sit in the dark.

David was well acquainted with the dark. He knew affliction, opposition, and the pang of his own sin. He knew what it was like to be utterly surrounded by enemies, to be deeply betrayed by a friend, and to be hunted down like an animal. Although he was keenly aware of his bleak circumstances, his eyes beheld the truth: the Lord, Creator and Sustainer of life, was his stronghold.

David learned that there is a certain wonderful security in feeling our frailty as we face adversity. The light of the gospel reveals that, even in our weakness, God's power is made perfect; when we are weak, then we are strong (2 Cor. 12:9–10). To be strong apart from the Lord is to be vulnerable to the most insidious of enemies—our pride. Pride separates us from the only source of protection, power, and life. Psalm 138:6 tells us that the Lord knows the proud "from afar." To be strong in the Lord is to know his presence, to desire it, to seek wholeheartedly after it, and to find ourselves hidden therein.

The powerlessness that comes from being beset by our enemies or by threatening circumstances is an opportunity to see reality. Our reaction to the barrage reveals where we place our trust. Do we justify ourselves? Are we incredulous at what is happening, believing that we don't deserve it? Do we despair and become skeptical of the Lord's character? Or do we, like David, cry out to the Lord and trust that we will see "the goodness of the LORD in the land of the living" (Ps. 27:13)?

As people walking the earth after the Messiah's first coming, we have the advantage of looking back on that which David could only hope for.

We can trust the Scriptures, as well as the testimony of those who came before us, that perfect Goodness walked, breathed, worked, bled, died, and rose again in the land of the living. The proof of God's character is seen in the Son. It is in light of his sacrifice and victory that we can trust him to be our light, our salvation, and our strength.

APRIL 25 · PSALM 32

Confession Is Good Medicine

GEOFF ALLEN

WHEN IT COMES to sinning, we're all experts. We've felt those stabbing pangs of guilt when we've sinned against someone, whether the Lord or our neighbors. We also know the welcoming relief that forgiveness can bring.

The hard part, for many of us, is *confession*. Confession is humbling, sometimes even embarrassing. In our image-saturated world, where every aspect of our being, from the way we look to the way we behave, is under constant scrutiny, the act of confession can seem particularly frightening and exposing. We feel as if a giant magnifying glass is poised above us for the whole world to analyze and pass judgment on our actions.

So we look for ways to circumvent confession in an attempt to protect ourselves, to salvage our image. We see this everywhere—from the latest news story about a public servant "caught in the act," to our own lives in the workplace and at home. An assignment we didn't do properly suddenly becomes someone else's fault. Inattention to a spouse or family member is presented as somehow justifiable because *they* have done something wrong. Sin has a way of creating within us an intense aversion to accepting and owning it. Instead, we spin, we assign blame, we deflect and deny, all so that we can protect our image from the painful exposure of the light of day. Yet even though our exterior image may be protected, on the inside guilt, like a cancer, is slowly eating away at us.

No one knew this better than David, the author of Psalm 32. After sleeping with Uriah's wife, Bathsheba (2 Sam. 11:1–5), David, rather than confessing to Uriah, tried to cover up the sin (2 Sam. 11:6–27). Like us,

David avoided confession, but his unwillingness to acknowledge his sin caused him great suffering (Ps. 32:3–4). It wasn't until he confessed his sin that he was able to boldly write of the many blessings we receive from the Lord when confession is made (vv. 5–7).

Sometimes our hesitancy to confess our sins is a result of forgetting that God is "a God ready to forgive" (Neh. 9:17). In fact, so eager is he to forgive that he gave his only Son as a sacrifice to cover every sin we will ever commit, past, present, and future. As a result, "There is therefore now no condemnation for those who are in Christ Jesus" (Rom. 8:1). When we sin, we can go to our Father, knowing he has promised that "if we confess our sins, he is faithful and just to forgive us our sins and to cleanse us from all unrighteousness" (1 John 1:9). In his presence, we are met not with judgment or disapproval, but with "shouts of deliverance" (Ps. 32:7).

APRIL 26 · PSALM 34

You Are Invited

JANI ORTLUND

I LOVE GETTING an invitation, especially from someone I admire. Psalm 34 is a sacred invitation. David has been delivered from danger (see 1 Sam. 21:10–15). Unable to resist praising the Lord, he invites us to join in! He begins by blessing the Lord. He urges us to humble our hearts and rejoice in what God has done for him. He calls us to adore God along with him, and to magnify God's greatness and goodness and power (Ps. 34:1–3). God's goodness is too glorious for us to keep to ourselves. He hears. He cares. He answers (vv. 4–7). And that makes a difference even in our appearance (v. 5)!

David goes on to welcome us into a deep personal experience with the Lord: "taste and see that the LORD is good!" (v. 8). It's as if David is saying, "He is real to me, and I want him to be real to you—as real as your next meal!" It is impossible for God not to be good to you. He would have to "un-God" himself if he did anything that was not good. It may not feel or look good from our present viewpoint, but God will make it good in his own time and way. That means that whatever I have right now must be good, and what I don't have, the Lord has withheld because of his goodness. "The LORD is good! . . . Those who seek the LORD lack no good thing" (vv. 8, 10)

David urges us to step further in, with a teachable, childlike spirit (vv. 11–14). Do you want to know whether you fear the Lord? Ask yourself if there is any deceit or conflict in your life—in relationships, in finances, in your devotion to God. David invites us into a long life of true flourishing, lived in reverent fear before God and demonstrated through our truthful speech and pursuit of peace.

Finally, David encourages us with the Lord's tender care for his own (vv. 15–22). His ears are toward your cries (v. 15). If you can cry out, you can pray. Both the righteous and the wicked will be afflicted (vv. 19, 21), but what a difference in the outcome. Those whose pride and stubbornness have been humbled under God's loving care will experience the nearness of the Lord (v. 18; 145:18; Isa. 57:15). They will be heard and healed, rescued and redeemed (Ps. 34:15, 17, 19, 22; 147:3; 1 Pet. 5:6–7). Our Redeemer will pay whatever price is needed to meet our needs (Ps. 34:22). But the wicked will be cut off and condemned.

What an invitation! Will you say yes? The Lord is near, redeeming the life of his servants, turning even bad things into good for his own. Believe it, even amid your own struggles. "Oh, magnify the LORD with me, and let us exalt his name together!"

APRIL 27 · PSALM 37

The Long View of Life

LAUREN CHANDLER

"HERE AND NOW" is the cry of our hearts from the very beginning of life. As babies crying out for comfort and nourishment, as children insistent on every want being met, as young adults convinced of invincibility—a long view of life seems to come only once we're old and gray, and perhaps not even then. This mentality can creep into our spiritual life as well. We want instant gratification. We want to trust and obey and see immediate results—God's discernible favor at once. But time and again, Scripture shows us another way.

This wisdom psalm exhorts us to adjust our sight from what appears to be to what *truly is*, from the here and now to the *there and then*. The way in which we do this is mentioned in the first few verses: "Trust in the LORD. . . . Delight yourself in the LORD. . . . Commit your way to the LORD" (Ps. 37:3–5). It is in the soil of trust, delight, and commitment that contentment, patience, generosity, and justice grow, the final fruit of which is an eternal inheritance.

Trusting in the Lord means that we believe and rely on God being who he says he is and doing what he says he will do. We trust that he is good and righteous. We trust that he has our best at heart. We trust that even when we suffer, this too is under the hand of a tender heavenly Father (Rom. 8:28). We believe that although it seems like those who mock God prosper while we who hold onto our faith struggle, our lot is secure.

To delight ourselves in God is to find great joy in who he is and in his presence, and to seek to have our every desire fulfilled in him. Not only do we trust that he is good; we aim to experience his goodness. This delighting molds our heart to desire what he desires for us—that which is ultimately gratifying to us, which he gladly provides. We begin to find contentment in what we have in him, rather than lamenting what we lack by the world's standards. Envy toward "wrongdoers" wanes with a right view of what is truly delightful and desirable.

Committing our way to the Lord means entrusting the path of our lives to his safekeeping. We acknowledge his sovereignty and trust that, whatever comes our way, he is not only aware; he is in charge. Those who are committed to their own way will ultimately be "cut off" (Ps. 37:34). But for those who are in Christ, he himself was cut off on our behalf, at the cross. In him, we are secure, safe, and ultimately satisfied. He is our all.

Hope for the Downcast

ELISABETH MAXWELL (LISA) RYKEN

WE ALL HAVE SEASONS of great joy and terrible sorrow in our lives. One day we may be in a festive procession, praising God in his sanctuary. The next day we thirst for God, feeling numb in our souls. Sometimes our souls are in turmoil, searching for God but not finding him. Our pillows are soggy with tears, while those around us wonder what's wrong with us. As waves of frustrating and disheartening events crash over us, we fear we will drown.

Psalm 42 is a beautiful word for the downcast. We do not know the exact circumstances that caused the psalmist to be in such distress. Many commentators believe David wrote Psalm 42 when he was fleeing from his son Absalom. Regardless of the exact circumstances, the psalmist is in a position that, to some degree, we have all experienced. He is discouraged to the point of wondering whether God cares for him at all (Ps. 42:9). Adding to his pain, he is taunted by adversaries who reject God.

The psalmist knows that the solution to his depression is God himself. He longs to be able to spend time with God. He remembers times when he was able to pour out his soul to God in corporate worship (v. 4). As he questions himself, trying to figure out why he is so downcast, he exhorts himself to hope in God and to remember God's goodness and faithfulness. He knows that God is still the solid rock that will carry him through his inward and outward turmoil (v. 9).

So, too, when we are facing the inner turbulence of our souls, we must remind ourselves of God's goodness and faithfulness to us. Remember God's work in the Old Testament—how he created Adam and Eve, made a covenant with Abraham, rescued Moses and the Israelites, set David on his throne, and brought his people back from exile. Recall also God's work in the New Testament—Jesus's saving work on earth and the Spirit's mission through the early church. Consider, too, how God has worked in your own life. How has God provided for your physical and spiritual needs? How has he comforted you in the past?

We all have days when we are downcast and our souls are full of turmoil. The real question is not why we are downcast, but what are we going to do about it? David's answer was to preach the hope of God to his downcast soul. Our ultimate hope is that "neither death nor life, nor angels nor rulers, nor things present nor things to come, nor powers, nor height nor depth, nor anything else in all creation, will be able to separate us from the love of God in Christ Jesus our Lord" (Rom. 8:38–39). Jesus himself is the friend of the downcast. Walk with him. Pour out your heart to him.

Our Mighty Fortress

GLORIA FURMAN

AS ORDINARY AS OUR days may seem, the world we live in is precarious. Each of us is affected by wars and rumors of wars (Matt. 24:6), national catastrophes, and personal crises. The unknowns we live with can threaten to overwhelm our faith and even our very lives. Where can we look for hope and security? "The LORD of hosts is with us; the God of Jacob is our fortress" (Ps. 46:7, 11). God alone is our hope in these troubled times.

The aspect of God's "very present help" (v. 1) describes his readiness and willingness to save (145:18; Deut. 4:7). God is our exclusive security when the world we live in falls apart. We all tend to place our trust in things like reliable friends, financial stability, and "sure things." But these temporary comforts can never serve as our sufficient refuge or foundation. The assurance of God's help is our hope even if the mountains crumble into the sea. He is the one who spoke everything into existence (Genesis 1; Ps. 33:6; 104:5–9), and by his word he can disintegrate it (46:6).

Dear one, do you lack the security of his presence and the confidence of his help when the morning dawns (v. 5)? To the wind and sea that threatened to capsize his disciples' boat, Jesus issued the rebuke, "Peace! Be still!" (Mark 4:35–41). There is coming a day in the future when Jesus will put an end to the rage of evil in this world, and his rebuke to the nations will stand: "Be still, and know that I am God" (Ps. 46:10). At Jesus's command, wars will cease and he will be exalted in all the earth (vv. 8–10).

It is no wonder that Martin Luther was inspired by this psalm to write his famous hymn, "A Mighty Fortress Is Our God." God exercises his indomitable power over all things—nature (vv. 1–3), our enemies (vv. 4–7), and the entirety of this violent world (vv. 8–11). Our unchanging God promises his "very present help" to his beloved children. Who is more willing to come to our aid than the God "who did not spare his own Son but gave him up for us all" (Rom. 8:32)? In the unknowns of our tumultuous earthly circumstances, we are assured that God is both mighty to save and steadfast in his love (Ps. 63:3). Anchored in the truth of the gospel, we find our refuge in Christ.

True Repentance

DAN DORIANI

PSALM 51 is the crown of the psalms of repentance. David wrote it after his sin with Bathsheba, the beautiful woman he had lusted after. He did not resist temptation, but took her, conceived a child with her, and orchestrated a cover-up that led to her husband's death. David's sin was public, irreversible, and callous. When God sent a prophet to confront David, he made no excuses. He confessed, "I have sinned against the LORD," and God forgave him: "The LORD also has put away your sin" (2 Sam. 12:1–13). No sin lies outside the perimeter of God's grace.

Psalm 51 reflects this truth and begins with a humble plea for grace: "Have mercy on me, O God, according to your steadfast love." (Ps. 51:1). David begs God to show mercy and covenant love. The appeal to love is essential—we will not properly confess sin unless we believe that God loves us.

David asks the Lord to wipe out the record of his sin, removing the defilement that bars him from God's presence. David confesses that he has offended God: "Against you, you only, have I sinned" (v. 4). His sin is all too visible to him; it is "ever before" him (v. 3), so he petitions God to blot it out, wash it away, cleanse it, and purify him.

David exemplifies the spirit of confession, which says, "I am unworthy to call on you, yet I do call on you." God is David's ultimate audience. David doesn't deny that he wronged people, but he insists that he mainly offended God (v. 4). He makes no excuses for his actions: "Behold, I was brought forth in iniquity, and in sin did my mother conceive me" (v. 5). His sin is neither accident nor aberration; it is his nature. David owns his actions, calling them "my sins" (v. 9).

False confessions are rushed and thoughtless: "Yes, yes, I sinned. Sorry! Let's move on," or, "I'm sorry if I offended you." True confession fully acknowledges our wrong, as David does here.

David's confession leads to hope that God will transform and renew him: "Create in me a clean heart, O God, and renew a right spirit within me" (v. 10). When Saul sinned, God withdrew his Spirit from him. But David pleads, "Cast me not away from your presence, and take not your Holy Spirit from me" (v. 11). He asks God to restore the joy of his salvation (v. 12), so that he might in turn teach others who have sinned against the Lord (v. 13).

After we confess our sins, we can praise God, offering him our "broken and contrite heart" (vv. 15–17). The repentant believer is restored, and he in turn prays for the restoration of "Jerusalem"—the community of all who seek God's mercy (v. 18).

MAY 1 · PSALM 56

In God I Trust

GLENNA MARSHALL

WHEN WE ARE faced with fearful circumstances or bouts of anxiety, our despair might cause us to think that God is aloof or even indifferent toward our suffering. But David shows us that God keeps track of every pain we feel.

David was on the run when he penned this psalm (1 Sam. 21:10–15). Knowing that David was destined for Israel's throne, King Saul was on a murderous rampage, bent on taking David's life. David fled to Gath, where he was unfortunately recognized and in danger of being taken prisoner. Feigning insanity, David escaped from the king of Gath while continuing to seek safety from his own king.

After appealing to God for grace in difficult circumstances, David declares that he will trust in God when he is afraid. We cannot miss the context of his confession, though: it comes *when* he is afraid. David is scared, and understandably so. He bumps into enemies while running away from his own king!

But what does David do with his fear? David's fear serves as a signal to put his trust in God (v. 3). Fear can be an indicator that it is time to capture our thoughts and to resolve to entrust ourselves to the Lord. And we have so many good reasons to trust him! As David asks, "What can man do to me?" (v. 11). God is sovereignly in control, and David trusts that God will deal with his enemies as he sees fit (v. 7).

Deeper still is God's intimate acquaintance with our sufferings. In verse 8 we learn that God keeps a record of our trials, collecting our tears in his bottle and marking down our sufferings in his book. God is not indifferent toward our suffering. He knows each and every one of our pains, and we can be confident that whatever he brings into our lives is for our good and his glory (Rom. 8:28).

We can share in David's confidence in God's trustworthy care for our lives. One day those who have believed in Christ, in the one whose greatest suffering has become our greatest treasure, will receive the comfort that ends all sorrows when they stand face-to-face with the Lord who has kept track of the tears they have cried. He will tenderly wipe away each and every one (Rev. 21:4), and his people will never have reason to fear or weep again. We can trust God with our lives because in Christ he is faithfully keeping us for eternity.

My Soul Thirsts for You

ANN VOSKAMP

WHOLE WEEKS and seasons and years can feel like a wilderness. In David's wilderness, his own son Absalom is seeking to kill him for the crown. It's a wilderness worse than we could imagine.

David calls to God in the wilderness—*My God*—using that audacious possessive pronoun. Who of us can pick up the phone in a crisis, call a friend, and say, "I need help, my Sally"? Whom can we *possess* with our problems? God alone is the One who lets our hurts possess his heart: "O God, you are my God; earnestly I seek you," cries David, "my soul thirsts for you; my flesh faints for you, as in a dry and weary land where there is no water" (Ps. 63:1). Sometimes, we need to experience God like we need to experience water!

David prays to God not for a strong life, not for a safe life, not for a serene life. David prays, "your steadfast love is better than life" (v. 3). There is a love that is better than we could ever imagine—a love better than *life*. A love that *is* life. If we have God's love—is there anything really left to have?

Chesed is the Hebrew word used in this verse to express "steadfast love." It is an unmovable love, an unchangeable love—a pledged love. God pledges himself to you, and his pledged love is *better* than life for you. Psalm 63 is an invitation to carry all that concerns you before God and whisper, "No matter what comes—your steadfast love is better than any outcome."

The Hebrew word for "clings" (v. 8) is the same Hebrew word as in Genesis 2:24: "Therefore a man shall leave his father and his mother and hold fast [cling] to his wife." If our soul clings to God, it holds fast to him in intimacy and in promised obedience. There is no experience of God unless there is obedience to God.

David determines to remember God "upon my bed, and meditate on you in the watches of the night" (Ps. 63:6). We make our lives a wilderness until we meditate on the word and the Word made flesh. To "set your minds on things that are above" (Col. 3:2) is the only way to begin setting things right in this world. Meditation is the migration of affection. Your soul has clung to other stuff. Meditation loosens that grip until your soul clings to Christ.

When God's love is better than life, your lips will praise him (Ps. 63:3); you will bless him as long as you live (v. 4), his praise ever resting on your joyful lips (v. 5). The only way to complete the joy of what you love is to complete that love with praise. Nonexistent praise is evidence of nonexistent love. Anyone who has truly experienced God will express gratitude to him. Their wilderness will become a well.

MAY 3 · PSALM 68

Our Great, Triumphant God

KAREN S. LORITTS

PSALM 68 is a joyful hymn of praise celebrating God's care for and protection of his people. "God shall arise, his enemies shall be scattered; and those who hate him shall flee before him!" (Ps. 68:1). With this triumphant call to praise, God's people are reminded of his power and might and are called to respond accordingly: "Sing to God, sing praises to his name; . . . exult before him!" (v. 4). "Ascribe power to God" (v. 34)!

David recounts God's faithfulness to Israel in the past (vv. 7–8) and rejoices in his help for today (v. 19). The wicked are no match for the God of Israel. The enemies of God are ultimately powerless; this emboldens us to stand firm and not capitulate to the enemy's threats. God triumphs over all the wicked.

The children of Israel have witnessed God's steadfast love and faithfulness. He restored his people and provided for them in the wilderness: "you restored your inheritance as it languished" (v. 9). It was only because of the assurance of his presence and his provision for their needs that Israel endured. His victory on their behalf is incomparable.

God is both defender and protector of the righteous. The fatherless have a Father, and widows a protector (v. 5). The lonely are not forgotten: "God settles the solitary in a home" (v. 6). He provides victory against all odds. Those who are captive or imprisoned find refuge (v. 6). The needy know of his goodness. It is a double blessing, goodness and mercy (23:6), that follows them. God's children could not be more secure than they are.

"Blessed be the Lord, who daily bears us up; God is our salvation" (68:19). What can truly threaten us when the omnipotent God bears us up, providing safety? "God is our refuge and strength, a very present help in trouble" (46:1). There is no need to fear, no need to flee. God is our salvation. "The salvation of the righteous is from the LORD; he is their stronghold in the time of trouble" (37:39).

In Jesus Christ, we see in concrete terms the length to which God will go in order to sustain his people. The psalmist writes, "Blessed be the Lord, who daily bears us up; God is our salvation" (68:19). This is a salvation secured centuries later by Christ, who died on a cross and rose again so that believers can be assured that God will daily bear us up, even despite our sins.

MAY 4 · PSALM 71

Always

MICHELE BENNETT WALTON

THOUGH GOD'S LOVING disposition toward us was settled at the cross, our feelings and circumstances often shake our confidence in who God is for us. We think of him as a glorified composite of reluctant benefactors, flawed parents, gracious strangers, and indulgent friends. And we know all too well how quickly human patience grows weary of human weakness.

Perhaps this is why we love Psalm 71. If you've wearied a friend with your tears or known the shame of crying hopelessly about *that thing* for the thousandth time, you begin to understand the power of the psalmist's declaration and request: "Be to me a rock of refuge, to which I may continually come." In this prayer alone he utters three petitions for deliverance, recounting the rich history of his relationship with the Lord in the process.

With each of these petitions, the psalmist declares that he depends "continually" on God. The Hebrew word for this, *tamid*, can also be translated "always." *Tamid* could be said to be the theme of Psalm 71, but not just because of the tenacity of the psalmist. Much more importantly, the psalmist puts the faithfulness of God on display. We see God actively involved in everything that touches the psalmist's life—protecting, defending, strengthening, saving, and teaching him. And we get a bird's-eye view of God at work over the course of a life—from birth to old age.

Our prayers likewise are uttered within the framework of a proven relationship. God has proven his faithfulness in our lives, in the lives of our brothers and sisters today, and in the lives of the saints in church history and Scripture no less than in the life of the psalmist.

God is not like us; he is unswervingly true to his promise. That's why we return to Psalm 71 and lean on (and learn from) the prayer of one who is actively rehearsing God's faithfulness. Through the psalmist's words of faith, we taste God's past faithfulness so palpably that present and future faithfulness seem equally sure. As the psalmist remembers and anticipates, we too are swept up in the expectation that such a righteous God will come through in the end.

Let your heart be swept up. Dare to hope. Dare to trust. Dare to believe. And run to God continually. "Now faith is the assurance of things hoped for, the conviction of things not seen. For by it the people of old received their commendation. By faith we understand that the universe was created by the word of God, so that what is seen was not made out of things that are visible" (Heb. 11:1–3).

MAY 5 · PSALM 77

Remember the Lord

KERI FOLMAR

WHERE DO YOU go with your trouble? To whom can you cry out when all around you is crumbling? Who will comfort your soul in the dark of night? The psalmist cries out in earnest prayer to a God he knows will hear. Although he feels deserted, his confidence is in this God of steadfast love, and he longs for the Lord's presence to again be felt among his people.

The psalmist asks a series of questions of God that are answered from within the questions themselves by descriptions of the character of God. The Lord will not spurn forever. He is favorably disposed toward his people. His steadfast love endures forever, and he fulfills all his promises. He is a gracious and compassionate God, whose anger will not last forever. These meditations on the character of God spur the psalmist on to appeal to the Lord based on his mighty work in the past.

The past gives the psalmist great hope for the future. God has been and is the great deliverer who cares for his people. The psalmist recounts God's wondrous deeds in bringing the people of Israel out of slavery in Egypt, into the Promised Land. God redeemed his people with his mighty arm of strength.

But that exodus was the shadow of a greater, ultimate exodus, where God would redeem his people from the slavery of sin and death. Jesus is the True Exodus. In the Old Testament, God parted the sea. In the New Testament, Jesus calmed the wind and the waves and walked on the water. God led his people "like a flock by the hand of Moses and Aaron" (Ps. 77:20). Jesus is the Great Shepherd who lays down his life for his sheep (John 10:11). He is the fulfillment of all of God's promises (2 Cor. 1:20). His death assuaged God's anger and redeemed his people to never again be separated from him.

The psalmist encouraged himself and his community by remembering— remembering God's character and his mighty works of old. When our sin weighs us down, when trouble comes our way, we, like the psalmist, must seek encouragement in remembering. Meditate on God's character, shown most gloriously in the crucifixion of Christ. Think of Jesus's mighty saving work completed at the cross. Allow the past to give you great hope for the future. Cry out to the God who hears. His footprints may be unseen (Ps. 77:19), but he is the Great Shepherd who will lead his people like a flock with his gentle but mighty hand.

God Withholds No Good Thing

CAROLYN MCCULLEY

THIS SONG OF praise is not only a song celebrating the pilgrimage to Jerusalem to worship at the temple; it is also a song to be sung today. Especially when our circumstances appear to be anything *but* celebratory—for "no good thing does he withhold from those who walk uprightly" (Ps. 84:11). *No* good thing. Period.

The Lord God is our protector. He shines down on us ("sun") and protects us ("and shield"). He is the one to truly provide favor and honor. But this psalm acknowledges that there are times when our life circumstances feel contrary to this promise. Verse 6 refers to the Valley of Baca. This is an obscure location, but *Baca* means "weeping," which may be a reference to any dark valley of despair and loss that we must pass through in various seasons of our lives. Whatever places seem barren of hope or joy can become fruitful "places of springs" as we see that our strength is in the Lord (v. 5). We know this to be true because of one important fact: our pilgrimage does not end in this life. We are on "the highways to Zion" (v. 5), going "from strength to strength" (v. 7) as we journey toward the moment when we appear before God in his dwelling place.

This is not an emotional song designed to cheer up our attitudes with flowery phrases. This is rock-solid *truth*. Our reward is found, not in this life but in the presence of the One who "bestows favor and honor" (v. 11). As we trust that the Lord will fulfill all his promises, we can survey our circumstances and declare with confidence that no good thing has been withheld from us. Marriage, children, jobs, finances, health—these things may or may not be part of our pilgrimage in this life. But they have not been withheld from us because we lack favor or honor in God's sight. No, this psalm declares that the very *best* thing has been freely given to us!

Look carefully at verses 11 and 12. They echo the promise given to Abram as he waited on God to fulfill his promise for a son and heir. Genesis 15:1 contains this promise from the Lord to Abram: "Fear not, Abram, I am your shield; your reward shall be very great." The Lord *himself* is our greatest reward. That's the incredible reason for declaring that "blessed is the one who trusts in you!" (Ps. 84:12). The presence of the Lord himself to comfort and shield us in the places of weeping will one day be fully revealed to us as we see him face-to-face in his courts, where we will dwell securely in eternal joy.

MAY 7 · PSALM 91

Danger and the Shadow of the Almighty

COLLEEN J. MCFADDEN

WHAT DO YOU do when danger abounds? There are numerous ways we may react, depending on what, exactly, we are facing. We may try to control the situation with the resources we have. We may ask for help from local authorities—or hide, and swear to "be good forever," should this fearful moment pass. Regardless of our circumstances, Psalm 91 is a beautiful, tender reminder that we are nowhere safer than in the "shadow of the Almighty" (Ps. 91:1).

This psalm is written in such a way as to personally address each of us: "For he will deliver *you*. . . . He will cover *you*. . . . *You* will not fear" (vv. 3–5). The danger described isn't specific, but rather all-encompassing, to show that no hazard or peril defies God's protection of those he loves. It is danger that can happen at any time (vv. 5–6), that can kill by plague or disease (vv. 3, 6, 10) or by devouring (v. 13). It might be an insurmountable danger with odds of ten thousand to one (v. 7)—but there is no danger too big for God.

For those who trust in him, God is a refuge and a fortress (v. 2). And how many are the ways in which he keeps us safe! He covers and shields us (v. 4), and he commands his angels to guard us and bear us up, out of harm's way (vv. 11–12). God promises to deliver us from those who are against us (v. 3), from enemies and from evil (vv. 7–8, 10). Ultimately, he will deliver us through salvation into everlasting life (v. 16).

So, what is our responsibility? In the face of danger, we must trust in the Lord Almighty. Note the personal nature of this trust: we do not trust in just any god, but in "my God" (v. 2). We have a personal faith in a personal God who has a dwelling place for us (vv. 1, 9). We belong to him; we speak with him and are with him (vv. 2, 15). We know his name, and he knows us (v. 14).

What does it mean to make the Lord our dwelling place (v. 9)? It means he is our home. He is the shelter and the shadow that covers us. When we call to him, he has promised to answer us—and not only that, but to "rescue" and "honor" us as well! (v. 15). As we dwell with him, we clearly see his faithfulness to us and have no fear (v. 5).

God sent his son, Jesus, to be a dwelling place on earth as he was God incarnate. In Christ, we dwell with our Creator. The Holy Spirit resides in us as a dwelling place for the Almighty. In Christ there is no need to fear. Look to this shelter of salvation in the face of temporary danger, which has been and will be overcome by the Most High.

MAY 8 · PSALM 96

Celebrating God's Perfect Judgment and Reign

KRISTYN GETTY

GOD'S PEOPLE HAVE always been a singing people. There must be a robust expression of our testimony to his grace, something not just seen in our lives but heard from our voices. The Psalms teach us why singing is important, showing us what to sing about, each song like a diamond revealing the many facets of God's character. Worship comes as a response to the revelation of God, and he has revealed himself to us in different ways. In Psalm 96, he is Creator, he is King, he is Judge. This final characteristic is the central cadence as we are called to rejoice in the perfect reign of God as the Judge of all heaven and earth.

The world is moving toward a time of judgment that will bring joy or terror, relief or dread, depending on the condition of our hearts. Judgment may not be something we are quick to celebrate in worship, but it is an attribute the psalmist David does not hesitate to exalt. We cannot understand God's love and grace without understanding his justice. And once we are secure in his grace, we are free to rejoice in his justice.

In Revelation, John mourns when it seems no one is worthy to open the scrolls of judgment. One of the elders replies, "Weep no more; behold, the Lion of the tribe of Judah. . . . has conquered, so that he can open the scroll" (Rev. 5:5). John's vision exemplifies how only Christ is worthy, for only he is able to bring ultimate justice to the earth; it is his sacrifice that accomplishes reconciliation between us and God.

All who have believed in Christ have been clothed in his righteousness. They no longer face condemnation. Every tear of injustice and scar of affliction finds its healing and hope in him. This is an incredible revelation of grace that stirs our hearts to worship. This is the good news we must sing about before the nations, where people are bound by many physical and spiritual chains. Judgment belongs to the Lord, and he will make things right. We cannot place our hope in other things to "fix" the world, nor do we despair about the world's current condition, for we know that when he comes, "he comes to judge the earth" (Ps. 96:13).

Are you singing words that bear the comfort and challenge of both God's justice and his grace to your heart and those around you? Are you choosing each day, by grace, to live in the joy and the readiness his return inspires, joining with the seas, fields, and forests to long for the perfect harmony of God and for his creation to be restored?

MAY 9 · PSALM 103

Believers Bless and Fear God

HEATHER HOUSE

PSALM 103 IS a psalm of thanksgiving, written by David, which encourages believers to "bless the LORD" and to "fear him." To "bless the LORD" is to praise God because his acts and character are worthy of it. To "fear him" is to respond in awe and obedience in light of who he is (Ex. 34:6–7). Both are appropriate reactions to God's work and character.

David provides a remarkable list of reasons to bless God, reminding us to "forget not all his benefits" (Ps. 103:2). The Lord forgives, heals, redeems, crowns, satisfies, and renews (vv. 3–5). He "works righteousness and justice for all who are oppressed" (v. 6), and he makes himself known to his people (v. 7). He is consistently "merciful and gracious, slow to anger and abounding in steadfast love" (v. 8). He will discipline and judge, but not forever (vv. 9–12). With fatherly affection, he lavishes us with forgiveness and compassion (v. 13). He understands that we as human beings are finite and fragile, and thus he is patient with us (vv. 14–16).

As David establishes what God does for humanity, the vast differences between the Creator and the created become evident. Humans sin; God redeems. People are frail; God is eternal. We are part of creation; God is the ruler of creation. The inequity is clear, but in his mercy, God passes over humanity's spiritual and physical weakness and preserves life, both temporal and eternal. He bridges the gap between his holiness and humanity's sinfulness through Christ's death and resurrection (Col. 1:15–23). Such generosity should be met with reverence, devotion, and obedience springing out of love.

Since this is so, the psalmist calls all creation to bless the Lord, including angels and other heavenly beings (Ps. 103:20–22). Believers join with them, but we have a special reason to praise God: because he has saved us. We have experienced the mighty Ruler as the tender, forgiving Savior.

God acts for individuals, for believers throughout time, and for future generations. David is aware of how God has rescued him (vv. 2–5). He also knows that God behaved in the same ways toward the Israelites in Moses's day (v. 7). And he is confident that God will continue to be faithful to those who trust him (vv. 17–18).

God's consistent character makes him dependable. For Moses and the Israelites, the congregation worshiping with David, believers today, and generations yet to come, God is unchanging. We can count on God's compassion, love, and forgiveness. Our response should be praise, awe, and obedience.

Give Thanks to the Lord

ANN VOSKAMP

DAYS AND HOURS and moments: all of our lives have these bookends, these beginnings and endings. Psalm 106 gives us God's commanded bookends for every moment, every breath. The psalm opens in praise—and closes in praise. It's called an *inclusio*, a Hebrew poetic pattern that repeats a phrase at both the beginning and end of a text, giving a sense of completion.

Praise the Lord! Praise the Lord! (Ps. 106:1, 48). There—*that* is God's given pattern for our lives, how we bookend our moments and lead complete lives. When we "give thanks to the Lord" (v. 1), our days are given a sense of unity. It keeps us in union with our Savior. If our lives are not characterized as giving thanks to God, our lives are then characterizing God as not good. We *must* give thanks to God, because God *is* good.

"Who can . . . declare *all* his praise?" (v. 2). If God's steadfast love knows no end, what could possibly make our thanks to him end? Calvin writes, "The stability of the world depends on the rejoicing in God's works. . . . If, on earth, such praise of God does not come to pass, . . . then the whole order of nature will be thrown into confusion."[3] Which is sadly and exactly how Psalm 106 unfolds; it reads like the history of the uncontainable grace of God—as well as the history of the ungrateful, unfaithful people of God. Disobedient, discontent, and disloyal, their story is more about giving God rebellious grief than giving him thanks.

Psalm 106 is a striking study in remembering. God's children keep forgetting their Father's faithfulness: they "did not consider [God's] wondrous works" (v. 7); "they did not remember the abundance of [God's] steadfast love" (v. 7); "they soon forgot [God's] works" (v. 13); "they forgot God, their Savior, who had done great things . . . wondrous works . . . and awesome deeds" (vv. 21, 22). *But God* . . . Remarkably, God never stops remembering his people: "Nevertheless, he looked upon their distress, when he heard their cry. For their sake, he remembered his covenant" (v. 44).

Christ remembers his covenant with covenant breakers—what could ever cause us to complain again? Every Christian should be a study in remembering. It's one of Christ's commands (Luke 22:19). It's what puts our broken pieces back together again. Remember. Remember what Christ has done for you, and give thanks. If we forget and do not give thanks, the whole world—*our world*—falls into confusion. The very stability of our world depends on our rejoicing in, remembering, and recounting the goodness of God.

MAY 11 · PSALM 110

The King-Priest at God's Right Hand

W. BRIAN AUCKER

INTO AND OUT of Psalm 110 flow important themes of the Psalms and of the entire Old Testament. Melchizedek, the ancient king-priest, trickles into this psalm from Genesis 14. The election of and covenant with Abraham results in victory over his enemies (see Gen. 14:19–20). The thematic river rises as David, a king-priest, rules in Jerusalem, wears priestly garments, offers sacrifices, and blesses his people (see 2 Sam. 6:14–19). The current surges forward with the Lord's pledge of victory for the Davidic king over his enemies (see 2 Sam. 7:9–11). Incapable of containing the rising tide, Psalm 110 bursts its shorelines. No Scripture is more quoted or referred to in the New Testament than this royal, messianic psalm penned by David. A king-priest who is greater than David and Melchizedek floods a glorious future.

The king-priest at God's right hand subdues all (Ps. 110:1). When Jesus quotes this verse to the religious authorities, he claims that the son of David is also the Lord of David (Matt. 22:41–46). God grants that Jesus Christ, David's Lord, may sit at the place of honor and power; his benevolent authority persists now and until the age to come (1 Cor. 15:25–28).

The king-priest at God's right hand is a priest forever (Ps. 110:4). The Levitical priesthood prepared God's people for the one to come but was not sufficient to deal with human rebellion once and for all. In contrast to this priestly line, the one "after the order of Melchizedek" (v. 4) combines the role of priest and king to intercede for his people forever (Heb. 7:11–28). He never ceases to be a priest, and yet, with the completion of his sacrificial work, he no longer stands, but *sits* at God's right hand as both priest and king (Heb. 10:11–14; see also 1:3; 8:1).

The splendors, perils, and complications of the world confront us. Rebellion, sin, and shame undo us. At such moments our voices echo the apostle Paul in his conflict with the fallen world: "Wretched man that I am! Who will deliver me from this body of death?" (Rom. 7:24). Jesus Christ, whose kingship excels that of David, answers this cry of the heart. He calls us to himself and subdues all his and our enemies (Ps. 110:1–2). And yet Jesus is also a priest forever. He offered himself willingly upon the cross to reconcile us to God. Those submitting to the authority of King Jesus and resting in his finished priestly sacrifice "will offer themselves freely" in service to him. Dressed in holy garments, we serve as a royal priesthood in his kingdom (v. 3; see Ex. 19:6; 1 Pet. 2:8).

MAY 12 · PSALM 116

I Love the Lord

KATHLEEN CHAPELL

I love You, Lord, and I lift my voice,
To worship You, O my soul, rejoice![4]

MY BOYS WERE four and two when first introduced to this praise song. Led by the valiant moms heading up the VBS that year, the children sang "I love you, Lord," in their clear, sweet voices, and I was moved to tears. There stood Colin and Jordan, my little baby boys, privileged to sing to the King of Heaven, "I love you!"

Psalm 116 is a love song to the Lord, a personal hymn of thanksgiving the psalmist sings to God for his gracious compassion and strong deliverance. "I love the LORD because he has heard my voice and my pleas for mercy" (Ps. 116:1). While many Psalms speak on behalf of many believers, or exhort believers to praise, these verses are an intimate, personal reflection on the Lord's care. With humble transparency the writer describes his despair: "The snares of death encompassed me; the pangs of Sheol laid hold on me; I suffered distress and anguish" (v. 3).

Then, weighed down by sorrow and despair, the psalmist turns to the Lord: "I called on the name of the LORD: O LORD, I pray, deliver my soul!" (v. 4). And the result: "When I was brought low, he saved me" (v. 6). More explanation follows: "You have delivered my soul from death, my eyes from tears, my feet from stumbling" (v. 8). The need was great, and the Lord's deliverance was complete.

Much of this Psalm is spoken directly to the Lord: "you have delivered my soul from death. . . . O LORD, I am your servant. . . . You have loosed my bonds" (vv. 8, 16). Other verses are written for an audience, proclaiming the Lord's care and his servant's devotion: "I will lift up the cup of salvation and call on the name of the LORD" (v. 13). Our love for the Lord is a deep and personal response to his grace to us. And yet, our gratitude to the Lord should swell beyond our private expression; our joyful praise should be irrepressible, so great is our love and thanksgiving (vv. 17–19)!

Consider this: among the countless blessings showered upon us by our heavenly Father, chief among them is the privilege of praising him. Broken, sinful people, stumbling along the path where he is leading, failing and falling—still he reveals himself again and again, picks us up again and again, comforts us again and again—we have every reason to praise him!

MAY 13 · PSALM 119:33-40

Teach Me, O Lord

KRISTIE ANYABWILE

WHEN I FIRST learned how to cook, I would just follow what Mom and Grandma did. First, I would ask lots of random questions while they busied themselves with preparation. Then, I would ask a lot of "why" questions, trying to understand not only what they were doing, but why it was done that way. Pretty soon I wanted to try it myself. They taught me ingredients and technique, and I followed their lead. I gained skills that would last a lifetime—and I now have great delight in serving my family recipes I learned as a child.

In this section of Psalm 119, the psalmist asks the Lord for instruction as he seeks to learn and live out God's commandments: "Teach me, O Lord, the way of your statutes; and I will keep it to the end" (Ps. 119:33). He progresses from asking for knowledge to asking for understanding of what he has learned. Why? "That I may keep your law and observe it with my whole heart" (v. 34). He wants to know and understand God's ways because he wants to obey him. As he seeks the Lord's guidance, he acknowledges that his heart can be distracted and drawn away from the things of God. Thus, along with knowledge and understanding, he asks God to incline his heart to him, lest he seek selfish gain (v. 36). He knows it can be tempting to use God's blessings and gifts for ourselves rather than for his glory.

When we focus on ourselves rather than on the Lord—when we hoard God's blessings rather than sharing them with others—we choke the life out of those blessings. Our lives feel empty, till we realize that joy comes through giving, not through selfish gain. For indeed, "it is more blessed to give than to receive" (Acts 20:35). How do we come back from this kind of emptiness? Only one thing can take our gaze off vanity and "worthless things" (Ps. 119:37): fixing our eyes on Jesus. God promises that if we draw near to him, he will draw near to us (James 4:8).

The Lord requires wholehearted devotion to him. We must keep our eyes firmly on him, rather than ourselves, lest the cares of the world cause us to stumble. But he does not leave us on our own as we seek to obey him—he is our Teacher, and he readily gives us knowledge and understanding of his ways and his commands, as well as the ability to live them out.

The Lord promises that if we delight ourselves in him, he will give us the desires of our heart (Ps. 37:4). Delighting in God will change our desires so that they are in line with his own. When that happens, our delight in God will grow and the death that vanity produces will give way to life everlasting.

Hold Close the Word of the Lord

JONI EARECKSON TADA

AFTER DECADES OF PARALYSIS, and almost as many years leaning on God's word, I often find myself running to these verses from Psalm 119. God has not kept me from affliction, but he has kept me from *perishing* in my affliction. How have these Scriptures kept me from caving in to despair? Let me share a few high points from this passage.

Forever, O Lord, your word is firmly fixed in the heavens (Ps. 119:89). Like the poet, you may feel yourself tossing about in a sea of trouble, nearly drowning in waves of despair and discouragement. Do what he does: stand on a safe and sure rock. The word of God is not fickle; it is our certain help. Should we wonder just *how* certain, the psalmist places the firmness of God's word in the heavens, ascribing to it the honored title, *Forever*. We can completely trust what God says.

If your law had not been my delight, I would have perished in my affliction (v. 92). Think of the many times you stake your life on God's word (and don't even realize it). Every morning he awakens you with grace. He grants you salvation, a home in heaven, escape from hell, and a purpose for living, all the while working everything for your good and his glory. He grants you the honor of bearing his name, safeguarding his reputation, representing his character, and sharing his gospel. These are promises that can't help but cause to swell within you a sheer delight in every declaration from God. And once they become your delight, you'll be quicker to reach for his promises when facing affliction. *That* will keep you from perishing.

I will never forget your precepts, for by them you have given me life (v. 93). The best evidence of your love for God's word is that you never forget it. And how could you? By it, God breathes life into your spirit, quickens your soul, and preserves your very body. The world, the flesh, and the devil may be hell-bent on draining every ounce of life out of you, but staying close to God's word will keep your spiritual vital signs healthy, keep you safe, and keep you on the path of righteousness.

I am yours; save me, for I have sought your precepts (v. 94). You and I are not our own. We are God's. He moved heaven and earth to send his own Son to a cruel cross for you. God's reputation is invested in what happens to you, and the best evidence that you belong to him is that you "have sought [God's] precepts." Make Psalm 119 your prayer at any time, and you know your words will have an audience before God—after all, you're speaking his language!

MAY 15 • PSALM 121

Our Help Is from the Lord

CAROL CORNISH

CHRISTIANS HAVE LONG found solace and reason for courage and hope in the words of this psalm. We live in a fallen world, a world full of trouble and danger. Protection is needed for traveling through this dangerous territory. Notice how the psalmist coaches himself—talking to himself and reminding himself of the truth of God's word. He identifies the source of his help as the Creator, "the LORD, who made heaven and earth." He reasons that since God is the Creator, he is also the sovereign ruler over all.

Because he is personally involved in both the mundane and the significant things in our lives, God knows the difficulties we face. He is able to keep us safe from anything that would do us real and lasting harm. Not only does he help us with immediate concerns; he also ensures that we will endure to the end (Phil. 1:6).

We are not promised that our lives will be free of hardships and tragedies. In fact, Jesus told us that we will have trouble in this world (John 16:33). His enemies are our enemies. A biblical perspective on life demands that we acknowledge this reality: trouble, difficulty, and hardship are the norm, not the exception. And yet, God promises that he is always with us (Matt. 28:20; Heb. 13:5).

All earthly sources of help have limitations. None is worthy of our ultimate dependence. So it ought to be our greatest comfort in trouble or danger to know that God's loving eye is always upon us—that he is our keeper. He is not distant, distracted, disinterested, or deficient.

God will never fail to help you. He cannot fail. Our utterly powerful, wise, and loving helper is the Lord Almighty. He is our faithful guardian. It is good to foster a sense of gratitude for God's help and for the knowledge that he stays close to us and guards our lives. Praise him for his kind and faithful help!

Psalm 121 provides a road map for life's journey. Lift up your eyes to the one and only sure source of help. The Lord hears the prayers of his people and is ready to answer in ways that will showcase his glory and shape us into the likeness of his Son. No trouble, no loss, no hardship, no disaster will do us ultimate harm. Walk in step with God's Spirit as he directs your going out and your coming in, so that all things mold you into the likeness of Christ and increase your joy in him. "The LORD will keep you from all evil" (Ps. 121:7). God proved this, ultimately, in the atoning work of his Son. In Christ you are invincible.

A Cry for Help

MARY A. KASSIAN

PSALM 130 IS the sixth of seven psalms designated by the early church as "penitential psalms" (Psalms 6; 32; 38; 51; 102; 130; 143). Being penitent means being sorry for and repentant of sin. It comes from the Latin *paenitentia*. We don't know who wrote this psalm, but whoever he was, he had gotten himself in a terrible predicament and felt desperate for God.

The psalmist cries to the Lord "out of the depths" (130:1). He was in severe distress. Perhaps he was going through interpersonal conflict, a marital breakdown, financial disaster, legal issues, health problems, persecution, or some other sort of crisis. Whatever the case, he had fallen into a hole of his own making. He was facing the awful awareness that there was absolutely nothing he could do to turn back the clock and undo the mistakes that had landed him there. The hole was deep and dark, and he could see no way out. Psalm 69:1–2 expresses a similar feeling: "Save me, O God! For the waters have come up to my neck. I sink in deep mire, where there is no foothold; I have come into deep waters, and the flood sweeps over me."

Most of us can relate. We've been there. We know what it's like to mess up and feel overwhelmed by troubles that are, in part or completely, our own fault. This psalm shows that we can cry out to the Lord for help, even when our difficulties are self-inflicted. We don't need to wallow in self-condemnation, or beat ourselves up with thoughts of "How could I have been so stupid?" Sin is a common malady: "If you, O Lord, should mark iniquities, O Lord, who could stand?" (130:3).

The psalmist appeals to God's mercy: "But with you there is forgiveness, that you may be feared" (v. 4). God's patience, kindness, and forgiveness make him "fear"—honor and trust—the Lord. It isn't God's harshness that motivates us to do what is right; it's his kindness (Rom. 2:4).

After confession and repentance comes the hard part: *waiting* on God. "I wait for the Lord, my soul waits, and in his word I hope; my soul waits for the Lord" (Ps. 130:5–6). The Psalms are full of admonitions to wait for the Lord (27:14; 31:24; 33:20; 37:7, 34; 62:5). But this "waiting" is not passive. Waiting on God means immersing oneself in his word, getting to know him and his ways, and patiently, expectantly, and attentively watching for his direction—"more than watchmen for the morning" (130:6). When you are sinking down into a pit of your own making, follow the psalmist's lead. Confess, repent, and then wait on God.

MAY 17 · PSALM 135

God Acts on Behalf of His People

STARR MEADE

IT'S A SHORT PSALM—only twenty-one verses—yet it calls upon us to praise or bless or sing to our God ten times. Redundant? Not at all, when we consider what this psalm says about the praiseworthiness of God.

Notice that almost every time we see the word "Lord" in this psalm, it is in small capital letters ("Lord"). That indicates the Hebrew word

YHWH (from which we get "Yahweh"), the covenant name God revealed to Moses. God revealed this name exclusively to those with whom he made his covenant. To know God as "the Lord" was a tremendous privilege for Israel and a reason for joyful praise. Sing to that name, the psalmist tells his countrymen, "For the Lord has chosen Jacob for himself, Israel as his own possession" (Ps. 135:4). There was no reason for Israel to have such a position of privilege, as we see in the use of the name "Jacob"—Jacob, the cheater, the swindler, the sinner—for the nation as a whole. The Old Testament often refers to God's people as "Jacob," perhaps to remind them that God chose them due to nothing about themselves, but only because of his infinite grace.

As God's people today, our privilege and reason for praise is even greater, since God, by his grace, has chosen us, sinners though we are, to know him under a better covenant, sealed by the blood of his Son.

The Israelites knew God as their Redeemer from earthly oppressors (vv. 8–12), the one who "will vindicate his people and have compassion on his servants" (v. 14). For this reason, they were to pour out blessing and praise to their God. Under the new covenant, we know him as the Redeemer from oppressors far more destructive than Pharaoh or Sihon. God has looked with compassion on us in our pitiful, self-chosen misery and has redeemed us from sin, death, and Satan.

The gods of Israel's neighbors could neither speak nor act on behalf of their worshipers (vv. 15–18), but Israel had heard God speak. They had seen him act. They knew him to be not only a God who can do things; they knew that "whatever the Lord pleases, he does" (v. 6). Nothing limits or hinders his sovereign will. He is God in the fullest sense of the word—and as God, he acts on behalf of his people. The psalmist calls on God's covenant people in all times and places to praise their sovereign God. He loves, redeems, and provides for them, not because they deserve it, but simply because he is a God of grace.

Searched and Known

ELISABETH MAXWELL (LISA) RYKEN

GO OUTSIDE ON a clear night and look up at the stars. Consider how many stars, planets, solar systems, and galaxies you see. Think about how many people live on Planet Earth today—more than 7 billion. Reflect on how many cells make up each of those 7 billion people. Then, try to comprehend how immense the God of the universe is, who cares for the largest galaxies and the tiniest cells. If we try to understand how big God is, we will not be able to wrap our minds around him. It is even more overwhelming when we begin to think of our own smallness in the universe.

Psalm 139 reminds us both of our place and of God's perfection, assuring us that, as small as we are, each of us has unique value in God's creation. The psalm highlights God's omniscience and omnipresence: he knows everything, and he is everywhere. God not only knows the location of every one of those seven-billion-plus people on earth at this very moment; he also knows what we are thinking and what we are about to say.

There is not one place we can go where God is not present. When James Cameron reached the deepest point of the ocean at 35,756 feet below sea level, God was there. When Neil Armstrong stepped onto the surface of the moon, God was there. And when you sit down in the kitchen for a cup of coffee, run to the store for groceries, or take a hike in the mountains, God is there. We can no more outrun the presence of God than we can outrun our own shadow. Which is good news: If you are looking for God, you do not need to search the entire world. He is right beside you, delighting to commune with you.

Because God is all-knowing and ever-present, there is nothing that happens anywhere in the universe that he does not know about. He oversees every single incident in our lives and the lives of everyone else on earth. God cares so intimately for each one of us that he knit together every cell in our bodies. He cares for us when we scrape our knees and break our arms, when we lose a job, and when we simply miss the train.

The more we know him, the more we understand his perfect character—not only his omniscience and omnipresence, but also his holiness, mercy, love, sovereignty, justice, kindness, and grace. And the more we know him, the more we praise him for who he is. We praise God for creating us with all our abilities and disabilities, knowing that he has a unique plan for each of us. And we trust the omniscient and omnipotent God of the universe to lead us all through life and then on to life everlasting.

How Great Is Our God!

SAM STORMS

ALL OF US HAVE stories of the way our children learned to pray. My daughters struggled to pray for everything at once, so at dinner they would slowly identify each piece of silverware and each item of food, pausing along the way to express their gratitude for them one by one! In the ancient world of Israel, it was customary to pray Psalm 145 before a communal meal. But this psalm is not so much about the food God provides as it is about the God who makes provision in all things.

We live in a world that has trivialized God, having reduced him to human proportions. God is now little more than an exalted man, a superhero at best, but not the all-powerful, majestic, sovereign King over all kings that we read about in Scripture. Here in Psalm 145 we see God for who he is, and we are given a model for how we ought to respond.

David speaks of the unrivaled glory, holiness, and altogether otherness of God. God alone is "great" (Ps. 145:3, 6). We can know him truly, but never exhaustively. David therefore directs our thoughts to God's majesty and his "glorious splendor" (v. 5). The radiant beauty of God's person and power outshine everything and everyone else combined.

But this "great" and "majestic" God is also "good" (vv. 7, 9), "gracious and merciful" (v. 8), and "abounding in steadfast love" (v. 8). It would be horrifying if God's power and majesty were used in the cause of evil. We rejoice in God because he turns his power and "righteousness" (v. 7) to bless and prosper his people.

It is because of who God "is" that what he "does" is marvelous and awe-inspiring. His "works" (vv. 4, 5, 6, 10, 12) are "mighty" (v. 4) and "wondrous" (v. 5) and "awesome" (v. 6). He exercises providential oversight of all his creation in such a way that his people give thanks and bless his name, speaking of his glory and telling of his power (vv. 10–13). He sustains what he has made and abundantly supplies whatever is needed (vv. 14–15). He is not only "righteous" in all his ways; he is also "kind" in all his works (v. 17). There is tenderness in his power, compassion in his sovereignty. He is a God who answers prayer and delivers his people yet destroys the wicked (vv. 18–20).

How else could we respond than to do what this psalm calls for: extol him, bless him, praise him, speak about him, think about him? Let us "sing aloud" (v. 7) and "give thanks" (v. 10) and "make known" (v. 12) all that he has done, and let it never cease (vv. 1, 2, 21). Let there be great praise for a great God!

MAY 20 · PSALM 147

Stars, Snowflakes, and Sovereign Grace

GLORIA FURMAN

WHEN WE SING psalms of praise, it is not our aim to revel in our own splendor. Our gaze is lifted to behold the majesty of God. The same is true when we consider the incredible world around us. Our worship is directed to God, whose providence and grace govern and sustain all things. Singing praises to ourselves is burdensome and soul-shrinking. Singing praises to God is freeing and fulfilling! It is good, pleasant, and fitting to sing praises to God (Ps. 147:1).

The psalmist issues a call to worship the God of the universe, expanding our horizon to behold the heights and depths of God's sovereign grace.

Our confidence is directed away from a futile focus on our own abilities: "His delight is not in the strength of the horse, nor his pleasure in the legs of a man, but the LORD takes pleasure in those who fear him, in those who hope in his steadfast love" (vv. 10–11).

The psalmist scans the universe to see the providential care of God for his creation, and how our cares and needs land squarely on the God who spoke the stars into existence. All the billions and billions of stars! We read elsewhere in God's word that "not one" of these stars "is missing" (Isa. 40:25–26). Our Father wields a power that is more than sufficient to address the needs and problems of his people. Even as we consider his provision for creation, it is tempting to entertain the notion that our miniscule existence in so vast a universe is beyond his concern. But the Bible tells a different story. God's care for each of us is unquestionable, and in the cross of his Son Jesus Christ, we see that God's willingness to save is also overwhelming (John 3:16; Rom. 8:32).

The God whose "understanding is beyond measure" (Ps. 147:5), who governs the path of every star and snowflake, is delighted to declare his word to Jacob and give his law to Israel (v. 19). How extraordinary that the all-powerful Creator would *give us his word*! Truly, God's people are dear to him. God has given us his word and his Son, the Word made flesh, all so that we might know his matchless worth and be satisfied forever.

We are weak; he is strong. The outcasts, the brokenhearted, and the humble look to the Lord for everything they need. God points us to himself as our sufficiency: "For I, the LORD your God, hold your right hand, it is I who say to you, 'Fear not, I am the one who helps you'" (Isa. 41:13). Praise to the Lord will erupt in song from hearts that are confident in his covenanted steadfast love.

Finding Wisdom

JOSEPH P. MURPHY

IN ELOQUENT POETRY contrasting wisdom and wickedness, Solomon instructs his son (Prov. 2:1) the best way he can. Drawing on all the wisdom
God has given him, he trains a future king in a way of life that will provide
blessing for himself and for those he will rule and lead.

The first step in wisdom is paying attention to instruction in it (vv. 1–2),
followed by the student's own desiring of it (vv. 3–4). However much
wisdom may engage the mind, it must be rooted in the heart. Wisdom
isn't gained accidentally or apathetically, but is sought diligently and with
persistence throughout our lives and with all our hearts.

Only wholehearted pursuit yields the knowledge of God, which includes a healthy fear of him (v. 5). To someone seeking wisdom in the
sense of worldly gain, the fear of the Lord seems superfluous and com-
plicating. Fearing the Lord, however, is reverent worship, delighting to
yield to his good ways, and this heart-transforming reverence is the difference between the wise and the wicked. Many today confuse wisdom
with worldly success, but when we are conscious of God, we cannot act
in any way whatever like the wicked (many of whom are "successful").
Biblical wisdom isn't just what works at a pragmatic level but what delights
our heavenly Father.

Righteousness and justice (v. 9), knowledge (v. 10), understanding and
discretion (v. 11), and integrity (v. 21)—all these are the fruits of wisdom.
Yet wisdom cannot be reduced to any of them. Defining wisdom is the
most difficult project of all. As with life itself, wisdom comes directly from
God. Life itself is perhaps the best way to conceive of wisdom: a life lived
trusting God.

The adulteress lies in wait for the son of the king, and she is the specter
of death no less today than in the ancient world (v. 16). But Jesus, who is
the Life (John 14:6) and is Wisdom himself (1 Cor. 1:30), becomes wisdom for those who have foolishly made a wreck of their lives. His grace

makes wisdom freely available to everyone who seeks it, even those who have spurned it in the past. God delights to give wisdom to those who ask (James 1:5).

MAY 22 • PROVERBS 6:20–35

Sexual Temptation

DAN DORIANI

THE LAW, the prophets, the apostles, and Jesus himself teach us that adultery is sinful. Here Solomon tells his sons that adultery, the taking of another man's wife, is also foolish and destructive. It causes more harm than other sins, including other sexual sins (Prov. 6:26). It enrages a wronged husband, whose revenge will be severe (v. 34), and it brings lasting shame, so that the adulterer's "disgrace will not be wiped away" (v. 33).

Society is awash in sexual temptation. The church rightly says no to sexual sin, but Solomon leads to a more comprehensive approach that doesn't only say no but also encourages his children to rejoice in the goodness of sex.

Solomon describes the strategy of the married woman who would seduce a prince. She is beautiful; she winks and flatters (vv. 24–25; 5:3; 7:15). She will "seize" a man and grab a kiss (7:13). She whispers: her husband is away, her bed empty (7:16–19). Her beauty and seductive words might lead his son astray, so Solomon labors to win his son. He invokes the boy's mother: "Keep your father's commandment, and forsake not your mother's teaching" (6:20; 1:8). Solomon commends his teaching in language that echoes Israel's *shema*: "Hear, O Israel: the LORD our God, the LORD is one" (Deut. 6:4), which should be on our mind all the time (Deut. 6:5–9). Like the law, these instructions should be on the heart and before the eyes, since they are a guide for life as one walks, lies down, and rises up (Prov. 6:21–23). As the law is a lamp for life, so these commands are light- and life-giving (vv. 23–24; Ps. 119:105).

Solomon's comments in this passage may surprise us. All sins offend God. Thus, adultery is no more sinful than other violations—but it *is* more destructive. When a man sees a prostitute, he makes a purchase—a foolish one, but still a transaction: "the price of a prostitute is only a loaf of bread" (Prov. 6:26). Adultery is more costly. It ruins a home, brings dishonor and destruction, and rouses a husband's jealousy (vv. 32–34). The adulterer burns his own flesh (vv. 27–28), suffers punishment, and bears lasting disgrace (vv. 29, 33–34). Solomon tells his son to weigh the consequences. Obedience *works*; wickedness *wounds*. If a starving man steals, people understand (though he still pays for his crime). But no one will "understand" the adulterer.

No adulterer "will go unpunished" (v. 29). A jealous husband "will accept no compensation" (v. 35). Even here, however, we are reminded of the gospel of grace, which scandalizes us with the good news that we can "go unpunished" because the Father accepted the Son's "compensation" for our sin.

MAY 23 · PROVERBS 8

Pursuing Wisdom

LYDIA BROWNBACK

OUR DESIRES—the things we want—govern our lives and our choices. Every moment of every day, we set our course toward the fulfillment of what we deem most desirable. Because that is true, it is vital that our desires be shaped by Scripture. Proverbs puts wisdom at the forefront of desirable acquisitions: "Wisdom is better than jewels, and all that you may desire cannot compare with her" (Prov. 8:11). In other words, nothing we acquire will prove as rewarding and satisfying as wisdom. Additionally, there is no guarantee that we will obtain the worldly things we so often want; but wisdom is promised to those who seek it (James 1:5).

Before we can set our hearts to go after wisdom, we first need to understand what it is. Proverbs links wisdom to "the fear of the LORD" (Prov. 9:10). Those who fear the Lord are those who orient their lives around him in humble reverence. They love what God loves and hate what God hates (8:13).

Our gracious God longs to give us this precious wisdom, which is made clear throughout Proverbs. We see this clearly in Proverbs 8, where wisdom speaks poetically in the voice of a woman. From her we see that wisdom is not some elusive concept available only to the super-spiritual. It is readily available to all who recognize its value and pursue it, as she calls upon us to do (v. 17). The pursuit of wisdom is pictured in Proverbs, not as an exhausting intellectual exercise but as wholeheartedness and sincerity. Those who humbly seek the Lord in order to know him more fully and to follow his ways will find what they are looking for. We spend our resources going after the desires of our hearts, yet once we recognize the supreme value of wisdom, we will want to harness our energies in diligent pursuit of that.

The poem of Proverbs 8 reveals that God wove wisdom into all of creation and into how the world operates, which teaches us a great deal about the practical benefits of obtaining wisdom for day-to-day life. As we pursue wisdom and grow in it, we will find that we live increasingly in sync with God's ways. Most of our discontentment springs from living out of sync with how God designed the world to work. The opposite is also true: wisdom enables us to experience contentment, joy, and usefulness in our everyday lives.

Because we are sinful, however, we are so often more foolish than wise. This is why Christ is essential in the acquisition of wisdom. Ultimately, he is our wisdom (1 Cor. 1:30). Apart from him we will not find the wisdom of Proverbs, but in him we are sure to experience its rewards.

MAY 24 • PROVERBS 11:9–13

Words

ANN VOSKAMP

OURS IS THE God who wields words. He speaks, and by the word of his mouth alone the universal black splits and cells divide and light sparks and mountains rise and oceans come thus far and no farther. The breadth of this world was created by the breath of his word (Genesis 1).

When God pulled on skin and came into this world, he came as *the Word*: "In the beginning was the Word, and the Word was with God, and the Word was God" (John 1:1).

In Luke 6:45, Jesus teaches, "The good person out of the good treasure of his heart produces good, and the evil person out of his evil treasure produces evil, for out of the abundance of the heart his mouth speaks." Jesus is saying that the tongue is the "tail" of the heart: how your tongue wags always betrays you—either the biting, cancerous sin in your heart, or a heart so overflowing with grace that it spills out onto others. You are what you speak. No matter the jarring, a cup of fresh water can't spill filthy water. When you are upset, you upset what's really in you.

In the words of a familiar quotation, "Cold words freeze people, and hot words scorch them, and bitter words make them bitter, and wrathful words make them wrathful. Kind words also produce their image on men's souls; and a beautiful image it is. They soothe, and quiet, and comfort the hearer."[5]

God spoke the world into being. And there is a way in which our words speak our own worlds into being. Bitter, cynical, sarcastic words make our worlds just that.

Whose mouth tears down the neighbor (Prov. 11:9)? Or whose mouth is known for rejoicing (v. 10)? Or shouts of gladness (v. 10)? Whose mouth is known as one quick to bless and build up (v. 11)? Or to attack and sneer and snap and overthrow (v. 11)?

Proverbs 11:9–13 offers that the tongue can be a very real tool of evil or of good in whole spheres of living, both personally and culturally. Belittle not, or you become little (v. 12). Speak only words that make souls stronger. Sometimes the way to show the greatest understanding is to let your tongue sit still (v. 12). *Speak only words that make souls stronger.* Tongues are daggers to slash or dressings to bind (v. 13). *Speak only words that make souls stronger.*

Dwelling in the Company of the Wise

W. BRIAN AUCKER

THE BOOK OF Proverbs reveals that God cares deeply about the particular behaviors of his people in all times and places. These proverbs instruct each person who loves the Lord to reflect his character in our everyday existence. If you hear, understand, and obey this instruction, the book of Proverbs places you in the company of "the wise." At its core, Proverbs calls God's people to a life of wisdom, which is simply skill in the art of godly living. Reflecting the wider themes of Proverbs, these verses, through a series of contrasts, encourage us to live as the just, speak as the righteous, and learn as the wise.

An initial set of contrasts encourages life as a just rather than proud person (Prov. 15:25–27). Again and again the Bible shows the value of widows, with particular warning to render assistance to them (Zech. 7:10). Oppression by the proud through injustice to widows ranks among the deepest concerns of the Lord (Deut. 10:18). Moving boundary markers of widows only multiplies this wickedness (Deut. 27:17; Hos. 5:10). The Lord will not tolerate this, and, if they truly desire to reflect his character, neither must his people. Care for those weakest among us, gracious words, and a rejection of injustice must distinguish us.

We must speak as the righteous rather than as the wicked (Prov. 15:28–29). "The righteous" person of Proverbs will lay hold of God's covenant and live in faithful compliance with his expressed will, while "the wicked" will continue to live in opposition. Confronted with a violation, real or perceived, we may choose to measure our words—or we may take the easy road and give free rein to our tongues and blurt out a reckless reply. To reflect before speaking may include a prayer, a plea for a proper response, which the righteous woman offers up to the Lord. The Lord will always hear such a supplication (v. 29; compare v. 8).

The Lord's school of wisdom provides "life-giving" instruction (vv. 30–33). It requires the ability to listen and to respond humbly to reproof. A teachable nature remains at the core of those desiring to "dwell among the wise." Those not evidencing any willingness to hear this message are not only foolish but self-despising (v. 32). And so we end where we began in Proverbs: the call to recognize that fearing the Lord places us in his school. The admission requirement is humility and the instruction is rigorous, but the result is life and honor.

MAY 26 • PROVERBS 19:16-23

The Fear of the Lord

MIKE BULLMORE

WHAT OCCUPIES this passage, as it does the whole book of Proverbs, is the character of a person as a reflection of the character of God. This godliness is the "wisdom" that Proverbs repeatedly sets forth and calls us to, whether it is positive traits to be pursued and practiced, like generosity (Prov. 19:17) and steadfast love (v. 22), or negative traits to be avoided, like unbridled anger (v. 19) or being a liar (v. 22). Proverbs relentlessly focuses on our character. The most important thing about us is not our social or economic standing but the godliness of our character.

So how do we get this godly character? From the outset, Proverbs tells us that "The fear of the LORD is the beginning of wisdom" (9:10; see 1:7). If "wisdom" describes a life that reflects God's character, then we have found the answer to our question. "Fearing God" is the path to godly character.

But what does Proverbs mean by the "fear of the LORD" (19:23)? Fundamentally it means to deeply revere God, with one result being that, when he speaks, we respond in exact accordance with what he says. If he speaks truth about himself, we take him at his word. If he speaks commands or instructions to us, we gladly obey. In either case, we are trusting him.

In other words, this "fearing" of the Lord renders a person humble before God and willing to "listen to advice and accept instruction" (19:20) from him. This leads to true "wisdom"—not just intellectual knowledge, but godliness of character.

But it will lead to far more than that. The fear of the Lord also leads to life (v. 23)! This "life" Proverbs speaks of is found only in God, and God makes this life available to us now in Christ (see 1 John 5:11–12). The New Testament teaches that this "life" will culminate in an unending perfect existence with God in the new heaven and new earth, but Proverbs is focused more on our present existence. Those who have this life will experience both restful satisfaction and God's protection here and now (Prov. 19:23).

Verse 16 helps us here. The contrasting parallelism in this verse tells us that a failure to keep God's commands is a "despising"—a devaluing of your own life. (An example is found in the wrathful man of verse 19.) This is simply another reminder that God's commands are not arbitrary but are designed for our good in this life—which, when lived in the fear of the Lord, is a foretaste of the fullness of the life to come.

MAY 27 • PROVERBS 24:10-12

Who Is My Neighbor?

MICHELE BENNETT WALTON

THE MAN KNEW what the law required: "You shall love the Lord your God with all your heart and with all your soul and with all your strength and with all your mind, and your neighbor as yourself." And somewhere within himself, he knew that he couldn't fulfill that perfect law. So Luke tells us, "But he, desiring to justify himself, said to Jesus, 'And who is my neighbor?'" (see Luke 10:25–37).

We too tend to make excuses for our complacent hearts. But when the One who weighs our hearts and keeps watch over our souls sees our inaction, he knows the real cry of our hearts. It is not ignorance. Luke explains that the young lawyer wanted to justify himself, and we are often no different. We embrace apathy, fear, or indecision; we buy the lies of the sluggard or the fool, and we reject the fear of the Lord.

Deep within the human heart is a desire to draw boundaries around our areas of responsibility and concern. Whether we want to limit the people to whom we are responsible (by defining "neighbors" narrowly) or to limit the matters in which we should get involved (by claiming we don't know), we shrink what God wants to expand. We acquit ourselves using reasons that may even sound like wisdom. But we will stand condemned for it.

The entire book of Proverbs shows us what real, God-fearing wisdom looks like in practical situations. This particular proverb should alert us to be suspicious of any so-called wisdom that consistently enables us to turn our backs on injustice. Although Proverbs extols the virtues of wisdom, wisdom must always bow the knee to faith (Prov. 3:5–7). When the seemingly wise path and the truly wise path part ways, we must choose to walk in the way of true righteousness (8:20).

"Rescue those who are being taken away to death; hold back those who are stumbling to the slaughter" (24:11). We have been commissioned by God to carry out his work on this earth, and this little proverb is a call to action. It has moved Germans to defy Hitler's orders, provoked American churches to protest abortion, and caused countless saints around the world to take action in specific situations.

Ask God to open your eyes today to those around you who are victimized, oppressed, or in danger. When he does, be quick to open your heart to them and call them "neighbor." Then ask the God who rescues to give you the wisdom and strength to pursue justice on their behalf, for his glory.

MAY 28 · PROVERBS 31:10–31

The Woman Who Fears the Lord

LYDIA BROWNBACK

"AN EXCELLENT WIFE who can find?" So begins the poem that concludes the book of Proverbs, and as we measure ourselves against this portrait of godly virtue, many of us cannot help but sigh in agreement and maybe even turn away in discouragement.

Although she is depicted as the ideal woman, however, we won't find her to be intimidating once we understand the purpose of the poem. What we are to glean from her is a heart attitude: what about her heart enables her to live the life she does? Her life is a picture of what happens when everything else in Proverbs is applied. She is a portrait of feminine wisdom. She embodies the full character of wisdom shown throughout the entire book of Proverbs.

First, she is wise as a wife, which is clear from the fact that her husband trusts her (Prov. 31:11) and praises her (v. 28); and because she faithfully carries out her wifely calling, her husband is able to excel at his own calling (v. 23). Additionally, no matter what task she is involved in, her overarching aim is the nurture of others. She provides food for those in her home, including the servants (v. 15); she extends her hand to the poor and needy (v. 20); and she watches over the ways of her household (v. 27). Those virtues and others she displays are the traits of wisdom taught throughout Proverbs.

One of the most prominent themes in Proverbs is the way in which our words expose us as either wise or fools. The woman in this poem "opens her mouth with wisdom, and the teaching of kindness is on her tongue" (v. 26). Another theme is diligence, which is woven all through this poem. The woman is purposeful with her time. How we use our time both reveals us as wise or foolish and determines which of those two paths will mark our destiny.

All her wise activities spring from her wise heart, which is rooted in the fear of the Lord (v. 30). And because she fears the Lord, she is depicted as a confident woman who is unafraid of what the future might hold (v. 25). This is the bedrock of all her wise behavior. She is a good wife and mother, and industrious, and financially shrewd, and kind, and charitable because she fears the Lord.

And in that way, we can indeed be like her. Redeemed by Christ and given a new identity by grace, a new life of wisdom opens up before us. She is the picture of wise living, but not primarily for how to be a better homemaker or a businesswoman. Rather, the overall picture of the poem is that those who fear the Lord are blessed and become a blessing to others.

Futility Is Not Forever

NANCY GUTHRIE

IN THE BOOK of Ecclesiastes we hear the voice of "the Preacher" (Eccles. 1:1). He has looked at life from every angle and is convinced that our lives have no lasting meaning or significance. He has seen everything "under the sun"—everything that can be seen from an earthly perspective—and his estimation is that "all is vanity" (v. 14). Our lives, he says, are like the visible vapors of our breath on a cold night—there for a second, and then gone. And yet, he says, God has "put eternity into man's heart" (3:11). God has implanted within the human soul a longing. We want who we are and what we do in this world to matter beyond our limited lifetime.

Of course, life in this world was not always such seeming vanity. In the garden of Eden, Adam and Eve lived with significance and satisfaction—until they sought for satisfaction apart from God. That's when everything changed. Their work, which was intended to bring great pleasure—caring for and exercising dominion over the earth—was reduced to exasperating toil. On that day, the entire creation was "subjected to futility" (Rom. 8:20).

It is this futility that the Preacher laments. He sees that people work their whole lives and then die, seemingly losing everything they've worked for. His recommendation is to eat, drink, and enjoy the fruits of your labor if possible, recognizing that we are "from the dust, and to dust all return" (Eccles. 3:20). And after death, who's to say? The Preacher has no clear sense of what will happen when this life under the sun comes to an end.

Fortunately, we can see something the Preacher could not see. We live in light of God's fullest revelation of himself in the person and work of Christ. So we know that there is life beyond the few years lived under the sun. We live in confident hope of resurrection life beyond the grave. We know that, though this life sometimes seems futile, Jesus has accomplished all that is necessary for all of creation to be set free from its futility. The world will not be this way forever.

Even now Jesus can fill our lives with meaning and purpose. We can be "steadfast, immovable, always abounding in the work of the Lord, knowing that in the Lord [our] labor is not in vain" (1 Cor. 15:58). Everything we've done in Christ, for Christ, and through Christ will matter forever. Life under the sun is not futile. Because of Christ, our lives will matter forever.

The Unpredictability of Life

CAROL CORNISH

GAINING PERSPECTIVE is a valuable pursuit. Throughout Ecclesiastes we read of "the Preacher" exploring various perspectives on life, since it often seemed empty and futile to him. Similarly for us, things often do not go the way we think they should. As we look at life, much of it can seem empty and meaningless. If we are not careful, this can lead to cynicism and bitterness. So, developing a biblical perspective on all of life is crucial.

It is wise to examine the point of view from which we are observing a situation or condition. When we fail to do so, we can be blind to our own prejudices, ignorance, and limitations. We may fall into the trap of limited and earthly views. Thankfully, we have God's word to provide a heavenly perspective. In the light of God's ways and words, we find clarity and confidence that whatever happens is under his sovereign control. Thus, though we may not be able to make sense of what is happening to and around us, we can rest in the knowledge that what is confusing and unclear to us is wholly within God's control and is an expression of his love.

Sometimes life seems particularly out of control and unpredictable. The things and people we count on let us down and may even leave us. Foolish people promote themselves and often gain a following, while wise people are frequently ignored and unappreciated. What we have built up might be destroyed by the evil actions of someone else. In situations such as these, the application of mere human wisdom will get us only so far. However, when we seek God's perspective, gleaning it from his word and from the way he works in our circumstances, we can have a much clearer view of life in this fallen and sinful world. If we are wise, we will also listen to and heed godly counsel. Ask the Lord to connect you with mature Christians who can offer sound biblical guidance.

Jesus said, "Therefore do not be anxious about tomorrow, for tomorrow will be anxious for itself. Sufficient for the day is its own trouble" (Matt. 6:34). Each day has its difficulties—sometimes tragic, sometimes mundane. But each day also has its own particular pleasures, and those are to be gratefully received and enjoyed. They are good gifts from God.

So, whether today is bringing you abundant delight or staggering trial, go to the Lord with both your joy and your sorrow. Let the pleasures humble you, since they are always undeserved, and let the sorrows drive you to take refuge in the only One who can be your enduring shelter.

MAY 31 · SONG OF SOLOMON 2:8–17

Behold, He Comes

NANCY GUTHRIE

THROUGH THE POETRY of the Song of Solomon, we get to peek inside the relationship between two married lovers. As the woman sees her beloved coming to her, overcoming every obstacle to get to her, she hears his voice saying, "Arise, my love, my beautiful one, and come away" (Song 2:10). He's inviting her to come to him and enjoy intimacy with him. Their secure belonging, each to the other, is expressed in her words, "My beloved is mine, and I am his" (v. 16).

Clearly, the Song speaks to us of the joy of sexual love within marriage. But we also know that our longings to be loved this way in this broken world often lead to great sorrow and intense frustration. We recognize that no human being can ever fully satisfy our cavernous needs and desires to be loved. So while this Song speaks to us of the beauty of sexual love inside the bonds of marriage, it also points us toward the only person who can love us in the way we most need to be loved—the Lover of our souls, Jesus Christ.

We tend to think that marriage is primarily about finding the love of our life who will make us happy. But marriage is most profoundly about putting the covenant keeping love of Christ for his church on display for the world to see, which infuses ordinary marriages with sacred meaning and purpose. Marriage is meant to declare the truth about the gospel—that Christ died for his church and he will never break covenant with his bride. That this is God's intention for marriage is spelled out by Paul, who quotes from Moses's account of the very first marriage and sexual union of Adam and Eve, saying that marriage has always been most profoundly about Christ and the church. "'Therefore a man shall leave his father and mother and hold fast to his wife, and the two shall become one flesh.' This mystery is profound, and I am saying that it refers to Christ and the church" (Eph. 5:31–32).

Just as the woman in the Song quickened at hearing the voice of her bridegroom, so we come alive when we hear the voice of our bridegroom inviting us to come to him. He says, "If anyone hears my voice and opens the door, I will come in" (Rev. 3:20). And one day, when Christ comes again, at the marriage supper of the Lamb, all who have been wooed by the love of our bridegroom, and cleansed by his blood, will be presented to him in purity and beauty. We who long for that day are comforted to hear the voice of our Beloved saying, "Surely I am coming soon" (Rev. 22:20).

JUNE 1 · SONG OF SOLOMON 4

How Beautiful Is Your Love

ZACK ESWINE

MEN NOTICE WOMEN. Female bodies rouse masculine whistles, stares, and calls. Flattery follows. He has learned that words work. So he uses his practiced lines. He tells her she is beautiful. She feels noticed. Noticed is nice.

But what flatters at first feels over time like being used. She thinks to herself, "He only touches me when he wants something." And if her appearance does not meet expected criteria, or if she begins to age, she wonders if he will look at all. She notices his eyes glancing at commercials, or the woman walking past in the restaurant—or at church.

Two can play at that game. She too knows what works. She likes what it feels like to get masculine glances when she enters a room.

In this cycle, a slandered version of sexual love gets handed down. We wouldn't recognize the pleasures of true attraction if it walked up to us. After all, few of us have ever witnessed it. "What does it actually look like for a man to romantically and truly notice a woman?" Chapter 4 gives an answer. To begin, married sex isn't dull! God doesn't "just say no." He just says "wait" till you are married. Then, unashamedly and without guilt, thoroughly enjoy his good gift to both of you.

Next, notice the man's words. A wife is created to hear them. The pick-up line steals what marriage was made to cultivate. Admittedly, his love poem makes us chuckle. Just remember, the images involve quality rather than resemblance. A "flock of goats" (Song 4:1) to describe his wife's hair demonstrates bounty. (At least he's trying!)

Moreover, this husband notices her whole body. His view does not narrow to only certain places. He meditates on her beauty when she is not around, puts words to it, writes to her about it, and delights in her. Obviously, then, much more than physical touch is involved here—and when touch has its time, the whole woman is in view. She is not a highway on which he speeds quickly from one place to another. Together they take the back roads. They slow down, take their time, and enjoy the scenery.

Finally, notice that she is not only his bride but his "sister" (vv. 9–10). Not biologically, but spiritually, with partnership and companionship—they are both friend and family. He places sexual longing within the commitment of shared companionship. Her love, not just her physical beauty, captivates him.

The result? She wants him too (v. 16)! Cherished by him; invited by her. Naked without shame. What a blessed relationship!

The Possibility and Promise
of Repentance

JOSEPH P. MURPHY

ISAIAH'S POETRY VIVIDLY proclaims the word of God in a time of societal and moral decline in Israel. Israel is religious rather than godly, a faithful spouse turned prostitute. Instead of genuine repentance, Israel clings hard to its religious actions without right intent, to the point that the One for whom their worship is meant is disgusted with them. This pattern has been repeated often in the life of God's people as a whole, and in individual lives.

Traditional ways of performing prayer, worship—and in Israel's case, sacrifice—are an integral part of the life of faith. God had established Israel's worship, including sacrifice, and obedience to his commands required practicing those prescribed ways. God's displeasure was thus not with the external things but with the fact that they had become *solely* external. Forms of worship are not the issue, but whether they actually express our hearts: Israel was presenting to God "*vain* offerings," "iniquity and solemn assembly" (Isa. 1:13).

Though it may be disagreeable to have our true motives exposed while we appear respectably religious, it should actually fill us with assurance and hope. It offers us, amid our hypocrisy, the opportunity for repentance. "Come now, let us reason together . . ." (1:18).

Rather than abandoning us to our own choices to do evil while cloaking it in the appearance of good, God calls us to soberly consider the truth—truth about him, ourselves, and his provision for our redemption. All is *not* lost. The truth *will* set us free—truth that puts into proper perspective God's action in redeeming us through the blood of Christ. Even if our hands are bloody from the suffering of those we have at least ignored, if not personally oppressed, through Christ we can be cleansed. We can turn again, we can learn new, truly good ways to the Lord and to those he brings into our lives.

The way forward is clear, and it won't change: the Lord has spoken. Each of us must embrace God's call to live lives that correspond to his gracious deliverance of us. Isaiah also provides a vision of the future to lift us above the seeming uncertainty of our personal struggles. What now has all the marks of failure and divine displeasure will yet become the source of lasting peace for humanity, bringing an end to warfare, external and internal. God's word shall not fail. He can be trusted.

JUNE 3 · ISAIAH 4:2-6

The Branch of the Lord

JEN WILKIN

THE PROPHECY OF Isaiah 4:2–6 is one of hope and permanence, drawing on images intensely familiar to Israel. In the time of Moses, God decreed that a tabernacle be built in the wilderness. It was a temporary dwelling place for the Lord, a place where God and man could commune. Admittance was gained by two means: a blood sacrifice burned on the bronze altar, and a cleansing with water at the bronze basin. Over the Most Holy Place, the Lord's presence appeared as a cloud of smoke by day and a pillar of fire by night. And over all the tabernacle was pitched a protective canopy of skins to shield it from the elements. As the Israelites stood at the foot of Mount Sinai, God declared that they should be to him "a kingdom of priests and a holy nation" (Ex. 19:6).

Though the tabernacle no longer exists, its function and purpose are now accomplished in the person of every believer. By means of the blood sacrifice of Christ (Heb. 10:11–14) and the ongoing "washing of water with the word" (Eph. 5:26), our very bodies become the dwelling place of the Lord—our hearts the Most Holy Place where God and man commune (1 Cor. 6:19–20). Indwelt by his Spirit, we live daily in the shelter of his care. Like Israel, we are called to be holy, as he is holy (1 Pet. 1:14–16).

But both the tabernacle and our earthly bodies offer only temporary residence for the Lord, acting as shadows of his permanent residence, the new Jerusalem described in Isaiah 4:2–6. Jesus Christ, the true and final

Branch of the Lord, once marred beyond all recognition and cut off, will be recognized as beautiful, glorious, and fruitful. An end will be made to sin: no longer will sacrifices or washings be required. The manifest presence of the Lord will be seen over the new Jerusalem, which will be a Most Holy Place, dwelling secure beneath the shadow of his wings. And we, whose names are recorded in the Lamb's book of life, will at last be holy as he is holy.

Imagine how Israel would have remembered this prophecy in her years of exile, dwelling as strangers in a strange land. Can you feel that same longing for the permanence and perfection of the dwelling place of the Lord? When all around you is hostility and brokenness, set your hope on this future home of peace and unbroken communion. May we be numbered among the faithful of whom it was said, "They desire a better country, that is, a heavenly one. Therefore God is not ashamed to be called their God, for he has prepared for them a city" (Heb. 11:16).

JUNE 4 · ISAIAH 6

Knowing God Changes Lives

SAM STORMS

THE MOST IMPORTANT lesson we can learn from this well-known episode is that *knowing God changes lives*. The only way to experience meaningful, lasting, Christ-exalting change in your life is through expansive and exalted thoughts about who God is.

The year was 740 BC, and King Uzziah had died. He became king while yet a teenager and ruled for fifty-two years. As disconcerting as the death of one's earthly leader may be, Isaiah is reassured that the King of kings never dies. His authority never passes to a successor. The power and rule of Uzziah have ended, but God's power is limitless and eternal.

The word "holy" doesn't mean a lot in our world today, but apart from it we can never hope to understand who God is. To say that God is "holy" (three times, no less!) is to say that he is separate from everyone and everything else. He alone is Creator. He is altogether and wholly other, both in his character and in his deeds. He is transcendently different from and greater than all his creatures in every conceivable respect. To put it in common terms, God is "in a class by himself." Holiness is moral majesty; it is transcendent beauty.

When Isaiah sees the holy God (Isa. 6:1–4), there is neither spiritual euphoria nor religious flippancy. Rather, the prophet experiences terror and self-hatred (vv. 5–8). He is not puffed up with a sense of self-importance. Indeed, he is *undone*! He sees himself as insufferably unrighteous compared to the infinite purity and transcendence of the King. Whereas we tend to measure sin in terms of how it affects others on earth, Isaiah sees it only in light of the majesty of the one true God against whom the sin is committed.

But here is the good news of the gospel: The infinitely holy God is also gracious and merciful and immediately provides cleansing and forgiveness. Isaiah's wound was being cauterized. The dirt in his mouth was washed away as the corruption of his heart was forgiven. He was refined by holy fire.

Personal transformation is the result not so much of seeing the ugliness of sin as of seeing the beauty of the Savior. Isaiah was awakened to the horror of his sin only because he saw the holiness of his God. It was only when he saw the surpassing and incomparable character of God that his heart was stung with the anguish of conviction. Personal holiness thus begins with an awareness of who God is. Perhaps that's why so few people are (or even care to be) holy. They've never really "seen" God. They know little of the magnitude of his holy majesty, his infinite righteousness. Isaiah saw God and was forever changed.

JUNE 5 · ISAIAH 9:1-7

Our Best Days Are Always Ahead

JANI ORTLUND

GOD HAS AN overarching plan of redemption for this world, and his followers have a place in that plan. Sometimes all we can feel is distress and anguish; all we can see is gloomy darkness (Isa. 8:22). But God is at work. Isaiah tells us to patiently trust in God during the hard times (8:17), because there is One coming—the promised Davidic King—who will shine his invincible light into the thick darkness, unleashing a flood of joy that will forever eliminate that darkness.

Isaiah sees this glorious future of Israel in a vision. Their current humiliation will come to an end (2:2–3)—a deliverance so sure, so real, that Isaiah prophesies in the present tense. Salvation will come through a child, a son, who will shine his light into the deep darkness (9:2, 6), and who will call his followers to walk in that light (Eph. 5:8).

Isaiah goes on to tell us that the faithful will no longer be a small remnant; God will multiply their nation (Isa. 9:3). Theirs will be an overflowing joy—like the joy of an abundant harvest or a decisive military victory. That joy is detailed in verses 4–7. God will break the rod of the oppressor as he did in the improbable victory of Gideon over Midian (Judg. 7:19–25). The cruel chains of tyranny will be replaced with the easy yoke of Jesus (Matt. 11:29–30).

What will our future look like? Our invincible Lord will take command (Ps. 2:7–9), exercising his authority over everything in heaven and on earth (Matt. 28:18). He will be our "Wonderful Counselor" (Isa. 9:6), making wise plans way beyond human capabilities (11:2). He is the "God of gods and Lord of lords, the great, the mighty, and the awesome God" (Deut. 10:17). His care for us will be that of a father full of compassion (Ps. 103:13), caring for our needs (Ps. 145:15–16); he will be our benevolent protector (John 14:18). He will be the "Prince of Peace" (Isa. 9:6). Think of a world where we no longer need West Point and the Pentagon, where there will be no more flag-draped coffins or wounded warriors, no more war, no more terror. Peace will flourish throughout all the world (2:4; 11:6–9).

And this kingdom will have no end (Luke 1:32–33). In fact, it will keep increasing in influence and peace. Can you imagine? How is this possible? The "zeal of the LORD" (Isa. 9:7)—his own miraculous, passionate intensity—will accomplish and sustain this.

Dear sister, whatever you are facing today will not last forever. Even in your darkness, look for his light. It is coming. It will be worth the wait. In Christ, your best days are always ahead.

The Root of Jesse

MARY PATTON BAKER

AN OLD-GROWTH forest is a wonderful place to observe the progression from death to life in nature. Often you will find a beautiful tree growing out of an old stump. This happens because when a tree is reduced to a stump from wind, fire, or cutting, it is actually still alive. The roots are still storing energy for a new tree to grow from the old root system. A new tree finds a way to sprout.

Isaiah uses similar imagery. The "forest" of the pride of the Davidic monarchy has been destroyed (Isa. 6:11–13). Yet a root springs from a seemingly dead stump: the root of Jesse, the father of David. By naming Jesse, the prophecy indicates that even David's kingdom is rooted further back than David. Its source is the covenant the sovereign God made with David's ancestors to be faithful despite their unfaithfulness. The root is therefore God's profound love for his people.

A new king, a new kingdom, and ultimately a new age will spring from the old. This new king will not be like the fickle Davidic kings. He will delight in God and be wise in his counsel. His judgments will not be based on what his senses perceive. He will not be swayed by power or wealth. In fact, he will take the side of the poor and weak. He will also be mighty in his rule, and will spread the knowledge and fear of the Lord. So much so, that in his reign "the earth shall be full of the knowledge of the LORD as the waters cover the sea" (11:9). Harmony and unity will be the hallmarks of this age.

Though one can look at this passage on many levels, most scholars agree that Isaiah's prophecy speaks far into the future—when the Messiah will come again to rule over a new heaven and earth. In this new creation, even the lion and the lamb will lie down together.

With prophecies such as Isaiah's, our response should be one of hope and expectation. Rather than looking only at the specifics of how such a prophecy will be fulfilled, we should look at our own role in the story. How do our lives reflect the character of our Messiah? He has sent us a down payment on his future kingdom by granting Christians the fullness of the Spirit. Thus, we can know the intimate knowledge of God that Isaiah speaks of. If we look, we can see God's presence in the world despite the pain and death. Like the new tree springing from an old stump, God's life and love will find a way as we yield to his gracious power.

JUNE 7 · ISAIAH 19:16–25

Salvation for the Egyptians

COLLEEN J. MCFADDEN

BEFORE THIS STUNNING picture of Egypt being saved, the Lord proclaims judgment on the Egyptians (Isa. 19:1–15). They will experience this judgment through war with one another (v. 2), oppressive leadership (v. 4), and economic collapse (vv. 5–10). Completely helpless to escape these things (v. 15), the Egyptians will be utterly terrified. "In that day the Egyptians will be like women, and tremble with fear before the hand that the LORD of hosts shakes over them" (v. 16). But this is precisely where the Lord wants them. He will reduce them to trembling so that his purpose may be accomplished.

What is that purpose? From the very beginning, God has promised that the nations will experience his salvation. He said to Abraham, "in you all the families of the earth shall be blessed" (Gen. 12:3). In Isaiah 19, we see that the Lord's deepest purpose in the world, even for Egypt, is one of deliverance. And the only way to make this happen is to break them first, to bring them to a point of utter ruin so that they will turn to him (Isa. 19:22).

And turn they will! If we omit the wording of "Egypt" or "Egyptians" in verses 18–25, we see a people who more closely resemble the Israelites, God's chosen nation, than God's enemies, as described in verses 1–17. For Egypt, too, will be transformed into God's people. Several urban centers will adopt the Hebrew language (v. 18). Altars and pillars will be built for the Lord (v. 19). The Egyptians will cry out, and the Lord will save them (v. 20). As he has dealt with Israel in the past, "the LORD will strike Egypt, striking and healing, and they will return to the LORD, and he will listen to their pleas for mercy and heal them" (v. 22).

What an amazing picture of God's plan of salvation extending beyond Israel and reaching all nations! For what is merely represented by five cities (v. 18) turns into entire nations—Egypt and Assyria—worshiping God alongside Israel (v. 23). Those who were once enemies will be brothers, incorporated into the family of God. The wall of hostility will be broken, and a road will be built for common worship. This is the gospel, a gospel that unites.

This gospel not only unites; it also blesses. God's kingly rule is very different from that of the worldly kings of Isaiah's day. The nations were known for oppressive rule, making people serve the king and his selfish desires. But the Lord of hosts rules his people with blessing and salvation (vv. 24–25). The Lord Jesus "came not to be served but to serve, and to give his life as a ransom for many" (Mark 10:45). Praise our Lord, who transforms his people to bring about unity and blessing through his gospel!

JUNE 8 · ISAIAH 25

Hope for the Hopeless

STARR MEADE

SO MUCH THAT goes by the name of "religious" or "inspirational" fails to face the horrors of a fallen world. We see daily accounts of disease and disaster, interrupting lives and marring them forever. We hear stories of evil, of people inflicting misery and death on others. And we live, moment by moment, with our own sinful hearts. Any hope or comfort we're offered must squarely face the darkness where we dwell.

Many people don't enjoy reading the Old Testament prophets. They contain too much wrath and judgment, it is thought. But really, the prophets confront human sin with all its attendant misery and then offer true hope and lasting comfort. Against a pitch-dark backdrop, the prophets shine a light almost blinding by contrast.

While there are glimpses of hope and glimmers of light in the first twenty-four chapters of Isaiah, we read mostly of the sin of God's people and the judgment they face. From chapter 13 on, we read of nation after nation—including Judah—whose sin has offended God and who will drink the cup of his wrath. In chapter 24, the entire earth lies broken before God (Isa. 24:19), and all its inhabitants face terror, the pit, and the snare (24:17)—every one, utterly without hope.

Then chapter 25 bursts onto the page with the salvation that God alone can bring (25:9). He does wonderful things for his people, plans formed from of old (v. 1), plans that took into account even our great sin. In spite of our sin, God made and carries out his plans because salvation is of the Lord. He delivers the poor and needy (v. 4), saving his people from their oppressors and from their own sin. He eliminates all enemies, either by destroying them (vv. 10–12) or by so changing their hearts that they come to glorify and fear him (v. 3).

God will spread a feast for people of all nations, a feast we begin to sample in the broken body and poured out blood of our Savior at Communion (v. 6). God promises to swallow up death and to wipe away tears, undoing the effects of our sin (vv. 7–8). Chapters 1–24, with their accusations and their threats of judgment, show us a world we recognize from newscasts and from glimpses into our own hearts, a world we are helpless to fix. God alone can provide a salvation adequate for such ruin—*and he does!* The hope found in God that Isaiah offers is all the more sure because the prophet has shown us, first, how hopeless we are on our own.

"Behold, *this* is our God; we have waited for *him*, that *he* might save us" (25:9).

JUNE 9 · ISAIAH 30

God, Ever Faithful

KAREN S. LORITTS

OVERWHELMED BY THE seemingly insurmountable threat of the Assyrian army, Judah abandons her faith in God's promise of protection. The nation disregards the Lord's counsel and plans an alliance with Egypt, who they foolishly believe offers more protection than the Almighty (Isa. 30:1–2).

Their disobedience brings "shame and disgrace" (v. 5) and sets them adrift from God.

Judah's actions were irrational and radically disobedient. Ironically, they returned to the very nation that had cruelly oppressed them, and from whose hands they had been miraculously delivered. What would cause them to lose faith in the God who had always acted so powerfully on their behalf?

Their refusal to ask God for his counsel and protection conveys pride. Pride is an enemy of God and a friend of the world. Paul describes prideful behavior as "swollen conceit" (2 Tim. 3:4). The depths of pride overshadow any desire to trust God.

Fear also clouded their thinking, as the rush for protection drove them toward a known enemy and away from their faithful God. Fear leaves one vulnerable to the wiles of the enemy, resulting in poor decisions, faithless plans, and a fearful heart. The alliance with Egypt would deliver humiliation, shame, and disgrace. Isaiah says there is no profit in sin (Isa. 30:5).

Judah's actions seem absurd. The fact that they would trust any nation (especially Egypt) to keep them safe, when God himself had promised his protection, is hard to understand. And yet, could it be that the things we place our trust in are equally ridiculous? Where have we strayed from God? What plans have we made that omit his counsel?

The later portion of Isaiah 30 offers a resounding promise of reconciliation and fellowship with God—for God's people back then, and for his people today: "The LORD waits to be gracious to you, and therefore he exalts himself to show mercy to you. For the LORD is a God of justice; blessed are all those who wait for him" (v. 18).

God offers his people rest and peace as they turn to him in repentance (v. 15). Judah must turn away from sin and back to God, as must we. Confession and repentance restore our fellowship with him (1 John 1:9). God offers his grace and mercy to those who wait for him (Isa. 30:18). Like Israel, we are often tempted to rush ahead with faithless actions. We "seek shelter in the shadow of Egypt" (v. 2). But it is God who will judge and defend us against any who would do us harm. It is in the "shadow of the Almighty" (Ps. 91:1) that we are safe and secure.

O Lord, Be Gracious to Us

GLENNA MARSHALL

WHEN WE OBSERVE the pervasiveness of evil in the world, we might wonder if God will ever bring the wicked to justice. Will he right the wrongs rendered toward his name and his people?

God is not oblivious to the wickedness of the nations or to the rebellion of our own hearts. He sees, and he sovereignly works his good purposes in his good timing. He will bring about the destruction of those who rebel against him as surely as he will preserve those who call upon his name.

Judah longed for the Lord to act on its behalf. As a result of Judah's chronic disobedience and failure to trust God, the nation suffered relentless attacks from the Assyrians, whose destruction seemed to go unchecked. But God would not allow evil to continue forever.

In Isaiah 33 God promises that he will destroy the Assyrians, just as they had destroyed his people. The cruel nation would indeed meet a decisive end by 612 BC. But the promises of Isaiah 33 are farther-reaching than the destruction of one army, for the enemies of God's people include more than the Assyrians. The greatest enemies of God's people are sin, Satan, and death.

Judah cries out, "O LORD, be gracious to us; we wait for you. Be our arm every morning, our salvation in the time of trouble" (v. 2). God's people plead for his grace while waiting for him to vanquish their enemies.

We too can cry out to God when we are suffering the pain of illness, the consequences of sin, or the betrayal of broken relationships. When Christ returns, he will right the wrongs of this world (Rev. 22:12). Those who call on the name of Jesus will see his certain victory over sin, Satan, and death.

While we wait for Christ and yearn for his return, we can know that he will keep his promises to preserve his people and forgive their sins because of his death and resurrection on their behalf. Upon his return, we will no longer suffer the repercussions of sin nor struggle with a sin-sick nature (Isa. 33:24). We will be safe in the presence of our King, knowing true rest and peace as we dwell with him forever (Rev. 7:15–17). The Lord is graciously *for* those who trust him, and through Christ we can wait with confidence, knowing that he will one day bring a good ending to his good story.

JUNE 11 • ISAIAH 35

God's Shalom

ELIZABETH W. D. GROVES

THE BOOK OF Isaiah as a whole moves from bad news (chapters 1–39) to good news (chapters 40–66), yet this passage in chapter 35 is as good a piece of news as one could ever ask for.

It describes a transformation of chalk wilderness into lush, vibrant gardens like Carmel and Sharon, and of parched, desolate, burning sand into reedy pools, even into *springs* so that they are not simply wet enough to survive—they become actual *sources* of water. Barrenness gives way to abundant life and health. The fearful are made strong and courageous, the disabled are miraculously healed, and all sadness is eradicated so that, most wonderfully of all, God's people finally arrive in his presence and experience nothing but joy. What a glorious picture! This is the Lord's shalom—peace, health, life, wholeness—coming to push back the effects of sin's curse.

Isaiah's readers may have assumed that the fulfillment of this prophecy would be in their return from the exile that Isaiah was predicting, or in deliverance from some other current oppression, and no doubt that was partially correct. But Isaiah also foretold the coming of the Servant, the Messiah, Jesus. While Isaiah's language was poetic and figurative, Jesus actually *did* heal the blind, deaf, lame, and mute. He brought shalom. Our God did indeed come, and he brought vengeance against our enemies—sin and death—and paid the recompense with his own life. He poured out his Holy Spirit into our dry souls, "a spring of water welling up to eternal life" (John 4:14), and he cleansed us so that we can walk on his Way of Holiness (Isa. 35:8). There may be hardships on that way, but our God will keep us safe, *and* we are heading to the best thing of all: eternity with our God, where he will wipe away every tear from our eyes and where there will be no more death, mourning, crying, or pain (Rev. 21:3–4), only everlasting joy.

Of course the complete consummation of those promises lies in the future; it will come with the new heavens and new earth at the end of history. But the age of the Spirit has already begun, inaugurated by Jesus's death, resurrection, and ascension. We have begun to experience God's shalom. Already he strengthens our hands and knees, conquers our fear, fills us with his Spirit so that rivers of living water flow out of our hearts (John 7:38–39), and leads us on the Way. Already, everlasting joy is upon our heads, even amid the sorrows that will one day completely flee away (Isa. 35:10).

God Is Our Comfort and Strength

HEATHER HOUSE

THIS WORLD IS MESSY, and sometimes it is an agony to endure. Maybe you are going through a difficult time because someone has wronged you. Or perhaps a sin in your life is the root cause. Maybe your circumstances happened for reasons you don't understand. Whatever the situation, you can be confident of this: during times such as these, God gives believers both comfort and endurance.

Isaiah has warned Israel that God alone can protect them from Babylon and Assyria, the international powers of the day. But instead of trusting the Lord, the Israelites choose to rely on military might, diplomatic maneuverings, and sacrifices to false gods to keep them secure—a decision that reflects a profound lack of faith in God. As a result of their persistent disobedience, Israel will soon be exiled from the land (Isa. 39:1–8; see also Lev. 26:14–33). Isaiah 40 looks ahead to the time when this punishment has ended and the people trust God to rebuild their shattered lives.

God will not abandon his people, despite their sin. Exile is designed to return their wandering hearts to him, and it will accomplish its purpose (Deut. 30:1–10). There will come a time when there will be no more need for punishment (Isa. 40:1–2). The Lord will appear before all nations to deliver his people (vv. 3–5). In the New Testament, the "glory of the Lord" (v. 5) is shown to be Jesus, whose arrival is announced by John the Baptist with words taken from Isaiah 40:3. That the Lord will indeed come to comfort his people is certain, because he has given his word (vv. 6–8). His word is trustworthy because *he* is.

God's care for his people is evident (vv. 9–17). He combines strength and tenderness in perfect balance. He is mighty enough to create the heavens and the earth, yet gentle enough to care for frail human beings. He is so powerful that the mightiest nations do not challenge him at all, yet he is tender enough to support the weak and needy.

Since this is true, Isaiah cannot fathom why Israel would ever think that an idol could measure up to this great God (vv. 18–20). Their unwillingness to trust God's power, control, knowledge, everlasting nature, strength, and support puzzles the prophet (vv. 21–26). Believers never need to look elsewhere for assurance and help.

During difficult days, God equips his people with power and strength (vv. 27–31). His endurance sustains those who are faltering. His power undergirds those who cannot persevere. His might upholds the weak. His people can endure in painful situations because God himself supports and comforts them.

JUNE 13 · ISAIAH 42:1–9

The Lord's Chosen Servant

BRYAN CHAPELL

THIS IS THE FIRST of the so-called "Servant Songs" in Isaiah—passages that relate some of the most tender and dear descriptions in all the Bible of the coming Messiah. The One who is described in these passages provides for others through his own suffering.

At one level these songs describe the nation of Israel, through whom blessing would come to all nations (Gen. 12:3; 17:4). But we need to remember that God referred to Israel as "my firstborn son" (Ex. 4:22) and, in doing so, made the nation representative of the character and care that would be evident in his ultimate "firstborn" son, Jesus (Matt. 3:17; Col. 1:15).

As the descriptions of Jesus's nature unfold, they give us great hope by displaying the heart of God as revealed in his Son and in his ultimate rule upon the earth. He will establish justice, open the eyes of the blind, release the prisoner, and turn back our darkness (Isa. 42:4–7). The injustice and suffering that we may experience do not have the final word—Jesus will set things right forever when he comes in final judgment upon all people and nations.

But we do not merely rejoice in what will happen in the future. Jesus's nature right now is such that he will not break a bruised reed or quench a faintly burning wick (v. 3). These are images of a powerful God acting with tender precision so as not to overwhelm those who are already broken and hurting.

This revelation of the "softer side" of God is all the more remarkable when we remember that Isaiah is writing to the nation of Israel during a time of rebellion, and prior to a period of divine discipline. The message is that even when God must deal with us according to our sin, he remains acutely sensitive to our needs and will not crush those who are precious to him.

God is aware that his children, who have been damaged by their own rebellion (as may be the case with our own children), often do not need more consequence for their sin as much as an assurance of care despite their sin. They need *grace*. The God who will not break an already bruised reed gives us permission to treat our children with such grace. For he will do the same with us.

JUNE 14 · ISAIAH 43

Stubborn, Rebellious, but His

ERIKA ALLEN

OUT OF ALL the nations in the world, God chose tiny, insignificant Israel to call his own. Not because of anything the people did to deserve it, but because God in his grace had bound himself to their forefather, Abraham (Gen. 12:2–3; Rom. 11:28–29).

Israel's purpose was, from the beginning, to reveal God's glory to the nations and to be the channel through which God would bless the entire world (Gen. 12:3). Called to be holy and set apart (Lev. 19:2), their lives were to be a living testimony to the holiness of God (Isa. 2:2–5). But rather than glorify his name, they profaned it again and again, resulting in God's judgment. Thus Israel is now a nation "plundered and looted," "trapped in holes and hidden in prisons" (42:22)—in bondage to the nations to whom they are supposed to be light.

Israel has forgotten who God is and who they are in relation to him. But in Isaiah 43, God reclaims his people for his glory. He will yet save Israel, so that through their salvation his name will be glorified (43:5–7). Though their suffering is well deserved, God says, "Fear not, for I have redeemed you; I have called you by name, you are *mine*" (v. 1). God's faithfulness to his people has not wavered. He will be with them and protect them even now (vv. 1–2). Why? "Because you are precious in my eyes, and honored, and I love you" (v. 4).

God reminds Israel that they are loved by none other than the all-powerful, *only* God of the universe: "Before me no god was formed, nor shall there be any after me. I, I am the Lord, and besides me there is no savior" (vv. 10–11). And his power—which he uses so mightily on their behalf—cannot be exhausted. He will never run out of ways to rescue them (vv. 18–19). God will move heaven and earth for his people, "that they might declare my praise" (v. 21).

Verse 25 is remarkable: "I, I am he who blots out your transgressions for my own sake, and I will not remember your sins." We don't deserve the Lord's love any more than the Israelites did. And yet, in his grace he blots out our transgressions in his Son, Jesus, "in whom we have redemption, the forgiveness of sins" (Col. 1:14).

Like Israel, we as believers are called to be light, pointing people to God so that he is glorified (Matt. 5:16). And, like Israel, we too will often fall short. But our hope is in Jesus, the true "light of men," who perfectly reflects the Father (John 1:4–5; see also Isa. 49:6). If we are in him, God says to us, "Fear not, for I have redeemed you; I have called you by name, you are mine." We are precious in his eyes, and honored. How he loves us!

Cyrus, God's Instrument

GEOFF ALLEN

HAVE YOU EVER received a blessing from God that surprised you? Perhaps through a person you least expected or a bad situation that turned out quite differently than you had anticipated? Scripture tells us that God has a long history of taking dire situations and working through them for the good of his people (Gen. 50:20; Joshua 2, Ruth 4; Esther 8–9; Rom. 8:28). So why should we as believers ever be surprised when God comes to our rescue in an unpredictable, amazing way?

In Isaiah 45, we see the Lord preparing two blessings for his people to receive in the coming years. The first blessing comes in the opening verse, where the Lord announces that Cyrus, a pagan king, will be God's "anointed," the one through whom he will work to deliver his people (Isa. 45:1). To an Israelite, this kind of anointing was unheard of, since only two kinds of people were typically anointed: rulers of Israel (1 Sam. 10:1) and high priests (Lev. 4:3). But in a display of his sovereignty, God declares to Cyrus that he will use him—"though you do not know me" (Isa. 45:5)—to ensure that his people are saved and returned from exile.

God knows his people and how they will respond, even before they do. He knows their shock and disbelief at the idea of a pagan king coming to their rescue. Through Isaiah, he warns his people not to question how he chooses to accomplish his purposes. He reminds them that they are a clay pot and he is the potter who formed them (vv. 9–11). As the Creator of the heavens and the earth (v. 12), God can use whomever he wants to liberate his people (v. 13).

The second blessing comes in the form of an invitation, but not to Israel. He instructs the nations to assemble together with their false gods and asks them to compare their wooden idols to himself, a righteous God and Savior (vv. 20–21). He graciously invites the nations to turn to him, the one true God, and be saved (v. 22), for in the end he will be to all either Savior or Judge, since "every knee shall bow" to him and "every tongue shall swear allegiance" (v. 23). It is striking to note that the chapter ends by foreshadowing the grafting of Gentiles into Israel (Romans 11). The Lord then declares that "*all* the offspring of Israel shall be justified and shall glory" (Isa. 45:25; compare Rom. 11:26; Gal. 6:16).

Ultimately, then, Isaiah 45 foreshadows the day when the Lord will, through the blood of Jesus, remove the "dividing wall of hostility," and "reconcile us both to God in one body through the cross" (Eph. 2:14–16).

JUNE 16 • ISAIAH 49:8-26

No Shame in Waiting

CAROLYN MCCULLEY

THIS PASSAGE INCLUDES a section of what is called a "servant song." These are four messianic passages of comfort and reassurance in Isaiah that portray the Servant of the Lord as the one who is chosen to carry his Spirit and offer hope for justice in this fallen world. Verses 8 to 13 in this passage include the end of the second Servant Song, a section that concludes with the exhortation of verse 13 to sing for joy because the Lord has comforted his people.

But this triumphant song of praise is immediately soured by the dissonant response from God's people, known here as Zion: "The LORD has forsaken me; my Lord has forgotten me" (Isa. 49:14).

Throughout the Bible, we see the temptation for God's people to survey their circumstances and then make assumptions about God's purposes— and worse, about his character. We know that our God is a worker of wondrous deeds, so when he doesn't appear to change our circumstances, we decide he is not faithful, nor does he love us. But the real display of faith is when we trust God's character even when we don't understand his responses or timing.

The illustrations Isaiah uses here speak to us as women. God compares himself to a mother nursing her child and says that even if such a woman has no compassion on her own children—a hard concept to imagine!— *he* will not be that way. As he restores the fortunes of his people, their joy will be like that of a bride dressing for her wedding or a mother welcoming her children. Even a barren and bereaved woman will experience the wonder of a sudden surge of sons and daughters. In these feminine and intimate emotional word pictures, the Lord speaks to us about his faithfulness.

These passages reach their climax in verse 23, where Isaiah writes, "Then you will know that I am the LORD; those who wait for me shall not be put to shame." That promise is timeless. As the psalmist wrote, "Those who look to him are radiant, and their faces shall never be ashamed" (Ps. 34:5). Waiting in faith on the Lord always has its rewards. And they are always much different—and far better—than we could have imagined. Let us walk through this day carried by Scripture's multiple promises of God's faithfulness, and let that rock-solid reality cause our hearts to overflow with joy and praise!

JUNE 17 · ISAIAH 52:13-53:12

The Substitutionary Atoning Death of Christ

LEE TANKERSLEY

THE TENSION THAT builds throughout the book of Isaiah should be, "How can a holy and just God cleanse and forgive a sinful people?" In the very first chapter we are told that the Lord will take a people who "have forsaken the LORD" and "despised the Holy One of Israel" (Isa. 1:4) and will make their scarlet sins as white as snow (1:18). They will be forgiven and cleansed. But how does this happen? How can the just God forgive a sinful people without compromising his just character? The answer is found in the work of Jesus Christ, whose sin-bearing death is nowhere more clearly pictured in the Old Testament than in Isaiah 52:13–53:12.

Centuries prior to the incarnation, Isaiah declares that Jesus, as God's servant, would be "despised and rejected . . . a man of sorrows and acquainted with grief" (53:3). Though he deserved to be exalted, he would be despised. Indeed, as Jesus suffered on the cross, we know that many mocked and derided him. Wicked men looked upon him, claiming that he was bearing the wrath of God. They "esteemed him stricken, smitten by God, and afflicted" (53:4).

And they were right! "It was the will of the LORD to crush him" (53:10) and put him to death. But what those standing around the cross failed to understand was that God was crushing him "for our iniquities," wounding him "for our transgressions," and laying on him "the iniquity of us all" (53:5–6). Isaiah foretells that Christ's death would be one of penal substitution for his people.

Jesus's death accomplished much. He demonstrated God's love for us (Rom. 5:8), destroyed one who holds the power of death (Heb. 2:14), and left us an example of faithful obedience (1 Pet. 2:21). Foundationally, however, Jesus died to pay the penalty for our sin as our substitute. This is central to the gospel message. On the cross, Jesus bore the very wrath of God which we, as sinners, deserved. Therefore, there is now no condemnation for us (Rom. 8:1). By his perfect life, penalty-bearing death, and justifying resurrection, our Lord made his people to "be accounted righteous" (Isa. 53:11).

Therefore, if your faith rests in Christ and you turn to him today to confess your sins, you need not worry whether God is in a forgiving mood or will decide to show mercy. Our forgiveness is rooted in the loving justice of God. We can trust in certain forgiveness because the righteous God poured out his wrath on Christ, our substitute, who willingly laid down his life in love so that we might justly be cleansed and forgiven.

JUNE 18 · ISAIAH 54

The Glorious Future of the People of God

KRISTIE ANYABWILE

SOON AFTER WE got married, my husband and I discovered that we were expecting our first child. The joy, excitement, fear, and anticipation of that moment was indescribable. However, just a few weeks later we experienced the terrible pain and grief of miscarriage. We were not yet Christians, and questions about God's purposes in suffering plagued us, leaving us feeling barren and with little hope of having a family.

The pain of desiring children but not being able to have them is something that no woman would wish upon her worst enemy. So is the agony of losing a spouse and being left without his companionship, protection, and love. A similar emptiness was in the hearts of God's people as we read chapters 40–55 of Isaiah, which are addressed to the Jewish exiles in Babylon. Israel is but a shadow of their former glory. They are bereft, their homes abandoned, families scattered, and pride shaken because of their sin.

But in chapter 53, God promises a servant who will suffer God's judgment on behalf of his people. He will bear the sins of many (Isa. 53:11–12). In light of this promise, God tells his people to prepare joyfully for their future! (54:1–3). He will be to them a gracious, loving husband who removes his bride's barrenness, widowhood, and abandonment (vv. 1, 4–6).

One pastor calls chapter 54 "an invigorating and uplifting breath of heavenly air." God calls Israel to ready themselves for an outpouring of blessing. He makes a promise to this barren nation: he tells her to make room, because she will grow far beyond what her current borders can contain (vv. 2–3).

When God restores his people to himself, his anger will be assuaged, his rebuke will be complete, his compassion will overflow to them, and his peace will reign. They will be comforted, protected, established, and preserved. After hearing of this suffering servant who will come in humility, who will die without sin, and who will be restored to life and reign with might, Israel is now encouraged to persevere. They have a bright future ahead of them.

So it is with all of us. In my own life, God used our season of heartache to introduce himself to us. He won our hearts. Two years after our miscarriage, our little family began to grow, and so did our awareness of the vastness of the family of God. But even if he hadn't done this, we would have every reason to sing praises to him and shout for joy! We are redeemed by Christ. We are the bejeweled city built by God, the recipients of his love and peace, protected and preserved in him until he returns.

An Invitation for All Who Thirst

BRIAN BORGMAN

THE SUFFERING SERVANT has accomplished the work of salvation through his substitutionary death (Isa. 52:13–53:12). Now the prophet stands like a street vendor, crying out to those passing by to come and buy his food. This food is nothing other than the lavish banquet of God's salvation. The amazing thing about his invitation, however, is that it is all free. Those who are thirsty and have no money are invited to come, partake of a meal fit for a king, and be truly satisfied. They are told to stop wasting their resources on what does not satisfy (55:2). The meal that has been set before them is described not only in terms of a sumptuous and delightful feast but also in terms of the covenant mercies given to David (v. 3). What seems like a confusing mixed metaphor is actually a wonderful promise, not only of the banquet of salvation but also of a restoration of the kingdom under the suffering servant who is also the Davidic King.

Isaiah continues his invitation and tells his listeners to seek the Lord, to call upon him, and to repent (vv. 6–7). Although Isaiah is offering free grace, he is not offering cheap grace. The proper response is clearly faith and repentance. Seeking the Lord and calling on his name express faith in God's word and character. Repentance acknowledges our sin and turns from it. When those demands are met, God promises compassion and abundant pardon.

Isaiah concludes this glorious invitation with a reminder that God is above us and his word is all-powerful (vv. 10–11). As the word goes out, it accomplishes God's purposes. God's word, the message of salvation, has inherent power. The final scene reflects the joyful response of those who experience God's salvation (vv. 12–13). It is like a new exodus. Even the inanimate creation rejoices over God's salvation as it anticipates the completion of God's saving work in the new creation. A full and free gospel message not only transforms sinners but one day will transform the whole earth.

This Old Testament passage is full of the gospel. It points us to the living water that quenches our soul's thirst. It points us to the living bread who alone can satisfy us. Ultimately, Jesus Christ himself is that living water and living bread. He alone satisfies. Those who come to him experience the joy and satisfaction of his salvation and his gracious rule over their lives. But who can come? According to Isaiah, there is just one prerequisite: you must be thirsty. You must know your need. All who know we are bankrupt and have nothing to offer except our poverty may come. When we come in faith and repentance, we experience compassion and full pardon.

JUNE 20 · ISAIAH 59

Your Redeemer Has Come

KERI FOLMAR

ISRAEL WAS A sinful nation. They had fallen into blindness, wallowing in the darkness and gloom of iniquity. Their sin separated them from God, and they could no longer see. They could no more help themselves than a dead man could climb out of the grave.

We are, by nature, no different from Israel, groping and stumbling in the darkness of sin. But God's hand is not shortened, nor is his ear dull. His own arm brings salvation (Isa. 59:16). He is limitless in his ability and readiness to rescue. "'And a Redeemer will come to Zion, to those in Jacob who turn from transgression,' declares the LORD" (v. 20).

The Redeemer is Jesus. He came to Zion to deliver the captives and open the eyes of the blind. On the cross, Jesus paid the ransom for those who would repent and believe (Mark 10:45). He paid with his life. Yet he did not remain a corpse but rose triumphantly from a grave that could not keep him. He is the Redeemer not only of one nation but of a people from every nation. "So they shall fear the name of the LORD from the west, and his glory from the rising of the sun" (Isa. 59:19). Through tears of repentance we can see his glory.

God's Spirit is upon this Redeemer. God's word shall dwell in his children forevermore (v. 21), vanquishing the darkness and gloom, giving light to walk in righteousness. We can have great confidence in approaching God as his children, with the righteousness of Christ as our breastplate and his salvation as our helmet (v. 17). This is our great hope. Our Redeemer saves and enables us to obey through his word and by the power of his Spirit in us. As we live lives of repentance, he gives life and ever-increasing sight until every bond of sin is exposed and broken, and we are presented perfect one day in glory.

So, sister, when you feel your sin, take heart. You cannot save yourself, but your Redeemer has come "to those . . . who turn from transgression" (v. 20). Don't wallow in the darkness and gloom. Repent and believe. Put on the breastplate and helmet of Jesus, and step into the light. Live for the glory of the One who is mighty to save, and proclaim his name from where the sun rises in the east to where it sets in the west. "Arise, shine, for your light has come, and the glory of the LORD has risen upon you!" (60:1).

JUNE 21 · ISAIAH 62

A Beautiful Picture of a Glorious Future

JENNY SALT

HAVE YOU EVER looked at a wedding album and marveled at how beautiful the bride and groom looked on their wedding day? Suppose the bride and groom were able to see those photos *before* the wedding had actually taken place. Imagine how helpful and encouraging it would be to see the "finished product" before the big day. That is the sense of Isaiah 62—the picture of the beautiful relationship of the Lord and his bride, with God rejoicing and delighting over his transformed people.

Some of God's people were still in captivity in Babylon, while others were back in Jerusalem but were disheartened by the state of the city as they remained under foreign rule. "Seeing" their glorious future would motivate them to hold on to the hope of their sure destiny, and to pray for that day to come.

The first five verses are from Isaiah's perspective. He will not stay quiet about the glories to come: "For Zion's sake I will not keep silent" (Isa. 62:1). He describes Zion in terms of a new identity, like the changing of a name in marriage: "you shall be called by a new name" (v. 2). Israel, once forsaken and desolate because of her sin, shall be known as "Married" (v. 4), with God rejoicing over his bride (v. 5). He will be like a devoted husband, focused on his bride and determined to love her.

In verses 6 to 12, God speaks about the watchmen, raised up by the Lord to pray with a boldness and persistence that "give him no rest" (v. 7). Bold and confident prayer is always appropriate when based on God's promises. We read of these promises in the verses that immediately follow: promises to establish Jerusalem and make her a safe and prosperous place to dwell.

The last three verses call for all people to enter into the salvation that is coming. This salvation is to be proclaimed by lifting up the signal or banner so that others may know and walk the ways of salvation.

What will our ultimate wedding day look like? We open the album and see the Lord God Almighty and his bride, the covenant people, beautifully dressed for her husband—something that far outshines any human marriage. How do we prepare for that day? We watch, and we pray, "Your kingdom come, your will be done, on earth as it is in heaven" (Matt. 6:10); we lift the signal for the nations, proclaiming the gospel of the Savior Jesus Christ and looking forward to the day when we will all dwell together as the Redeemed of the Lord.

JUNE 22 · JEREMIAH 1

The Call of Jeremiah

GEOFF ALLEN

HAVE YOU EVER been given a task that you knew was going to be difficult? Did you try to beg out of it because you felt you were not the right person for the job? If anybody understood this feeling, it was Jeremiah when God called him to prophetic ministry during the last days of Jerusalem.

Jeremiah was given the unhappy task of confronting Judah regarding her unfaithfulness to God.

As you can imagine, being the bearer of such a message to a people who don't want to hear it would be difficult for any seasoned prophet. But Jeremiah didn't even have that going in his favor, as he was still a youth when the Lord called him (Jer. 1:6). Add to that the insecurities that come with any young person having to speak to older community members, and you have all the makings of a reluctant and cowering prophet.

Yet throughout Scripture we see the Lord commissioning weak and inadequate people to carry out his will. An aged and childless Abraham to father a nation; Moses, with his speech impediment, to speak before Pharaoh; the young shepherd David to slay the giant and establish a royal line leading to Jesus the Messiah. Jeremiah was one of many who thought themselves the wrong person for the job, until the Lord touched his mouth and promised him the words would be there to speak when needed (vv. 9–10). Armed with this assurance, Jeremiah could then arise and dress for the work he was called to do (v. 17).

God does not tell Jeremiah that he will be spared from pain, ridicule, persecution, or affliction. The Lord knew Jeremiah before he formed him in the womb (v. 5), and he knew the numerous tribulations—from being beaten and imprisoned (ch. 37) to being thrown into a cistern by wicked officials (ch. 38)—that Jeremiah would have to endure to fulfill his commission. But God nonetheless commanded Jeremiah not to be dismayed by his hostile audience (1:17). He promised to make him "a fortified city" (v. 18) against the land. God himself would fight for and protect Jeremiah: "They will fight against you, but they shall not prevail against you, for I am with you, declares the LORD, to deliver you" (v. 19).

God often calls us to tasks that are entirely too much for us to handle in our own strength. He does so in order that we would depend not on ourselves, but on the power of Christ (2 Cor. 12:9). He faithfully equips us with his word (2 Tim. 3:16–17) and the power of the Holy Spirit. Indeed, he will "equip you with everything good that you may do his will" (Heb. 13:21). If you are in Christ, there is absolutely nothing that can prevail against you (Rom. 8:31–39).

A Call to Repentance

STARR MEADE

REPENTANCE IS BASIC to any relationship of sinful human beings with a holy God. This passage urges God's Old Testament people, the Israelites, to repent. Repentance is required for entering into eternal life, but a close walk with God as a believer is also a lifestyle of daily repentance. We never graduate beyond repentance.

Repentance is costly. It requires giving up things we never should have loved, but do (Jer. 4:1). Repentance is painful (4:3–4a). It requires acknowledging what we really are: guilty rebels (3:13), faithless children (3:14), adulterous spouses (3:8, 20). Repentance requires a drastic turnaround, a complete change in direction. But it is the only way to a relationship with a God who hates our sin.

Of what must we repent? We must repent of every time we rebel and refuse to do what God has given us to do (3:13); of all the times we pervert our way, being so much less than God created and called us to be (3:21); of each time we forget our covenant God (3:21); of the days and years we give to that which cannot save us (3:23–24). We must even repent of our repentance, since it so often lacks sincerity (3:10).

Repentance isn't pleasant. But in his eagerness to do us good, God pours out encouragements to repent. If we repent, he will not look on us in anger, for he is merciful (3:12). He is our Master and Father who longs to bless us, so we owe him repentance and renewed obedience (3:14, 19). If we will repent, we will be among those with whom his presence dwells forever (3:16–17).

And yet, look at how often we've repented before. Look at our pitiful tendency to turn back to our sin. The Lord our God, in whom is all our salvation (3:23b), will not leave his people to wallow in their sin forever. He promises shepherds who will feed us with knowledge and understanding (3:15) so that we will know the hatefulness of sin, like he does, and understand how devastating it is, as he does. He promises that, when we return to him, he will heal our faithlessness (3:22). He will forgive us *and* change us. These are wonderful promises, given first to God's people, Israel, under the old covenant, and fulfilled, for them and for us, in the person and work of Jesus Christ. Jesus is himself the true and final Shepherd.

For those who will not repent, but go on in their own way without turning, God is faithful to warn: Repentance is required "lest my wrath go forth like fire, and burn with none to quench it, because of the evil of your deeds" (4:4).

JUNE 24 · JEREMIAH 7:1–8:3

Standing at the Gate

JENNY SALT

THERE IS AN old saying that is not quoted much these days: "going to hell in a handbasket," which refers to something or someone who is on course for disaster. It has fallen out of popular usage, probably because the concept of hell is neither popular nor politically correct today. But it would not have been out of place if Jeremiah had used it as part of the message he preached at the temple gates in Jerusalem in Jeremiah 7.

During Jeremiah's ministry, the people of Judah were going to the temple, sacrificing in the prescribed manner, zealous in their religious observance—and yet they were completely out of step with Yahweh and his ways. Their trust was not in Yahweh but in the outward trappings of religion—a dangerous state to be in. In his commentary on the book of Jeremiah, the Reformer John Calvin put it this way: "Sacrifices are of no importance or value before God, unless those who offer them wholly devote themselves to God with a sincere heart."[6]

The people of Judah were treating the temple as a kind of safe house. It didn't matter how they lived; it didn't matter if they worshiped other gods (Jer. 7:18, 30–31); it didn't matter if they stole, swore falsely, murdered, or committed adultery (7:9), as long as they came into the temple and said, "We are delivered!" (7:10). How foolish! Despite the warnings, despite the evidence of the history of Israel, they failed to listen. "Go now to my place that was in Shiloh, where I made my name dwell at first, and see what I did to it because of the evil of my people Israel" (7:12). "Yet they did not listen to me or incline their ear, but stiffened their neck" (7:26).

It is no different today. We can do our mental calculations and ask ourselves questions like, Do I go regularly to church? Check. (In fact, I haven't missed a week in ages!) Have I read my Bible today? Check. (My daily devotions have never been more regular!) Am I giving up my money and my time to serve in the local church? Check. (I have even been asked to disciple some other women in my church!) All these aspects of the Christian life are good, but if we put our confidence in these things as a way of being right with God, we are in danger of thinking the same way as Jeremiah's contemporaries. No, our righteousness comes from God and is by faith in Jesus Christ (Phil. 3:9).

The "handbasket" may look very impressive, but it is heading in the wrong direction unless our confidence is based solely on Jesus's work at the cross, as we "glory in Christ Jesus and put no confidence in the flesh" (Phil. 3:3).

JUNE 25 · JEREMIAH 10

The Idiocy of Idolatry

ELISABETH MAXWELL (LISA) RYKEN

JEREMIAH HAS FEW heartwarming passages. Yet, amid gloom and destruction, there are reminders of God's goodness and faithfulness to those who obey (Jer. 3:12). After eight chapters of woe and destruction, chapter 10 offers a glimpse into God's awesome character. It is both a psalm of praise and one of the most sarcastic passages in the Bible. Jeremiah warns his people not to learn the ways of nations or to be dismayed by their religious customs (10:2–3). He shows the futility of idols and the absolute worth of the living God.

Jeremiah's description of idols and their worshipers would be humorous if it were not so deadly serious. He describes how an idol is a tree, cut down and shaped by a craftsman and then covered with precious metals and jewels. The completed idol is nailed into place so it will not fall. The Philistines of 1 Samuel 5 learned this; they forgot to nail their god, Dagon, to the floor when they stashed the ark of the covenant in his temple. The next day, Dagon was lying facedown on the floor beside the ark! He could not stand before the living God.

Jeremiah exposes the idiocy of worshiping idols. They are man-made. They cannot speak or walk. They have no power to influence our lives, which makes the people who follow them either stupid or delusional (vv. 14–15). Idols "shall perish from the earth and from under the heavens" (v. 11), and their worshipers will face God's wrath (v. 10).

In contrast, Jeremiah pours out praise to the true God. He is the living God, the everlasting King, and the Creator. Whereas idols are impotent, God stretched out the heavens and makes lightning (vv. 12–13). His wrath makes the earth quake and nations tremble (v. 10). God is everything that idols are not. As the "portion of Jacob" (v. 16), the Lord puts idols and their followers to shame by providing everything his people need.

We laugh at pagans carving gods and nailing them down. But before we laugh, consider *our* idols. What do we worship? Where is our trust? Some worship clothing or technology. For some it is the perfect family. Others crave sex, money, or power. Any idea or object that takes God's place in our lives—that demands our allegiance or devotion—is an idol.

Idols may not be wood covered with gold and jewels. They may be pixels or plastic or human. If Jeremiah saw them, he would be as sarcastic about our idols as he was about ancient idols. He would declare them utterly worthless. Yet, from Jeremiah's day until now, the living God is still the Creator, the everlasting King, and the Lord of hosts. In Christ he has drawn near. Only he is worthy of our trust—and only he satisfies.

Looking Up from Despair

TASHA D. CHAPMAN

WHAT ARE SOME of the most daunting jobs you have faced recently? How did you respond to the challenge? Trials at work can lead us to such discouragement that our hope and joy in our vocational calling dries up.

We tend to fear and avoid public speaking and conflict management. Just imagine Jeremiah's job! It had to be one of the most challenging in history. As a prophet, he was called to preach words from a holy God to a rebellious people—words that foretold national destruction for his homeland. Although obediently performed, his work provoked the very people he loved to slander him and even to plot against his life (see Jer. 11:18–23). Jeremiah called the people to give up their idols and to turn back to the living God. Yet they repeatedly refused to heed his warnings of the destruction that would come if they didn't repent.

In his fear, isolation, and seeming failure, Jeremiah does not give up. He does not hide. He does not reject his God-given responsibilities. Instead, he complains loudly and angrily to his Boss. With poetry and rhetorical questions, he expresses his painful doubts, even accusing God of treachery (15:18). And God answers him personally. He reminds Jeremiah of his many promises: Jeremiah's identity and calling (1:4–10); the coming judgment and destruction of Judah; and God's continuing presence, restoration, and salvation for Jeremiah (15:11–14, 19–21). Jeremiah persevered in his discouraging work for decades (1:1–3)—even though he knew that he himself would witness, and suffer from, the devastation he was trying to prevent.

In writing this book about his life's work, Jeremiah told of his weaknesses, anger, and pain, as well as his faithful perseverance. He showed how God was near and able to help. When the going got tough, Jeremiah looked up. He looked to the One who called him and who would sustain him for impossible tasks. And God's presence and perspective renewed Jeremiah's hope. Success was not about getting results or respect. His efforts were for far greater purposes: God's redemptive plans, for God's own glory.

When our work leads to despair, Jeremiah's story can embolden us to bring our complaints and pain to God. In looking up to our loving God, we will find a higher perspective and renewed hope, for he has called us to good work (Eph. 2:10), he is always with us (Rom. 8:31–39), he knows our pain intimately (Heb. 4:14–16), and he can redeem our efforts for his glory (Rom. 8:28). Like Jeremiah, we can find success in faithfulness to God and his words (Gal. 1:6–10).

JUNE 27 • JEREMIAH 17:1–13

Sin: Good News and Bad News

BETHANY L. JENKINS

LET'S START WITH the good news. The good news is that sin is not fundamentally about what we do or don't do. It is not mere behavior. That is great news. The bad news, however, is that sin is much deeper. It is about a heart that does not treasure God. This means that if we want to avoid sin, our hearts must be transformed from the inside. Is that even possible?

Jeremiah condemned the Israelites for worshiping other gods (Jer. 1:16; 2:28), believing false prophets (5:30–31), mocking the temple (7:9–11), and sacrificing children to idols (7:31; 32:35). Yet their main problem was deeper than any of their sinful acts. God indicted them in the following way: "My people have committed two evils: they have forsaken me, the fountain of living waters, and hewed out cisterns for themselves, broken cisterns that can hold no water" (2:13). In other words, they turned from trusting God to trusting themselves. Their sin was "engraved on the tablet of their heart" (17:1).

Sin is deep because it is a matter of where we put down our roots. In ways that echo Psalm 1, Jeremiah 17 tells us that if we put down our roots in ourselves, then we are like shrubs in a desert—living in a parched and uninhabited land, without hope for seeing any good (vv. 5–6). If, on the other hand, we trust in the Lord, then we are like trees by a river—staying calm even when heat and drought come—because the steady river, not the fickle rain, is our life source (vv. 7–8).

How do we know where we have sunk our roots? We look to where our minds and hearts wander. What am I anxious about? What, if I lost it, would make me angry? What, if I did not get it, would make me frustrated? Where does my mind go when I have nothing else to think about—things, relationships, social causes, hobbies, work? Whatever we "must have" or whatever our mind effortlessly contemplates is where we have put down our roots.

Jeremiah understood the predicament of our human condition: "The heart is deceitful above all things, and desperately sick; who can understand it?" (v. 9). Hundreds of years later, however, a man whose roots were planted by the river of God was uprooted for our sake. Jesus lived in the desert, where he was tempted (Matt. 4:1) and forsaken (Matt. 27:32–50), so that we might put down our roots by the river. He changes our hearts and reconciles us to God. As Paul writes, "if anyone is in Christ, he is a new creation. The old has passed away; behold, the new has come" (2 Cor. 5:17).

JUNE 28 · JEREMIAH 23:1-8

The Righteous Branch

MIKE BULLMORE

THERE ARE PASSAGES in the Bible that are profoundly beautiful. This is one of them. The beauty here is not so much in its poetry, although it possesses no small measure of that. The real beauty is in the presentation of a deeply-longed-for reality that captures our imagination and stirs our hearts with hope.

The prophet Jeremiah was called to speak into an already bleak and rapidly darkening situation. The people of God had forsaken their God and, despite the prophet's call to repentance, they had refused to repent. The most grievous thing was that the spiritual leaders had turned away from the work God had given them to do. So Jeremiah is called to speak these words of "woe to the shepherds" (Jer. 23:1–2). But into this dire situation God also speaks words of hope. He promises to restore his people (v. 3) and provide care for them with faithful shepherds (v. 4). It is amid this message of hope that a profoundly significant and beautiful word is spoken.

Jeremiah shifts suddenly from speaking of multiple shepherds to one Leader-King who is called "a righteous Branch" who "shall reign as king and deal wisely, and shall execute justice and righteousness" (v. 5). These words are part of a powerful stream of messianic prophecy (see esp. Isa. 9:1–7 and 11:1–9). In hearing them, a deep longing for such a possibility, a longing that resides somewhere in every human heart, is touched.

Three truths become clear in this passage. First, God will not abandon his purposes for his people. He knows who are his and, though he disciplines, he will restore. Even amid Israel's sin and faithlessness God still speaks of them as "my people" and "my flock" (Jer. 23:1–3), and he promises that they will "dwell securely" in the end (v. 6).

Second, God wants his people to *know* that he will accomplish his purposes for them, so that they will turn and again put their hope in him. There is the emphatically repeated refrain "declares the LORD" (vv. 1, 2, 4, 5, 7). God wants to assure his people that he will accomplish his purposes.

Third, in Christ and through his righteous reign, God will set all things to perfection. This "righteous branch" will be called "The LORD is our righteousness" (v. 6), and he will execute perfect righteousness. In him there will come a deliverance that will completely overshadow even the great deliverance of the exodus (vv. 7–8).

Let the sheer beauty of this truth—of this Christ—capture your imagination, stir your affection, and cause your hope to flourish!

JUNE 29 · JEREMIAH 26

The Pursuit

JESSICA THOMPSON

ISRAEL HAS ONCE again fallen into great sin. Their hearts are far from God and their actions are evil. Yet despite their faithlessness, God longs for his people to return to him. He graciously sends Jeremiah to confront Judah and to warn them of the consequences of their sin: "It may be they will listen, and every one turn from his evil way, that I may relent of the disaster that I intend to do to them because of their evil deeds" (Jer. 26:3).

Jeremiah is obedient to the Lord's command, but Judah's response is far from penitent. Rather, the people grab the prophet and yell, "You shall die!" (v. 8). Jeremiah is brought before the officials of Judah, where again he is threatened with death for daring to speak against Jerusalem and the temple—a message his audience considered to be blasphemy. Jeremiah doesn't falter, but once again proclaims his message of repentance and judgment. His concern is not for his personal safety but that the will of the Lord be accomplished. His confidence in the sovereign purposes of God is startling: "But as for me, behold, I am in your hands. Do with me as seems good and right to you. Only know for certain that if you put me to death, you will bring innocent blood upon yourselves and upon this city and its inhabitants, for in truth the LORD sent me to you to speak all these words in your ears" (vv. 14–15).

This story of pronounced judgment and a call to repentance resulting in the death of a prophet is a scarlet thread throughout the whole Bible (see Matt. 23:37). Time after time we see prophets warning God's people, pleading with them to repent; and time after time we see the people respond in anger and attempts to silence God's messengers. They try to silence the voice of their own conscience by killing the one who brings the message.

Ultimately, we see this culminating with Christ, who like Jeremiah pronounced his confidence in God and did not try to escape those seeking his life. But unlike Jeremiah, Jesus indeed died at the hands of his accusers. And it is his very death that makes a way for rebellious, hateful lawbreakers to be reconciled to their God. God still pursues us with the cry to repent— to turn to him and live. A price must be paid for sin. Someone must die. But consider the scandal of grace: We can be eternally condemned, or we can accept that the price was paid by our Savior, whose death makes a way for us to be restored to the Father forever.

Seek Me and You Will Find Me

ROBERT A. PETERSON

AFTER THE JEWS of the southern kingdom of Judah rejected all of God's prophets, God drove them into exile in Babylon. Jeremiah's letter to those exiles assures them that God has not forgotten or abandoned them. Following proper protocol, Jeremiah addresses the letter to Nebuchadnezzar, king of Babylon. It is striking that while this powerful king and his armies had overthrown Judah and taken the people into captivity, the Lord says *he* sent them into exile: "Thus says the LORD of hosts, the God of Israel, to all the exiles whom I have sent into exile from Jerusalem to Babylon . . ." (Jer. 29:4). Human responsibility is genuine; for its sins, Judah reaped what it sowed. But God is in control even of the powerful nations that do not acknowledge his lordship.

Even though false prophets say otherwise, the exiles should prepare for a long stay in Babylon (vv. 5–6). God's counsel through Jeremiah might surprise us: "Seek the welfare of the city where I have sent you into exile, and pray to the LORD on its behalf, for in its welfare you will find your welfare" (v. 7). Christians today around the globe do well to follow this sage advice and be a blessing wherever God has placed them.

God condemns the false prophets who have misled his people. He warns the exiles not to heed their prophecies, because he did not send them, and they speak lies (vv. 8–9). The New Testament instructs us that false prophets will continue until Jesus comes again. God warns us, like the Israelites of old, to cling to his word and reject the words of such prophets (Matt. 24:24; 2 Pet. 2:1–3).

God promises to return his exiled people to Israel when their seventy years of captivity are completed (Jer. 29:10). Then he adds words filled with grace that have been a blessing to countless believers since Jeremiah's time: "For I know the plans I have for you, declares the LORD, plans for welfare and not for evil, to give you a future and a hope" (v. 11). The Lord followed through on his words of warning and punished his wayward and idolatrous people by sending them into captivity, but his delight is to return them to their land and restore their fortunes.

Jeremiah's letter to the exiles contains other famous words—words that speak to the hearts of believers everywhere always. God calls to repentance Christians who have turned away from him, and he promises, "then you will call upon me and come and pray to me, and I will hear you. You will seek me and find me, when you seek me with all your heart" (vv. 12–13).

Seek him. Call upon him. He delights to draw near.

Rescued from Exile

LEEANN STILES

JUDAH'S LEADERS HATED Jeremiah and his announcements of doom. They didn't want to think about their sin or the fact that God might judge it. They assumed the Lord was on their side, and that he would never let their enemies defeat them. But he did. The Lord handed them over to the Babylonians.

Amid all of this, the Lord gave Jeremiah a message of hope, which begins in this chapter and continues through chapter 33. These four chapters are known as the "Book of Consolation." We read in chapter 30 that Judah and Israel would be delivered from a time of deep distress (Jer. 30:5–11). Their grievous wounds would be healed (vv. 12–17), and the nation would be rebuilt (vv. 18–20). In spite of their rebellion, God would restore his people. And he would raise up a prince who could intercede for them (vv. 9, 21). That's a promise Judah needed to hear. Yes, foreigners had dragged them into captivity. This was God's judgment on their waywardness. But he never abandoned them.

We're much like the Israelites. We want to ignore our sin and think there won't be any consequences. But sin drags us into captivity. We can't escape God's judgment any more than Judah could escape the Babylonians.

But the Lord hasn't abandoned those he's chosen—then or now. We must remember the hope he offers. Jesus Christ fulfills Jeremiah's prophecy completely, for all time. Verses 23–24 explain this: "Behold the storm of the LORD! Wrath has gone forth, a whirling tempest; it will burst on the head of the wicked. The fierce anger of the LORD will not turn back until he has executed and accomplished the intentions of his mind. In the latter days you will understand this."

God does punish the rebellious. He doesn't just overlook our sin. He releases his fury and will not turn back until it is avenged. But at Calvary, God vented his fierce anger on Jesus. When Jesus cried out from the cross, "It is finished" (John 19:30), he announced that he had accomplished God's will, "the intentions of his mind." His resurrection confirms that God's wrath is fully satisfied for those who repent and believe. We can be healed; we can be fully reconciled to him. Isaiah 53:5 puts it this way: "But he was pierced for our transgressions; he was crushed for our iniquities; upon him was the chastisement that brought us peace, and with his wounds we are healed."

God fulfilled Jeremiah 30. He brought the Israelites back to the Promised Land. He has made the way for us to be rescued from the exile of sin as well. Place your hope in Jesus. His wounds bring spiritual healing and give everlasting life.

JULY 2 · JEREMIAH 31:31–40

The New Covenant

JEN WILKIN

SEEKING TO BRING hope and comfort to exiled Judah, Jeremiah foresees a time when God will end his rejection of them and restore them to himself. But how? How could a people characterized by disobedience and faithlessness be changed into a people who seek after the Lord with heart, soul, mind, and strength? God's answer to this dilemma is to establish a new covenant, one that will do what the old covenant of the law could not do.

As New Testament believers, the term "new covenant" is familiar to us. Though whispers of a new covenant can be found throughout the

Old Testament, Jeremiah 31:31 is the only place where the actual phrase occurs. It is spoken here, and then it is not spoken again until it is uttered in an upper room from the lips of Jesus. Taking in hand the cup, he announces the arrival of what Jeremiah had foretold six hundred years before: "This cup that is poured out for you is the new covenant in my blood" (Luke 22:20).

Jeremiah's description of this new covenant paints a picture of hope on four fronts. Unlike its predecessor, the new covenant *renews*, *relates*, *reveals*, and *reconciles*:

1. *It renews.* "I will put my law within them, and I will write it on their hearts" (Jer. 31:33). This new covenant allows God's law to be written, not on lifeless tablets of stone but on living hearts renewed by the gospel. Rather than external obedience, the new covenant enables obedience that flows from internal transformation—right actions springing from right motives (Ezek. 11:19).

2. *It relates.* "And I will be their God, and they shall be my people" (Jer. 31:33). The new covenant allows for relationship on an intimate level. No longer does God dwell in a temple made by human hands; he makes human hearts his very temple (1 Cor. 3:16).

3. *It reveals.* "And no longer shall each one teach his neighbor and each his brother, saying, 'Know the LORD,' for they shall all know me, from the least of them to the greatest, declares the LORD" (Jer. 31:34). Through the Holy Spirit, the knowledge of God's character is given in a new and personal way to *all* of God's people (John 14:16).

4. *It reconciles.* "For I will forgive their iniquity, and I will remember their sin no more" (Jer. 31:34). This new covenant, ratified by the blood of Christ, means not just a covering for sin but a complete removal of our guilt. God will forgive sin to the extent that he will not remember it any longer. No grudges will be held. All will be forgotten.

God Is a Promise Maker and Keeper

COLLEEN J. MCFADDEN

GOD IS A promise maker. God is a promise keeper. Have you heard that refrain before? Our God makes covenants, or promises, and he carries those covenants to the end. He will not break his promises.

While we know this is true, it is hard to believe it amid difficult circumstances. Jeremiah had every reason to question whether God would keep his end of the deal. Jeremiah was locked up in prison (Jer. 32:2; 33:1), awaiting the inevitable destruction of his city and exile of his people (32:28–29). The future did not look promising. Even outsiders looking in on the situation thought that the Lord had abandoned his people (33:24). But God doesn't break his promises.

The main promise in focus is God's covenant with David. God promised King David that his kingdom would last forever (see 2 Sam. 7:8–17). That is, it would "never lack a man to sit on the throne of the house of Israel" (Jer. 33:17). So certain is it that God will fulfill this promise, that the Lord compares it to the inevitability of day and night: "If you can break my covenant with the day and my covenant with the night, so that day and night will not come at their appointed time, then also my covenant with David my servant may be broken" (vv. 20–21). And what is more, the kingdom will be so large, it will be beyond number (v. 22). What an amazing promise in the face of ruin and exile!

The Lord will provide a king in the line of David to rule forever. And he goes on to promise a priest to make atonement for sins forever (v. 18). The book of Hebrews speaks of a priest like this: "he has appeared once for all at the end of the ages to put away sin by the sacrifice of himself" (Heb. 9:26). The forever-reigning king and once-and-for-all priest is the man Jesus Christ. As God's perfect Son, he acts as high priest interceding for us. "For by a single offering he has perfected *for all time* those who are being sanctified" (Heb. 10:14). This is our priest. This is our king.

God is a promise maker. God is a promise keeper. How sure can we be that his covenant will be kept? He says it again: As long as sun and moon go round, so will my love for you (Jer. 31:35–36). Not only will the land be restored (33:7, 11), but mercy will abound. What a great hope for Jeremiah and those facing exile! And what a sure foundation for us today as we rejoice in our priest-king, Jesus Christ, who executes justice and righteousness (v. 15). These promises are a sure thing.

JULY 4 · JEREMIAH 39

Devastating Judgment and Divine Love

LEE TANKERSLEY

IT IS HARD to describe the devastation portrayed in the opening two verses of Jeremiah 39. It reads like a simple note of history: "In the ninth year of Zedekiah king of Judah, in the tenth month, Nebuchadnezzar king of Babylon and all his army came against Jerusalem and besieged it. In the eleventh year of Zedekiah, in the fourth month, on the ninth day of the month, a breach was made in the city" (Jer. 39:1–2).

Babylon laid siege to Jerusalem, and about eighteen months later they broke through the walls of the city and laid waste much of it. But this is no simple historical note.

When the Babylonians laid siege to Jerusalem, it was for the purpose of starving the people, and that is exactly what happened. As Jeremiah had prophesied (19:9), starving mothers boiled and ate their own children in those days (Lam. 4:10). Then, when there was no food left and no strength to fight, the Babylonians broke down the walls, took the people captive, and burned much of the city. It was a terrible scene.

Yet we must remember that it was a terrible scene of *divine judgment*. This was the Lord's work, bringing judgment to a people who had forsaken his ways and rebelled against his laws. The severity of such judgment is hard to look at, and it may well make us want to move on from this Bible story to another. However, if we will allow ourselves to pause here for a moment and look at this portrait of divine judgment, it will do us good.

Such pictures of divine judgment should make us consider the nature of our own sin. All of us can go through times when our sin doesn't feel very weighty to us. Perhaps we excuse it by noting that others struggle in similar ways. Is our gossip, obsession with body image, or covetousness of our neighbor's life really all that bad? To answer that question, we need look no further than this picture of divine judgment on Jerusalem. Let this shadow of divine wrath remind us that our sins are not trivial and must be fought on all sides.

But this picture should also help us to see more clearly the love our God has for us. When we were his enemies and deserving of his full wrath, God demonstrated his love for us by sending his Son, who willingly bore divine judgment for us on the cross (Rom. 5:8). Therefore, out of gratitude, let us fight sin and pursue holiness. Christ shed his blood so that we might never know divine condemnation.

JULY 5 · JEREMIAH 50

Jeremiah Preaches Destruction and Restoration

DONNA THOENNES

NO ONE ENVIED Jeremiah—not then, not now! What a tough calling—to be God's spokesman, tasked with delivering mostly undesirable messages! Jeremiah is unique in that he leveled accusations against God's chosen people for 45 chapters! But in chapters 46–51, his prophetic voice is more consistent with the prophets who proclaimed divine judgment against foreign nations.

In chapter 50 Jeremiah addresses Babylon, and devotes more space to God's judgment on that nation than he did for all the other nations combined. Babylon was an influential powerhouse in the region and had a history of destruction against God's people. God calls Babylon "plunderers of my heritage" (Jer. 50:11). Babylon had sinned against God himself by

tormenting his people. God is righteously angry and declares, "Go up.....
Kill, and devote them to destruction" (v. 21).

Babylon would endure the same destruction and anguish she had
brought on God's people. "Repay her according to her deeds; do to her
according to all that she has done" (v. 29). Great nations from the north
would come with swords and leave Babylon desolate.

While Babylon's future is desperately bleak, Jeremiah communicates
hope for Israel. At this point in their history, God's people had little reason to believe that deliverance would come. But Jeremiah reminds them
of God's sovereign plan. There was reason to hope that they would be
restored to their homeland. The people of Israel and Judah will be united
(v. 4) and seek the Lord together "in an everlasting covenant that will
never be forgotten" (v. 5). God's people will go forth with exuberance,
with newfound freedom (v. 8). The good shepherd promises to bring
his flock back to pasture: "I will restore Israel to his pasture, . . . and his
desire shall be satisfied" (v. 19). Even more astonishing, God's people
will be spiritually restored, forgiven, and pardoned (v. 20). The future
is full of promise.

This glimpse into Jeremiah's prophetic ministry displays God's sovereignty over all nations. His full character is on display as Jeremiah declares
him to be both a wrathful judge and a loving, covenant keeping shepherd.
"Their Redeemer is strong; the Lord of hosts is his name. He will surely
plead their cause, that he may give rest to the earth, but unrest to the
inhabitants of Babylon" (v. 34). God would bring about two seemingly
impossible things: Babylon would be overthrown, and the Jews would be
restored to their homeland.

Jeremiah was faithful to preach God's anger over injustice and his mercy
toward his flock. In the face of injustice, may we trust God to both defend
his own and judge the unjust according to his sovereign will.

Great Faithfulness

ELISABETH MAXWELL (LISA) RYKEN

IN 589 BC, King Nebuchadnezzar II of Babylon laid siege to Jerusalem. A few years later, the city was captured and destroyed. Most of its inhabitants were taken as captives to Babylon. Few of us can comprehend the grief and horror of living through the siege of Jerusalem. Imagine the hunger, thirst, and uncertainty. Imagine seeing family members killed. Imagine watching friends and neighbors dragged into captivity. Imagine everything you have ever known and loved being destroyed.

While the rest of the nation was grieving, one eyewitness to the destruction—probably Jeremiah—wrote five laments to memorialize their suffering and give expression to their sorrow. The laments can also be thought of as elegies—formal funeral poems.

Lamentations 1, 2, 4, and 5 are focused on the nation's grief. But chapter 3 focuses more on the author's own pain and sorrow. He talks about how his skin has wasted away and his bones were broken. He talks about his darkness and bitterness. His faith almost gone, he is close to giving up. "My endurance has perished," he says, "so has my hope from the LORD" (Lam. 3:18).

Yet just at the point of utter desolation, the author remembers something that stabilizes his soul and redeems his hope. He remembers that "the steadfast love of the LORD never ceases; his mercies never come to an end" (v. 22). This one great truth—the faithful love of the Lord—halts his slide into the pit of despair and gives him hope.

Once he looks heavenward and contemplates the situation from God's perspective, the author sees both righteous punishment for sin and merciful redemption. God had warned Judah that the consequences of her sin would be punishment and exile. But the nation had responded by ridiculing and imprisoning God's messenger, Jeremiah. Thus, the author of Lamentations knows that their punishment was just. He also knows, however, that if the people repent and return to the Lord, even now he will rescue and redeem them.

He reminds the people of God's goodness and the certainty of his salvation: "The LORD is good to those who wait for him, to the soul who seeks him. It is good that one should wait quietly for the salvation of the LORD" (vv. 25–26). While most of us will not live through the siege and destruction of a city, we too need the faithful love of the Lord amid all the small calamities and large disasters of our lives. And with Jeremiah, we too can proclaim, "Great is your faithfulness" (v. 23)—and with far deeper meaning, for we have seen this faithfulness take on flesh and blood on our behalf (John 1:14).

JULY 7 · EZEKIEL 2-3

Telling Good News to Bad People

KERI FOLMAR

EZEKIEL LAY ON his face, having just seen the likeness of the glory of the Lord. After this extraordinary experience, God commissions the prophet in chapters 2 and 3. Ezekiel's call is a difficult one: he must proclaim God's words of lamentation and woe to a nation of rebels who will not turn away from their sin.

Notice God's word and his Spirit working together in this passage. God commands Ezekiel to stand, but Ezekiel does not stand and hear God's word until enabled by the Spirit. The Spirit sets him on his feet (Ezek. 2:2). Ezekiel did not have the ability to obey God's word without the Spirit. We, likewise, do not have the ability to obey God's word without the power of his Spirit. But, oh! What power *with* the Spirit. The same power that raised Jesus from the dead now works within us to enable our obedience (Rom. 7:6; 8:4; Eph. 1:19). With our Bibles and the Holy Spirit, we have all we need to live a godly life (2 Pet. 1:3).

God asks Ezekiel to eat a scroll full of his words. Surprisingly, the scroll, although full of woe, is as sweet as honey. The prophet accepts God's word and God's providence as sweet. He fills his stomach with it (Ezek. 2:8–3:3). We too are invited to fill ourselves with the word of God, nourished by its fortifying sustenance and letting its sweetness linger in our minds. "You are what you eat." When the word of God nourishes us, our mouth is opened with wisdom, our work is enabled, and our hearts are transformed. We become like the Author as we receive his words in our hearts and hear it with our ears (3:10). Similarly, we should accept all of God's providences as sweet, as they are sent for our good and God's glory to conform us to the likeness of the Son (Rom. 8:28–29). God knows how best to accomplish his purposes.

Ezekiel was given hard words to say to hostile people. He was to warn the wicked as well as the righteous, whether they listened or not. Just like Ezekiel, we are responsible for speaking God's word to both the wicked and the righteous. Yet the news we proclaim today doesn't stop with the bad but includes good news of great joy! Jesus has come (as anticipated throughout the prophets). He died and took God's punishment for rebels who would not listen, turning them into his friends.

Ezekiel heard bad news and was willing to proclaim it. How much more should we be willing to proclaim the good news of Jesus that we ourselves have heard and received!

JULY 8 · EZEKIEL 11:14–25

The Love That Will Not Let Go

BRYAN CHAPELL

THIS PASSAGE CONCLUDES one of the saddest accounts in the Bible: the departure of God's glory from the temple of Israel due to the people's unrelenting idolatry and sin. Many consequences of the people's rebellion have already been experienced; they have been scattered among the nations and sent into exile (Ezek. 11:16). Yet, despite this discipline for their sin, God keeps reassuring his people of his faithfulness and love.

He reminds them that he himself has been a sanctuary for them, despite their exiled distance from the physical temple (v. 16). He promises that one day he will gather the people from their scattered existence and return them to the Promised Land (v. 17). He promises to provide his Spirit to make hearts tender toward him (v. 19). Finally, God sends the prophet Ezekiel to live among the exiles and tell them of the hope that is theirs (vv. 24–25).

These spoken assurances of God's continuing care for his rebellious people are remarkable. However, no evidence of grace is more striking than the stages of the departure of the glory of God (represented here by the cherubim chariot in v. 22) from the temple. This passage concludes the three-stage process of the removal of God's glory—the same "Shekinah" glory that had led the nation from slavery, filled the tabernacle and temple at their dedications, and rested upon the ark of the covenant as a perpetual testament of God's dwelling among his people.

This glory represented not only the presence of God but also his heart of such great love for his people that he would make his dwelling among them. Now that glory departs from the people due to their rebellion, but the departure is not without obvious signs of God's grief for his people's departure from him.

In its first stage of departure, the glory moves from the Most Holy Place to the threshold of the sanctuary (10:3–5). In the next stage, the glory moves to the east gate of the temple courts (10:18–19). Finally, the glory that represents the heart of God for his people moves beyond the city to the mountain east of the city (where the Messiah will also return one day—see Zech. 14:4).

God's departure is not cold or callous; he lingers over his people. Like a parent leaving the airport after a child has departed for college, God keeps turning back. Even his staged departure is evidence of his love—a love that culminates in the provision of Jesus, who reflects God's infinite glory indwelling, and never departing from, his people (2 Cor. 4:6).

JULY 9 · EZEKIEL 18

Turn and Live

ZACK ESWINE

OPEN A BOOK that you have not read and turn to its middle chapters. Start reading. What will you likely find? Confusion. Why? Because, you neither know how the book started nor what led its storyline to this point. Some books, however, offer summary chapters. A reader is fortunate if she starts in the middle of a story and by chance lands upon one. This Ezekiel passage offers such a fortunate middle. Here you have the gospel summarized in the Old Testament.

To begin, this passage exalts the centrality of God. God is present. He speaks, listens, and engages us (Ezek. 18:1–4). He also commands, takes issue with ways of life that run contrary to his convictions, and declares justice and mercy. God wants people to love him and to love each other (vv. 5–8). We love him by having no other gods but him (v. 6). We love each other by our respect for marriage and sex, by our unwillingness to oppress another human being, by our protecting rather than stealing from one another, by our aversion to murder and violence, and by how we handle money with integrity and use our resources sacrificially to advocate for those who have none (vv. 6–18).

Next, this passage exposes fallen people. Families damage one another. Neighbors hurt each other. To account for this, people create their own proverbs to navigate life (v. 2). For example, if a parent sins, the child is stained and must pay for the parent's mess. In reverse, if a child sins, the parent must pay for the child's sins (vv. 19, 20).

But God's wisdom differs. Individual souls belong to him (v. 4). Those who turn toward God's convictions on the basis of God's forgiveness find new life. Those who turn from God and against neighbor, will be judged accordingly and die (v. 30). So God earnestly pleads with us. He takes no pleasure in judgment that leads to death for anyone, even death of the wicked (vv. 23, 32). Mercy and love forge his desire for us. And his judgment is not mean. It says, "enough!" to those who sin against God and their neighbors. It therefore defends those who are victimized, as well as the repentant.

No wonder, then, that Jesus, the Lamb who takes away sins, started his first sermon with "the kingdom of God is at hand; repent and believe in the gospel" (Mark 1:14–15). No wonder, too, that he died as a judged soul so that you can receive the welcome of a pardoned one. He rose to new life so that you can leave the old one. Our ruin is not God's goal. "Why will you die?" the Lord beckons. "Turn, and live!" (Ezek. 18:31–32)

God Rescues His Flock

CAROLYN MCCULLEY

THIS PROPHECY IN Ezekiel denounces the rulers of Israel who have lived large at the expense of the people, feeding themselves but not caring for the weak, sick, and lost of their communities. Using the metaphor of a shepherd, Ezekiel says these leaders have been enriching themselves from the flock, not tending to it, and he rebukes them for it.

Unfortunately, selfish shepherds still exist today. Many in the flock have been hurt by leaders who have exploited the trust, finances, and support of their church members. Others have been fed twisted teaching instead of the complete word of God. When spiritual abuse happens, people tend to withdraw from God and his church. Wounded sheep, they become cynical and distrustful.

God has a message for those who have been hurt by deceptive shepherds: "Behold, I am against the shepherds, and I will require my sheep at their hand and put a stop to their feeding the sheep. No longer shall the shepherds feed themselves. I will rescue my sheep from their mouths, that they may not be food for them" (Ezek. 34:10). He does not approve of their behavior, nor will he tolerate it. He promises to intervene, and he will take this on himself: "I, I myself will search for my sheep and will seek them out" (v. 11).

If you have withdrawn from fellowship with other believers because you have been hurt by exploitative leaders, the Lord has a comforting word about pursuing you in your isolation. He will not leave you to fend on your own: "I will seek the lost, and I will bring back the strayed, and I will bind up the injured, and I will strengthen the weak, and the fat and the strong I will destroy. I will feed them in justice" (v. 16). He is so serious about this that he concludes this rebuke with the most solemn oath that can be uttered: "I am the LORD; I have spoken" (v. 24). He is the One who spoke the entire universe into being; there is no higher authority than his own word.

This prophecy is fulfilled in the Messiah, Jesus Christ. Jesus is the ultimate embodiment of the good shepherd of Psalm 23: "He makes me lie down in green pastures. He leads me beside still waters. He restores my soul. He leads me in paths of righteousness for his name's sake" (vv. 2–3; see John 10:1–18). Jesus will lead you to righteous fellowship, to pastures that nourish you, and he will restore your soul. He will not leave you weak, sick, and lost. He will preserve his flock. "You are my sheep, human sheep of my pasture, and I am your God, declares the Lord God" (Ezek. 34:31). Sweeter words than these can never be heard.

JULY 11 · EZEKIEL 36:16-38

The Lord's Concern for His Holy Name

KRISTEN WETHERELL

NO ONE LIKES to be misrepresented. Whether through malicious slander or through misunderstanding, when someone fails to represent us properly, we can feel violated. There are certain truths about ourselves that we want upheld, and it bothers us—even enrages us—when they are not. How much more is this true of our holy God, the only one whose character and ways are perfect and who alone is worthy of worship?

In this passage God speaks to Ezekiel about a problem, makes an incredible promise, and restates his ultimate purpose, all in relation to his concern for his holy name.

The problem lies with Israel, who has brought shame upon God's name through its rebellion and subsequent exile (vv. 17, 20, 23), and with Israel's enemies, who have irreverently rejected God (v. 23). The people's sin results in the profaning of his name—but, rather than rejecting his people forever, as their sin deserves (v. 18), God mercifully includes them in an incredible promise.

God promises to take his people out of exile (v. 24), to cleanse them from sin (v. 25), to rebuild their land (vv. 33–35), and to give them his Spirit in order to change their desires and ways (vv. 26–27). *God* will do this, apart from anything his people have done or deserved; it will be a free gift "for the sake of [his] holy name" (v. 22).

This clearing and upholding of his name is God's ultimate purpose. In fact, this purpose grounds the whole of Ezekiel's prophecy: "Then they will know that I am the LORD" (v. 38). God states this more than twenty times throughout the book. God's name is wrapped up with his dealing with human sin and his fulfillment of his promises; we are completely lost and without hope, unable to change our situation or save ourselves, unless he acts. This is why the coming of Jesus Christ is so amazing; he is God's way of dealing with our sin once and for all (John 3:16), making good on God's promise to give his people new hearts (John 3:3) and ultimately upholding his holy name for all eternity (John 17:1–2). Salvation brings God honor and glory!

Ezekiel's prophecy runs against the grain of much of western Christian culture, whose version of Christianity has become "me, and the God who helps me." Although our salvation certainly involves us and benefits us, we are reminded that it is all about God, for the sake of his holy name. "From him and through him and to him are all things. To him be glory forever. Amen" (Rom. 11:36). We are wrapped up in a magnificent purpose!

JULY 12 · EZEKIEL 37:1-14

Overturning Death

ELIZABETH W. D. GROVES

NOTHING IS IMPOSSIBLE for God. Not even overturning death. In Ezekiel's vision, what he saw was not bodies that had been without a heartbeat for sixty seconds or without oxygen for five minutes, so that there might be some hope of resuscitation. The bodies in his vision had long since rotted away or been scavenged by wild animals. The bones themselves had been exposed to the elements until every bit of flesh was long gone. Can you imagine such bodies living again? It's almost a macabre thought.

Ezekiel acknowledged that God alone determines what is possible (Ezek. 37:3). God declared that he would bring those bodies back to life, and that's exactly what he did, breathing life into them just as in Genesis 2. Why? So that they would know he was the Lord, who can even overturn death.

Israel in exile was, as a nation, as hopeless as those dried-out bones, yet God brought them out of their graves (Ezek. 37:12–13), restored them to life against all odds, like the mighty army of verse 10, and returned them to their own land. God had a purpose for Israel, to bring hope to the nations, and he would not let that purpose fail. The covenant keeping God restored life to his exiled people to fulfill that purpose and so that they would know he was the Lord (v. 14)—who can even overturn death.

Jesus lay dead in the grave for three days, and no doubt his disciples were as confused and hopeless during that time as anyone has ever been on this planet. Yet God the Father, impossibly, raised him to life, breaking the power of death itself.

All of us are born dead in sin until the Holy Spirit breathes life into us and causes us to be "born again to a living hope" (1 Pet. 1:3). There is probably no more astonishing miracle than that spiritual rebirth. Then the Holy Spirit sets about the process of forming us into the image of Christ, so that his body, the church, becomes "an exceedingly great army" (Ezek. 37:10), called to battle evil and injustice and to bring his shalom to the world. And as we are united with Jesus, death's power over *us* is broken too! Its sting is gone. We don't fear it, because we know it is simply our entrance into glorious life with him.

We all experience "death" of many kinds—the loss of hopes, dreams, relationships, loved ones, our own physical life—but Jesus's resurrection guarantees the hope of the abundant life he came to bring to his people. *Nothing* is impossible for the Lord, not even overturning death.

JULY 13 · DANIEL 2

Compassionate, Humble, and Bold

JONI EARECKSON TADA

COSMOPOLITAN MAGAZINE would have sold well in Babylon. In the ancient world, it was the New York City of style, opulence, beauty, and astrology. Our society isn't that different. On my way to work this morning, I counted three houses with the "Psychic Reader" sign out front. And this evening, a TV commercial came on for the *California Psychic Hotline*. Creepy. Like Babylon, our society is fast, affluent, and enamored with new-age mysticism.

This is why Daniel is so relevant today. Chapter 2 is an amazing account of how a believer should live amid an idolatrous, sensual culture where the latest astrological reading is the hot topic of the party.

Nebuchadnezzar has a bizarre dream, and he demands that his astrologers not only interpret it but also recount it. And if they can't, it's "off with their heads!" In response, Daniel shows deep concern, not only for himself and his friends but also for hundreds of others who are about to be cut into pieces. He *cares* about the society in which he lives, and he's not about to let fanaticism destroy an entire strata of Babylonian society.

This is a model for how we should relate to the people of *our* day. For it is Daniel's exemplary character that gains him favor; the king's official is about to spread terror, but Daniel stops him with tactful, wise words (Dan. 2:14). Given a reprieve, Daniel then urges his friends to pray diligently, demonstrating his utter dependence on God (v. 18). Daniel shows tremendous compassion toward the magicians and astrologers who are about to lose their lives; he pleads on their behalf because he knows the king's edict is unjust (v. 24). He is humble before the king and careful to give glory to God for what he is about to say (vv. 27–28). (And how did Daniel finally arrive upon the details of the dream and its interpretation? Note that he devoted 90 percent of his prayer to praising the greatness of God's name [vv. 20–23].)

Daniel does not mince words before the most powerful man on earth but boldly unveils God's awesome plans. And what is God's plan for the ages, after all earthly kingdoms fail? "The God of heaven will set up a kingdom that shall never be destroyed" (v. 44). The stone described in verse 45 is none other than Christ, on whom the church is built (Eph. 2:19–22).

The lesson for us in today's society? Tact and reason will take you far. When threatened, depend wholly on God. Enlist the prayer support of others. Then, be humble but don't mince words: boldly proclaim the Rock of your salvation.

Living in Fire

JOSEPH P. MURPHY

NEBUCHADNEZZAR'S SELF-AGGRANDIZEMENT, and the complaint against the Jews for their failure to bow to his gold statue, exhibit typical human behavior. His behavior is by no means the worst we could cite, even in our own day. At least he acknowledges God (Dan. 3:28; 4:34–37). But he displays an insecurity matching his ego, requiring everyone—with great public fanfare—to pay homage to the statue.

Idolatry is involved whenever humanity places itself in the position of God, attributing glory, honor, and majesty to itself. In a day or place where religion is closely tied to politics, any expression of religion apart from that of the political power might be viewed as treason, as it was by Nebuchadnezzar.

How likely was it that Shadrach, Meshach, and Abednego would survive that blazing fire? It was about as likely as a man being raised from the dead, permanently, never to die again. Yet that is at the heart of the Christian faith, for in raising Jesus from the dead, God declared him to be his Son (Rom. 1:4). Similar resurrection is promised to all who place their faith in Christ (John 11:25). Likewise, the book of Daniel not only reveals the fact of future resurrection (Dan. 12:2), but here it reveals that the redeemed of the Lord will dwell with him, the one who is a consuming fire (Deut. 4:24; Heb. 12:29). Such miracles are not often repeated but have been recounted here to provide an anchor for faith in our God, our future, and our true identity. A sword ablaze was the last thing seen by humanity exiting the garden of Eden (Gen. 3:24). Humanity was made to live with God, but now that sin has come into the world, God's presence poses a threat to us. But by the grace of Christ, those who trust and obey him shall be like him when he comes (1 John 3:2), an end that Nebuchadnezzar seems to have glimpsed in the blazing kiln: *four* figures, alive!

For these three ancient Jews, that end of resurrection in God's glory had not yet been revealed. Consequently, they teach us much, for they were settled in their faith. Even if God did not save them, they would still live so as to worship only the God of Israel (Dan. 3:18). Obviously, to so choose without thought of eternal life means they were thinking not of themselves but of God. He alone is worthy of all the honor we can show him in life, to the point of giving life itself for him. For Jesus Christ has given his life for us (Mark 10:45).

JULY 15 · DANIEL 4

Pride and Humility

KAREN S. LORITTS

"NOW I, NEBUCHADNEZZAR, praise and extol and honor the King of heaven, for all his works are right and his ways are just; and those who walk in pride he is able to humble" (Dan. 4:37). The pathway to spiritual transformation is often hard. King Nebuchadnezzar found it to be costly and humbling.

In the preceding chapters of Daniel, we find the pagan king of Babylon ambitious to build a mighty kingdom. Nebuchadnezzar commands his subjects, including the Hebrew exiles, to yield to Babylonian culture and pay homage to its pagan gods. But Nebuchadnezzar's admiration and respect for uncompromising, humble Hebrews such as Daniel and his friends gives him pause. He has just witnessed Shadrach, Meshach, and Abednego being rescued by God from the fiery furnace. The king acknowledges that "there is no other god who is able to rescue in this way" (3:29). But as the powerful, willful king relishes the prosperity of his kingdom, the shadow of pride follows him. He is conflicted.

And yet as chapter 4 begins we see glimmers of a spiritual transformation in his life. The king is terrified by a second dream. Daniel is again summoned to interpret, and the news is not good. Nebuchadnezzar's authority and kingdom will be greatly reduced. Furthermore, he will be drastically humbled, until he knows "that the Most High rules the kingdom of men and gives it to whom he will" (4:25). But even with the impending doom, God provides a way of escape if Nebuchadnezzar will simply reform his life (v. 27). The king refuses, once more boasting in his kingdom (v. 30).

Here we have a prideful king, claiming to have built his kingdom by his own hands, facing humiliation and ruin when the King of heaven extends mercy as a way of escape. The truth is that swift repentance quickens reconciliation with God. Yet King Nebuchadnezzar continues his "walk of pride" for the next twelve months. He forgets what he has witnessed in the lives of the Hebrews, and how God works on behalf of those who trust him (Prov. 21:1). Sadly, he resists the life-giving, pride-destroying path of repentance, and his nightmarish dream comes true.

At the end of God's appointed time of judgment, however, Nebuchadnezzar comes to his senses, acknowledges his sin, looks heavenward, and worships the Most High (Dan. 4:34–37). He is restored and gains even greater renown. The story of Nebuchadnezzar is an Old Testament example of a crucial theme throughout the Bible, one that Jesus himself will emphasize: God humbles the proud and exalts the humble (Luke 18:14). This powerful king, who had destroyed Jerusalem and persecuted God's people, was humbled by God's grace and brought to confess God's mercy.

JULY 16 · DANIEL 6

Daniel and the Lions' Den

GLENNA MARSHALL

IF SOMEONE DEVISED a plan to get you into trouble, would your faithfulness to God be something he or she could use against you? What does it say about a person that the most consistent thing about her is her devotion to God?

Daniel was a faithful follower of Yahweh. Even though he lived most of his life as an exile far from Jerusalem, Daniel worshiped God and devoted himself to prayer daily. His excellence of character led to his receiving an honored position as an official under King Darius, who planned to put Daniel in charge of the entire kingdom.

This caused other leaders and government officials to become jealous and seek to remove Daniel from his high position. But they soon realized that the only thing they could possibly use against him was his utter devotion to God. They convinced Darius to prohibit prayer to anyone other than the king for thirty days. Whoever ignored this decree would be thrown into a den of lions. The edict was irrevocable, since in Medo-Persian governance a king could not renege on his edict without shaming himself. His word was law.

"When Daniel knew that the document had been signed, he went to his house. . . . He got down on his knees three times a day and prayed and gave thanks before his God, as he had done previously" (v. 10). Daniel knew about the new law, yet he faithfully kept his habits of prayer just as he always had—and just as the other leaders knew he would. These men gleefully turned Daniel in, reminding Darius of the consequences of Daniel's actions.

Grieved, Darius sent Daniel to the lions' den and appealed for Daniel's God to save him. The king neither ate nor slept all night, running to see about Daniel's fate early the next morning. The Lord had kept Daniel safe, a miracle that led the king to write a new edict declaring that all people should fear "the living God" (v. 26).

Daniel's night in the lions' den points to the greater prophet, Jesus Christ, who would suffer death because of his faithfulness to his heavenly Father yet would be raised from the dead by that same Father. His faithfulness, suffering, and vindication become ours as we are joined to him in faith. And when we walk after him in new obedience, we begin a life of faithfulness like Daniel's. Daniel's faithfulness was shaped by prayer. Is your devotion to Christ known to those around you? Today is the day to proclaim with your habits and priorities that Jesus your Rescuer is your very life!

Undeserved Mercy and a Call to Great Love

LEE TANKERSLEY

WHEN THE PHARISEES complained about Jesus letting a "sinful woman" touch his feet, anointing them with oil, he noted that this woman loved much because she had been forgiven much, just as those who are forgiven little, love little (Luke 7:47). In light of that declaration, some of us may assume that we are doomed to love little. We might not feel, after all, that our sins are of the same magnitude as those of this "sinful woman." However, the picture of our sin against the Lord in Hosea 1:1–11 shatters that misconception.

In this first chapter, Hosea is commanded to take a wife who will be adulterous, unfaithful to her marriage covenant (Hos. 1:2). The result is that when Gomer conceives and bears her second and third children, these children are likely the product of her adulterous unions. Consequently, the children bear the names "No Mercy" (v. 6) and "Not My People" (v. 9). It is a terrible, heartbreaking picture of adultery and its consequences.

Yet the events of this story are by design. After all, it was God who commanded Hosea to take a wife who would be adulterous (v. 2), and it was God who gave Hosea the names that he assigned to the children (vv. 6, 9). God called Hosea to this difficult task because he was displaying the sin of his people, Israel, who, by "forsaking the LORD" (v. 2), were committing spiritual adultery. This was a picture of Israel's sin.

Before we sit in judgment on Israel, however, we must realize that they are a picture of all of humanity, as we by nature prefer to worship the creation rather than our Creator (Rom. 1:25). We all have rebelled against our God and thus have been unfaithful, committing spiritual adultery against the One to whom we owe all devotion.

However, the Lord promised great mercy toward his undeserving people, telling Hosea, "In the place where it was said to them, 'You are not my people,' it shall be said to them, 'Children of the living God'" (Hos. 1:10).

This great promise has fallen on us whose faith is in Christ. We who have proven ourselves spiritual adulterers are now part of Christ's cleansed bride. We who were not his people are now "members of his body" (Eph. 5:30). We who were in great need of mercy, and deserved none, have become the objects of God's merciful forgiveness and grace. The reality is that none of us is doomed to love little, for we have all been forgiven much. Let us then devote ourselves in love to the One who loved us when we had fallen far short of loving him.

JULY 18 · HOSEA 6

Repentance

SUSAN HUNT

WE READ HOSEA 1 and ask, "How could she?" We come to Hosea 3 and, wonder, "Why would he?" Then, by God's grace, we realize that we are the unfaithful ones and God is the relentless Lover of our souls. Chapter 3 should conclude, "And they lived happily ever after." Gratitude should propel us to be a faithful bride to our heavenly bridegroom. But we continue to scandalously stray. A major theme of Hosea is our need for repentance.

The narrative provides a vivid contrast between true and false repentance. Chapter 5 concludes with a tutorial on repentance (Hos. 5:15). Chapter 6 begins with a call to repentance. The blessings of repentance are breathtaking (Hos. 6:1–3): God will heal, bind, revive, raise up—but rather than turn to the Lord, Israel turns away (vv. 4–11). There is no fruit of repentance. Their love is shallow and short-lived. They do not forsake their sin or seek the Lord.

Gospel repentance is deep and daily. It goes to the darkest places in our hearts and grieves over our sinful condition and our specific sins. It does not just acknowledge the consequences of sin; it sorrows over the guilt of sin. True repentance cries with the psalmist, "Turn my eyes from looking at worthless things" (Ps. 119:37), and with the tax collector, "God, be merciful to me, a sinner!" (Luke 18:13).

Like Adam (Hos. 6:7) we are covenant breakers, but God is a covenant keeper. After the first man and woman sinned, God did not forsake them. He gave the gospel promise to provide a Redeemer (Gen. 3:15), binding himself to them in covenant faithfulness. When Adam heard the promise, he named his wife Eve, which means life-giver (Gen. 3:20).

Gomer shows us what we become when we go our own way. Yet Hosea sticks by Gomer, giving us a picture of God's love for us. The book of Hosea ultimately shows us that, if we are in Christ, he never leaves us to self-destruct.

The story of Hosea and Gomer tells the grand story of the triune God's sovereign, transforming, and ultimately triumphant love for his church. His love will not let us settle for counterfeit repentance. His emotion-packed response to our unfaithfulness is, "How can I give you up?" (Hos. 11:8). His Spirit presses hard until we submit and ask him to turn us back. The grace of repentance radically liberates us to see our sin and his mercy, to hate and forsake our sin and to turn in renewed faith and obedience to our Rescuer. Gospel repentance transforms God's daughters from life-takers to life-givers, from Gomer to glory (2 Cor. 3:18).

JULY 19 · HOSEA 11:1–12:1

He Will Not Abandon Us

BRYAN CHAPELL

MATTHEW USES THIS passage in his Gospel in a way that surprises us. He says that when Jesus, Mary, and Joseph fled to Egypt to escape the wrath of King Herod (Matthew 2), that journey led to a fulfillment of Hosea 11:1: "Out of Egypt I called my son" (see Matt. 2:15). Our difficulty lies in the fact that Hosea is not referring to the Messiah returning from Egypt; he is referring to the nation of Israel. Was Matthew wrong?

The answer must be no, and the explanation lies in remembering that God referred to the nation of Israel as "my firstborn son" when commanding Pharaoh to release the Hebrews from slavery (Ex. 4:22–23). God's people are as precious to him as his own child; he even refers to them as having the identity of his son. In this way, the nation becomes a symbol of God's care, and much of what happens to Israel becomes symbolic of what God will do through the ultimate representation of his care, Jesus Christ.

The message to us should be even more plain: if God cares enough about sinful and wayward people like the Israelites to give them the identity of his son, then he also cares for us who have the identity of Christ by virtue of his grace.

Though it may be hard for us to conceptualize, when we become believers, our old identity—which was characterized by sin and shame before God—dies. In place of that identity, we now possess the identity of Christ (Gal. 2:20). He took our sin on himself, so that we might have his righteousness (2 Cor. 5:17, 21). We are now as precious to God as Jesus is, because we have his identifying characteristics (1 John 3:1).

A simple illustration of what it means for believers to have the identity of Christ was given long ago. A Christian wrote of God giving every believer a special mirror. On one side of the mirror is a natural reflection showing all our flaws. But on the other side of the mirror is the image of Jesus Christ. And, when God looks at us, he chooses to see us from the Jesus side of the mirror—identifying us as his own child.

This is very similar to what Hosea is saying. Even though the nation of Israel has sinned and been unfaithful to their Lord, God declares that he will not forsake them. He sees them as his own child and loves them! Though they will face his discipline, they will not face his rejection, because they are his. His heart "recoils" at the notion of abandoning them and his "compassion grows warm and tender" (Hos. 11:8). So also is God's love for us. Though he has every reason to abandon us in response to our sin, he refuses to forsake us because we have the identity of his child.

A Plea to Return to the Lord

KRISTEN WETHERELL

IF YOU ARE a parent, you know what it is like to be sinned against by your child. You also likely know when your child feels genuine sorrow. There is a difference between an apathetic "I'm sorry" and a tenderhearted "I was wrong," between regret over sin's consequences and sadness over sin (2 Cor. 7:10).

Hosea's prophecy ends with a call for God's child, Israel, to pursue the latter: genuine repentance for sin, with the promise of God's healing mercy and steadfast love. The whole book culminates in this final plea, encouraging us with the fact that even the most wayward sinner can receive forgiveness and reconciliation with God.

What does genuine repentance look like? Hosea tells Israel what God yearns for the nation to do: "Return, O Israel, to the LORD your God" (v. 1). Hosea's Spirit-given plea teaches us the life-giving nature of repentance; it is not a mere obligation but a holy opportunity. It is not a begrudging practice but a beneficial privilege.

First, genuine repentance involves identifying and owning our sin (vv. 1, 3). Unless a doctor diagnoses a specific ailment, the remedy remains obscure. When we confess sin in generalities, we miss a chance to see how God has particularly been gracious to us. As Israel confesses her idolatry (v. 3) in all the ways she has been faithless to God and received his discipline, God promises to be faithful to Israel and to bless his people, to "heal their apostasy" and "love them freely" (v. 4)—satisfying them (v. 5), flourishing them (vv. 6–7), and protecting them (vv. 7–8). We too ought to confess specific sins and enjoy the blessing of remembering God's specific character and promises.

Second, genuine repentance involves rediscovering God's mercy (v. 3). Jesus Christ is God's only begotten Son, the one who never sinned yet took our punishment. In every way that Israel was bent on turning away from God (11:7), Jesus walked uprightly and aimed to please his Father.

Nevertheless, God's just anger toward sin did not turn from Jesus (v. 4) but was laid upon him at the cross. For those who have trusted in Jesus Christ for forgiveness of sins, we can remember and rejoice in God's eternal pardon of forgiveness (v. 2), his acceptance of us in Christ (v. 2), and the peace we now enjoy with God (v. 4), knowing that his anger has forever turned from us.

What a motivation to repent and return to the Lord!

JULY 21 · JOEL 2

Return to the Lord

JONI EARECKSON TADA

TIMES WERE GOOD during the early reign of Joash, the young king of Judah. There were grapes, apples, grain, wine, and oil in abundance, and also herds of cattle and sheep. The people of God lived in security and prosperity. But after the high priest Jehoiada died, things began to go downhill. Priests of Baal and other bad characters now came out of their holes. Joash and his people fell under their bewitching influence, broke their covenant with God, and opted for a life of ease and luxury.

Enter Joel, God's man for the hour, with this soul-shaking message to these comfortable, affluent, and spiritually unfaithful people. Almost overnight, the abundance of the land was decimated. Joel's thundering message was, "Awake, you drunkards, and weep, and wail, all you drinkers of wine, because of the sweet wine, for it is cut off from your mouth" (Joel 1:5). God snatched back his own wine and oil, which was being used for the worship of Baal, and he sent legions of insects and locusts to devour and destroy the corn and grapes—with the Lord himself at the head of this formidable army.

Such images can sound archaic and antiquated. We console ourselves, thinking, *God wouldn't do such a thing nowadays. Besides, we're not idol worshipers.* Or are we? Who or what gets most of our time? Takes up most of our thinking? When the Spirit whispers, *Turn off the Food Network and spend extra time in my word,* what is our response? Think of the blessings of abundance God has given. Are we equally generous, giving others the "shirt off our back," feeding the poor, or helping someone who is homeless? Is our idea of sacrifice opting for a less expensive vacation, not dining out as often, or limiting the number of hours spent at the computer? If handed a financial windfall, do we give most of it away to kingdom causes, or does it end up widening the comfort margins of our family life? We must be honest about the way we are wired. We're not unlike the people during the time of Joel.

This is why Joel's clarion call is as relevant today as it was then: "'Yet even now,' declares the LORD, 'return to me with all your heart, with fasting, with weeping, and with mourning'" (2:12). This is a wonderful thing—God is not required to speak to us or to send us his warnings. If he *is* speaking to us, it means he has not forsaken us! And what is he saying? Turn from your ways, turn back to me, and I will bless you. In drawing us back to his heart, God will even restore the years the locusts have eaten (see v. 25). Amazing!

JULY 22 · AMOS 3

The Lion Has Roared

ERIKA ALLEN

WHEN LIFE IS GOOD, we often neglect our relationship with the Lord. We tend to think we're doing okay on our own. We don't feel our need for God as acutely as we do in times of hardship, and we aren't as sensitive to our sin. Amos ministered during a time when things were going well for Israel politically and economically. Israel not only thought they were doing okay on their own; they saw their prosperity as a sign of God's blessing. As God's chosen people, they believed he would protect them no matter what. Oblivious to their sin, they happily went about their business, awaiting the day when God would subdue their enemies and make Israel ruler of the world. Life was good!

Amos's message to Israel in chapter 3, then, comes as quite a shock. Through his prophet, God informs them that disaster is on the way—and it's coming from none other than the Lord himself, precisely because of their relationship with him (Amos 3:2). Amos uses a terrifying image to express God's coming judgment: a lion that has roared because it has spotted its prey and is about to attack (vv. 4–8).

Israel will be held accountable for two specific sins: false, ritualistic worship, and abuse of the poor (vv. 13–15). The nation's wealth has come at the expense of the needy among them, who are being heartlessly exploited and subjected to slavery (4:1; 8:4, 6)—a direct violation of God's command (Deut. 15:11). Israel believed that as long as they were performing the right religious practices, God would be pleased and would overlook their sin. But Amos says that the people's worship actually has served to "multiply transgression" (Amos 4:4–5). Far from appeasing God's anger, their sacrifices will actually ensure it.

Through her disobedience, Israel has forfeited God's protection (see Deuteronomy 27–30) and incurred his wrath (Amos 3:9–11). Verse 12 is chilling: "Thus says the LORD: 'As the shepherd rescues from the mouth of the lion two legs, or a piece of an ear, so shall the people of Israel who dwell in Samaria be rescued.'" Absolute destruction is about to befall Israel.

And yet, despite the severity of God's judgment, a glimmer of hope remains. God will spare a tiny remnant (5:3). Because of his steadfast love and faithfulness, he will yet provide the promised heir of David, through whom his people—and the entire world—will be blessed.

Scripture speaks of God again using the imagery of a lion: Jesus is the Lion who conquered our sin by being the Lamb who was slain. Though obedience is required of us no less than it was of Israel, as followers of Christ we do not fear God's punishment or his wrath. For "behold, the Lion of the tribe of Judah, the Root of David, has conquered" (Rev. 5:5).

God Wants His Family Back

CAROLYN ARENDS

THINGS ARE GOING well for Israel. Church attendance is up, and so is the economy—two seemingly obvious indicators of God's favor. The prophets have foretold a "day of the Lord," when God will judge the unjust; the Israelites can't wait for their enemies to get what's coming to them! So imagine their unhappy surprise when a herdsman-turned-prophet named Amos declares that God's coming judgment is aimed most squarely at Israel herself (Amos 5:18–20).

It turns out that, far from being an indication of God's blessing, Israel's wealth has actually come from their exploiting the poor (v. 11). Their religious observance is nothing more than an attempt to manipulate God (vv. 21–23). The coming day of the Lord can hardly be good news for such an unjust nation—one who, as God's chosen people, should know so much better. Amos predicts their impeding doom—"'I will send you into exile beyond Damascus,' says the LORD"—chillingly forecasting the Assyrian exile at a time when Assyria seems harmless (v. 27).

It's all very bad news. And yet, situated between oracles of warning, doom, and woe is an oracle of entreaty (vv. 1–17)—God pleading with his people to "Seek me and live" (v. 4). It's not too late; there's still hope for Israel, or at least for a faithful remnant. Pulsing at the heart of this passage is the reality that Philip Yancey says is the overarching story of the Bible: God wants his family back.

What would it mean for God's family to "seek him and live"? First, they would see him for who he really is—not a wish-granter on a par with pagan deities, but the Creator and Keeper of everything (vv. 8–9). Second, their right relationship with God would express itself in right relationships with people.

Rituals, offerings, and songs are just noise to God if the "worshipers" are also miscarrying justice and oppressing the poor (vv. 21–23). "How great are your sins," he laments through Amos, "you who afflict the righteous, who take a bribe, and turn aside the needy in the gate" (v. 12). God declares what he really wants in a stirring passage that has reverberated on the lips of radical justice-seekers like John Woolman and Martin Luther King Jr.: "Let justice roll down like waters, and righteousness like an ever-flowing stream" (v. 24).

This is God's dream for his people: inexhaustible justice and righteousness. How is his family doing today? Do justice and righteousness characterize our lives? Or do we confuse wealth and religiosity for right relationship? It's never too late to "seek him and live." Through Christ, the way is open. God always wants his family back.

JULY 24 · AMOS 9

We Are Always His

KATHLEEN CHAPELL

ONE OF OUR children's favorite books is Margaret Wise Brown's *The Runaway Bunny*. As you turn page after page, you hear a little bunny devise a number of plans by which he would run away from his patient mother—and she continues to explain how she will not let him go: "I will become a little boy and run into a house," he finally threatens, but she assures him, "I will become your mother, and catch you in my arms, and hug you." At last the little bunny gives up: "Shucks," he says, "I might just as well stay where I am and be your little bunny."

In Amos 9, the Lord speaks to his people of his unrelenting love, but he speaks in a much stronger—and rather scary—tone to his wandering children. The Israelites have fallen into deep sin and idolatry. The prophet tells of God's impending judgment: "If they dig into Sheol," warns the Lord, "from there my hand shall take them; if they climb up to heaven, from there I will bring them down" (Amos 9:2). The people might try to hide in heaven or hell, on the highest mountain or the deepest sea, but God will find them!

And yet God's ultimate purpose in judgment is not destruction, but restoration. Verse 8 turns the tone from anger to provision: "I will not utterly destroy the house of Jacob, declares the LORD." Indeed, the line of Jacob—that sinful, broken hero—will be preserved as the Lord continues to work his plan of restoration and salvation. The Lord promises to restore his people. He will never stop pursuing his beloved. Like the glad father running to meet and embrace the Prodigal Son in Luke 15, God will never cease to love and welcome his erring child.

In a beautiful parallel of this relentless love the Lord has for his children, the psalmist reflects on his faithful Father: "Where shall I go from your Spirit? Or where shall I flee from your presence? If I ascend to heaven, you are there! If I make my bed in Sheol, you are there! If I take the wings of the morning and dwell in the uttermost parts of the sea, even there your hand shall lead me, and your right hand shall hold me" (Ps. 139:7–10).

Our Lord shows us both sides of the same coin: the strength and power of the Lord pursuing and disciplining his sinful and rebellious people; and the heavenly Father of those children, always present, always caring, always redeeming his own. His children may seek to hide from him, may flee to heights and depths, in schemes and broken promises and relationships, but he will still pursue us, still love us, still catch us in his arms and hold us.

JULY 25 · OBADIAH

Judgment and Blessing

ELIZABETH W. D. GROVES

THROUGHOUT THE OLD Testament we see that God was grieved by sin— the sin lodged in his own people's hearts, and the sin of his enemies. In faithfulness to his covenant promises, he sometimes judged and punished his people for their sin, always with the goal of turning their hearts back to him and restoring them so that they could become a blessing to the nations. Often, he used other nations to judge and purify Israel. However, when those nations were overzealous in doing so, the Lord then judged them in turn. Edom was one such nation, and the book of

Obadiah foretells the judgment that would fall on Edom because of its harsh treatment of Israel.

Does Obadiah therefore teach that "those who hurt us will get zapped"? No, not so simply. There are many things that remain the same today as they were at the time of Obadiah, but the life, death, and resurrection of Jesus shed a new and surprising light on many Old Testament realities, and we have to understand them through our union with him.

What remains the same as in Obadiah's time? First, God's fiery judgment still looms for his enemies. Second, God still hates sin in his people. The cross shows us just how much God hates sin. Sometimes even those who claim Christ's name commit heinous sins against others, and when they do, it grieves him. The Holy Spirit teaches us to increasingly grieve over our own sin, and he still sanctifies us (transforms us to be more like our Lord), sometimes even allowing us to experience wrongs at the hands of others as part of that process.

What has *changed* since the coming of Jesus? First, "God's people" are no longer biological, ethnic Israel, but rather all those who flee to him for forgiveness through the atoning blood of Jesus, and who are united to him by faith. Gentiles are welcomed in, at last fulfilling God's long-standing promise to bless all nations. Second, God himself, in the person of Jesus, has borne the judgment for his people's sin. This is astonishing. Judgment no longer hangs over our heads, since he bore it in full. Third, surprisingly, when others do us wrong, we are called to forgive and to bless them!

Although fierce judgment still awaits those who refuse to come to Jesus for forgiveness, one day *there will be no more sin* (Revelation 21). For those who are in Christ, judgment is past, and a glorious kingdom of blessing stands ahead (Obad. 21b), purchased and guaranteed by his death.

The Goodness and Greatness of Our God

LEE TANKERSLEY

THOSE OF US who grew up with Christian parents may have recited a blessing around the dinner table that began, "God is great. God is good." We likely uttered such blessings during a time when our greatest frustrations revolved around early bedtimes and eating our vegetables. And just as that blessing may have faded from our minds, so have the days long gone when our troubles were so light. Now we likely find our fears revolving around the struggles of raising our children well, caring for our elderly parents, or simply living with a constant reminder of death. Yet, as much as our troubles may have changed with the passing of time, our need to anchor our souls with the reminder of God's goodness and greatness hasn't changed. This is why Jonah 1 should be a source of great encouragement for us.

In this first chapter of Jonah, the greatness of God's sovereign control is on display. After Jonah runs from God, we are told that God "hurled a great wind upon the sea" (Jonah 1:4), stopped the raging sea once Jonah was thrown in (v. 15), and "appointed a great fish to swallow up Jonah" (v. 17). None of these events happened by chance. In his sovereignty, God was directing every element in the story to bring about his good purpose of sending Jonah to the Ninevites. We see clearly in this chapter the greatness of our God.

Yet it is not merely the greatness of God's sovereignty that shines forth in these events, but also his goodness and love. Jonah did not want to go to the Ninevites, as their wickedness was well known. But God was aware of far more atrocities committed by these people than Jonah had known, and God's personal offense at their evils was much greater than anything Jonah had felt. Yet, unlike Jonah, God did not distance himself from the Ninevites but eagerly extended to them his mercy and compassion. He exercised his sovereign control in these events so that, in love, he might show his goodness to a people who had made themselves his enemies. Such love, Paul tells us, "surpasses knowledge" (Eph. 3:19).

Therefore, as we are weighed down by the struggles of our lives today, we can remind ourselves again that our God is great, and he is good. As in the days of Jonah, he still controls the events of our world and lovingly directs them toward his good purposes. Should we ever doubt this, we can remember that years after Jonah, God again demonstrated his goodness and greatness as he sent his Son to a people who were his enemies so that, by his death and resurrection, we might become his children.

JULY 27 · JONAH 4

A Sovereign and Compassionate God

LYDIA BROWNBACK

GOD WILL HAVE his way. Jonah learned that truth when he tried to run from the presence of the Lord (Jonah 1:3). He could not escape. The real question is, why would Jonah or any of God's people seek to run from him—the sovereign, compassionate Lord of creation? Fleeing him makes no sense. However, we are likely to follow in Jonah's path if our focus is on ourselves and our ways rather than on God and his kingdom.

God had instructed Jonah to go to Nineveh to preach a message of repentance, but Jonah didn't like God's plan, so he boarded a ship for Tarshish. Out on the sea, a big storm arose, and eventually Jonah was tossed overboard and swallowed by a large fish. There, in the belly of the fish, Jonah repented of his willfulness, and afterward the fish vomited him onto dry land. Jonah proceeded to Nineveh to fulfill his God-given mission. He could not outrun God, and neither can we. God got Jonah where he wanted him, and God does the same with us. God will have his way, and he works sovereignly in and through his creation to bring it to pass.

Jonah fulfilled his missionary calling, but he did so grudgingly. His heart wasn't in it. Deep down, he resented the fact that God was involving him in showing mercy to a people who historically had been a great source of strife to Israel. As chapter 4 opens, Jonah's resentment has bubbled up into suicidal anger, but despite Jonah's hard heart, God is tender with him. To show Jonah the hardness of his heart, God asks questions, and he appoints a plant, a worm, and a scorching east wind. Through these means God demonstrates both his power and his compassion and exposes Jonah's self-centeredness.

An inward focus warps our view of God and leads to personal misery. A self-centered life is never a contented life or a productive one. It is a small life. As with Jonah, God will take steps to bring us to repentance. His covenant faithfulness to his people demands it. If we are tempted to flee from God's presence, it is only because we have a wrong view of him. And if we have a wrong view, it is because we are focused elsewhere.

The path back begins by looking away from ourselves and toward all that God has done for us in Christ. As we reset our focus, we can't help but see that we no more deserve mercy than the Ninevites did, yet God has lavished it upon us. The more we behold our God—his character and his ways, supremely revealed in Christ—the more our hearts will soften and enlarge. We won't want to run away from him anymore, and we will increasingly reflect his compassion to the lost around us.

JULY 28 · MICAH 6:1-8

"What the Lord Requires" and Why

MICHELE BENNETT WALTON

MICAH'S CHARGE TO "do justice," "love kindness," and "walk humbly" was not a new one for God's people. In fact, it could stand as a summary of the messages of other Old Testament prophets like Amos, Hosea, and Isaiah. But we should note Micah's particular context as we seek to understand the verse. Here's the picture: "[Israel's] heads give judgment for a bribe; its priests teach for a price; its prophets practice divination for money" (Mic. 3:11). Chapter 6 catalogs ways in which the rich were taking advantage of the poor, showing that the corruption was not confined to leadership. Injustice reigned from the top down.

God originally entered into covenant with Israel in Deuteronomy, giving them a plain statement of what he required: "And now, Israel, what does the LORD your God require of you, but to fear the LORD your God, to walk in all his ways, to love him, to serve the LORD your God with all your heart and with all your soul, and to keep the commandments and statutes of the LORD, which I am commanding you today for your good?" (Deut. 10:12–13). Israel was called to be different as a perpetual living testimony to God's holiness and righteousness. God's redeemed people were not keeping the covenant.

While the whole book of Micah portrays Israel's unfaithfulness, verses 6 and 7 of chapter 6 show specifically how Israel divorced their religious practices from God's moral standards. Micah depicts their frenzied religious activity climaxing in the pagan practice of child sacrifice. The problem was not Israel's desire to bring sacrifices, for in the Old Testament forgiveness of sin was received through sacrifices. But the law clearly put forth ethical responses to God's salvation that were required from his people. These could not be ignored.

In fact, the same ethical standards are upheld in the New Testament, as we see in Christ's words: "Woe to you, scribes and Pharisees, hypocrites! For you tithe mint and dill and cumin, and have neglected the weightier matters of the law: justice and mercy and faithfulness. These you ought to have done, without neglecting the others" (Matt. 23:23). Both the Old and New Testaments show that good works do not save a person. Doing justice will not earn us a righteous standing before God any more than the Israelites' pagan sacrifices could earn it for them. God's perfect sacrifice for us in Christ is the gracious means of salvation. But our response to such a staggering gift must be the glad-hearted delight in doing justice, loving kindness, and walking humbly with the God who saves us.

The Shepherd-King's Steadfast Love

BRIAN BORGMAN

WHEN SIN IS EXPOSED, it can be devastating. It can seem like everything is falling apart; like things will never again be the same. We can wonder if we have sinned too many times, or if our sin is simply too big this time. In Micah's time, things were rapidly falling apart. The moral and spiritual decay described in verses 1–6 of this passage is striking. Families had collapsed. False religious leaders were feeding cheap grace to a disintegrating people. It is a sad commentary when people's lives are unraveling because of their sin and they choose superficial remedies instead of real healing grace. But God has his remnant. God's true people are not sinless, but they are broken and repentant. They refuse the false security of phony grace and respond to the word of the Lord.

In verses 7–20, Micah responds to the Lord. He represents the faithful, who are full of confident expectation in the Lord. Sin is no match for Micah's covenant keeping God. This passage is a song of victory and praise. Micah, with his faith freshly reinvigorated, knows that his Shepherd-King will cause his grace to triumph over sin.

Do you know how to believe God like this? Amid brokenness and sin, are you confident that he will pick you up and take your side? Micah asks for more grace (Mic. 7:14–17). Why not? Why ask for only a little grace when God is not on a budget? He then asks, in verse 18, "Who is a God like you?" (This is a play on Micah's name, which means "Who is like Yahweh?") Who forgives like you? Who has unchanging love like you? Who else offers genuine compassion and real forgiveness?

So often, we think small thoughts about God and his love! The cross of Jesus Christ is our Father's grand display of unchanging love and real forgiveness. Christ, our Shepherd-King, through his blood and righteousness, brings pardon and comfort to those whose lives are falling apart. Perhaps you fear that your sin is too great. Meditate on verses 18–20, and then dare to take God at his word. God forgives not because we deserve it but because he delights in his own steadfast love. His Son is the incarnation of his steadfast love. We can always count on his steadfast, unchanging love, even when things seem to be falling apart.

JULY 30 · NAHUM 1

God's Wrath against His Enemies

BRYAN CHAPELL

HERE GOD PRESENTS himself in warrior imagery, riding upon the whirlwind and making the storm his chariot as he brings havoc upon the nation that opposes him and his people (Nah. 1:2). These and the other references to natural elements harnessed to dispense the wrath of God are not the images that we tend to associate with the God of grace, who is "slow to anger and abounding in steadfast love" (Ps. 103:8; see also Nah. 1:3). But we forget that one of the aspects of God's grace is his protection of his people, including the overpowering of their enemies (vv. 7–8).

We understand God's promise to overcome the enemies of his people as evidence of his grace when we have experienced oppression, abuse, or injustice. Then we know that God's grace is revealed not only when he forgives our sin but also when he defends us, brings justice, and—as one historic statement of Christianity relates—"restrains and conquers all his and our enemies."

In this passage God promises his judgment upon Nineveh, a cruel and evil city that has regularly oppressed Israel. God's promise to judge sin should help us in two ways. First, we should be encouraged that the grace of God has delivered us from such ultimate devastations of his wrath as will fall upon the enemies of his people. Gratitude for his grace should make us long to live for him. The grief that we have for the suffering that Christ experienced on the cross in our behalf makes service to him a privilege and joy.

The second reason that God's promise of judgment upon his enemies should help us is that it cautions us not to disregard his wrath against those who are opposed to him. Nineveh and Babylon are consistently used in the

Bible to represent all those who will not turn from evil. If we are living in unrepented rebellion, we had best read these judgment passages as healthy warnings to turn from our sin. God's warnings about the consequences of sin are not ungracious. If he did not love us, he would not warn us.

In contrast to these warnings about God's warfare against those who oppose him and harm his people is the proclamation of the good news of peace for those who turn to him (v. 15; see also Rom. 10:15). Though Israel herself has rebelled against God and therefore deserves his wrath, God shows his grace in bringing the good news of his peace to her. This peace is ours, too, despite our sin, as we take refuge in Christ's grace.

Where Is Justice?

TASHA D. CHAPMAN

THE PROPHET HABAKKUK witnessed terrible evil during the corrupt final days before Judah's fall to Babylon. We witness similar signs of godlessness today: materialism; celebrity worship; denial of God's existence; immoral and violent entertainment; children sacrificed to parental selfishness; and pornography, drug, and gambling addictions.

Like Habakkuk, we have a deep desire for justice. How can a sovereign, just, and holy God allow such evil? More specifically, Habakkuk wondered, how could a loving God use the wicked Babylonians to punish his own people? Habakkuk doesn't understand, so he waits expectantly for God to explain (Hab. 2:1). God answers Habakkuk and directs him to record the answer to instruct others: God will bring judgment and justice to *both* the Israelites *and* the Babylonians, but it will come in his own timing. And in the end, God's glory will be known throughout the world (v. 14). In light of his ultimate divine judgment (v. 20), there will be no more complaints or confusion.

God does not minimize Habakkuk's pain and doubts; nor does Scripture minimize ours. But the Lord does call us to a bigger perspective concerning his redemptive work. He calls us to respond in faith. What does it look like to live by faith (v. 4)? Throughout this book we observe Habakkuk growing in faith in several ways. First, God assures him of his unchanging character. Habakkuk can be confident that God is sovereign, faithful, merciful, omnipotent, just, and holy.

Second, Habakkuk learns that the Babylonians will not disturb God's plans for Judah. Others cannot hinder God's work in our lives or his redeeming work in the world. But faith involves waiting patiently for God's timing, not demanding our own, and leaving ultimate justice to him.

Third, living by faith requires active listening to God, as Habakkuk did, especially when we are confused with doubts.

Fourth, a faithful response to God's love involves trusting him enough to obey him—unlike the Babylonians, whom God condemned in the "woes" for greed, pride, injustice, violence, and idolatry.

Finally, to live by faith is to grow in confidence in God's salvation—confidence based on his character and loving promises, not on our attempts at good works. The Israelites around Habakkuk were practicing idolatry, yet God promised to cleanse and restore them. No matter how bad circumstances seem, our response in faith can bring joy and strength to wait on God our Savior (3:18–19).

AUGUST 1 · HABAKKUK 3:17–19

Habakkuk Rejoices in the Lord

MARY PATTON BAKER

THROUGHOUT HABAKKUK'S ORACLE, we have listened to him rail against his circumstances. Like Job, he questions why the just must suffer injustice, enslavement, and violence. He cries out to God twice, and twice God responds to him. The book of Habakkuk then ends with the prophet's final response to God. No longer complaining, he now utters this beautiful prayer.

The prayer begins with a recitation of praise for the mighty acts of God in creation and in his victories over the oppressors of his people. The remembrance of God's great power causes Habakkuk to tremble. He recognizes the sheer force of God's will in human history, and foresees the violent destruction not only of Israel but eventually of her invaders.

Yet remembering the past also brings an end to Habakkuk's questions and complaints. Habakkuk finally comprehends the nature of faithful suffering. His circumstances have not changed. The wicked still rule, the poor still suffer, the worship of false gods still pollutes his community, and the wars have not ceased. So how can Habakkuk now rejoice?

The answer lies in looking to the three stages in Habakkuk's final words. First, Habakkuk comes to accept suffering. He does not turn away from the answers he receives from God. Instead, he faces them head-on and determines that even if all the basic sources of food are taken away, he will still trust God and rely on him.

Second, he rejoices "in" God (Hab. 3:18). The joy he takes in God can find its source only in God's presence. Rather than wallowing in the circumstances before him, Habakkuk leans into God's love.

Third, he experiences God's strength. He uses the imagery of a deer, known for its sure-footedness on treacherous mountaintops. For Habakkuk, this signifies the security of God's presence even in dangerous circumstances. Habakkuk is secure because God cares for him every step of the way. He is no longer looking only at his personal circumstances but now has the big picture: God's kingdom will be established on earth.

Habakkuk teaches that it is not wrong to have questions. It is where we go with our questions that will ultimately determine our character. God wants to be in dialogue with us. He wants to have a relationship, and so as Christians we have been given the fellowship of the Holy Spirit. Through daily communion with God through prayer, worship, and meditation on his word, we make ourselves available to him. He will hear us and grant us that inner joy that reaches beyond any human circumstance.

Worshipers Who Gladden the Heart of God

KRISTYN GETTY

GOD CREATED US to worship him. If we do not worship God, we will worship something or someone else, and worship of anything but God is self-destructive. If we worship God alone, however, he fulfills us. This is seen in Zephaniah's prophecy as he describes the city of Jerusalem in two very different conditions—in a state of rebellion and distance from God, and then in a state of restoration and fellowship with God.

At the heart of the contrast is misdirected worship stemming from the disease of pride. Pride shuts down the flow of worship, is toxic in our lives, and fools us into serving false gods. Humility is the medicine—when we turn and humbly seek God, a life of joy and righteousness results. God gives us "pure speech" and transforms us into true worshipers as we accept his grace and yield to his lordship over all things (Zeph. 3:9). As both our Judge and Redeemer, God is the "mighty one who will save" us from ourselves (v. 17).

God's redemption was ultimately fulfilled in Christ and, unlike Zephaniah's listeners, who knew only in part, we are privileged to know this fully and live in the joy of it. Through Christ we become citizens of the restored city of worshipers, living an earthly expression now of our heavenly hope. We join with God's ancient people, singing aloud to praise the Lord for removing the judgment we deserve (v. 15).

God delights in freeing us to worship him. The Israelites were not the only ones singing in chapter 3. Verse 17 says God loudly sings over his people, extravagantly rejoicing in their restoration. The gladness of God's heart when sinners turn to him echoes throughout Scripture. In Luke 15:10, Jesus says, "There is joy before the angels of God over one sinner who repents." God desires all sinners everywhere to turn to him (2 Pet. 3:9).

Am I ready? Is the worship of my heart and direction of my steps in my home, in my church, and in my community revealing loyalty to Christ and the fragrance of the City of Heaven? Do I yearn and pray for others to be freed from false idols, thereby increasing the joy of our Savior? The One who sang his creation into being will one day see his people completely renewed as the worshipers they were meant to be and will rejoice over his work of grace as he marvels at the work of his hands.

Fear Not, I Am with You

LYDIA BROWNBACK

SIX CENTURIES BEFORE Jesus was born, God's people were carried captive to Babylon, and the city of Jerusalem and its temple, God's earthly dwelling place, were destroyed. After many decades of exile from their homeland, God brought his people back to Jerusalem and stirred up their hearts to begin rebuilding the temple (Ezra 1:1–7). But the work stalled, and the people got wrapped up in their own affairs and set the work of the temple aside. Fifteen years later, in 520 BC, God reissued the call through Haggai to resume the rebuilding campaign. But before long, discouragement set in. Zeal for the work began to lag again.

That's when God brings a word of encouragement through Haggai. First, God pinpoints the reason for the people's discouragement: no matter how hard they work, the new temple cannot possibly be as glorious as the former one. "Is it not as nothing in your eyes?" (Hag. 2:3). The people are comparing the glorious temple of the past with the much less glorious project of the present, and they are tempted to give up. How often we do the same during difficult or seemingly unfruitful seasons of kingdom work. When we fail to see results from our labors, we find ourselves looking backward, or at the successes of others. We begin to question the value of our efforts.

But God didn't leave his people in the throes of discouragement. He led the restored exiles forward with a command and with promises. The command was clear, and it had two parts. The first part was issued to everyone involved—the governor, the high priest, and the people: "Be strong" (v. 4). The second part of the command was attached to a promise: "Work, for

I am with you. . . . My Spirit remains in your midst. Fear not" (v. 5). In other words, God's people were not to be driven by visible success or by how current efforts matched up with past successes. They were to serve God with their talent, time, and goods and trust him for the outcome.

From our vantage point today, we might wonder why restoring a building, in the overall scheme of kingdom priorities, was so vitally important. Before the coming of Christ, the temple was where God met with his people, so God's call to restore it indicated his desire to be with them. When "the Word became flesh and dwelt among us" (John 1:14), the "temple" was Jesus's physical body (2:19–22). Now, in the new covenant, the body of Christ, the true church, is the temple in which God lives among his people (1 Cor. 3:16). One day, when Jerusalem is made completely new, there will be no temple, "for its temple is the Lord God the Almighty and the Lamb" (Rev. 21:22).

AUGUST 4 · ZECHARIAH 1

Return to Me, and I Will Return to You

BETHANY L. JENKINS

WHEN PEOPLE HAVE lied to us, betrayed our confidence, or wronged us in some other way, we tend to distance ourselves from them. We think, "I would never do to anyone what they have done to me." As we look to God, however, we see that all of us are sinners. Even our best deeds are like dirty clothes before God (Isa. 64:6). Yet as we see our sin more clearly, we begin to wonder whether God distances himself from *us* when we have wronged him.

The Israelites were not in exile by accident. God had warned them that he would send them to a foreign land if they disobeyed his law (Deut. 28:36). But they did not listen. They embraced idolatry and immorality for centuries—under judges, kings, and prophets. Finally, he sent them to Babylon.

Seventy years later, when Persia defeated Babylon, the exiles were sent back to Israel. Yet there were problems. First, many of them felt more at home in Babylon than in Israel. Second, other people now occupied their land. Third, the temple, which represented God's presence with his people, was destroyed. Thus, as they traveled home, remembering that they had been sent into exile because of their sin, they wondered, "Are we still God's people? Will he meet us again?"

God sent Zechariah to them, saying, "Return to me, . . . and I will return to you" (Zech. 1:3). He then gave Zechariah eight visions to confirm that promise. In Zechariah 1:7–21, we see two of those visions. First, God showed Zechariah that his envoys (the "red, sorrel, and white horses"; v. 8) were watching his people (the "myrtle trees"; v. 10), who would "again overflow with prosperity" (v. 17) at the right moment. Second, God showed Zechariah that he would bring justice to the nations by oppressing those who had once oppressed Israel (the "horns"; vv. 18–21).

Hundreds of years later, a prophet greater than Zechariah came in the name of the Lord, saying in essence, "Return to me, and I will return to you." Jesus proclaimed, "The time is fulfilled, and the kingdom of God is at hand; repent and believe in the gospel" (Mark 1:15). The moment was right. In Christ, his people would "again overflow with prosperity," and his justice would reign.

Have you wronged the Lord? Has he distanced himself from you? Do you wonder if he will meet you again? No matter how long you have been in exile, you will again overflow with prosperity, and his justice will reign. For God extends this call and promise to you through Christ: "Return to me, and I will return to you."

AUGUST 5 · ZECHARIAH 9

Our King Has Come

JEN WILKIN

ISRAEL HAD BEEN without a king for a hundred years when the prophet Zechariah spoke of a coming king. Still another five hundred years would pass before the prophecy found its fulfillment in Christ (Matt. 21:5). In the intervening years, enduring the oppression of foreign kings, the Jews came to cherish the hope of a future king who would rule in military might, overthrowing their oppressors and establishing an earthly kingdom. Believing that their king would deliver them from the tyranny of Rome, however, they became, in effect, prisoners of a false hope.

But God's plan to liberate his people exceeded anything they could have hoped for. He intended liberation from the tyranny of sin itself. The messianic prophecy of Zechariah 9:9–13 speaks not of a warring king but of a king who brings an end to war; not of a king dressed in battle regalia and seated on a war horse, but of one humble, seated on a donkey, feet dragging in the dust. No wonder the Jews did not recognize Jesus as the Messiah. By earthly standards, he was no king at all.

In fact, however, Jesus is the true King, putting to shame the kings of the earth. Though earthly rulers practice injustice to serve their own ends, this king is righteous. Though earthly rulers serve self-interest at the expense of their subjects, this king brings as his gift salvation itself—offered in utter selflessness, at great expense, for the good of his people. Though earthly rulers are marked by pride, this king is marked by humility.

Believer, rejoice. Your king has come to you—righteous, having salvation, humble. Do not miss what the Jews missed. Deliverance has come for the prisoner in the most unexpected form. His kingdom is a kingdom for those who would, like their king, become "gentle and lowly in heart" (Matt. 11:29); it is a kingdom for the poor in spirit, the meek. Those who are citizens of his kingdom will know the end of tyranny as they tread with joy the path of lowliness he trod.

Because our king came to humble himself, even to the point of death on a cross, the tyrannical reign of sin is ended. No longer must we be ruled by our unrighteousness—our king has come to us in utter righteousness. No longer must we be ruled by our selfish ambition—our king has come to us bearing salvation. No longer must we be ruled by our pride—our king has come to us in gentle humility. Rejoice, believer. Your captivity is ended. Your king has come.

Justice

LEEANN STILES

EVERYONE LONGS for justice. We pull for the good guys to win and the bad guys to lose. We believe those who do wrong should be penalized. People who prey on the poor ought to be punished. Yet immorality seems to go unchecked. We look forward to the day when things will be made right.

The Israelites fretted about injustice, too. They had returned from exile twenty years before, expecting to rebuild the city and the temple. But so much was against them. Hostile neighbors plagued them. They wondered why their oppressors went unpunished. Some of their own turned from the Lord and his ways. They yearned for God to intervene.

So Zechariah's words couldn't have been more timely. Zechariah foretold a day when the Lord would again raise up Israel, right down to the feeblest person (Zech. 12:8), and would reestablish the house of David. Powerful images such as panicked horses with mad riders (v. 4) and flaming torches (v. 6) describe the destruction of Israel's enemies. They would be victorious! Israel longed for this day as surely as we long for it: the day when the wicked will get what they deserve and the righteous will be delivered.

But there's a big problem about the day of judgment, even for the "good" guys. That's because "there is none who does good, not even one" (Ps. 14:3). No one is without sin. Everyone deserves judgment. That's why Zechariah's prophecy takes a strange twist in verse 10 of chapter 12. It pictures weeping, grieving, and pleas for mercy coming from God's own people (Zech. 12:10–14). This happens when they "look on me, on him whom they have pierced" (v. 10). We know from the New Testament that ultimately this is about Jesus. In fact, the apostle John quotes this very verse when the Roman soldiers pierce Jesus's side at the crucifixion (John 19:37).

We remember, then, that our wickedness is judged, too. Payment for our rebellion came at a high price—the death of God's firstborn. "He was pierced for our transgressions; he was crushed for our iniquities" (Isa. 53:5). Our reaction is a sorrow over sin that should lead to repentance.

But God doesn't stop at repentance. He desires to purify us as well. Zechariah 13:1 gives another promise: "On that day there shall be a fountain opened . . ." Jesus—in his life, death, and resurrection—cleanses us from all unrighteousness. Come to that fountain now!

AUGUST 7 · MALACHI 3:6–12

Put God to the Test

KAREN S. LORITTS

IN MALACHI, the people of God are in spiritual decline. Perhaps idolatry isn't as rampant as in the past, and Judah's beliefs are relatively orthodox. But their worship is halfhearted at best. Rather than worshiping God with all their heart and soul and might (Deut. 6:5), Judah is basically offering him their leftovers. This is particularly evident in the behavior of priests, who grudgingly perform their duties and offer polluted sacrifices: "The lips of a priest should guard knowledge, and people should seek instruction from his mouth, for he is the messenger of the LORD of hosts. But you have turned aside from the way. You have caused many to stumble by your instruction" (Mal. 2:7–8).

In chapter 3 the Lord rebukes Judah for two specific sins. The first is a failure to keep his commands: "From the days of your fathers you have turned aside from my statutes and have not kept them" (3:7). This implies apostasy, a falling away from devotion to God. God had promised Israel that all would go well with them if they kept his commandments (Deut. 6:1–3). But Israel disregarded this promise and fell into sin and corruption.

The second sin God condemns is "robbing" God: "Will man rob God? Yet you are robbing me. But you say, 'How have we robbed you?' In your tithes and contributions" (Mal. 3:8). The people were to support the Levites and priests with their tithes (Num. 18:21–28), but they were not doing so. Perhaps this was partly in response to the corrupt service rendered by the priests; nevertheless, it was a sin for Israel to withhold these gifts. Tithes were not to be given in proportion to the service of man but rather in response to God's generous provision. It was therefore God, not men, that the people were robbing.

This passage is a hard one even for us today; parting with resources isn't any easier now than it was for the people of Israel. And when we *do* give, sometimes it is with wrong motives. The passage invites self-examination: am I giving from a cheerful, grateful heart (2 Cor. 9:6–9)? God says that if we are faithful in our giving, he will be faithful to meet all our needs. "Put me to the test, says the LORD of hosts" (Mal. 3:10); test him and just see how much he will bless those who are generous!

Trust God, dear sister, and he will be close to you. Bring your tithe to him, and he will bless abundantly. Put God to the test; he will be faithful to keep his promises. "Honor the LORD with your wealth and with the firstfruits of all your produce; then your barns will be filled with plenty, and your vats will be bursting with wine" (Prov. 3:9–10).

AUGUST 8 · MATTHEW 1:18-25

Immanuel: God with Us

STARR MEADE

ADAM FORFEITED immeasurable good when he chose sin: life, health, righteousness, a perfect world. His most tragic loss, however, was his enjoyment of God's presence. Genesis 3 gives us the pitiful image of Adam and Eve cowering in their fig leaves as they try to hide from God.

Yet not even sin thwarts God. From eternity past, God had planned to have a people for himself, among whom he would always dwell. God found Adam and Eve and promised to repair the devastation they had worked (Gen. 3:15).

When God led the Israelites out of Egypt, he commanded them to make a tabernacle and promised to dwell among them there (Ex. 25:8). Later, Solomon, acknowledging that no house is big enough to contain God, still asked him to dwell in the temple his people had built, and God answered with the cloud of his glory entering that temple (2 Chron. 6:12–7:3). It was Israel's great privilege to be so favored, but these physical representations of God's presence were limited and temporary. They all pointed to a time when God, in his fullness, would dwell among his people forever. They all pointed to Christ.

Now, as Matthew writes his Gospel of Jesus Christ, he deliberately points back, time and again, to Old Testament promises fulfilled in Jesus. He does it first here, where he points back to Isaiah's promise of a son born of a virgin, whose name would be "Immanuel," even pausing to make sure we know that "Immanuel" means "God with us" (Matt. 1:22–23).

How does Jesus usher in a whole new era of God dwelling among his people? First, in Christ, the second person of the Trinity takes on humanity and lives on the earth. Second, Jesus will remove the sin that has, for all these centuries, kept people from a perfect closeness with God. He will be called Jesus, "for he will save his people from their sins" (v. 21).

Thus Matthew begins his account with three stunning facts about his subject: Jesus has no human father, for God is his father. Jesus comes to save his people from their sins. And Jesus fulfills the age-old promise and purpose of God to be with his people, perfectly and forever. Matthew will move through his narrative, demonstrating by Jesus's life and words that Jesus is who he claimed to be, able to save those who trust in him. Then Matthew will close his Gospel with Jesus's promise to continue as "Immanuel" to his people: "Behold, I am with you always, to the end of the age" (28:20).

AUGUST 9 · MATTHEW 3:1-12

Prepared for the Lord's Coming

CLAIRE SMITH

SEVEN HUNDRED YEARS before John the Baptist began preaching in the wilderness of Judea, Isaiah had prophesied about a voice crying in the wilderness, saying, "Prepare the way of the LORD" (Isa. 40:3). Four hundred years before John, the prophet Malachi likewise prophesied of one who would prepare the way of the Lord (Mal. 3:1; 4:5–6). There had been no true prophets since.

But the silence was now broken. God had promised to visit his people, and he had promised a messenger to prepare his way. John was that promised messenger—the prophet about whom these earlier prophets had prophesied. He was the herald announcing the arrival of the King, and preparing the people to meet this King. Jesus, God's promised Messiah, was coming, and people needed to turn from their sin and accept his rule. John was preparing the way for the King, just as God had foretold all those years earlier through the prophets.

Although those prophecies were centuries old, John's message was urgent: the kingdom of heaven is *at hand*. The king was coming, but so too was the wrath of God. People needed to be warned, so that they would repent from their sin while there was still time.

Repentance is not about outward appearances—simply undergoing a religious ritual, or saying one thing but believing and living another. It means confessing sins and turning away from sin. It means having changed hearts and lives. It means death to the old way of life, and submission to the rule of the King. Jesus's coming rule demanded an urgent and whole-hearted response.

So we see two timelines at work in John's ministry. First there is the long, slow fulfilment of prophecy—seven hundred years of waiting for the voice in the wilderness and the coming of the King. But second is the urgent need to repent and be ready for the King, to avoid the coming wrath. We must not be fooled by these timelines, as if the apparent slowness of the first cancels out the urgency of the second. God is true to his word. Isaiah and Malachi may not have known through whom, or when, or how God would fulfill his promises, but they knew that he would (1 Pet. 1:10–12; 2 Pet. 3:8–10).

God has promised that this same Lord Jesus, whose way John prepared, is coming again to judge the living and the dead, and only those who trust in him will be prepared at his coming, and will avoid the coming wrath (2 Thess. 1:8–9). He is coming again! The time to prepare is now.

Jesus and the Law

MARY BETH MCGREEVY

JESUS WAS CONSTANTLY being criticized by the religious authorities for not relating to the Law as they thought he should. This was especially true when it came to his handling of the Sabbath, when he was known to perform healings or to allow his disciples to pick grain (Matt. 12:1–2; Mark 3:1–6). Jesus explains that, far from doing away with the Law and the Prophets (that is, the entire Old Testament), he has come to fulfill them. He fulfilled the moral law by his perfect obedience to it; the prophecies, in the specific predictions of the life of the Messiah; and the sacrificial system, by his substitutionary atonement. Much of what happened in Israel's history pictured his life, and the Wisdom Literature described his character. All of the Old Testament pointed to him.

Rather than abolishing the Law, Jesus confirms the Bible's authority. Not the smallest letter (the *iota* in Greek or the *yod* in Hebrew) will pass away until all of it is accomplished. Much has already been accomplished through Jesus's earthly life, death, and resurrection. One day he will come again for the consummation of all things that have been foretold. For this reason we can understand why he holds accountable anyone who does not obey the Law or teach it as relevant and authoritative.

The standard that Jesus places upon his hearers is shocking: if we would enter the kingdom of heaven, our righteousness must exceed that of the scribes and Pharisees, who were known for their strict outward observance of the smallest details of the law. But that is just the problem: their hearts did not conform to their outward professions and piety (23:23). They ignored the Law's intent to promote justice, mercy, and faithfulness as they scrupulously followed its minutiae. What they needed was a new heart.

God provides this new heart when he brings believers to spiritual life through faith in Jesus Christ. This regeneration not only imputes Jesus's perfect obedience to the Law to our account to give us right standing before God; it also provides the motivation and power to obey and serve him.

Now, when we as believers find ourselves actually obeying God's word, we do not take credit for it as the Pharisees did. No, we recognize that all the glory goes to God, by whom we attain true righteousness and by whose power alone we can obey in any measure. The Law now becomes for us not restrictions that condemn, but the revelation of God's character and gracious work in redeeming a people who love and serve him by his enabling power.

Worry, Unbelief, and Our Father's Welcome

ELYSE FITZPATRICK

WORRY: WHO DOESN'T DO IT? Whether it's a minor discomfort or a full-fledged panic attack, we all know what worry is. And because worry is such a universal experience, our Savior addressed it. In this passage, Jesus pinpoints the sources of our enslavement to worry. Our worries are rooted in life as it is lived out in this world: we need food, drink, and clothing. Yes, of course we need these things to survive, but the life Jesus is pressing us toward is something more than scratching out a living by our own devices. He's pressing us to trust in his ability to provide everything we need, including basic necessities. We worry because we're not convinced that he is both willing and able to provide for us. So we trust in our own abilities to control our circumstances, to work things out, to provide for ourselves—and worry grows. Why? Because we know we cannot control anything.

Why do we trust in ourselves when our experience shows that it is futile to do so? It is because of our unbelief. We are those "of little faith" (Matt. 6:30). Every moment I've spent worrying conflicts with what I say I believe. I confess that he is "God, the Father Almighty, Maker of heaven and earth," and I worry as though he were a feeble, unloving demigod.

But Jesus doesn't condemn me in my weakness or the frailty of my faith. No, instead he reassures me that, even though I'm acting like a "Gentile," an orphan estranged from a caring Father, I still have a heavenly Father who knows what I need and will provide for me. "All these things will be added to you," he assures us (v. 33). He is our loving Father.

Finally, rather than trusting in our own ability to provide for ourselves, we're told to seek after God's kingdom (rather than our own) and his righteousness (rather than our own) (v. 33). It is right here that we come to the crux of our worry and distress. Simply put, we worry because we're trying to build our own kingdom, failing to believe that it is his "good pleasure" to give *his* kingdom to us (Luke 12:32). We worry because we're trying to construct our own righteousness, to prove that we're worthy to be cared for. We fail to believe that it is God's pleasure to give us *his* righteousness (2 Cor. 5:21).

What is the answer to our unbelief, misplaced trust, and worry? It is not a determination to pull ourselves up by our own bootstraps, but rather a call to believe the gospel. To believe that our Father loves us and has provided all we need—a King, a kingdom, and a righteousness that ensures our free welcome into it.

AUGUST 12 · MATTHEW 7:24–29

Foundations and Storms

LAUREN CHANDLER

THE WORD INCARNATE preaches a sermon so significant that it has been preserved on the pages of Scripture for two millennia. A crowd of disciples, townspeople, and religious leaders has gathered to hear the man who speaks with unparalleled authority. In his conclusion, the part of the sermon listeners most often carry home with them, he lays before them four basic warnings: they must choose between two gates and roads (Matt. 7:13–14), two kinds of prophets (vv. 15–20), two kinds of disciples (vv. 21–23), and two foundations (vv. 24–27). Would they be with Jesus or against him? Would they trust his word to the point of action, or would they continue to live according to what they "felt" was right—for the religious, legalism; and for the irreligious, licentiousness?

Jesus gives a peek into his hearers' future. He uses the image of one's home: the place where we dwell, where we lie down to sleep, where we keep safe what is most precious to us. And he uses the image of a storm, an indomitable threat that has the potential to destroy all that we hold dear, even our very lives. He speaks a prophetic word that is for each person in the crowd: storms will come, and they will reveal what you have built your life upon.

The home is where we seek security, so it's important to us that it be built in a manner and in a place that is immovable. During the summer heat, the sand around the Sea of Galilee would harden on the surface. To the untrained or foolish eye, it would seem a sufficient site for a foundation. However, a wise builder knew that he must dig through the impacted sand to the bedrock several feet below in order to establish a secure foundation.

Jesus says the way to ensure a firm foundation—building on the rock instead of the sand—is to hear his words and do them. Many can hear his words and even find them remarkable, but unless one lets them settle into the heart, nothing has changed. Trust will continue to be put in what is seen, heard, and felt, not in what can endure the storm. To build upon the rock means to do the hard work of digging, of self-examination, of active faith in Jesus. The great news of the gracious heart of God is that even when the storm washes away what we thought was firm beneath our feet, we are invited to build again—this time on what will last. We get the opportunity to take him at his word.

AUGUST 13 · MATTHEW 9:9–13

Follow Me

GLORIA FURMAN

WHAT WOULD THE holy Son of God ever want to do with sinners? We may wonder if we will ever be "enough" to follow Jesus. But discipleship does not necessarily mean what we think it means.

Matthew recounts the day he left his former way of life behind him (see also Luke 5:28). Perhaps it started as just another day at the office. Perhaps he had a sense that his life was about to change. One thing is clear: Jesus called Matthew to follow him, and Matthew obeyed. He left everything and followed the man who is the Way, the Truth, and the Life.

Discipleship was not a dismal prospect for Matthew. He celebrated with a great feast! His associates came to the party and dined with Jesus and his disciples. This text also highlights who *wasn't* there to celebrate. The religious leaders would have been able to join this great feast, but they refrained so as not to come in contact with the "sinners" and absorb their uncleanness.

Jesus's desire to enjoy fellowship with the unclean defied the religious leaders' way of understanding purity. Here was a religious man who socialized with the irreligious. "Why does your teacher eat with tax collectors and sinners?" (Matt. 9:11) This was not a request for clarification; it was a criticism. Much is revealed about the nature of Jesus's mission in his rebuke to the Pharisees. The eternal Son of God is not impressed with their self-righteousness, nor does he congratulate their self-promoting deeds. Pharisees were content to judge the sin they saw in others. Jesus's instruction to "go and learn" (v. 13) is a call to understand God's desire to show loving kindness (Hos. 6:6).

Lest we be quick to judge the Pharisees, we should remember that our own self-righteousness separates us from God, too. The irony is that the Pharisees' mistake can quickly become ours, as we consider ourselves better than the Pharisees and look down on them. By God's grace we need to see ourselves in light of his radiant holiness: we are sinful beyond hope, except for his saving grace.

Jesus, who is the epitome of the perfection commanded in God's law, came to save sinners, calling us to repentance and faith in him. Not only does Jesus fellowship with the unclean and come away untainted by sin himself, he also cleanses and forgives our sin. Being his disciple is costly, to be sure, but we gain a prize of immeasurable worth when we follow "the upward call of God in Christ Jesus" (Phil. 3:14). We gain Christ!

Clinging to Christ through Persecution

TRILLIA NEWBELL

JESUS HAS JUST instructed his disciples to go to the "lost sheep of the house of Israel" and proclaim that "the kingdom of heaven is at hand" (Matt. 10:6–7). Later he tells them the sobering news: doing so will lead to your persecution and likely death. The disciples weren't being sent out to proclaim Christ to people ready and willing to hear; they were being sent out in the midst of wolves ready to devour their prey (v. 16). If these wolves hated Jesus, why would they embrace the message from his disciples (v. 24)?

The disciples *were* persecuted. Though we don't have a record of all that they endured and how each of them died, we do know that James was likely beheaded (Acts 12:2) and Peter was crucified as Jesus prophesied in John 21:18–19. We know that many others suffered similar fates, such as the martyrdom of Stephen (Acts 7:54–60).

For most of us, persecution won't come in the form of being beaten, flogged, or hanged as it did for Christians in the early generations of the church, or as it still does for believers in many places in the world. Our lives are relatively normal and mundane. Persecution will come, however, in the form of being shunned, laughed at, ridiculed, slandered, and ignored. And, remarkably, such mistreatment may very well come from those closest to us. Jesus warns that we may be hated even by our own families for his name's sake (Matt. 10:21–22).

As we seek to share the gospel—"as sheep in the midst of wolves" (v. 16)—Jesus says that we must be wise and yet also innocent (v. 16). Paul reminds us of this holy calling: "Do not be conformed to this world, but be transformed by the renewal of your mind, that by testing you may discern what is the will of God, what is good and acceptable and perfect" (Rom. 12:2).

Speaking boldly about Jesus may mean rejection, even by those we hold most dear, but we do not need to fear. Our confidence is found in knowing that God is for us. Who, then, can be against us? (Rom. 8:31).

The only one to fear is the Lord God himself; all others can only kill the body, but the Lord has the power to cast the soul into hell (Matt. 10:28).

Jesus's promise, though, is that as we acknowledge him before men he will acknowledge us before his Father (v. 32). We can rest in the promise of God's everlasting love, knowing that ultimately "neither death nor life, nor angels nor rulers, nor things present nor things to come, nor powers, nor height nor depth, nor anything else in all creation, will be able to separate us from the love of God in Christ Jesus our Lord" (Rom. 8:38–39). We are forever his.

Heart Matters

KAREN S. LORITTS

IN THE GOSPEL according to Matthew, Jesus uses parables to reveal truths of the kingdom, separating the truly committed from the merely curious. The Greek word for "parable" literally means to place one thing beside another for comparison. Many profound spiritual and moral lessons can be found in the parables.

The parable of the sower uses an agricultural illustration. A sower sows his seeds. Normally, germination would occur, yielding a fruit-bearing harvest. But because the seeds land in four different types of soil, there are varying results. Some fell "along the path" (Matt. 13:4), while others fell "on rocky ground" (v. 5). Some seeds "fell among thorns" (v. 7), and others fell "on good soil" (v. 8). The seeds that fell on three out of the four types of soil failed to bear fruit. It was only the seeds that fell on the good soil that produced an abundant harvest.

This parable is obviously not a lesson on how to reap a literal crop—rather, its message is spiritual and concerns the kingdom. As Jesus goes on to explain in verses 18–23, the seed is the message (the "word") of the kingdom. The soil is the human heart. As the word of God is sown, there are varying responses among the hearers.

The impenetrable, hardened heart hears the message, yet the enemy, the devil, takes it away before it takes root. "The thief comes only to steal and kill and destroy" (John 10:10). The unstable heart hears the message with joy, but adversity proves that the person was never truly a follower of Christ, united to him (John 15:1–6). The wishy-washy heart hears the message but, being weighed down by "the cares of the world and the deceitfulness of riches" (Matt. 13:22), she vacillates and is unfruitful. "Do not love the world or the things in the world. If anyone loves the world, the love of the Father is not in him" (1 John 2:15). The world, the flesh, and the devil are enemies of the heart.

The persevering heart hears and receives the message with understanding, applies what she hears, and perseveres with sure obedience, reaping an abundant, fruitful harvest: "So shall my word be that goes out from my mouth; it shall not return to me empty, but it shall accomplish that which I purpose, and shall succeed in the thing for which I sent it" (Isa. 55:11).

Kingdom people surrender to the indwelling authority of the Holy Spirit, who cultivates hearts that bear good fruit for his kingdom.

AUGUST 16 · MATTHEW 16:13–28

The Cross of Christ

DAN DORIANI

IN MATTHEW 16:13-28, Jesus leads his disciples away from the crowds for instruction. He begins with a question: "Who do people say that the Son of Man is?" (v. 13). Peter, inspired by the Spirit, confesses, "You are the Christ, the Son of the living God" (v. 16). This confession is the rock, Jesus says, on which "I will build my church" (v. 18). Yet because the title "Christ" is widely misunderstood among the Jews, Jesus has to define his role as the Christ, God's anointed. He will not *initially* be a glorious, conquering king. No, he must go to Jerusalem, be killed, and on the third day be raised (v. 21). Jesus's suffering is essential to his work as Messiah. By his sacrifice on the cross, he saves his people.

Peter erupts: "This shall never happen" (v. 22). Peter dares to believe that he knows better than Jesus; he cannot imagine that Jesus will die at the hands of his own people. But Jesus rebukes him: "Get behind me, Satan!" (v. 23). When Peter denies that Jesus must die, he is speaking for Satan, who tempted Jesus to seize glory without facing the cross. Peter's mind is set "on the things of man," but the cross of Christ is the centerpiece of "the things of God" (v. 23). There is no Christianity without the cross and the empty tomb. Eventually Peter grasped the centrality of the cross—and preached it. He said Jesus "bore our sins in his body on the tree, that we might die to sin and live to righteousness. By his wounds you have been healed" (1 Pet. 2:24).

Jesus's crucifixion and resurrection are both the source of redemption and the paradigm for discipleship: "If anyone would come after me, let him deny himself and take up his cross and follow me" (Matt. 16:24). Jesus died once to atone for sin, and we, rescued by this grace, are given the glad summons of sacrificing for others as he did. He bore the ultimate cross for us; we bear little crosses for others.

Jesus commends this life in three ways. First, if we lose our life for Jesus's sake, we find it (v. 25). A life of self-gratification is shallow, then deadly. But a life spent in service to the Lord is truly enriching, both in the present and in eternity. Second, there is no benefit if a person "gains the whole world and forfeits his soul" (v. 26). Third, when Jesus returns, "he will repay each person according to what he has done" (v. 27), for he forgets no good deed, and no sacrifice misses its reward.

Lose your life—and thus save it. Trust him this much. He is worth it.

AUGUST 17 · MATTHEW 18:15–20

Sin and Reconciliation

MARY A. KASSIAN

THE LORD WANTS ME to take a radical, zero-tolerance approach to the sin in my life (Matt. 18:8). But what do I do when I encounter sin in another believer's life—particularly if it directly impacts me? Matthew 18 presents a strategy for dealing with sin and breaches in interpersonal relationships. According to Jesus, the solution is not to sweep other people's offenses under the carpet. Rather, we are to deal with them in a manner that optimizes the opportunity for healing and reconciliation.

It's not accidental that the instructions for confronting someone else's sin are preceded by a requirement to deal with the "log" in my own eye first (7:3–5). In chapter 18, the instructions are sandwiched between teachings on the importance of humility (18:1–5), radical personal holiness (vv. 7–9), God's compassion and mercy toward wandering sheep (vv. 10–14), and a lesson on unlimited forgiveness (vv. 21–35). I cannot properly deal with another person's failings if I don't have the right spirit and attitude.

If a sister sins against you, first *address the matter privately, one-on-one* (v. 15). Speak with her alone, with a spirit of humility and gentleness, and a genuine desire for restoration (Gal. 6:1). Take care not to gossip, malign, harbor resentment, or return evil for evil. The word translated "restore" in Galatians 6:1 is a Greek medical term that refers to the process of setting a broken bone. The same kind of tenderness and care is needed to set a relationship right.

If she does not listen, *engage help from others* (Matt. 18:16). Meet with her and one or two mature, dependable believers whose aim is to provide godly counsel. If she still will not listen (v. 17), *take the problem before the elders*, the governing authority of the church. The authority to *bind* and *loose* mentioned in Matthew 18:18 conveys the sense of *convict* and *acquit*, and probably alludes to cases of church discipline. The church has authority to pronounce judgment in God's name, and also to release persons from that judgment and restore them to fellowship (see also 1 Corinthians 5; 2 Thess. 3:6–15; 2 Tim. 2:23–26; Titus 3:10).

Civil authorities execute God's justice, and some offenses require their involvement (Rom. 13:1–4). The goal of the above process is not to secure a legal judgment but to make every possible attempt to restore a struggling believer and nourish further fellowship. "My brothers, if anyone among you wanders from the truth and someone brings him back, let him know that whoever brings back a sinner from his wandering will save his soul from death and will cover a multitude of sins" (James 5:19–20).

True Worshipers

KRISTIE ANYABWILE

IN THIS PASSAGE, majesty and mercy meet. Jesus demonstrates his majesty by removing defilement from his temple. He demonstrates his mercy by healing those who come to him. But the buyers and sellers, as well as the religious leaders, are oblivious. Selfishness, greed, and unbelief cause them to miss this pinnacle of Jesus's earthly ministry.

In his triumphal entry into Jerusalem, Jesus prophetically and humbly shows himself to be Israel's Messiah (Matt. 21:4–5). The next day, he returns to the temple so that all might see the majesty, the mercy, and the message of the Messiah. His majesty is seen as he uses his divine authority as King of kings to throw out false religion and robbers from the temple, to make room for his mercy. As false religion goes out, true worshipers come in. The lame and blind now have free and full access to Christ, and he heals them (v. 14). Remembering his triumphal entry from the day before, children continue shouting their hosannas to the Son of David.

True worship occurs as Christ affirms and accepts the praise of the children. Likewise, the physically blind and lame who come to Christ for healing exhibit true worship. But the spiritually blind (those who have read and know the Scriptures but do not see the Son of God standing before them) and the spiritually lame (those who come to offer sacrifice to God but stumble and fall in greed and trickery for selfish gain) continue in their infirmities, unaware of the healing that their souls desperately need.

The temple was to be the place of worship. From the first portable tabernacle to the current temple, God had continually called his people to meet him in this holy place so that he might "tabernacle" (dwell) with them and that they might fellowship with him. The priests, who were given charge to ensure that all that took place in the temple happened just as the Lord had commanded, had completely forfeited divine command for earthly commerce. The place of worship was turned into a "den of robbers," a hiding place for evil, a marketplace for moochers. In Christ's last week of preaching and teaching in the temple, he exposes this degradation and affirms his true worshipers.

True worship begins with a temple cleansed from ungodliness, a people cured from sin, and hearts corrected toward righteousness, so that we might continue the mission for which the Lord Jesus called us. May we be among those true worshipers.

AUGUST 19 • MATTHEW 22:34–40

Love above All Else

MARY WILLSON

FOLLOWING HIS ACCOUNT of Jesus cleansing the temple (Matt. 21:12–13), Matthew recorded several intensified encounters between Jesus and the religious professionals of the day. Before the crowds gathered in the temple courts, these religious leaders pummeled Jesus with questions and sought to undermine his authority. Yet their schemes consistently backfired, since their conspiracies were no match for Jesus's wisdom. Their public challenges unwittingly generated even greater astonishment over Jesus's teaching (22:33).

These particular Pharisees sought to leverage the Scriptures against Jesus. Surely, they must have thought, his answer would offend some fraction of the crowd, diminish his appeal, and perhaps provide grounds for his arrest. Little did they know that they were testing the very Word made flesh, the one who had come to obey and fulfill the Law and the Prophets (5:17)! Jesus's straightforward summation of the law proved his intimate knowledge of God's heart, and his direct and simple answer suited God's intention for his commands (Deut. 30:11–14).

Jesus boiled down God's law to one central purpose: love. By "love," Jesus did not mean sentimental emotion or attachment. Jesus proved his love for God preeminently by an unyielding commitment to obey him, even in the most bitter circumstances. God calls all of his people to complete devotion to him (Deut. 6:5), and the chief display of love in all of human history took place when Jesus willingly sacrificed his life for the sake of sinners like us, all for the glory of his Father. As the apostle wrote, "By this we know love, that he laid down his life for us" (1 John 3:16).

In the life of Jesus, we see what God means by these two great commandments (Matt. 22:37–39). We imitate Christ's obedience as we honor God's purposes and listen to his voice. We offer all that we are and have at the feet of our great King, and we commit ourselves to love others with the sacrificial love of Christ.

But Jesus is more than our example. Jesus is also our Savior. He perfectly fulfilled God's righteous requirements in our place and secured justification for us on the cross. It is only because Jesus perfectly obeyed these great commandments that we are now set free to obey God's commands as his dearly beloved children (Eph. 5:1). Jesus's obedience is the *source* of our salvation, whereas our obedience is the *fruit* of salvation. Only those who have received Christ can truly follow him, and only those who follow him have truly received him (1 John 4:7–5:5).

In response to such grace, love the Lord your God with all your heart, soul, and mind, and love your neighbor as yourself.

Take Heart! The End Will Come

KERI FOLMAR

CONTRARY TO SOME popular "power of positive thinking" Christian teaching, this world is not a comfortable place for faithful believers. Persecution, betrayal, natural disasters, false teachers, and moral permissiveness characterize this age and will continue to the end. Sorrow and trouble invade the life of every Christian sooner or later. This is why Jesus warns his disciples in Matthew 24. Jesus is realistic about this fallen world and knows that, just as he is headed to the suffering of the cross, his true followers will also suffer in this age.

But history, far from being meaningless or random, is going somewhere. We see in Matthew 24 that no events, international or individual, surprise Jesus. He knows what the future holds, for he orchestrates it all for his glory and the believer's good. He is Lord over all.

That very cross toward which Jesus resolutely marched, that instrument of torture and death, was also the instrument of salvation "for all who believe" (Rom. 3:22–26), and it is the tool that enables a groaning creation to be reconciled to its Creator. There will be no more conflict or hardship, no more hatred or torment, no more lies or evil, no more trouble or sorrow, no more death. All things will be put to rights at the close of the age because Jesus took the Father's punishment for the sins of those who would become the children of God. He has made peace for us "by the blood of his cross" (Col. 1:20). We know this because after Jesus died, God raised him from the dead to send him back one day in glory.

Take heart! We do not have to figure out what our future holds. Adversity and trials will come, but the same Lord who upholds the universe holds us in his hands. We have only to endure, relying not on our strength but on "his glorious might" (Col. 1:11) and "the immeasurable greatness of his power toward us who believe" (Eph. 1:19). The same power that raised Jesus from the dead is working in us (Rom. 8:19) to enable us to resist temptation, stand firm during persecution, face hardship, and reject false teachers. As we endure, we have the privilege of proclaiming this gospel of the kingdom, and then the glorious end—a new beginning for us—will come. All will have been worth it. The glory then will far outshine the present pain.

A Beautiful Waste

JANI ORTLUND

IT IS AFTER Jesus's triumphal entry into Jerusalem, and everyone is anticipating Passover. Jesus and his disciples are in Bethany, about two miles outside Jerusalem, at the house of Simon the leper, sharing a meal together. Perhaps Jesus had healed Simon and Simon had invited him to his home. No one would have come if Simon was still diseased, since lepers were required to live apart from other people. Whatever the nature of the invitation, Matthew opens the door for us to see Jesus reclining at the table as a meal is being served.

Into this scene comes Mary, the sister of Martha and Lazarus, who all lived together in Bethany (John 11:1). Maybe Jesus was lodging with them. Mary comes in and does something that stops the flow of food and conversation. She takes an alabaster flask full of a pound of pure nard (Mark 14:3; John 12:3), breaks it, and pours it on Jesus's head.

This expensive, fragrant oil was a perfume used for solemn acts of devotion. Usually, more common oils were used to anoint guests, but Mary chose her best. It was an extravagant choice. Mark tells us it was worth a year's wages for the average worker!

As the luxurious fragrance fills the room, so does the disciples' indignation. They scold Mary and shame her, pointing out her excessive waste (Mark 14:5).

But Jesus defends her extravagance, shielding her from their accusations, supporting her unrestrained devotion. He tells them to leave her alone and stop troubling her. They call it a waste—"This could have been . . . given to the poor" (Matt. 26:9). But Jesus calls it a "beautiful thing" (vv. 10–12), reminding them that they will have continual opportunities to serve the poor, but not many more chances to show their love for him.

What act could be judged as too extravagant for Jesus, especially in light of what he was about to do for us? Jesus honors a woman who honors him. Mary's anointing was an act of love and devotion. And it turned out to be the only anointing Jesus's body received, as the women who later came to anoint his body at the tomb found it empty (Mark 16:1–6)! Jesus esteemed her worship so highly that we are still talking about her today (just as Jesus said we would; see Matt. 26:13).

Jesus gladly accepts our extravagant acts of worship and calls them beautiful. This is what he honors. He is worth it. There is no devotion too great, given his great and undeserved love for us. What will you break open to pour out for Jesus today?

The Command to Make Disciples

ROBERT A. PETERSON

THE "GREAT COMMISSION" (Matt. 28:18–20) is aptly named. Before Jesus's return to the Father in heaven, he met with his eleven remaining disciples. Strangely, we are encouraged by their mixed response to Jesus: "When they saw him they worshiped him, but some doubted" (v. 17). They expressed both praise and doubt. How like us!

Jesus comforts them by proclaiming his power. "All authority in heaven and on earth has been given to me" (v. 18). Jesus does not send his disciples in their own strength. Far from it! He sends them in *his* strength. He, the crucified and risen Lord, has been invested with the authority of God himself.

On the basis of his divine authority, Jesus sends his disciples to "all nations" (v. 19). In God's providence, this fulfills his promise to Abraham in Genesis 12:3, as Paul explains in Galatians 3:8. Jesus commands his followers to make disciples, baptize them, and teach them. The command to make disciples assumes prior evangelism. People must believe in Jesus as Lord and Savior before they become his followers. According to Jesus, baptism is part of the discipling ministry of his church. Baptism is to be performed in water by a minister of the gospel. It is to be performed in the threefold name of Father, Son, and Holy Spirit.

Baptism has many meanings biblically, including cleansing from sin, renewal, and dedication to God. But its most profound meaning is union with Christ. Using the picture of changing clothes, Paul writes, "As many of you as were baptized into Christ have put on Christ" (Gal. 3:27). Baptism portrays putting on Christ as a person puts on a garment. That is, baptism signifies being united to Christ. In fact, according to the Great Commission, baptism signifies union with the Trinity! It is amazing to think that God loves us enough to put the name of the Holy Trinity upon us and claim us as his own children.

God wants his children, saved by his grace, to live for him. The disciples are to teach new believers "to observe all that I have commanded you" (Matt. 28:20). Salvation is by grace alone, through faith alone, and not by works. But the faith that saves is never alone! Rather, saving faith *works* (Eph. 2:8–10).

Jesus prefaced the Great Commission with encouraging words concerning his divine authority. He follows that same commission with encouraging words concerning his divine presence: "Behold, I am with you always, to the end of the age" (Matt. 28:20). Jesus does not send the disciples into the world as orphans; he promises to be with them until his return. We today can draw great comfort from these words. Jesus is with us!

Authority

SUSAN HUNT

MARK IS A MAN on a mission to establish the identity of Jesus as the Son of God, and thereby to defend Jesus's call to discipleship. His strategy is a fast-paced "docudrama" that presents the life and teaching of Jesus. At times his footage leaves us breathless, but it never leaves us in doubt that Jesus is no mere man. Mark begins by showing that Jesus is the fulfillment of all the Old Testament promises and prophesies (Mark 1:2–12). Jesus is the Messiah. He is God. He is the King that the Father enthroned on his holy hill (Ps. 2:6).

The next clip gives a succinct summary of Jesus's teaching (Mark 1:15) followed by the calling of his first disciples (vv. 16–20). Then Mark presents convincing evidences of the power and authority of King Jesus. Jesus went to the synagogue, and two kingdoms collided. The power of Jesus's presence and the authority of his teaching demand a response. We bow in submission to his authority, or we rebel and shriek, "What have you to do with us?" (v. 24). There is no middle ground.

Jesus left the synagogue and went home with Simon and Andrew. In this quiet place he took the hand of a sick woman and lifted her up. The fever obeyed his touch and left her; she responded by serving them. No convalescence was needed. Here is a strong and sweet picture of the power and fruit of the gospel.

At sundown, when the Sabbath was over and people could travel without breaking the Sabbath traditions, the people of the town thronged around Jesus. While man-made regulations keep us from Jesus, God's word and Spirit woo us to him. Jesus healed the sick and cast out demons, validating his authority and displaying the merciful character of his kingdom.

The contrast between the kingdom of light and the kingdom of darkness inevitably brings conflict. They cannot be synthesized. No one can serve two masters (Matt. 6:24). If Jesus is God—and he is—it changes everything. Jesus's compelling call to discipleship leaves no place for indifference and inertia. There are only two options: trust and obey myself, or trust and obey him. Transferring authority from self to Jesus is not just radical—it is impossible apart from God's sovereign initiative in our lives.

A relationship with Jesus is the essence of discipleship. Obedience to him is the evidence of discipleship. The disciple of Jesus continually asks, What will it mean to submit my life to the authority of God's word and to live for his glory?

AUGUST 24 · MARK 4:26–29

Crops and the Kingdom

LEEANN STILES

I LOVE TO GARDEN. I enjoy tilling the soil, spreading fertilizer, and planting rows of seeds. In a week or so a stem starts to sprout, then a leaf. Gradually that seed turns into a plant that produces vegetables for a family feast. Even though I know a bit about photosynthesis, I don't really grasp how these things happen.

Mark 4:26–29 portrays a similar wonder. Jesus is explaining what the kingdom of God is like. Someone scatters seeds that grow, though he doesn't understand how. Yet he reaps a full harvest. It's a simple illustration, but rich in meaning. It explains some things we need to pay attention to if we want to have the kind of ears described in verses 9 and 23: ears that hear.

First, our "sowing" role is sharing God's word (Mark 4:14), specifically the gospel. Jesus announces that "the kingdom of God is at hand; repent and believe in the gospel" (1:15). The gospel is the good news that Jesus, God's Son, came into our world, fulfilled God's commandments, and then became the sacrifice for sinners like us. His death and resurrection open the door to forgiveness and salvation for all who repent and believe.

We also recognize that the Holy Spirit—not us—fulfills the "growing" role. Some people think we can increase God's kingdom by our own actions—that when we help the poor, for example, we are bringing in his kingdom. Jesus's teaching corrects that. Acts of service are good and right, but they don't establish the kingdom. They do give opportunities to tell the gospel message, but kingdom growth involves the redemption of people's souls, and only the Spirit can make that happen.

Next, kingdom expansion is a long-term process. Jesus spoke to crowds who thought he would quickly establish a kingdom on earth. Sometimes we expect instant blessings in our lives, too. But this parable describes something different: God's kingdom goes from something hardly noticeable and continues to increase in size over time until it will reach its full glory at Christ's return. Over decades and centuries, people come to faith and grow as Christians.

Finally, the growth of God's kingdom is sure. It spreads steadily even in ways we don't comprehend. It increases in spite of all opposition. Therefore we can be confident that, when we sow seeds by explaining the gospel, some will take root. Some people will respond. The Holy Spirit is working. The kingdom of God will come to fruition—as surely as a seed of wheat comes to harvest. And those who hear and believe Jesus's words will "from the Spirit reap eternal life" (Gal. 6:8).

Jesus Rejected

KATHLEEN B. NIELSON

MARK 6 OFFERS a vivid picture of the rejection that Jesus often encountered. The picture both warns us about ourselves and teaches us about Jesus, who at the end of Mark experiences the ultimate rejection.

These are Jesus's hometown neighbors and acquaintances, ordinary people like us. They can't fit Jesus into their ordinary lives; for years he was just a carpenter, part of a local family, and now he's performing miracles and teaching with authority in the synagogue. *Who does this man think he is?*, they ask. They're astonished, not in a positive but in a negative way: they take offense at him (Mark 6:3). Jesus causes offense. How could he not? He is God incarnate breaking into human history, disturbing all our ordinary complacency. The people of Nazareth are glimpsing who he is—and rejecting him.

This story shows rejection of Jesus, and it shows his response. First, he sees it and names it. When Jesus speaks about a prophet not being without honor except in his hometown (v. 4), he is setting himself in a long line of prophets rejected by their own people (see 2 Chron. 36:16; Jer. 35:15). He is also accusing these people of letting their familiarity with him harden their hearts, so that they are unwilling to believe (Mark 6:6). They are refusing to believe in God's final prophet.

Jesus not only sees and names their rejection; he answers it accordingly. Such rejection brings consequences: verse 5 does not mean that Jesus was constrained by their unbelief but that he will *do no mighty work* where he is rejected. Those who reject him reject his blessing—eternally.

Jesus "marveled because of their unbelief" (v. 6). Their rejection certainly did not take him by surprise. Part of what Jesus is doing here is surely training his disciples, getting ready to send them out and preparing them for similar rejection. What a haunting picture: the Son of God himself marveling at the refusal of human beings to accept his coming to save them! Unbelief is not rejection of a religion or a set of propositions; it is rejection of Jesus the Son of God, who receives that rejection personally.

Jesus's final response is to leave Nazareth and go on teaching (v. 6). Mark shows clearly that Jesus came to accomplish his mission: "not to be served but to serve, and to give his life as a ransom for many" (10:45). The Son of God knew he was the servant "despised and rejected by men" that Isaiah had long ago prophesied (Isa. 53:3). Ultimately, Jesus our Savior responded to human rejection with divine love: he went to the cross.

AUGUST 26 · MARK 7:1-23

The Heart of the Law

MICHELE BENNETT WALTON

FROM OUR SAFE historical distance, we can be tempted to look scornfully at the hypocritical Pharisees. But the truth is that they were *attempting* to worship God. The traditions they guarded were originally aimed at honoring God. But in practice, they ended up anxiously carrying out not God's law but their own. What happened?

Legalism results whenever we add to God's law. In this case, the tradition of *corban*—which was intended to provide for God's work—often practically nullified the commandment to honor one's parents. So, while adding rules to God's law might seem like a way to safeguard it or make it clearer, the truth is that additions to the law of God end up subtracting from it.

Jesus didn't quibble with the Pharisees about their traditions but went directly to the heart of the matter: how is a person defiled? He told them, "There is nothing outside a person that by going into him can defile him, but the things that come out of a person are what defile him" (Mark 7:15). His words still shake pharisaical hearts to the core.

Because the Pharisees assumed that their hearts were pure, they looked anxiously for what the rabbis called a "mother of defilement"—an external source of contamination. Then they built up a fortress of laws to protect their "pure" hearts. But Jesus, knowing the heart of man, assumed something wholly different. No Pharisee, no legalist—*no human*—starts with a righteous heart.

We can turn the New Testament Pharisees into a caricature of a certain group in ancient history, dismissing their wayward behavior as a peculiar brand of stubborn sinfulness. But we would be better served to look with sober eyes at their plight and humbly learn the lessons that Scripture intends to teach us. As we attempt to worship God in our own context, we should be aware of the subtle temptations of legalism. Are we fearful of unbelieving people, places, and things? Do we withdraw from our neighborhoods and communities in order to protect our "purity"? If our self-protection inhibits our ability to carry out Jesus's command to "go and tell," then we may find hints of legalism in our own hearts.

Take a few minutes to review the first few chapters of the Gospel of Mark. Look for the ways Jesus interacts with people considered "unclean" before the law. Then ask God to open your eyes to the spirit and not just the letter of his law.

AUGUST 27 · MARK 10:35–45

Greatness as Service

HEATHER HOUSE

JESUS ASKS HIS followers to do many things that are the opposite of what our sin-broken world expects from us. He tells us to love our enemies (Matt. 5:43–48), to take the more difficult path (Matt. 7:13–14), and to lose our lives in order to save them (Matt. 16:24–26). He also upends our ideas of what it means to be great.

In Mark 10:35–45, James and John are heading toward Jerusalem with Jesus. The Lord has just been telling his disciples (a third time) that he will soon die and rise again. But apparently James and John don't understand. Perhaps they believed that Jesus was saying he was about to restore David's earthly kingdom. The two disciples brazenly ask for places of authority in his coming empire. Jesus knows that James and John have no idea what they are requesting from him. He has no cushy governmental office to offer, no personal influence to wield, no chariots to command. Instead, what James, John, and the rest of the disciples will have as members of his kingdom is servanthood and suffering.

That doesn't sound like a better position, does it? The world teaches that we have achieved something when other people do the things we do not want to do ourselves, and when our lives are easy and enjoyable. Jesus teaches that we are great when we value others more than ourselves.

Jesus, who deserves worship, adoration, and service, is instead about to drink a cup of wrath, enduring punishment for the sins of the world (Rom. 3:21–25). He is about to sink under the waves of death, a baptism that will destroy his body (Isa. 53:2–5). He is about to give up his life in order that others might be free from eternal separation from God (2 Cor. 5:21). And we who are known by his name are called to show others the same kind of love. So instead of desiring to be our own boss, or to be someone else's boss, we seek to serve. Creating a community known for its compassion and service shows that we value what God values.

To the world, it sounds bizarre to spend time with social outcasts. It seems odd—foolish, even—to use a medical degree to serve the poor rather than to make as much money as possible. Or to give money to an out-of-work man or a spare room to a homeless family, when you could have a new sound system or home gym or great vacation. It also looks absurd to give your life for people who hate you (John 7:7). But that is the kind of greatness that Jesus wants us to desire. It is how he has treated *us*.

A Surprising Kind of Rescue

JEN WILKIN

JESUS DOES NOTHING by chance; nor does he bend to anyone's expectations. Perhaps nowhere is this more clearly seen than in his triumphal entrance into Jerusalem. The book of Zechariah, recorded some five hundred years before Jesus's birth, spoke of a coming king who would bring peace to Israel, depicted as "humble and mounted on a donkey, on a colt, the foal of a donkey" (Zech. 9:9). The prophecy was well known among the Jews of Jesus's day, who looked for a king to deliver them by force from Roman oppression.

So when Jesus instructs his disciples to bring him a donkey colt from a nearby village, he does so with purpose. Even the way he states his request indicates awareness and deliberate action. He intends to go to the cross, and he understands exactly what must be done to accomplish that end.

The colt is found, and Jesus mounts it to ride the short distance into Jerusalem. The journey was only two miles, and most pilgrims made it by foot. Significantly, in all four Gospels, this is the only recorded instance in which Jesus rides rather than walks. Why? Because he is making a statement. He is announcing unequivocally that he is Israel's Messiah. He is, in effect, enacting a living parable. The people respond immediately to its implicit message, laying cloaks and branches in his path, as in the anointing of Old Testament kings. They cry out "Hosanna!"—"Save now!"—acknowledging Jesus as the Promised One, the Christ.

And yet the salvation for which they clamor is a deliverance from earthly oppression. When their expectations of a warrior-king are not met, their shouts of "Hosanna!" will turn to shouts of "Crucify him!" Yet, with steady deliberation Jesus steps into the prophecies of old, initiating the sequence of events that will indeed result in peace, a final exhalation of his breath that speaks peace to all nations, just as Zechariah had prophesied. After thousands of years of waiting, he will indeed "save now," though not as his people expected.

If the Jews had eyes to see that their coming King was also their Passover Lamb, their shouts of Hosanna might have rung until the Passover was spent and the Paschal Lamb slain. What about you? Has Jesus failed to meet your expectations? Have you looked for him to intervene in power and found yourself disappointed? Consider that he is deliberately acting for your good, though perhaps not in a way you expected. Know that the one to whom you cry "Save now!" is able to save to the uttermost.

Jesus Sees

ANN VOSKAMP

JESUS SEES. Jesus sits down across from the treasury, and he sees how the wealthy put in their large sums. And Jesus sees how the widow puts in her large heart. Jesus sees how the widow puts in these two small copper coins—two "*leptai*," the smallest coins in circulation at the time, less than the worth of a penny today. Jesus witnesses the willingness of the widow, and he tells those who are his disciples that what matters most in our giving is not the sum but the sacrifice.

Jesus tells those who are his disciples, what you give out of your abundance is not the same as what you give out of your affection. What some people put in is their leftovers. What other people put in is their life. There are those who are comfortable giving God something; then there are those who aren't comfortable until they give God everything.

The Greek word Jesus uses to express what the widow gave is *bios*. A wooden, literal translation would read something like, "She put in everything, even her whole life." Jesus's words startle and sober and shake the slumbering awake. There are rich people of God who give out of their margin. And there are real followers of God who give out of their *marrow*.

After we give to God, do we eat any differently? Margin, or marrow? After we give to God, do we dress any differently? Travel any differently? Live any differently? Margin, or marrow? Are we giving God some of our money? *Or all of our lives?*

When we give, we too often give only what ensures that we don't lose comfort or control. But when the widow gave her mites, she gave not only her money but her marrow. She gave away not only her comfort but her control. She gave till she had to trust God.

Jesus was born in a barn to parents who were poor. His life was one of poverty: "Foxes have holes, and birds of the air have nests, but the Son of Man has nowhere to lay his head" (Matt. 8:20). Jesus lived the life of a homeless man. And he died on the cross as a completely naked and utterly penniless man. Jesus gave up control of everything for us.

While the widow was willing to *risk* giving her life for God, Jesus unequivocally *did* lay down his for you. What could ever stop you from giving your trust, giving control of your life, giving the marrow of your life, to the only One who gave up his life for you?

AUGUST 30 · MARK 14:32-42

The Way of the Cross

JENNY SALT

TRAVELING FROM point A to point B often involves working out the best way to go and asking whether there are options. Is there a faster way? Is there a way without tolls? Is there a more scenic way?

When we think about the way to God, there may be similar types of questions: are there different ways, and is one way easier than the other? For all of us there is a point A, sin and separation from God; and a point B, peace and reconciliation with God. How do we get from point A to point B? The Bible tells us that there is only one way: the way of the cross.

Mark 14:32–42 places the reader at the night before Jesus's crucifixion. Jesus would soon experience the horror of separation from his Father. The desolation of the cross and the words "My God, my God, why have you forsaken me?" (Mark 15:34) will echo out over Calvary. The "hour" (14:35, 41) had come, and it was not a matter of going through the motions or just getting it over and done with. On this night, the night that Jesus would be betrayed into the hands of sinners (v. 41), Jesus was "greatly distressed and troubled" (v. 33).

His disciples were with him in the garden of Gethsemane. Jesus took Peter, James, and John further with him, and, telling them of his distress, he asked them to watch and pray. Sadly, even after three years of witnessing Jesus's ministry, these disciples failed to do what Jesus asked, and failed to understand what Jesus had come to do: take upon himself the sin of the world. For Jesus, the way of the cross was submission to his Father: "Remove this cup from me. Yet not what I will, but what you will" (v. 36).

The failure of the disciples to watch and pray as Jesus asked highlights just how significant the work of the cross is. These men had glimpsed the glory of Jesus at his transfiguration (9:2–13). They had heard him teach about his mission (Matt. 16:21). And yet they failed to understand what Jesus was about to do. From our perspective it seems far more obvious. But we are just like them. Following Jesus, knowing peace with God through faith in Jesus, does not guarantee that we will always trust and obey God. All of us fail in this regard.

What is the way forward? The *only* way is the way of the cross: keeping our eyes fixed on Jesus, "the founder and perfecter of our faith, who for the joy set before him endured the cross, despising the shame, and is seated at the right hand of the throne of God" (Heb. 12:2). How comforting to know that the way to God does not depend on what we do, but on what Jesus has done at the cross.

AUGUST 31 • LUKE 1:39-56

God Delights to Exalt the Humble

LYDIA BROWNBACK

A SHARED BLESSING. Surely that is why Mary made haste to visit her relative Elizabeth. Who else could grasp the wonder they were both experiencing—the miraculous conception of a child! Yet Mary and Elizabeth were not the first among God's people to receive this miracle. We find many instances, beginning with Sarah in Genesis, of God's provision of children to barren women—children who would be key figures in redemptive history. Through overcoming barrenness, God demonstrated that he is able to overrule every circumstance to accomplish his purposes.

Elizabeth's womb carried John the Baptist, the forerunner of the Messiah, who was the child in Mary's womb. Much about the character of God and his kingdom is seen in his choosing an elderly, childless woman to mother the forerunner of the Messiah, and a young girl of humble means to mother the Messiah himself. God values humility. Elizabeth's humility is evident when she says to Mary, "Why is this granted to me that the mother of my Lord should come to me?" (Luke 1:43). Mary's humility is seen in her song of praise, traditionally called the "Magnificat," in which she extols the mercies of God in blessing the "humble estate of his servant" (v. 48).

God's choice of Mary and Elizabeth shows the great reversal brought about by the in-breaking of God's kingdom. With the coming of the long-awaited Messiah, God scatters the proud, brings down the mighty, fills the hungry, and sends the rich away empty.

We see God's love for the small and despised, his compassion for the weak, whether the weakness of sin or of social inferiority. Mary was among the weak due to both her poverty and her gender, as were the other four women in the Messiah's family tree (see Matt. 1:1–16). Tamar, Rahab, Ruth, and Bathsheba were either social outcasts or morally compromised, or both.

Mary's song is similar to the song of Hannah long before her (1 Sam. 2:1–10). Both women extol God's strength and praise him for his power. However, Mary's song goes beyond Hannah's. Foreshadowing the mission of the Messiah, she declares that from this time forward she would be known as blessed. Both Mary's song and her meeting with Elizabeth foreshadow the saving work of the child Mary carries, and the nature of the kingdom he brings. Here we find the presence of the Holy Spirit, the entrance of joy, and abundant mercy.

SEPTEMBER 1 · LUKE 2:22–38

A Hole in Her Heart

JANI ORTLUND

BABY JESUS IS almost six weeks old. His godly parents, having circumcised him on the eighth day (Luke 2:21), now want to perform "everything according to the Law of the Lord" (v. 39). They present him to the Lord as their firstborn at the temple in Jerusalem and offer a sacrifice for Mary's purification before they leave.

Imagine yourself as Mary, cradling your infant son as you and your husband make your way into the noisy, crowded court of the temple. You see a man approaching. The people around you greet him as Simeon, and you sense their respect for him. Luke tells us he was a God-fearing man, patiently waiting for the One who would come to deliver Israel (1:78–79). Simeon lived in the presence of the Holy Spirit (2:25, 27). In fact, the Holy Spirit had revealed to him that he would see the consolation of Israel before he died.

You are surprised to find yourself placing your tiny son into his outstretched arms as you see the wonder in Simeon's face. A baby! He never expected a baby. So this is the one he has been waiting for. This tiny baby boy is the Christ! Salvation has come in the form of a gurgling infant. Simeon tells all around him that this child will be a light to the Gentiles and will bring glory to Israel. You and Joseph wonder at his words.

As he places Jesus back in your arms, Simeon's eyes gravely lock with yours. Solemnly, he tells you that your son will face opposition in his role as Judge and Savior. And it will cost you greatly, too. It will be like a sword piercing through your own soul. You gasp, fearing his words and yet recognizing truth behind them, and you hold your baby to your chest. The tears begin to pool in the corners of your eyes. You look to Joseph. What does all this mean?

Just then you see a dignified elderly lady making her way toward you. You recognize her as Anna, the aged prophetess, known for her humble dedication to God. Her gentle smile lifts your anxiety as she begins thanking God for your baby, telling others that he is their hope. Her thankful heart reminds you that God is at work. He has been faithful to you over all the strange and hard events of the past eleven months. Even now, bringing this sweet, godly lady to lift your troubled heart—can the Lord not be trusted with every day ahead of you?

It always costs for Christ to come. God gave up his Son. Mary paid the highest price a mother can. But God is faithful. He gives his Spirit; he fulfills his promises; he sends his servants to help us along the way. He can fill any woman's heart with the faith she needs to follow him.

Tried and Tempted

MARY BETH MCGREEVY

SOMETIMES, WHEN WE are tempted, we feel sinful. But it is not a sin to *be* tempted. The Lord Jesus Christ, when "full of the Holy Spirit," was led by the Spirit into the wilderness to be tempted by the devil (Luke 4:1–2).

At stake was the heart of Jesus's identity. Was Jesus really the Son of God? A voice from heaven had just declared, at his baptism, "You are my beloved Son; with you I am well pleased" (3:22). Now the devil comes with half-truths to try to undermine that declaration:

- Would God allow his Son to go hungry? Wouldn't he want him to use supernatural powers to turn stones into bread? If you really are the Son of God, why not do it?
- Doesn't God intend to make the nations his Son's heritage, and the ends of the earth his possession (Ps. 2:7–8)? Then why not worship me, avoid the cross, and rule them right now?
- Wouldn't God use angels to protect his Son? Then make an irrefutable entrance into your public ministry by jumping off the temple so everyone can see angels rescuing you!

Because Jesus was fully human (as well as fully divine), these were real temptations. After forty days without food, Jesus was hungry. Anticipation of his suffering on the cross would have been cause for dread. And it would have been natural for him to want everyone to acknowledge who he was and come to him without the criticism of the religious authorities and the doubts of those who knew him only as "Joseph's son" (Luke 4:22). How easy it would be to doubt God's provision and timing!

Is this not our great temptation as well? "If I really am God's child, why would he allow me to go through such hard times?" "Why would he make me wait so long to get married? To have a baby?" "Why can't I just compromise God's ways to accomplish what I know he wants me to do?"

To *be* tempted in these ways is not a sin. God allows us to be tempted to test us and ultimately to strengthen us. But he also gives his enabling grace so that we can trust him amid the temptations. Just as Jesus answered the devil's temptations with quotes from Deuteronomy, God gives us his word to answer the half-truths that assail us. He fills us with the Spirit of Christ to lead us through our wilderness. And as we trust God to accomplish his will in his time, we experience the kind of gospel living that brings glory to God and defeats temptation.

SEPTEMBER 3 • LUKE 7:36–50

For the Love of Judgment

MICHELE BENNETT WALTON

JUDGMENT IS THE posture of the self-righteous person, setting himself over the world to catalog the rightness or wrongness of all things. In verse 39, we see Simon the Pharisee busily passing judgment. With the words, "If this man were a prophet" (Luke 7:39), he decries the Savior of the world as less than a prophet. Then he goes on to condemn the "woman of the city" (v. 37), unable to see her even as a candidate for God's mercy. In one verse, Simon has judged Jesus, the woman, and the whole situation wrongly—denying faith, withholding mercy, and ignoring love.

But if Simon's words expose his heart, surely this woman's actions tell us even more about her. She knew that in presenting herself before these Pharisees and scribes, she would be subjected afresh to their scorn. Certainly she could see the familiar shadows of judgment passing over Simon's face as he eyed her from his seat of honor. But she didn't care about proving her righteousness to these men. She came to see Jesus, bringing a bottle of costly perfume and her pride, both of which she would pour out at his feet.

That's why Jesus turns our attention to the woman. Her posture could hardly be more different from that of Simon. She abandons any pretense of self-righteousness as she clings to Christ's feet, anointing and kissing them in an act of loving gratitude. Her faith in Jesus's righteousness on her behalf expresses itself in overflowing love for him. Galatians 5:6 tells us that faith-fueled love is what counts, not law-keeping: "For in Christ Jesus neither circumcision nor uncircumcision counts for anything, but only faith working through love."

Preoccupied with his own righteousness, Simon considered neither faith nor love. So Jesus confronted him with the hard truth. By presenting the sinful woman's behavior as a model of faith and a rebuke to Simon's self-righteousness, Jesus makes it clear that Simon has even judged himself wrongly. He lacks the righteousness that the sinner has found in Christ.

Which character do you identify with in this story—Simon or the woman? To all who will abandon their self-righteousness at his feet, Christ says, "Your faith has saved you; go in peace." But to those like Simon who prefer to stand in judgment, Scripture cautions, "For with the judgment you pronounce you will be judged, and with the measure you use it will be measured to you" (Matt. 7:2). Ask God to expose any ways in which you may be passing judgment on yourself and others, and allow his Spirit to turn your attention back to Jesus—the one who has shown such mercy to you, despite the judgment you deserve.

SEPTEMBER 4 · LUKE 8:40–56

More Than a Healer

ELYSE FITZPATRICK

MANY OF US know what it's like to have a physical ailment that goes on and on without relief. We hear about some new remedy and begin to hope in it, only to discover that we're no better and perhaps even worse. We're not all that different from two other women, one young and another older, who learned that there was a Physician who could heal diseases—and could do much more than that.

An important religious leader named Jairus met Jesus. Falling at his feet, Jairus implored Jesus to come immediately to heal his twelve-year-old daughter, who lay dying. Undoubtedly, this man had tried everything—

had called in all the best physicians and religious leaders to prescribe and pray—all to no avail. He was desperate and powerless. Then, to his great relief, Jesus agreed to come with him. Hope began to rise.

While Jesus was on his way to Jairus's home, a woman who had been ill for twelve years, who had "spent all her living on physicians," approached the crowd (Luke 8:43). Unlike Jairus, though, she was an outcast. Rather than being a religious leader, this nameless woman was unclean, destitute, and alienated from every means of approach to God. She too was desperate and, like Jairus, had no idea whom she was dealing with.

So she snuck up behind Jesus, pressing though the crowd, and did the unthinkable: she touched a holy man. And instantly she was healed. The Lord knew what had happened and demanded to know who had touched him. Why? Did he really not know who it was? He knew, but he pressed her to confess her need because he wanted to be more to her than merely a magician or healer. She didn't need a magic-healer, she needed a Savior, so Jesus didn't let her slink away through the crowd.

Meanwhile, Jairus heard the dreaded news: "Your daughter is dead" (v. 49). But Jairus, too, was about to learn that Jesus is more than a teacher who heals the sick. He's a Savior who raises the dead. "Do not fear," Jesus said, "only believe" (v. 50). Jesus said, "Child, arise," and "she got up at once" (vv. 54–55).

Jesus always does more than we expect. Jairus was hoping for a miraculous healing from a respected teacher. Instead he experienced the resurrection power of God. The unclean woman was hoping to scrape by with a healing. She discovered her Redeemer. Jesus insists on being more than what we expect, more than a handyman to fix our troubles. He won't let us get by with just trying to use him. Instead, he will love us and make us his own so that we might really know him.

The Joy Set before Us

JOSEPH P. MURPHY

IN NUMBERS 14:21, the Lord declared that all the earth would be filled with his glory. On the mountain with Jesus, three of his disciples saw that glory come. The shining brightness, visible in Jesus, must have been overwhelming!

Yet God's concern lies elsewhere. Earlier with Moses, the Lord addressed the problem of those who saw his glory yet persisted in disobedience. God himself became man in Jesus, and on this mountain the veil is pulled away. The disciples see him as he is. Unlike Moses, Jesus doesn't strike fear into his disciples when they see the glory of God upon him. They know and love Jesus, and know his love for them. Their love isn't perfect, of course, but through this and many more experiences, it will grow. Jesus's love, however, is perfect. It is such that they never turn away from him. When they abandon him at his death, it is out of fear for their lives at the hands of men, not fear of or rejection by Jesus. Jesus loves us perfectly, and that is what leads him to his death for us. How blessed we are!

Therein lies our problem. Seeing such awesome glory, and knowing the presence of One who loves us perfectly, we fail to grasp the implications of what we see and know. This isn't the time to pitch a tent and enjoy ourselves (Luke 9:33). The kingdom of God *is* coming, and it *has* arrived in Jesus Christ, but its full expression delays—because it is meant to include us! What's needed now is for us to *follow* Jesus, to the cross. John, having seen Jesus this day, later declared, "Beloved, we are God's children now, and what we will be has not yet appeared; but we know that when he appears we shall be like him, because we shall see him as he is" (1 John 3:2). John links our future with Jesus's present. The manifest glory, and the joy, that awaited Jesus that day, was on the other side of his cross. The same holds true for us. In a real but limited sense, we must share in his death so that we will also share in his resurrection. How shall this occur?

"This is my Son, my Chosen One; listen to him!" (Luke 9:35). Moses, through whom God gave the Law, and Elijah, the greatest of the prophets who called Israel back to the Law, stand in living testimony to Jesus Christ in the sight of Jesus's disciples. All that they said and did in expressing God's word points to Christ. Jesus is the Word of God. God's concern is that we continue to hear and trust that Word. Listen to him—especially, listen to his words that tell of his great love for sinners like us.

SEPTEMBER 6 · LUKE 12:13-21

The Parable of the Rich Fool

KRISTEN WETHERELL

AMBITION AND GREED taint the air as thousands of curious people follow Jesus. The crowds have been increasing in size as they seek a sign from him (Luke 11:29), even trampling one another to get close (12:1). A man in the crowd demands that Jesus get involved in his financial affairs; after denying that request, Jesus warns his disciples to *watch out for covetousness*.

To covet is to yearn for what others have. It is greed motivated by a desire for security and satisfaction—in other words, for *life*. Such is this rich man's dilemma. His problem is not that he is wealthy, for riches are not inherently evil; nor is his problem necessarily the storage facilities he has built for his crops. Money and possessions are gifts from God, to be stewarded for his purposes.

Yet, as the rich man addresses his soul, we identify his problem. He confidently seeks security and satisfaction—*life*—in riches. Rather than offering his soul and his stuff to God, he hoards it. He is driven by greed and compelled by covetousness.

But we may ask, if covetousness is a yearning for what others have, then how can we accuse the rich man of it? Are the crops and barns not his? Jesus anticipates our question, and his answer is an emphatic no. Everything belongs to God—our stuff and especially our souls. He has created us to treasure him above all else and to offer our earthly riches to his service. If we had everything we could ever want *except* Jesus, we would not only lose what we possess on earth but would lose our very souls for eternity.

The point of Jesus's parable is not that we must reject earthly things but that we must prioritize eternal ones, allowing everything earthly to point us to the Creator and Giver of every good gift. While riches and possessions will never satisfy nor save us, God does. And how does he do so? Jesus, the richest person in the universe (he is God!), became poor, taking on human flesh, so that by his poverty we might become rich (2 Cor. 8:9) in the truest, most everlasting way.

When we receive Christ as our greatest treasure, along with all the immeasurable riches of his mercy, grace, kindness, and glory, he helps us fight against covetousness and greed and to pursue generosity toward God and others. What do you have that you did not receive (1 Cor. 4:7)? Entrust your most valuable possession—your soul—to Christ, and then be rich toward God as you use what he has entrusted to you for his purposes.

SEPTEMBER 7 · LUKE 15:11–32

A Prodigal Son and a Resentful Brother

STARR MEADE

THIS PARABLE USUALLY goes by the name of "the prodigal son." And to be sure, the younger son *does* receive a great deal of attention in the story, and all true believers can relate to him. We know that, like him, and in spite of our Father's goodness and generosity, we have not only sinned against our Father but have sinned outrageously. When we're honest, we see ourselves in this young man, demonstrating, by our favorite sins, that we despise our Father's gifts. We relate to the Prodigal Son, and we love the story because the father forgives and welcomes him anyway.

Yet Jesus intended the story, as well as the two parables before it, as a rebuke to those religious people who feel they have *earned* their place in the family of God and who resent the ease and freedom with which those who have not earned it are welcomed in (Luke 15:1–3). Imagine yourself as the older brother. You're always responsible, faithful, and obedient. Imagine the righteous indignation you feel when your little brother not only breaks your father's heart but then converts into cash the land and livestock earned over a lifetime so he can waste it all on loose living! Then imagine coming in from the field to the sounds of that brother's party. Shouldn't there be some sort of consequence for his wretched behavior? Instead, he receives gifts and honors you've never had. Where's the justice in that? You deserve better!

What the scribes and the Pharisees and the older son lacked were the perspective of God and the heart of God. When God looks at people apart from the righteousness of Christ, he doesn't see both good people and sinners; he only sees sinners. He sees none who deserve his gifts. Yet his heart is such that he lavishes those gifts anyway. To both the moral and the immoral he says, as the father told the older brother, "all that is mine is yours" (v. 31). In both cases, it is pure gift and never deserved.

Christ came to call sinners of all kinds to repentance: tax collectors *and* Pharisees, prodigal sons who sin blatantly *and* older brothers who count themselves righteous just as they are. And when anyone repents, God's response is never grudging. His forgiveness never hangs back; it runs to welcome the penitent.

Christ calls all God's children to have the heart of their Father. He calls us to welcome repentant sinners of all kinds, rejoicing in every manifestation of God's extravagant grace.

SEPTEMBER 8 · LUKE 16:14–17

Make Your Choice

CLAIRE SMITH

JESUS'S STATEMENT THAT "you cannot serve God and money" (Luke 16:13) immediately tells us that the Pharisees had a problem, because they were "lovers of money" (v. 14). As teachers of God's law, their life's work should have been in the service of God—but they had made their choice, and they had chosen to love money, not God. And because they did not love God, they lived their lives to impress people, and not God. They tried to win approval and esteem from people with their apparently righteous and religious lives—perhaps by their actions even trying to impress people with their "love" for God.

But just as you cannot serve both God and money, neither can you please both people and God. It is one or the other. What fallen human beings celebrate is not what God celebrates. It is an abomination to him. So being a people-pleaser is not just useless when it comes to pleasing God; it works against us. It is an offense to God. The Pharisees were earning God's judgment even as they were earning people's praise. But God knew the true state of their hearts. He knows what is in every human heart.

Although they claimed to be experts in the Law and the Prophets, the Pharisees failed to see that the kingdom promised therein had arrived in the person of Jesus. To ridicule Jesus is to ridicule the person promised by the Law and the Prophets. To reject Jesus is to refuse to enter the promised kingdom.

Jesus is the fulfillment of the old covenant. The Law and Prophets had not been wrong. Far from it! Not one word from them could pass away, exactly because the kingdom they pointed to had now arrived in Jesus—and his kingdom is a permanent kingdom. The word of God had not changed, but the times had.

The Pharisees, like all people, had to choose. They were lovers of money, but they could not serve both God and money. They wanted to be justified, but they could not please both people and God. They wanted to be experts in the Law and the Prophets, but they failed to see that, in Jesus's preaching, the promised new era in God's purposes had arrived. And like all people, they were being urged to enter forcefully into that new kingdom (v. 16), and yet were ridiculing and rejecting the only one whose teaching—and subsequent death and resurrection—could bring them in.

They had ignored all the promises and the warnings, and made the wrong choice at every turn (see vv. 29–31).

What Do You Trust?

JESSICA THOMPSON

JESUS TOLD THIS parable about a Pharisee and a tax collector "to some who trusted in themselves that they were righteous, and treated others with contempt" (Luke 18:9). The Pharisee's prayer is really just a list of his accomplishments—perhaps intended to remind God how great it is that he is on his team. He self-righteously compares himself to a tax collector who is praying at the same time. The Pharisee boasts that he is not "like this tax collector" (v. 11). Like a peacock with his feathers on full display, each feather representing a spiritual achievement, the Pharisee struts around, making sure that all who see him are aware of what a holy person he is.

In stark contrast is the tax collector, who stands far off and cannot even look up when he prays. Overcome by his shame, he beats his chest and cries out in anguish, "God, be merciful to me, a sinner!" (v. 13). The tax collector has no beautiful feathers to display. He has no merits to brag about. He has only the promise of mercy for those who call upon the Lord.

Jesus concludes the parable by saying, "I tell you, this man went down to his house justified, rather than the other. For everyone who exalts himself will be humbled, but the one who humbles himself will be exalted" (v. 14). This exemplifies one of the major themes of Luke: the first become last, while the last become first. The proud are humbled, while the humble are exalted.

Ironically, it is easy to sit back in judgment when we look at the Pharisee and say, "Thank God I'm not like him." We see how ugly pride and bragging are. But it is sobering to realize that we aren't always that different from him—we are often simply more sophisticated and subtle with our boasting. Where do we place our confidence when we pray? Before coming to God, do we mentally rehearse the ways in which we have been "good"? Do we try and make sure that we are acceptably clean? Or do we come with naked confidence before the throne of grace, remembering that it was not our good behavior that got us there in the first place?

We must ever be on guard against the notion that God's goodness toward us is in any way based or contingent on our behavior or accomplishments. We are saved by grace alone, and it is the accomplishment of Another that makes us acceptable. As we pray, may our insufficiencies and failures never keep us from our Savior, who is "a friend of tax collectors and sinners" (7:34). May we run to him with all of our messiness, finding that in that moment he meets us with grace, love, and forgiveness. His love will exalt us out of the mire, into rich communion with him.

SEPTEMBER 10 · LUKE 19

Identifying with Zacchaeus

ANN VOSKAMP

YOU KNOW THAT sting of not being liked. You know the people who would avoid you in the grocery store. Who would look the other way if they saw you in the parking lot. People who would mutter and would begin to grumble (Luke 19:7). We all have Zacchaeus moments when we feel as disliked and shunned as a tax collector.

Six times the socially rejected tax collectors are mentioned in the book of Luke—and *every single time positively*. It's a pattern into which you can weave the ends of your frayed heart: Jesus is drawn to the rejected, and the rejected are drawn to Jesus.

And it's the people who draw themselves up as the respectable who find Jesus repelling. Why? Because when you feel essentially respectable, you want religion. And when you know you are essentially rejected—you want the *gospel*. In religion, it's the "respectable" who search for a God to impress. But in the gospel, it's God who searches for the rejected to *save*.

The only "respectable" people who become Christians are those who realize they aren't. It's not that *even* the rejected are accepted by Jesus—it's that *only* the rejected are accepted by Jesus. Only those who confess that their reliance on self-sufficiency and supposed morality is as sinful as any other sin. It's only when you realize you aren't respectable, that you are no better than the rejected, that you are fully accepted.

Jesus speaks straight into the ache of our hearts: "Today salvation has come to this house" (v. 9). Not that salvation will come, but salvation has come. Jesus is here. You don't have to perform, or be perfect, or pretend. You need simply to know a *Person*—One who pursues you. Jesus doesn't give Zacchaeus a checklist before he shows up. Jesus just shows up, right where we are. Salvation isn't about keeping rules. It's about keeping at rest in the work of Christ, keeping company with the grace of Christ, keeping your joy through the strength of Christ.

Like Zacchaeus, you have to position your heart to see Christ in all things. Zacchaeus climbed the limbs of a tree; we turn the pages of Scripture.

Zacchaeus had to make himself look less than respectable in order to see Jesus. To be like Jesus, we, too, must be willing to look less than respectable. If we've positioned our lives to see Jesus, we must go to the rejected, eat with the less than respected, and make time for the run-down and the reviled and rebuffed. These are the words of Christ: "I must stay at your house today" (v. 5). This is our Zacchaeus moment, we the accepted: and we "received him joyfully" (v. 6).

Who Is the Greatest?

BRYAN CHAPELL

THIS ACCOUNT IS all the more striking and sad because of its immediate context. The disciples are with Jesus at the Last Supper (see Luke 22:10–14). He has just told them that, though he is the Son of God—the long-expected Messiah and prophesied Davidic King—he will give himself to save his people (vv. 15–22) and to bring in the fullness of his kingdom (vv. 16, 18).

We expect the apostles to beg Jesus not to go through with such a plan of self-sacrifice. Surely they would, instead, offer themselves in sacrifice for God's purposes. Yet no such selfless objections or offers arise. The response of the disciples to Jesus's announcement of his sacrifice to bring in his kingdom is not heartrending gratitude, but a dispute—first about who will betray Jesus (v. 23) and, then, about who will be greatest in the kingdom established by Christ's suffering (v. 24).

The scene is similar to (though much sadder than) that of teenage children whose mom has fainted from the exhaustion of caring for them, arguing first about which of them loves their mother more, and then arguing about who gets to drive the car to the hospital!

Luke uses the irony of the apostles' insensitive dispute about their future prospects to underscore Christ's sacrifice and what should be the priorities of all who would live according to his kingdom's purposes. In contrast to our tendency to put ourselves first and live for our own priorities, the gospel calls us to put others first, as did Jesus.

The difficulty of living according to such selfless priorities is emphasized by the fact that this same dispute about who will be greatest among them has arisen before in Luke's Gospel (9:46–48). The sinful repetition of the apostles' concern for self-promotion should remind us that freedom from selfish living requires a heart transformation that only the gospel provides. A greater love for Christ and his priorities displaces love for ourselves, as the magnitude of his selfless sacrifice for us touches and transforms our hearts (Phil. 2:1–10).

SEPTEMBER 12 · LUKE 23:26–49

The Mystery of the Cross

SAM STORMS

LUKE'S ACCOUNT OF the crucifixion of Jesus threatens to overwhelm the reader, as the details of his abuse at the hands of his executioners rush upon us like a relentless flood. It is painful enough to envision our Lord as the object of scorn, ridicule, and mockery. That the sinless, spotless Lamb of God should then be subjected to the vile taunting and torturous mistreatment of such men is more than we can fathom.

What can we say when the Lord of Glory is nailed to a cross? We say this:

We know that at the cross God was rightfully angry toward us, yet we also know that he was loving us, so much so that he gave his only begotten Son.

We know that our great triune God is unchangeable and that the union between Father, Son, and Spirit is unbreakable. Yet we also know that on the cross hung God the Son, forsaken by God the Father.

We know that God is the essence of all life. He is its source and sustainer. Yet we also know that somehow at Calvary the God-man, Jesus, died.

We know that God is infinitely righteous, pure, and holy—that in him there is no defect, and of him nothing evil can be said. Yet we also know that for our sake God "made him to be sin who knew no sin" (2 Cor. 5:21).

One of the most wonderful declarations in Scripture is Paul's assurance that no matter what we encounter in life or in death, nothing "will be able to separate us from the love of God in Christ Jesus our Lord" (Rom. 8:39). It is here in Luke's narrative that we discover why the apostle could speak with such robust confidence. To put it simply, we shall never be separated from the love of God because Jesus, in our place, was separated and forsaken, and suffered the wrath we deserved.

All of us have experienced some season of loneliness. You may be immersed in it right now. But as painful and depressing as it may be, of this you may be absolutely certain: your heavenly Father will never, ever turn his back on you. He will never, ever turn away his face. He will never, ever forsake you. How can you be so sure? Look to the cross. The only God-forsakenness that you ever had cause to fear was endured to an infinite and immeasurable degree by your Lord and Savior, Jesus.

Hopes Resurrected

CAROLYN ARENDS

TWO DESPONDENT TRAVELERS make their way from Jerusalem to nearby Emmaus. Only a week ago, they were riding the high of Palm Sunday, hailing Jesus of Nazareth as the long-awaited hope of Israel (Luke 19:28–39). Now, their hopes are in ashes, vaporized at the foot of a cross where, two days earlier, Jesus was crucified like a common criminal. They encounter a stranger, apparently the only man in Jerusalem who hasn't heard about what happened. He asks what they are talking about, and they explain the terrible events of the weekend. "But we had hoped that he was the one to redeem Israel," they confess (24:21).

As readers of the Emmaus story, we're in on the most wonderful twist in the universe; the "stranger" is in fact the risen Savior. Death has been defeated! The travelers, however, are in the dark. And so this passage, one of the longest and most detailed stories in the New Testament, is significant not only as an eyewitness account of the resurrection but also as a guide to handling our own doubts.

We see, first, that it is possible to be in the company of Jesus and not realize it (v. 16). While it's always good to seek God's presence (Jer. 29:13), we needn't take seasons of emotional or spiritual dryness as proof of his absence. God said he would never leave or forsake us (Deut. 31:6); the promise holds whether we "feel" him near or not.

Second, we see the importance of naming our doubts. Jesus takes his time, refusing to rush his companions to the right answers, and instead asks them to share "what things" have been happening in their city—and in their hearts (Luke 24:19). It's only once they've been able to process their own questions and heartaches that they are ready to recognize the truth.

Third, we see how important it is to understand Jesus—and relationship with him—in the light of the entire biblical witness. "Beginning with Moses and all the Prophets, [Jesus] interpreted to them in all the Scriptures the things concerning himself" (v. 27). In the context of the whole story,

Christ's suffering—and ours—cannot be seen as a sign of God's defeat or his absence, but as the expected path to God's everlasting glory (v. 26).

Receiving Jesus

STARR MEADE

IN CHURCH CIRCLES, we often hear the phrase "receive Jesus" to describe the act by which a person enters into salvation. It's often expanded into the expressions "receive Jesus as your personal Savior" or "receive Jesus into your heart." Neither expression is particularly helpful, however, nor is either one found in Scripture. John calls on us to "receive" Jesus, but as more than just a "personal Savior" from sin's punishment. He uses his whole Gospel to show us what we must receive Jesus *as*, and introduces those ideas here in his opening prologue.

In receiving "the Word," we receive him as the eternal God (John 1:1). To the Jews of John's day, this was blasphemy. To the Gentiles of John's day, it was silliness—one more "son" of mythological gods. To modern humans, there either is no God, making Jesus of Nazareth just a good man, or Jesus is divine only in the sense that we all are. People today tend to "receive Jesus" as a moral teacher but nothing more. John calls on his readers to receive Jesus as God in the fullest sense of the word: infinite while we are finite, completely other than we are.

John calls on us to receive Christ as the one who created all that is (vv. 3, 10). That includes us. As creatures, we are accountable to Christ. He is our Creator, so he has the right to command us. He sets the rules and demands our obedience. If we want Christ as a "personal Savior," we cannot balk at having to humbly obey him as Creator as well.

John calls on us to receive Christ as "the light of men" (v. 4) and "the true light" (v. 9). To receive him is to allow his light to shine on our darkness and expose our sin. It is to turn from our dark deeds to him. John explains later that, for this very reason, many refuse to come to Jesus. They love their darkness too much to give it up for the true light (3:19–20).

To receive Jesus is to receive the only one who can give us life (1:4, 12–13). We will never earn life through the law of Moses (v. 17) nor through our own choices or decisions (v. 13). We must receive, as beggars, the grace Jesus brings (vv. 16–17), giving up all ideas of our own worthiness. We must acknowledge that we have nothing to commend us to God—nothing but the fullness and grace of this one John urges us to receive, this Word made flesh who came to dwell among us (v. 14).

SEPTEMBER 15 • JOHN 2:1-12

From Empty to Full

SUSAN HUNT

AN ORDINARY WEDDING in an obscure village is host to the Word who is God (John 1:1; 2:1–12). Here, as throughout John, Jesus demonstrates the fulfillment of the covenant promise—"I will be your God; you will be my people"—that weaves its way from Genesis to Revelation. In Jesus, God has secured his presence among a sinful people.

The Cana wedding is rich with redemptive significance as the Savior takes water pots used for the Old Testament ritual of purification and changes the water to wine. The prophesied feast of the kingdom begins! "On this mountain the LORD of hosts will make for all peoples a feast of rich food, a feast of well-aged wine . . ." (Isa. 25:6).

In the Old Testament, wine was a symbol of joy and blessing (Ps. 104:15; Prov. 3:10). At the Last Supper, Jesus spoke of the wine as a symbol of his life-giving blood (1 Cor. 11:25). This inaugural miracle of the messianic age points to redemption in Christ. This sign manifested his glory and caused the disciples to believe in him (John 2:11), accomplishing the purpose of the miracles and of his life (20:30–31).

How fitting that Jesus's first miracle takes place at a time of rejoicing. His birth brought joy to the world (Luke 2:10). He is the source of joy (John 17:13). In his presence is fullness of joy (Ps. 16:11).

Mary's instruction to the servants—"Do whatever he tells you"—is the key to experiencing the transformation from emptiness to fullness in our

341

own lives. The servants obeyed, and water was transformed into wine. When God's grace changes our status from rebel to redeemed, we are empowered by his Spirit to obey him. We are transformed by the renewing of our minds (Rom. 12:2) into his likeness (2 Cor. 3:18). Joyful obedience is the evidence of our love for Jesus (John 14:15).

The gospel is about the grand reversal from emptiness to fullness, from spiritual death to abundant life (10:10). But before Jesus could effect this change in us he had to endure the reverse of this reversal himself. Jesus, in whom "the whole fullness of deity dwells" (Col. 2:9), emptied himself, took the form of a servant, and was obedient all the way to the cross (Phil. 2:6–8). The result: "from his fullness we have all received grace upon grace" (John 1:16). He gives us his joy so that our "joy may be full" (15:11) as we anticipate the day when he declares, "Behold, the dwelling place of God is with man. He will dwell with them, and they will be his people, and God himself will be with them as their God" (Rev. 21:3).

SEPTEMBER 16 • JOHN 3:16–21

How Does God Show His Love?

HEATHER HOUSE

JOHN 3:16, perhaps the most famous summary of the gospel in the Bible, seems simple enough. After all, this is one of the first verses children memorize. People paint the reference on signs and hold them up at sporting events, implying someone could understand the gospel from reading this one verse. And yet, although this verse is straightforward in concept, it is incredibly deep in application. It plainly describes both God's love and humanity's need to accept that love as the solution to their separation from him. For all people in all times, our eternal destiny rests in either believing or rejecting these unadorned words.

John 3:16 is part of Jesus's conversation with Nicodemus, a Jewish religious leader. In verses 1–15, Jesus offers a changed life through a new spiritual birth, but Nicodemus is unsure how this could be true. Verses 16–21, then, show how it is that one can be born again and have eternal life.

By providing a way for us to have eternal life, God demonstrates his devotion to the people he created (John 3:16–18). This eternal life manifests itself through abundant joy and blessing on this earth, but it also goes beyond this material world by guaranteeing believers a place in God's presence forever. Living with a holy God is not possible for those who have sinned, and all humans have (Rom. 3:23). Therefore God sent his own Son to provide the means by which anyone can be justified (Rom. 5:15–21). Jesus accomplished this through his own death when he took on the guilt of his people (1 Cor. 15:3). Through the sacrifice of his only, innocent Son, God has given everything needed for us to be saved from the punishment we deserve (Isa. 52:13–53:12).

Sadly, people can and do reject Jesus's work. Those who refuse to recognize him for who he is remain separated from God and will face judgment (John 3:19–20). Knowledge of God ("light") arrives in Jesus, but many prefer the darkness because they want their evil actions to remain hidden. They would rather continue on the path they have chosen than admit that God created them and therefore has a rightful claim on them. Others are appalled by the notion that they cannot make themselves right with God through their own effort. Whoever recognizes what God offers through Jesus comes to the light because God gives him or her faith to believe (v. 21).

God loves us so much that he offered a solution, at great cost to himself and his Son, to the problem of sin that humanity had created. How will you respond to this truth? How will you share it with others?

SEPTEMBER 17 • JOHN 4:1-45

Quenching Our Deepest Thirst

LAUREN CHANDLER

THE SAVIOR AND a Samaritan. The Messiah and a mess. The Way, the Truth, and the Life—and a sidelined, shamed sinner. They are an unlikely pair. According to tradition, Jews were to have nothing to do with Samaritans (the descendants of Jews who had gone astray by marrying Gentiles). However, this text reveals that it was the will of God for Jesus and this woman to meet and exchange a deep theological discussion that has everything to do with everyday life.

The woman's midday trip to the well is a hint of her social status. It is likely that she chooses this time of day to avoid the disapproving looks from those who know of her immoral lifestyle. Rejection is something she has come to know intimately. By birth, she is rejected by pious Jews. She has been rejected by her husbands, and seemingly rejected by God. Because of her scandalous living situation, she is rejected by her own people and is not respected by the man with whom she shares a bed. So, she goes to the well to seek some kind of escape from the scorn, as well as water to temporarily quench her thirst.

Jesus meets her at her well. He meets her at the very place where she has tried day after day to find satisfaction for her parched soul. She is surprised by the fact that he approaches her. Her hesitation with him reveals her wounds. Why would he, a Jewish man, come in such close contact with a Samaritan woman, unclean in countless ways? What is he trying to sell, this one who claims to have an endless supply of water? Oh, but her soul is so thirsty. This thirst goes deeper than she knows. Jesus puts his finger on the deepest wound: "Go, call your husband" (John 4:16). The woman answers truthfully but then deflects attention from herself with a theological question. The Wonderful Counselor guides the conversation back to the heart of the matter: worship—that cavernous desire for something more that has failed to be met by every other "well" in her life. Finally, it is met in a man—Jesus.

But it wasn't just the woman who gained strength and hope from this conversation at the well; one could say it also strengthened and encouraged the very Son of God: Jesus tells his disciples, who had just come back from the village with food, that he was already full (v. 34). Like the satisfaction that comes from a perfectly balanced meal, the kingdom work of pursuing, engaging, and revealing the "gift of God" (v. 10) to this woman gave Jesus renewed strength for his ministry.

The Authority of the Son

KRISTEN WETHERELL

ONE OF THE most important questions every person must answer is, "Who is Jesus?" Responses vary. Some say he is a good moral teacher, worthy of our imitation but not our worship. Others call him a prophet but not the Savior. The religious leaders in Jesus's day had their own opinion, boldly calling him a law-breaker and, worse, a blasphemer, since he was making himself equal with God (John 5:18).

Every person must come to terms with Jesus's claim of unity with the Father. Is he indeed a blasphemer, telling profane lies about God? Or is he telling the truth? John would have us listen to Jesus's own words about his authority.

First, Jesus claims authority to give life (5:21, 25–26). Even before time, at the start of creation Jesus was the giver of life. He spoke the world into existence, which is one reason John calls him the Word (John 1:1–3). But Jesus is the giver not only of earthly life; he gives eternal life to those who hear his word and believe in him (5:24). He also promises resurrection life at his return, when the saints will receive imperishable bodies and enjoy new heavens and a new earth in the glorious presence of Christ himself.

Second, Jesus claims authority to execute judgment (5:22, 27–30). In calling himself the Son of Man (5:27), he is declaring that he is the fulfillment of Old Testament prophecy (see Dan. 7:13–14). He is the King of kings whom all Scripture anticipates, and he will exercise final authority when he returns to judge every person and claim a people for his own possession. His judgment will be perfect and impartial. He will discern between those who have received him and those who have rejected him, and he will accordingly reward and punish those two groups.

Jesus also claims authority to receive worship (John 5:18–20, 23). It is impossible to love, obey, and trust God the Father apart from loving, obeying, and trusting his Son. Contrary to what popular culture and alternative religions believe, Jesus is the only way for unrighteous sinners to be accepted by a holy God (14:6). The Judge is also the giver of eternal life! This is good news for those who are often wary of authority. When we come willingly under Jesus's authority, we discover that he is *for* us, not against us (Rom. 8:31).

What would it look like for you to submit to King Jesus today? In what ways is he calling you to hear his word and joyfully obey him as an act of worship?

SEPTEMBER 19 · JOHN 6:22-71

The Bread That Truly Satisfies

JESSICA THOMPSON

JESUS HAS JUST performed an astounding miracle. He has fed five thousand with only two loaves of bread and some fish. After witnessing this miracle, the crowd pursues Jesus, addressing him as "Rabbi." But Jesus knows they are seeking the gift rather than the Giver. He confronts the crowd with their desire for physical gifts. The purpose of the miracle, he explains, was so that they could see beyond the physical and be amazed by God's power—to be lifted into the spiritual. The sign was performed in order to open their eyes to the Son of God, who has the power to supply every need.

Rather than seeking after "the food that perishes," the people should long for "the food that endures to eternal life" (John 6:27). But their eyes are clouded and their hearts darkened. They ask Jesus, "What must we do, to be doing the works of God?" (v. 28). Jesus at this point decimates all of their religious presuppositions. The answer is not a matter of doing, but of believing. "This is the work of God, that you believe in him whom he has sent" (v. 29).

Astonishingly, the crowd responds by asking Jesus to perform a sign so that they can believe in him. It's as though they have already forgotten the miracle they have just witnessed! Jesus replies, "I am the bread of life; whoever comes to me shall not hunger, and whoever believes in me shall never thirst" (v. 35). This was the point of the miracle the day before. Jesus is better than the bread he provided. He is better than the manna that their fathers ate. He will satisfy eternally, because he is the true and better bread from heaven. All those who believe this message will have eternal life (vv. 49–51).

Jesus said, "No one can come to me unless the Father who sent me draws him" (v. 44). No amount of human seeking, no amount of human understanding, no amount of religious rule-keeping will open our eyes to Christ. The Father must draw us. This is a source of enormous comfort, assurance, and confidence for us who believe—for Jesus has said that it is impossible for him to lose that which has been given to him by the Father (v. 39). If you believe, you have been drawn and you are kept forever. You cannot be lost. Glorious praise to the one who satisfies, draws, and keeps!

SEPTEMBER 20 · JOHN 8:48–59

A Problem of Identity

MARY PATTON BAKER

THIS PASSAGE RECORDS the conclusion of an extended discourse that Jesus held in the temple during the Feast of Booths, where he proclaimed that he was the light of the world. From the beginning of the discourse, the Jews had argued with him. By the end, many who initially had been attracted to his teaching took offense as well.

The crux of their disagreement concerned identity. Not only did they fail to recognize who Jesus was; they also failed to understand what it meant to be a true child of Abraham. So when Jesus challenged their sense of identity based upon their Jewish bloodline and religious traditions, they turned from praising his wisdom to hurling the worst insult imaginable: they called him demon-possessed.

How offensive for Jesus to insist that being a child of Abraham is a matter of faith, not of privilege, and then to point out their separation from God and enslavement to sin! How dare he proclaim that he was in relationship with the Father of all truth and life, and that their father was the devil, the father of lies! Surely, Jesus must be mad to hold out the promise of eternal life to all those who would obey his words. But the last straw came when Jesus made this ultimate claim: "before Abraham was, I am" (John 8:58).

This man must be demon-possessed to claim divine preexistence and divinity! And so this Jesus had gone too far: he must be killed.

Yet, as Jesus pointed out, the problem with this Jewish audience was not intellectual, but spiritual. Jesus threatened their secure self-righteous identity wrapped in their religious traditions. Their inability to hear confirmed their enslavement to a system with no room for the Lord's Anointed.

So too, Christians must never become complacent, thinking they know it all, as did those Jews at the temple. The New Testament carries many warnings about falling into the snares of the devil. This danger lies not only in the desires of the flesh but also in spiritual pride (1 Tim. 3:6–7). Submitting in faith to God's word is still the best antidote. We must immerse ourselves in its teaching to counter the unbiblical messages ingrained in our culture's media and entertainment. Ultimate truth claims are no longer popular; as we find our true identity in Jesus, we also will encounter hatred and name-calling, for as the world hated Jesus, it will hate his followers (John 15:18). Yet this is where the truest, deepest communion with Jesus himself lies.

SEPTEMBER 21 · JOHN 9

Was Blind but Now I See

MARY A. KASSIAN

THE EVENTS OF John 9 take place right after the Feast of Tabernacles, a week-long festival commemorating Israel's time in the wilderness. The Jews built and lived in temporary booths during the week. They came to the temple every night carrying oil lamps for the most interesting and entertaining part of the festivities—the fire ceremony and torch dance. Four huge golden menorahs set on bases fifty feet high (as high as the walls of the temple) were ignited in the courtyard. The Levitical musicians played while a circle of young men danced and threw flaming torches high into the air.

On the last night of the fire ceremony, the Scripture readings were all about "the light." The people were reminded that God's presence faithfully led them through the wilderness in the great pillar of fire. The priests urged them to look forward to the time when the true "Light," the promised

Messiah would "tabernacle" with his people and reflect his light to every nation of the earth. It is said that the lights in the temple blazed with such brilliance during the ceremony that all Jerusalem was illuminated.

It was in front of the extinguished torches the next morning that Jesus announced, "I am the light of the world. Whoever follows me will not walk in darkness, but will have the light of life" (John 8:12). As Christ left the temple, he portrayed what happens when the light shines: some people, like the man born blind, will see—while others, who think they have sight, will turn away blind (9:39–41). The blind man progressed from calling Jesus a prophet (v. 17) to defending him against the Pharisees (v. 25), to inviting them to become Christ's disciples (v. 27) and correcting their doctrine (v. 34), to confessing Jesus as Lord and worshiping him (v. 38). The Pharisees, by contrast, remained oblivious to their spiritual blindness. The previous night they had given their wholehearted assent to the Scripture: "The people who walked in darkness have seen a great light; those who dwelt in a land of deep darkness, on them has light shone" (Isa. 9:2). But ironically, they couldn't see that the Light of the World was standing right in front of them.

The prophets foretold that the Messiah would heal the blind (Isa. 29:18; 35:5; 42:7). In the ministry of Jesus, there are more instances of his healing blind people than of any other type of miracle (Matt. 9:27–31; 12:22; 15:30–31; 21:14; Mark 8:22–26; 10:46–52; Luke 7:21–22). These miracles, of course, symbolized Jesus's ability to cure spiritual blindness. John Newton's familiar hymn sums it up: "Amazing grace, how sweet the sound, that saved a wretch like me; I once was lost but now am found—was blind, but now I see."

Come into This Picture

KATHLEEN B. NIELSON

IN JOHN 10 Jesus offers a picture, one of many pictures he uses to tell us who he is and what he came to do. I am, Jesus says, the bread of life . . . the living water . . . the light of the world . . . and, here, *the good shepherd*. Jesus takes time to develop this picture of the shepherd and his sheep, turning it around, inviting us in. From every angle he's showing himself to us—and calling us to follow him (like sheep).

We can never sum up such a picture in mere propositional statements; we're meant to look into it deeply—to step into it, in a sense. But we can note the picture's main colors, or themes.

First, this shepherd is all about life. He comes to give life, abundant life (John 10:10)—in contrast to the thieves and robbers (vv. 1, 8, 10) or the hired hand who leaves the sheep to be snatched by wolves (vv. 12–13). Clearly, many others will try to take these sheep—but any beside the one good shepherd will bring death, not life. Just as shepherds in Jesus's time would often lie down at night across the opening to the sheepfold, making themselves the door, so Jesus our shepherd is the door (v. 7)—the only way to life.

To give us life, this shepherd lays down his life. Jesus repeats this grand truth of our salvation (vv. 11, 15, 17), pointing us to the cross to see truly what will happen there: the Son, sent by the Father, will die to save sinners. Our Savior here looks straight ahead both to the cross and to the resurrection (vv. 17–18). He knows what he will do, and he knows the ones for whom he will do it (vv. 16, 27). What an amazing shepherd—who will go to this length to save his sheep.

This shepherd demands a response, the very response John seeks in his book: "that you may believe that Jesus is the Christ, the Son of God, and that by believing you may have life in his name" (20:31). What does believing look like? It looks like a sheep hearing its shepherd's voice and following him (10:3–4, 16, 27). John 10 goes on to show people who do *not* believe (vv. 25–26, 38). The contrast between them and those in Jesus's flock is a contrast between destruction and utterly secure eternal life (v. 28).

The Jews had been looking for a shepherd for a long time (see Psalm 23 and Ezekiel 34). Jesus comes, points to himself, and says, "Here I am." This good shepherd laid down his life to give us eternal life. This picture invites us in, to hear his voice and follow him.

He Is Who He Says He Is

KRISTIE ANYABWILE

THE BOOK OF JOHN IS "written so that you may believe that Jesus is the Christ, the Son of God, and that by believing you may have life in his name" (John 20:31). As we learn of Lazarus's miraculous recovery, we see this belief that leads to life beautifully demonstrated.

Everyone has been questioning Jesus—the scribes and Pharisees, the Jewish crowds, even the disciples. And many don't like his answers. When Jesus identifies himself as the God of Abraham and Isaac, some of the Jews who had previously believed in him are enraged and attempt to stone him (8:58–59). When Jesus makes the bold claim that "I and the Father are one," other Jewish leaders "picked up stones again to stone him" (10:30–31). But Jesus escapes and leaves Judea.

While he is away, his friend Lazarus becomes ill and dies. The Bible makes it clear that Jesus loves Lazarus (11:3, 5). And yet, when told that Lazarus is ill, rather than go to him Jesus chooses to stay "two days longer in the place where he was" (v. 6). Why would he respond in such a way? Jesus certainly did not allow Lazarus to die out of malice or a lack of concern. Rather, he allowed him to die precisely *because* of his love for him. Jesus knew that Lazarus's death would give his beloved friends the opportunity to see firsthand that he was exactly who he claimed to be—the one with the authority to lay his life down and to take it up again (10:18). John 11:45 says that many of the Jews believed in Jesus after seeing Lazarus raised from the dead.

In the same way, Christ died for our sins because of his great love for us. "But God, being rich in mercy, because of the great love with which he loved us, even when we were dead in our trespasses, made us alive together with Christ—by grace you have been saved" (Eph. 2:4–5). What must we do to be saved? We must believe that Jesus is who he says he is: the Son of God. We must believe that he died on the cross for the sins of all who would trust in him. We must believe that he triumphed over death so that all who trust in him, though they die, shall live (John 11:25).

Those of us who have this life in him must continue to trust in Christ, regardless of our circumstances. We must have faith that the Lord always acts out of his love for us, even if it means temporary pain, suffering, or loss. What we see now is not the end. What we see is always a means to an end—that is, the glory of God revealed more fully to us and through us as we continue to trust Christ for what we cannot see.

SEPTEMBER 24 • JOHN 14:15–31

Obedience: A Sign of Love

TRILLIA NEWBELL

CARRYING A CHILD in the womb is a glorious but often painful experience. Ligaments tear, joints soften, and everything stretches. God designed our bodies to be transformed, over the period of pregnancy, to make room for the most excruciating part of the adventure: giving birth. Childbirth, for most, is painful. God said it would be (Gen. 3:16). But once the child is born, the sorrow and pain is diminished by the joy of seeing and holding the child. Jesus, understanding the distress of childbirth, uses it as an illustration for his death and resurrection (John 16:21).

The disciples were confused and sorrowful at the thought that Jesus would be leaving and returning in a "little while" (14:18–19). Jesus continually prophesied his death and resurrection, but they did not understand. But Jesus had another promise—that he would never truly leave them, but would send a helper. God's comfort to the disciples, and his comfort to us, is that we are not orphaned children left to walk out our faith alone (v. 18). Rather, we are beloved children of God, assisted and guided by the Holy Spirit. Jesus promised us his presence. He dwells in us, and so does the Spirit (vv. 17–20, 23).

It is also by the Holy Spirit that we are enabled to keep our Lord's commandments. Jesus says that we keep his commandments as a sign of our love for him (v. 15). This is the difference between the Christian and the non-Christian. Those who truly belong to Jesus, who are truly his disciples, will trust him enough to obey his commandments. This is the evidence of saving grace.

We often confuse obedience to the Lord with legalism. Legalism is the effort to earn God's favor through obedience. But true obedience, flowing from a heart that understands God's grace, is not mere behavior: it is love. "For the love of Christ controls us" (2 Cor. 5:14). It isn't our obedience that saves us. It is through faith alone by grace alone that we are saved (Eph. 2:8). Then, because of the Spirit and the grace in us, we are compelled to obey. We delight to do so. It is our deep joy to honor our loving Father.

Just as Jesus told the adulterous woman, "Neither do I condemn you; go, and from now on sin no more" (John 8:11), he also tells us to receive his forgiveness as a free gift of his grace and then to forsake sin in light of that grace. Such holy living is made possible because God has sent us a helper who will teach us all things and illuminate God's word to us, so that we remember Jesus's commands (14:26).

SEPTEMBER 25 · JOHN 15:1–17

The Joy of Abiding in the Vine

GLORIA FURMAN

JESUS IS THE true Vine, and the branches that are truly in him necessarily bear fruit. The Father prunes these fruit-bearing branches so that they might bear even more fruit—to the praise of his glory. Continual reliance on Christ is essential to our fruitfulness. Simply mimicking the fruits of spiritual vitality only creates cheap imitations of the real thing. The Word who is God is incarnate revelation (John 1:1)—a truth we cannot fully comprehend with our finite minds. Truly, a sinner being "in Christ" and obtaining spiritual life from that union is the most supernatural thing in the history of the world.

Jesus's promise of joy makes it resoundingly clear that obedience to God is not something to do grudgingly. He says that his obedience to the Father is for his own joy, a joy that we will share if we obey him. Could there possibly be anything more fulfilling in this life than having our joy made complete in God? Surely our obedience to Jesus can bring nothing short of the most comprehensive and lavish soul satisfaction we could ever know. This is what we were made for!

For the joy set before him, the eternal Son of God died on behalf of sinners (Heb. 12:2)—for his own joy and for our joy in him. The cross is rightly understood as the apex of divine love. Christ's love is sovereign, irresistible, and unconditional. His love is effusive and compelling (see 2 Cor. 5:14). His love animates our ministry and is a distinguishing mark of his followers. "By this we know love, that he laid down his life for us, and we ought to lay down our lives for the brothers" (1 John 3:16).

As friends of Jesus, we are objects of his great love, and we are obedient to him. Our obedience is not what *qualifies* us to be a friend of Jesus, but it is what *characterizes* us. The fruit we bear is broad in scope, but the focus on evangelism and mission is central. Our union with Christ Jesus was never meant to be a privatized and complacent relationship, but an overflow of Christ's love to others who do not yet know him. Being united to Christ not only necessitates our need to share his love with others; it also produces the fruit that will last. This lasting fruit is accomplished through prayer in Jesus's name, which assures that the God of salvation receives the glory he so rightly deserves.

SEPTEMBER 26 · JOHN 16:4–15

Our Helper

MARY WILLSON

JESUS CAME TO lay down his life for his people, and when he spoke with his disciples in this passage, he knew his time on earth was drawing to a close. Jesus would return to his Father after completing his work of salvation (John 16:5). Can you imagine the sorrow Jesus's disciples felt as they heard him speak of his imminent departure? After years of walking with him, hearing his teaching, witnessing his merciful power, and being served by him, these disciples desperately loved him. How would they carry on without him? Jesus knew their grief and tenderly addressed their troubled hearts.

As the Father had sent Jesus, Jesus promised he would send the Helper. This Spirit of truth would come in Jesus's name and abide with them forever (14:16–17). The word Jesus used for "Helper" has a range of meaning that includes "Advocate," "Comforter," and "Intercessor." The Holy Spirit would guide them and bear witness to Jesus as they abided in him, followed his commands, and testified about him (14:26; 15:26–27). The Helper would encourage them when they experienced hostility in their gospel mission (15:18–16:4).

Contrary to what his disciples were feeling, Jesus declared that his parting would actually be advantageous for them. Rather than being confined by flesh, the Spirit moves as he wills and operates on human hearts in any place at any time. In this way the Spirit would amplify Jesus's public ministry. While the Holy Spirit ministered mightily throughout old covenant days, his new covenant ministry brings expansion (promised in Joel 2:28–29), heart-renewal (promised in Ezek. 36:27), greater fruitfulness (promised in Isa. 44:1–5), and increased unity (promised in Ezek. 11:19–20). Furthermore, before Jesus's return, the Spirit convicts the world of sin, righteousness, and judgment by exposing the sin of unbelief, opening eyes to God's judgment against his enemies, and revealing Jesus's righteousness even in his bodily absence.

The Trinity has invested wholly in our safeguarding: The Spirit, sent by Jesus, guides us into all truth as the authoritative mouthpiece of God's Son. His intimate counsel testifies to the gospel and applies gospel truths to our lives. He speaks to us about Jesus on our Father's behalf.

If you have received Christ Jesus in faith, the Spirit will glorify Jesus through your life. As Jesus assured his disciples, he does not leave us alone in this world to flounder in self-reliance or despair. Rather, "the Spirit helps us in our weakness" (Rom. 8:26), and we rely on him in all our efforts to follow our Messiah in this world as we await his return. Rejoice in the nearness of your Helper!

Jesus Prays for Us

SAM STORMS

AS PARENTS OF two grown daughters, my wife and I often reflect on the years of their infancy and childhood and wonder how they survived as well as they did. Small children rarely realize the dangers and obstacles that lurk in their world. Our prayer as parents is that as they mature both physically and emotionally, they will grow to recognize the threats all around them.

The same is true in the spiritual life as well. New Christians, mere infants in Christ, rarely sense the reality of the spiritual conflict in which they've been placed. They are often naive to the schemes that Satan and his demonic hosts have set in place. One indication of spiritual adulthood is a growing awareness of the war that is waging within us and a readiness to prepare ourselves for battle.

Jesus knew all too well the battle that we as Christians would be compelled to fight. He knew, even as he prepared to die, that the forces of darkness were preparing themselves for an all-out assault on the church. This must be why Jesus prayed for us as he did in John 17:15. Only hours from his betrayal and crucifixion, we were on his mind!

Whereas it might have been easier had he prayed that we be taken "out of the world," his request was that the Father "keep" us "from the evil one." Physical removal from this earth into the glory of heaven would have saved us the agony of a fight, but God wants us *here*, to bear witness to his saving grace, to demonstrate his all-sufficiency as we rely wholly on him in our conflict with the enemy, and to make known the good news of the gospel to a lost and dying world (John 17:18, 21).

What Jesus prayed on the night of his betrayal, he continues to bring to our heavenly Father, for "he always lives to make intercession for" us (Heb. 7:25). People often leave our presence with a promise, "I'll pray for you." We never know for certain if they carry through with their pledge. Perhaps most of them do. But doubt lingers in our minds.

But we need never question the faithfulness of Jesus in praying for his people. What comfort to know that our Lord Jesus Christ has not ceased to argue our case! What encouragement to know that he "is at the right hand of God . . . interceding for us" (Rom. 8:34). Although Satan may tempt us, he cannot destroy us. Although he may accuse us, he cannot condemn us. For the Father always hears the Son when he prays for his people. If your faith is in him, Jesus is praying for you.

SEPTEMBER 28 · JOHN 18:33–40

Help Us to Listen

KATHLEEN CHAPELL

"WHATEVER." Who hasn't heard that response—usually accompanied by a shrug.

"This was not up to my expectations."

"Whatever."

"You may not speak to me that way!"

"Whatever."

Whatever. So what? Who cares? It's not important. This is essentially Pilate's response when Jesus says, "For this purpose I was born and for this purpose I have come into the world—to bear witness to the truth" (John 18:37).

"What is truth?" Pilate asks (v. 38).

Whatever.

How ironic! The man charged with determining truth in this matter dismisses the importance of truth. "What is truth, after all?" he asks. And so he turns over to the mob the very one who *is* the Truth.

I have sometimes read this account of the hours leading up to the crucifixion and felt a strange sympathy for Pilate. He seems to be trying to find an answer. Back and forth he goes, from interviewing this Jesus—this problematic, perplexing man—to trying to placate the crowd outside. There doesn't seem to be an easy answer. Jesus doesn't seem to be a threat to Rome, to Caesar, to Pilate himself; he seems innocuous enough. He says he has a kingdom, but not of this world. Why do these angry folks want him dead?

Oh, Pilate, if only you had listened—really listened to what Jesus was saying! "Everyone who is of the truth listens to my voice," Jesus says (v. 37). "I am the way, and the truth, and the life" (14:6). "I am the good shepherd" (10:11). "I am the resurrection and the life" (11:25). Pilate, if only you had *listened*.

"I can't find any guilt in him," Pilate tells the mob.

"Release Barabbas!" responds the crowd. They demand that Pilate release the robber, the criminal, the murderer, and punish the innocent. Release the sinner, and crucify the sinless! The demand makes no human sense. But even in this short, confusing, frustrating interaction, God reveals his plan of salvation. The sinless will suffer, to save the sinners who trust in him.

Lord, help me listen to you! Help me hear you when you speak truth. Help me remember always that I am the sinner you released—I am the one for whom the sinless Jesus was crucified! He is my Passover Lamb, and his blood has washed my heart clean!

SEPTEMBER 29 · JOHN 20

See

JONI EARECKSON TADA

HAVE YOU NOTICED how people try to "tame" the resurrection of Jesus? They cover it with sentimental images portraying him with his hair parted down the middle, holding a lily, and surrounded by angels and bluebirds. We have gilded the real Savior with so much "dew on the roses" that many people have lost touch with the earth-shaking facts of his resurrection.

After all, only minutes before Mary Magdalene arrived at the tomb this man was stiff, gray, and stone-cold dead. The lifeless corpse then opened its eyes, rose from its grave, and as the stone mysteriously rolled aside, Jesus walked out into the dark, cool garden night. If this were not the Gospel account, we'd think we were reading a scene from a horror novel. No wonder many of the people who first saw the resurrected Christ were frozen with fear—hours earlier, Jesus was a corpse. Now he was alive!

Why do we prefer a romanticized image of the resurrection? For one thing, a sentimental idea of Jesus rising from the dead requires nothing from us. A tame, nostalgic picture requires no conviction or commitment. It lacks power because it lacks truth. So, for a moment, brush aside the birds and the lilies and *think* about the facts: a dead man walked out of his grave. And as he did, this man, alive with the glory of God permeating every fiber of his being, was conquering all the demonic forces of darkness. He was satisfying the wrath and judgment of God and defeating the last great enemy: death. The resurrection of Jesus became the firstfruits of the harvest of the resurrection of all Christians (1 Cor. 15:20–22). If you belong to Jesus, you will one day receive a body like his, perfectly suited for the new heavens and the new earth—and this world that we love so much, when compared to that one, will be like a candle compared to the sun. All because he arose.

The resurrection message is Mary's testimony, "I have seen the Lord!" (John 20:18). The other disciple who reached the tomb first also "saw and believed" (v. 8). So may I ask: *what do you see?* Do you see a syrupy, sweet picture of Jesus with cherubs and children? A picture on a Sunday school wall that demands nothing of you? Or do you see the death-defying, victorious Christ who defeated sin so that you might have resurrection power to live a life that pleases him? Today, *see* the risen Lord, and *see* every benefit of the resurrection that is now being poured out on you. *See* this day as a chance to live a life that honors him.

SEPTEMBER 30 · ACTS 1:6–11

Equipped for the Task

CAROLYN MCCULLEY

WE ALL HAVE a habit of looking for our own solutions and timetables. Children want to know, "Are we there yet?" Hungry teen boys want to know when dinner will be served. Bored workers mind the clock, looking forward to the end of another day. It's quite common to believe that the thing we anticipate will provide the relief we seek.

So it was with the early disciples. Once they recovered from the shock of seeing the resurrected Jesus, they returned to their preplanned agendas: "Lord, will you at this time restore the kingdom to Israel?" (Acts 1:6). It's a natural question, as so much of their faith history was centered on the physical kingdom of Israel. But Jesus was doing much more than restoring the kingdom to Israel—he was establishing his own kingdom. Their faith wasn't to be established on knowing when something would happen in the future. Their faith was to be established on Christ's work. Therefore, the last words of Jesus to his disciples were about their task to be his "witnesses in Jerusalem and in all Judea and Samaria, and to the end of the earth," and about how they would be equipped to do it: "you will receive power when the Holy Spirit has come upon you" (v. 8). Then Jesus ascended into heaven, completing his work on earth.

So too, we live in the time between the ascension of Jesus and his triumphant return. We have the same task and the same empowerment. We may have different questions—"Lord, will you at this time restore my marriage/children/job/health/church?" But he has the same answer. As believers in Jesus, we are empowered by the Holy Spirit to build the church and be Christ's witnesses today. Our daily concerns are very real, but they are not the end goals. Knowing what we are ultimately called to do helps us to endure when our circumstances are dark and difficult *and* when our circumstances are happily distracting. We are witnesses to the life-changing power of the gospel, and we are empowered by grace to stand firm even in the most confusing and tragic times.

The Lord is building his church and advancing his kingdom. We know he has a purpose, even when our limited perspectives don't allow us to trace those purposes in our circumstances. The One-in-Three God has given himself to us and promises never to leave us—the Father ordains our lives for good, the Son has completed his sacrifice on our behalf, and the Spirit has been given to us as a guarantee of our inheritance. That knowledge is more than enough for today. We can trust him for our tomorrows.

The Day That Changed Everything

MARY PATTON BAKER

THE PROMISED DAY finally arrived! A sudden wind filled the house in which the disciples were staying, which alerted them to a momentous event that was about to happen. All those assembled in the upper room then saw fire, the great sign of God's presence. This fire took the shape of tongues and rested on each of them. And "they were all filled with the Holy Spirit" (Acts 2:4).

Those gathered in the upper room had been told by Jesus to wait for this day (John 16:7–15; Acts 1:4–5). It was the day the people of Israel had been waiting centuries for—the day promised by God through the prophets, such as Jeremiah (31:33), Ezekiel (36:26), and Joel (2:28–30). This day would bring an end to the futility of trying to fulfill God's law with hearts of stone. The day when all people, regardless of age, gender, or social status, would be empowered with the Spirit to live obedient lives of joy with new hearts of flesh.

Each disciple in the upper room received the miraculous gift to speak the wonders of God in another language. The simple fisherman Peter, once a coward but now emboldened by the Spirit, preached such a powerful sermon that three thousand people became believers and were baptized. Hearts convicted by the Holy Spirit turned to Jesus and also received this new filling of the Spirit.

The promised Spirit fills the believers, and the Spirit does not go away. This is Luke's ultimate message—so the story does not end with the Day of Pentecost. Acts goes on to tell of the lasting effects of that day by describing what happened in the day-to-day lives of the young church. The believers "devoted themselves" to teaching, fellowship, the breaking of bread, and prayers (Acts 2:42). This new fellowship, they realized, was not simply human companionship but the unique sharing of the Spirit among Christians. They broke bread together daily to give thanks and to remember their salvation in Jesus Christ. And because only the Holy Spirit can bring about such a change, the text tells us, "The Lord added to their number day by day" (v. 47).

As with the early church, the Spirit has been given to us so that we may be obedient from the heart. He enables us to enjoy the sweet fellowship of Christian love as well as to be witnesses for Christ. But we also must do our part. To "devote" oneself means to be persistent. Are you persistent in seeking the fellowship of the Spirit with God's people? Acts 2 demonstrates that true Christian growth happens when Christians share together God's word and fellowship in the breaking of the bread.

OCTOBER 2 • ACTS 4:23–31

Praying to Be Bold Witnesses

BRIAN BORGMAN

HAVE YOU EVER been reluctant to speak out for Christ? Do you remember a time when you had an opportunity to witness to someone and you were gripped by fear? Such feelings are common among Christians. Although there are many resources at hand to help us share our faith boldly, the first step is not learning a technique or mastering a method. Praying is the real secret to being a bold witness.

The church in the book of Acts gives us a stirring example of God-centered, Christ-exalting, Scripture-saturated, Spirit-empowered prayer for boldness. In Acts 4:23–31 we see the church at prayer. Peter and John had just given their report of their recent imprisonment and run-in with the religious authorities. The church went immediately to prayer. The believers "lifted their voices together to God" (v. 24). The church was praying together in unity.

The church then addressed God as "Sovereign Lord, who made the heaven and the earth and the sea and everything in them" (v. 24). As they approached God, they acknowledged him as the unrivaled Lord of everything. Even their persecution was a result of his sovereign will (v. 28). Their prayer was also rich in Scripture. They saw Christ clearly in Psalm 2 and directly applied it to their situation. They were not just praying their own thoughts and ideas; they were praying God's word back to him. Then they prayed that God would grant them to speak his word with all boldness and that God would accompany their witness with his supernatural power. God answered their prayer immediately and visibly (Acts 4:31). The next few chapters of Acts demonstrate God's answer to their prayer as they spoke the word with boldness in the power of the Spirit.

As we consider the greatest prayer meeting ever recorded, we can learn some important lessons to help us pray to be bold witnesses. The first is that we must join together with our brothers and sisters in praying for boldness, not praying in isolation. There is power when the church prays together. Second, our prayers should be filled with God's word. If we want to speak God's word in power, we should learn to pray God's word in power. Finally, as we pray we need to stay focused on the One to whom we pray. He is the Lord over all things. He is the sovereign king. Nothing is too difficult for him. So join in with other believers and ask God to fill you with his Spirit and with boldness. Ask him for opportunities to speak of God's Son and his grace. Then rely on the Holy Spirit to give you boldness in your witness.

OCTOBER 3 · ACTS 6:8–7:60

Rejection of Christ Is Rejection of God

COLLEEN J. MCFADDEN

STEPHEN'S SPEECH IS the longest discourse in Acts. It is a response to Jews who misunderstand the temple and the law. Appealing to the authority of the Old Testament, Stephen focuses on two realities the Jews were unable to grasp: God is not bound to the temple; and God's people have continually rejected him and his law.

God graciously manifested his presence among his people through the tabernacle and the temple. But despite the undeniable significance of these places of worship, he was never bound to either earthly structure. Rather, throughout history, God's presence has been with those who love and follow him. He was with Abraham in Mesopotamia, Haran, and Canaan

(Acts 7:2–4). He was with Joseph in Egypt (7:9) and with Moses in the wilderness (7:31, 38). Even when he allowed Solomon to build the temple (7:46–47), the Lord made it clear that "the Most High does not dwell in houses made by hands" (7:48).

But the Jews did not want to accept this truth. They were "stiff-necked," just as their fathers were (7:51). As Israel had forsaken their God in the past, so now the Jews rejected Jesus, "the Righteous One" (v. 52), whom God sent to fulfill the law. And just as God's prophets had been rejected and persecuted by Israel in the past, so now Stephen is scorned and reviled.

As the first person to die for his faith in Jesus, Stephen is an example of one who follows and trusts the Lord, regardless of the cost. What else can we learn from his speech and his character? First, we recognize our own tendency to try and "contain" God. Are we tempted to contain him to Sunday morning or to the church building? Are we, like Israel, tempted to make an idol out of the place of worship? We must be ever mindful that Jesus came as our Immanuel: *he* is God with us. And he has filled us with the Holy Spirit (Eph. 2:11–22), so that God's presence is with us always and everywhere.

We should also look to Stephen as a model of how to treat our adversaries. Even as they were preparing to take his life, Stephen pleaded with the Judge to forgive them (Acts 7:60). Didn't Jesus express the same compassion on the cross? "Father, forgive them, for they know not what they do" (Luke 23:34). As God's people, we must care for our adversaries in the same way, speaking the truth with compassion and grace—even when they wish us harm.

God is with us. Trust him. Trust him enough to act in bold faith, as Stephen did. One day we, too, will look upon heaven (Acts 7:56) and be welcomed in.

Love without Boundaries

CLAIRE SMITH

NEVER UNDERESTIMATE the lengths to which God has gone and will go to save. There is no person beyond his embrace. There is no place beyond his reach. There is no cost that has not been paid, and no limit to which he has not gone.

Consider the Ethiopian eunuch. He was a high-ranking official of a distant non-Jewish nation. He was in charge of great wealth. Materially, he lacked nothing. He was a God-fearer, but he could not enter the temple as others could (Deut. 23:1). Although he had been in Jerusalem to worship, and although he had read the Scriptures, he was returning home without knowing who it was who perfectly fulfilled the salvation that the Scriptures promised—even for outsiders like himself (Isa. 56:3–5).

But God had other plans. The gospel was to cross boundaries, just as the risen Lord Jesus had told his disciples it would, and it would do so by the power of the Spirit of God (Acts 1:8).

Christ's followers had been scattered by the persecution of the church in Jerusalem, and as they spread, so did the gospel—geographically, ethnically, and religiously. Philip was one of the messengers. He preached first in Samaria, where the Holy Spirit was poured out on the new believers.

Then the Spirit directed him to cross still more boundaries with the gospel. An angel led him into the desert, where the Spirit told Philip to approach the Ethiopian, who was reading aloud the Spirit-inspired prophecy of Isaiah. In God's providence, the text was about God's innocent servant, who was humiliated and rejected and suffered an unjust death. But the eunuch did not know who this suffering servant was, so Philip—brought there by the Spirit for just this purpose—began with this text and told him the wonderful news of Jesus and of sins forgiven (see Isa. 53:4–8). There was now nothing preventing the eunuch being fully part of the people of God, and so he believed and was baptized, and went on his way rejoicing, taking with him the gospel "to the end of the earth" (Acts 1:8).

That mission completed, the Spirit whisked Philip away to take the gospel to the center of Roman rule in Judea, the Greek-speaking city of Caesarea. It was another step in the spread of the gospel that finally embraced all nations, extending to the seat of power in Rome and beyond (28:11–31). Even today, through the lives and words of his people, this gospel continues to spread throughout the world, because God saves through a gospel without boundaries.

OCTOBER 5 · ACTS 9:1–31

A Changed Life

KAREN S. LORITTS

THE REGENERATION of Saul, ruthless persecutor of the Way, was the providential work of God. Saul viewed Christianity as a threat to Judaism, so he made it his personal mission to silence converts to Christianity and demolish its influence. As a Pharisee, he was blinded by religiosity, tradition, and cultural mores. But a dramatic confrontation with Christ lifted him out of that dark place to face the Light: "But I received mercy because I had acted ignorantly in unbelief, and the grace of our Lord overflowed for me with the faith and love that are in Christ Jesus" (1 Tim. 1:13–14).

The mercy of Christ means that we do not get the punishment we deserve, and the grace of Christ means we do get blessings that we do not deserve. Saul, who was "breathing threats and murder against the disciples of the Lord" (Acts 9:1) even as Jesus sought him out, certainly deserved to be condemned for his cruelty. Instead, he receives forgiveness and redemption—he receives salvation. This salvation comes out of nowhere. Saul does not ask for it. He does not pray for it. God himself sovereignly works to confront and soften this hardened man.

And there is immediate evidence of change in this regenerate, forgiven man. Though Saul is hungry, thirsty, and alone for days, he fasts (9:9). Self-denial and dependence on Christ replaces his self-righteousness. Once on a rampage, he now obediently waits in darkness. Contrition and humility are marks of the redeemed. Saul-turned-Paul becomes a passionate voice for Christianity, boldly proclaiming the truth, indifferent to personal safety. Though the proclamation of truth may be costly, its results are everlasting. The impact of Paul's redeemed life echoes down through history.

The conversion of Saul teaches us that none are beyond the reach of God's grace and mercy. We sometimes worry that our sin is too great—or too frequent—for him to truly accept, love, and forgive us. But the Bible tells us otherwise: "If you, O LORD, should mark iniquities, O Lord, who could stand? But with you there is forgiveness, that you may be feared" (Ps. 130:3–4).

Like Saul, our sin makes us deserving of death and separation from God. But because of the mercy of our Savior, instead we receive grace upon grace (John 1:16). The story of Saul is a remarkable testament of the wonder and work of Christ Jesus.

OCTOBER 6 • ACTS 10:34-43

Cross-Cultural Evangelism

LEEANN STILES

IT WAS A LONG journey from Joppa to Caesarea. Not particularly in physical distance (31 miles), yet for Peter, sociologically, it might as well have been a trip to Mars. His world revolved around Judaism. Gentiles were unclean; befriending them was unheard of. But the Lord made it clear in a vision (Acts 10:9–20) that he, not Peter, determined what was clean, whether animal or human (vv. 15, 28). This shattered Peter's worldview. It overturned laws and attitudes that had long separated his people from everyone else. Peter's perceptions had to change drastically before he even opened his mouth to speak God's word to a Roman named Cornelius.

Fortunately for those of us who are Gentiles, Peter obeyed God, crossing cultural and ethnic barriers with the good news. He learned that God shows "no partiality, but in every nation anyone who fears him and does what is right is acceptable to him" (vv. 34–35).

The message Peter shared in verses 34–43 reflected God's plan to save people from all kinds of backgrounds. Although this crowd knew about Jesus

(vv. 37–38), Peter witnessed and understood some things that they didn't. He told them about Jesus's death and resurrection (vv. 39–41). He explained God's plan of redemption: all who believe in Jesus are forgiven of their sin (v. 43). Then, to the utter amazement of Peter and those who had traveled with him, these Gentiles believed the gospel and received the Holy Spirit.

Sometimes our perceptions, like Peter's, need to change. We lack faith that God can move among certain types of people or those in circumstances different than ours. Or we believe he can't use us. But God is never limited in these ways. He has determined that one day redeemed people from every nation and tongue will stand before his throne and give him glory (Rev. 7:9). He's called every Christian to be part of his plan to bring salvation to many regardless of their ethnicity, language, age, religious background, economic status, or political persuasion.

I desire to be a person who takes risks for God's kingdom. If you follow him, I suspect you do, too. Peter is a model for us. He listened to God's instruction. He put aside preconceptions and traditional ways of doing things. He went to an unfamiliar place. He knew how to communicate the gospel clearly and boldly. He marveled at the Spirit's power to draw people to Christ. We can do that, too—whether our journey takes us next door, across town, or to the other side of the world. After all, God the Son crossed from heaven to earth to draw us to himself.

OCTOBER 7 · ACTS 13:13–52

From Skeptic to Believer

BETHANY L. JENKINS

"WHEN ANYONE TELLS ME," said the eighteenth-century skeptic David Hume, "that he saw a dead man restored to life, I immediately consider with myself whether it be more probable that this person should either deceive or be deceived." He reasoned that anyone who supposedly witnessed a miracle was most likely duped: "It forms a strong presumption against all super-natural and miraculous relations that they are observed chiefly among ignorant and barbarous nations."[7]

As a Roman citizen and a Pharisee, Paul was not ignorant or barbarous. In fact, he was just as skeptical as Hume. Although Paul believed in God, he did not think that God could be incarnate, and while he believed in the resurrection on the last day, he did not think it could happen in the middle of history. Thus, the claims of Christianity—that Jesus was God incarnate, and that he rose from the dead—seemed so ludicrous to Saul that he set out to stop its spread by killing its adherents.

When Paul (at that time called Saul) met the risen Christ, however, he had to deal with the reality of Jesus. In a moment he turned from being a skeptic to being a believer. During his first missionary journey (Acts 13–14), Paul and his colleagues visited the synagogue at Antioch in Pisidia, where the religious leaders asked him to speak.

Paul began by surveying the course of God's relationship with Israel, from the election of the patriarchs to the royal accession of David (13:17–22). He then moved directly from David to Christ, arguing that Jesus was the One in whom the divine promises given to David were fulfilled (vv. 23–37). Paul then gave a call to action: "Let it be known to you therefore, brothers, that through this man forgiveness of sins is proclaimed to you, and by him everyone who believes is freed from everything from which you could not be freed by the law of Moses" (vv. 38–39). In response, some people were intrigued (v. 42), others were jealous (v. 45), and many joyfully received the gospel (v. 48).

Today, too, we have to deal with the reality of Jesus. We may think we cannot believe in Christianity because we do not like its teaching on this or that issue, but our not liking particular teachings does not mean that Jesus did not rise from the dead. When Paul looked at Christian teachings, he rejected them; when he looked at Jesus, however, he followed the truth of the resurrection wherever it led him—even if it meant that some thought him a fool (1 Cor. 1:23).

Always Grace

JESSICA THOMPSON

THE CHURCH IN Antioch is growing and flourishing. Gentiles are hearing the message and believing. Then some Jewish men come from Judea and tell the Gentiles that they must be circumcised in order to be saved. Having heard and received the message of free grace, these new believers are now being told that their salvation depends on adherence to the Mosaic law.

Paul and Barnabas will have no part in demanding that these Gentile Christians be circumcised. After "no small dissension and debate" (Acts 15:2), they are sent to Jerusalem to meet with the apostles and elders—including Peter and James—to discuss the matter.

Peter defends Paul's ministry to the Gentiles and reminds the Jewish Christian leaders that all are saved by grace alone, through faith in Christ—that God has made no distinction between Jew and Gentile. Why then, asks Peter, are the Jewish believers "placing a yoke on the neck of the disciples that neither our fathers nor we have been able to bear?" (v. 10).

James agrees that the Gentiles should not be required to observe the entirety of the Mosaic law. He proposes a solution to the matter, which he introduces by saying, "we should not trouble those of the Gentiles who turn to God" (v. 19). Hear the heart of our Savior in those words! They are reminiscent of Jesus's invitation in Matthew 11:28–30: "Come to me, all who labor and are heavy laden, and I will give you rest. Take my yoke upon you, and learn from me, for I am gentle and lowly in heart, and you will find rest for your souls. For my yoke is easy, and my burden is light."

Those in the early church who had at one time believed that the law would save them needed this reminder as much as the Gentiles did. They needed to remember the lavish grace that is given when we simply believe. They needed to remember that there is rest for our souls in Christ.

The council's response was one that would establish fellowship between Gentile and Jewish Christians, avoiding unnecessary offense—or unnecessary burden—to either group. Gentile believers are to be instructed simply "to abstain from the things polluted by idols, and from sexual immorality, and from what has been strangled, and from blood" (Acts 15:20).

When the Gentile believers read the council's letter, "they rejoiced because of its encouragement" (v. 31). Such should be our hearts' response when we remember that the law has been perfectly fulfilled by our strong Redeemer. May we also rejoice as we revel in the grace that saved us from first to last!

OCTOBER 9 • ACTS 16:16–40

Radical Obedience

LAUREN CHANDLER

IT IS OFTEN assumed that if we walk by the Spirit and obey God's commands, we will live a cushioned life, impervious to hardship and suffering. Time and again, Scripture shows us otherwise.

Consider Paul. The apostle walked in a power only a few have experienced. He carried authority, as Jesus did. This was seen when he commanded (in the name of Jesus) the spirit of divination to come out of the slave girl. If anyone should have had a pain-free life because of radical obedience, it would have been Paul. But on this day, his obedience meant chains.

By delivering the young woman from demonic possession, Paul brought trouble upon himself and Silas. The girl's owners realized they could no longer profit from her oppression. Paul's actions should have attracted a crowd in awe of the power of Christ. Instead, a mob gathered in protest. Paul and Silas were not only verbally maligned; they were physically beaten, stripped of their dignity and their clothes, and thrown into prison.

Human nature would suggest a throwing up of hands in exasperation that the Lord had failed to deliver his disciples. Protest would no longer be relegated to the mob; it would find its place in the hearts and mouths of the imprisoned. The mind of the Spirit, however, compelled a different response. Paul and Silas lifted their voices in prayer and songs of praise, convinced of God's deliverance despite the heavy chains that had them bound. Doubts have trouble getting a word in edgewise when lungs are filled with worship. The power of the One they praised literally shook the foundations of the prison. The doors flew open. Surely this was their deliverance.

What Paul and Silas beheld with their eyes was interpreted differently in their hearts. Most would perceive the miracle as a sign from God to run and not look back, but they saw an even more miraculous work ahead. It was not their deliverance and safety that they valued most—it was the jailer's. With spiritual eyes they saw his deep need to be freed from the bondage of sin. His chains far outweighed the shackles that burrowed deep into their skin. Because they counted the jailer as more significant than themselves, and looked not only to their own interests but also to his (Phil. 2:3–4), an entire household was brought into the family of God.

The seeds planted in that dank cell grew into a gathering of slaves set free—the Philippian church. From the beginning, it was a people marked by obedience no matter the cost. The example set before them in Paul and Silas was but a reflection of Christ Jesus, who "humbled himself by becoming obedient to the point of death, even death on a cross" (Phil. 2:8).

OCTOBER 10 · ACTS 18:24–28

Getting It Right as Servants of the Gospel

JENNY SALT

SOMETIMES NOT "getting it right" has devastating consequences; sometimes it hardly matters at all. Accidentally using salt instead of sugar in a recipe will have an impact on the taste of what you are making, but it won't kill you. But accidentally getting sugar and arsenic mixed up is much more serious!

When it comes to the gospel of Jesus Christ, getting it right (that is, understanding it rightly and applying it accurately) is very important, but there may be degrees of "rightness" that will determine the consequences. Here, Luke includes a short account of Apollos in Ephesus, which also acts as context for Paul's ministry in Ephesus (Acts 18:23–21:16). This larger section of Acts gives us an insight into the movement of the gospel while also highlighting the misunderstandings of the gospel among people in that city.

For example, in the verses following 18:24–28, Luke records the account of the twelve disciples of John the Baptist who knew nothing of the Holy Spirit (19:1–10). Then there are the sons of Sceva (itinerant Jewish exorcists) who used Jesus's name to exorcise evil spirits, but with no true faith or repentance (19:11–20). Finally, we read of pagan shrine-makers led by Demetrius who rise up against Paul, resulting in "no little disturbance concerning the Way" (19:23). In other words, Luke records increasing degrees of "getting it wrong" in Ephesus.

Which brings us back to Apollos in 18:24–28. We are told that he was an eloquent man, a Jew from Alexandria, competent in the Scriptures, who "spoke and taught accurately the things concerning Jesus" (v. 25). This suggests that Apollos was a true believer, and yet there was a gap in his knowledge: "he knew only the baptism of John" (v. 25). Priscilla and Aquila heard him as he preached boldly in the synagogue, and took him aside to explain to him "the way of God more accurately" (v. 26). There were gaps in Apollos's understanding, but after Priscilla and Aquila's quiet, private instruction, he had a more accurate understanding of the gospel, perhaps especially concerning the gift of the Spirit (see Matt. 3:11). With this instruction and the encouragement of believers in Ephesus, Apollos went to Achaia, where he was able to preach boldly and powerfully, "showing by the Scriptures that the Christ was Jesus" (Acts 18:28).

"Getting it right" when it comes to the gospel is important. This passage reminds us of the importance of encouraging each other to speak faithfully about Jesus. Not only that, but these verses reflect an overall theme in Acts: that under God's good hand, believers are empowered by the Spirit to preach the good news of Jesus Christ, and as they do, the church grows.

The Work of an Elder

ZACK ESWINE

HAVE YOU EVER attended a going away party for a friend? Can you imagine grown men weeping there? They might not see their friend again. Audible cries from masculine hearts fill the room. They hold onto each other, speak into each other, and kiss the cheek of their leaving friend. These verses invite us into such a scene.

The men gathered are elders called to the spiritual care of a Christian community. This passage reveals the calling of an elder's life. Surprisingly, an elder's work begins with tears. This passage refers to tears three times (Acts 20:19, 31, 37). Tears come from trials endured (v. 19); from heartfelt love for those who need instruction and help (v. 31); and for times when dear friends must part for the sake of the Lord's call, taking watch for the challenges ahead (v. 37). This tearful work is forged by personal testimony to the Lord's grace in the elders' own lives. Paul uses the word "I" repeatedly. He describes his life and ministry among them as testimony (vv. 21, 24, 26). He has given not only the gospel of grace, but *himself* to them—and this with integrity of character (vv. 33–34).

Personal testimony and tears join together in the larger purpose of teaching what is "profitable" in light of "the whole counsel of God" (see vv. 20, 27). Paul offered this ministry of God's word in family living rooms as well as in public settings (v. 20). We might say that his Bible rested on both coffee tables and pulpits as he opened it and taught.

This teaching ministry pointed to the person, work, and teaching of Jesus. It overflowed into practical help for neighbors in need (v. 35), no matter who those neighbors were (v. 21). Moreover, an elder's call is Spirit-founded (vv. 22, 23, 28). Because the Spirit of God leads them, one might suppose a smooth future. On the contrary, the work of God's Spirit does not exempt us from life under the sun. Rather, it empowers us to purposefully walk into the heart of fallen things for the glory of Christ. Immunity? No. Purpose and strength? Yes! Therefore, by this

Spirit, elders "pay careful attention . . . to all the flock." They remain "alert" (see vv. 28, 31).

Pray for your elders' tears, testimony, teaching, neighbor-help, and alertness. Commend them to God and to God's grace. To God for their life and purpose; to God's grace for their shortcomings, limits, and sins, as well as for their true source of power. He is able to build them up (v. 32).

OCTOBER 12 · ACTS 21:37–22:29

Witnessing to Hostile People

SUSAN HUNT

JESUS STATED UNEQUIVOCALLY that his followers will be his witnesses (Acts 1:8). His confidence was not in us but in his provision of the Holy Spirit. Paul elaborates on this miracle of grace when he explains that the power in us is the same power that raised Jesus from the dead (Eph. 1:18–20). The immeasurable power of the Holy Spirit in us changes us from spiritually dead people to people who are bursting with the abundant life of Christ. This life cannot be contained. As we decrease and Jesus increases, his goodness will show up in every situation and every relationship.

The story of this Spirit-empowered witness progresses, and in this passage we come to Paul's witness to a hostile audience. His method and message are a tutorial for us as we face difficult situations and relationships.

Paul's graciousness to the tribune opened the way for him to speak. When he faced those who opposed him, he spoke their language. He told enough of his story to identify with them, then quickly transitioned to the gospel story of a voice calling his name. The two questions Paul asked the Voice are the essential questions: Who are you? What do you want me to do?

Once Paul knew the identity of the One who sovereignly initiated a relationship with him, he was never the same. Neither are we. When the Holy Spirit shines the light of the gospel into our hearts, the inevitable response of this new life in us is to acknowledge Jesus as the risen Lord and submit to his will.

Paul could fearlessly face the hostile crowd because he no longer lived for himself. He was a servant of the risen Christ. He knew that his story was part of the Grand Gospel Story, and that everything that happened to him was an opportunity to advance the gospel (Phil. 1:12). So it is with us. We are to show and tell what we have been empowered to see and hear.

It is staggering to consider that we have been appointed to know God's will and to see and hear the Righteous One as he reveals himself to us in his word (Acts 22:14–15). God sovereignly purposed our salvation and ordained the times and places where he wants us to be his witnesses. We can show compassion to difficult people in our family, our neighborhood, and our workplace because we are sinners who were once hostile to the gospel until God called us by name. When we gain permission to speak about Jesus, we do so with the assurance that he has promised to never leave us.

OCTOBER 13 • ACTS 26:12-32

Faith on Trial

ELISABETH MAXWELL (LISA) RYKEN

ACTS 26:12-32 CONTINUES the account of Paul's appearance before the Roman proconsul Festus and King Agrippa (begun in 25:13). Since Agrippa was familiar with Jewish law, Festus has enlisted his help in hearing Paul's case and documenting the charges against him for his hearing before Caesar.

For the third time in Acts, Paul speaks of his conversion. He tells about his upbringing and credentials (26:4–11). But how did this impeccable Pharisee come to be so hated and reviled that Jewish leaders were demanding his death? Paul explains: he had been traveling to Damascus to persecute those who believed in the resurrection of Jesus. He was a man on a mission; nothing would have diverted his vengeful fury. Nothing, that is, except the King of kings commanding him to stop. The risen Christ himself spoke to Paul, instructing him to take the gospel not only to the Jews but also to the Gentiles.

For Paul, his change of attitude and behavior was a matter of obedience to the King. But the Jews believed Paul had committed blasphemy, which was punishable by death. Paul knew how seriously the Jews took blasphemy. He had seen Stephen stoned (7:54–60). Paul also knew that he had done nothing wrong, and that if proper judicial procedures were followed, whether Jewish or Roman, he could be released.

As he faced trial, Paul had confidence in God's promise to protect him (26:17). Whether his future held freedom or chains, Paul trusted his Lord's sovereign goodness. Paul was obedient to God's command to proclaim the gospel. Starting in Damascus and continuing right up to that very day, Paul had testified "both to small and great" (v. 22). This was his opportunity to present salvation to these rulers, and if his appeal were granted, he might have the same opportunity before Caesar.

When Festus suddenly declared that Paul was crazy (v. 24), Paul dismissed the ruler's claim by asserting that the things he had said were both true and rational. He contested that Agrippa, the Jewish governor, must be familiar with recent events and realize that Paul spoke the truth. Paul prodded Agrippa to acknowledge that the words of the prophets were true and that Jesus was the logical fulfillment of their prophecies.

Paul longed for everyone—then and now—to believe in the death and resurrection of Jesus. We must either reject or accept Paul's claims. If we accept and believe, then our response is to gladly entrust ourselves to King Jesus and speak of his salvation.

OCTOBER 14 · ACTS 28:17-31

Thy Kingdom Come!

SAM STORMS

ALTHOUGH THE BOOK of Acts ends here, the kingdom of God does not! How fitting that Paul's final days of ministry would be filled with proclamations of the "kingdom of God" and "the Lord Jesus Christ" (Acts 28:31). But what does this mean?

Jesus claimed that the fulfillment of Old Testament hope was present in his person and ministry. But the *fulfillment* was taking place without the final *consummation*. The prophetic hope of the messianic kingdom was decisively begun but not finally completed in the person and ministry of Jesus. The kingdom is both the present spiritual reign of God and the future realm over which he will rule in power and glory. It is here, and it is not here.

What, then, is the kingdom of God? What would Paul have said to those who were coming to him (v. 30)? God's kingdom is not a geographical realm with clearly defined boundaries, such as those that separate the United States from Canada and Mexico. It is not to be identified with any one nation or political body.

The kingdom of God is not that place we call heaven—at least not yet!

The kingdom is not the church. The church is the people through whom the reign of God's presence and power is manifest.

The kingdom is not a place, but a power. It is not a static thing, but a dynamic and living reign. It is not land, but lordship!

The kingdom is not yet deliverance from political oppression (but it will be).

The kingdom is not yet renewal of creation (but it will be).

The kingdom is not yet material prosperity (but it will be).

So what is the kingdom that Paul proclaimed and that we too must make known?

The kingdom of God is the presence and powerful lordship of the King—Jesus! The kingdom is known and seen wherever Christ is acknowledged, where his subjects are saved, where his enemies are vanquished, and where his ways are obeyed. The kingdom of God is anywhere or anytime or anyone over whom Jesus Christ exercises lordship. It is the King reigning in hearts and minds.

God's dynamic and sovereign presence is now among us in Jesus. The kingdom is God in strength, God in saving action. And the one in and through whom this kingdom reign is manifest is Jesus Christ, his Son!

No Good News without
Bad News First

BRIAN BORGMAN

THE GOSPEL IS "the power of God for salvation" (Rom. 1:16). But salvation from what? In order to understand salvation, we must first understand our sin and the necessary consequences of it. We will never see the need for the power of God until we see our powerlessness under sin. We will never celebrate the good news until we understand the bad news. Paul spells out the bad news for us in Romans 1:18–32.

Paul begins his exposition of the good news with a very unpleasant portrait of humanity. He says that God is personally angry with our sin because he is holy, righteous, and loving. Although there is natural revelation that tells us about God as Creator, we reject that revelation. In our pride we refuse to submit to the Creator, and instead we manufacture manageable objects of worship. As Calvin said, our hearts are "idol factories" that crank out little deities that we love and serve.[8] This is high treason against God. This idolatrous path of rejecting the true God is cosmic rebellion. This is the path of self-deceit that exchanges the truth of God for a lie. This is how each one of us comes into the world.

God does not take treason lightly. His glory is too valuable for him to allow creatures to trample and belittle it. God reveals his wrath against our sin by giving us over to *more* sin (vv. 24, 26, 28). The failure to honor God as we ought is met with God giving us over to moral degradation. The ever-increasing speed of the downward spiral of sin is God's judgment against sin—and not only the so-called "big sins," but other sins such as deceit, gossip, malice, and pride (vv. 29–31). The Bible is clear: we know better. But instead of seeking God's help, we look around to approve the sins of others so that we can feel better about our own sin (v. 32).

This picture is frightening. We love our sin and are trapped in the whirlpool and cesspool of our own depravity. We need a radical rescue that only God can provide. We don't merely need a helping hand; we need

God to exert divine power through the gospel of his Son. God's saving righteousness is our only hope for salvation. When we feel the weight of this bad news, then the good news is really good. The British preacher Charles Spurgeon put it so beautifully: "Too many think lightly of sin, and therefore think lightly of the Savior. He who has stood before his God, convicted and condemned, with the rope about his neck, is the one to weep for joy when pardoned."[9]

OCTOBER 16 · ROMANS 3:9-31

But Now

ROBERT A. PETERSON

FIRST, THE VERY BAD NEWS: "all," both Jews and Gentiles, have sinned and are condemned before God (Rom. 3:9). "None is righteous, no, not one" (v. 10). Paul quotes several Old Testament verses to show what he will later spell out: "You once presented your members as slaves to impurity" (6:19). He speaks of our using throat, tongue, lips, mouth, feet, and eyes as instruments of sin (3:13–18). His point is unmistakable: "the whole world [is] accountable to God" (3:19). Anyone who thinks he can merit God's favor should forget about it: "For by works of the law no human being will be justified in his sight" (v. 20).

Then, the very good news. After showing the universal need for salvation, Paul returns to the theme of 1:16–17: the saving righteousness of God in Jesus. This salvation is received by faith alone, as Paul says eight times in 3:22–31! Faith saves. But is it true that it doesn't matter what you believe, as long as you are sincere? Not according to Paul. He insists that saving faith must be directed toward Jesus Christ.

Paul presents Jesus's saving accomplishment as a redemption and a "propitiation" (vv. 24–26). Redemption pictures us as slaves of sin, unable to rescue ourselves. Christ delivers us by offering himself as our ransom. Faith connects us to this saving work. But what about "propitiation"? This takes us back to the Old Testament, where the Lord decreed animal sacrifices as atonement for sin. But animal sacrifices were not the ultimate basis for forgiveness: "It is impossible for the blood of bulls and goats to take away sins" (Heb. 10:4). So, in a sense, God wrote IOUs to himself when he forgave Old Testament believers (Rom. 3:25). And this is where propitiation comes in. Propitiation means that, through Jesus's crucifixion, God satisfied his own justice. He "made good" on his IOUs. Christ took God's wrath for us. His death showed God's "righteousness at the present time, so that he might be just and the justifier of the one who has faith in Jesus" (v. 26). Because of Christ's work on the cross, God could save us without compromising his moral integrity.

It is no wonder, then, that this leaves no place for human boasting! (v. 27). Such boasting is excluded by faith in Christ's death and resurrection. Paul invites any who do not know him, "If you confess with your mouth that Jesus is Lord and believe in your heart that God raised him from the dead, you will be saved" (10:9). We are sinners, "but now" (3:21) God has given us his Son. Now we are counted righteous. Amazing grace!

OCTOBER 17 · ROMANS 4

The Truly Blessed Life

ZACK ESWINE

IF YOU WANTED YOUR friends to have a blessed life, what would you wish for them? For Paul, the blessed life begins with forgiveness (Rom. 4:6–8). Why is this?

When someone relates to you on the basis of your worst moment, you are to them always the one who sinned. Their conversation condemns. Their silent treatments accuse. Now imagine that a particular thing they accuse you of is true. You regret this and berate yourself. No excuse can relieve you. No amount of effort or change can undo the done thing.

This is why a blessed life requires the grace of forgiveness. No more accusation or guilt; finally at home again with God. The old hymn "And Can it Be" captures what it feels like to be ungodly and yet for God in his mercy to justify us anyway (v. 5):

Long my imprisoned spirit lay,
fast bound in sin and nature's night;
thine eye diffused a quickening ray;
I woke, the dungeon flamed with light;
my chains fell off, my heart was free,
I rose, went forth, and followed thee. . . .
No condemnation now I dread;
Jesus, and all in him, is mine.[10]

The unforgiven, unblessed become like the blind men beside the road who hear Jesus walk by. We care nothing for decorum. Not anymore. We fill our desperate lungs and yell, "Mercy!" But who can receive such merciful blessing from God? "Anyone," Paul says (vv. 9–12). How do we get this blessing? "It is a gift of God's grace," Paul writes (see v. 16). And as he writes this, maybe Damascus road flashes in his memory: the bloodied knuckles of violent hands; the meanness which he perpetrated in God's name upon innocents. Maybe when he speaks of David (vv. 6–8), he remembers David's sins too.

"Don't trust your efforts," he continues. "Those have always got you into trouble anyway. You must appeal with empty hands to Christ's work, not yours." But how? "Believe," Paul says. Because of Jesus, God will credit your fledgling faith as if it were a strong oak of faith. He will treat the broken thing as if it were solid, like a toddler's drawing displayed on the fridge. The muddled art gets credited as if it were expert, and all who gather know what the parent is doing. They join in, give thanks, and make much of the child's offering. So it is with faith. So it is with God. Grace comes, and the blessed life begins.

He Loved Us Then; He'll Love Us Now

DANE C. ORTLUND

IT IS NOT hard for many of us to believe God has put away all our failures that occurred before our conversion. Sure, maybe we lived a particularly rebellious life before our new birth—but that was, after all, before we had heard the gospel. We did not know of God's love. Of course we screwed up a lot then.

What is hard is to believe that God continues to put away all my present failures, now that I am supposedly "better." We so easily view the Father looking down with raised eyebrows: "How are they still such failures after all I have done for them?" we see him wondering. After all, a Christian conscience is a resensitized conscience. New birth makes us feel more deeply than ever the ugliness of sin.

That's why Romans 5:1–11 is in the Bible.

After exulting in the peace we now enjoy because of the gospel (vv. 1–5), Paul says roughly the same thing three times over. "*While we were still weak,* at the right time Christ died for the ungodly" (v. 6). "*While we were still sinners,* Christ died for us" (v. 8). "If *while we were enemies* we were reconciled to God by the death of his Son, much more, now that we are reconciled, shall we be saved by his life" (v. 10). Three times Paul says that God did something to save us when we hated him. Weak. Sinners. Enemies. We didn't have to clean ourselves up first. He didn't meet us halfway. He himself pulled us up into peace.

That's great news. But that's not even Paul's main point in these verses. He's after something else. What's the ultimate point Paul is driving at in Romans 5:6–11? Paul's burden is our present security, given that past work. He mentions Christ's past work to drive home this point: If God did that back *then,* when you had zero interest in him, then what are you worried about *now*? The whole point of Romans 5:6–11 is captured in the "since" of verse 9: "*Since,* therefore, we have now been justified by his blood, . . ."

This really calms us down. He drew near to us when we hated him. Will he remain distant now that we want to please him? He suffered for us when we were failing, as orphans. Will he sternly cross his arms over our failures now that we are his adopted children? His heart was gentle and lowly toward us when we were lost. Will his heart be anything different toward us now that we are found?

"While we were still . . ." He loved us in our mess then. He'll love us in our mess now.

OCTOBER 19 • ROMANS 6

Free to Fight

LYDIA BROWNBACK

"WHERE SIN INCREASED, grace abounded all the more," Paul has just written (Rom. 5:20). Since that is the case, why bother to strive against sin? In one sense, asking that question indicates that we are beginning to grasp the nature and extent of grace! But as Paul makes clear in chapter 6, those who are truly in Christ will not want to keep on sinning. Before conversion, we are *not* able *not* to sin. But once we have been united to Christ, we are *able not to* sin. In Christ we are free—not free to sin but free *not* to sin.

Through Christ's atoning work, the power of sin has been broken in those who believe, yet the presence of sin remains with us, and because of that, we will have to battle against it every day of our lives. Paul's words are a call to fight against sin and to grow in holiness, trusting that as we continually engage in the fight, the Holy Spirit is at work in us, conforming us more and more into Christ's likeness, a process theologians call "progressive sanctification."

Paul encourages us with a promise: "Sin will have no dominion over you, since you are not under law but under grace" (6:14). Sin's dominion was broken at the cross, at which time we died with Christ and were raised with him to newness of life (v. 4).

Continuing willfully in sin is not only an abuse of God's grace; it is also personally destructive. If we obey sin, we become slaves to sin (v. 16).

Grace enables us instead to "become slaves of righteousness" (v. 18)—and this "slavery" is true freedom. Fighting against indwelling sin feels like a battle because it *is* a battle. But the war has already been won for those in Christ. That is Paul's message here. We have already been set free from the penalty and the power of sin, and one day we will be set free from its presence. In the meantime, we strive to avoid giving in to our sinful inclinations. Although our old sin nature clamors to be fed and filled, we need not give in to it, because, in reality, we have died to sin (vv. 2, 7, 11–13).

Elsewhere Paul writes, "The grace of God has appeared, . . . training us to renounce ungodliness and worldly passions, and to live self-controlled, upright, and godly lives in the present age, waiting for our blessed hope, the appearing of the glory of our great God and Savior Jesus Christ, who gave himself for us to redeem us from all lawlessness and to purify for himself a people for his own possession who are zealous for good works" (Titus 2:11–14). That is the essence of the Christian life. As we live it out, we are walking the road to eternal life.

OCTOBER 20 · ROMANS 8:18-30

Our Faithful Father

JONI EARECKSON TADA

PANIC. This is what I felt shortly after the diving accident in which I broke my neck. I learned that I was a quadriplegic and that my paralysis was total and complete. It didn't help that my friends were going off to college and getting jobs, while I was stuck in a hospital bed. Life in a wheelchair looked bleak and frightening, and a dense fog of depression settled over me. I cried out to God. I wanted assurance that my world wasn't ripping apart at the seams. I longed for someone to promise that everything was going to be okay.

This is the heartfelt plea of *anyone* who suffers. We want assurance that somehow, someway, things will work out in the end—that our world is orderly and stable and not spinning off into nightmarish chaos. We want to know that God is at the center of our suffering, not only holding our lives together but holding *us*, just like a father who holds his crying child, pats him on his back, and says, "There, there, honey . . . everything will be okay; Daddy's here, it's okay." That's our plea. We want God to be Daddy like that.

In Romans 8 we have the massive promise of that assurance: "And we know that for those who love God all things work together for good, for those who are called according to his purpose" (Rom. 8:28). Here God tells us that he is so supremely in charge of the world that all the things that happen to Christians are ordered in such a way that they serve our good. And this is true whether we face tribulation, distress, persecution, famine, nakedness, danger, the sword, or broken necks. The robust hope of the believer is not that we will escape a long list of bad things, but that God will make every one of our agonies an instrument of his mercy to do us good—in the here and now, and in the hereafter.

Here is all the Fatherly assurance we could want in our sufferings. And the assurance goes beyond the promise that "everything will be okay." Verse 29 reveals a far more splendid purpose in that, through our sufferings, we are predestined to be conformed to the image of his Son, Jesus Christ.

Friend, you need not panic over your problems. Paul says that your sufferings are small and short when compared to the weight of glory they are accruing for you in heaven. So bear with the headache and hardship a bit longer—these things are stretching your soul's capacity for more joy, worship, and service in heaven than you can possibly imagine. "Wait for it with patience" (v. 25). Wait and trust in the Lord. Your present hope and expectation will not disappoint you.

OCTOBER 21 · ROMANS 10:5–21

Faith Comes from Hearing

ROBERT A. PETERSON

THERE IS MUCH confusion today, even among evangelical Christians, as to whether people need to hear and believe the gospel to be saved. This passage alone should clear up the confusion. As is his custom, Paul contrasts relying on one's own works versus believing in Christ as ways of salvation. It is true that those who keep the law perfectly will attain eternal life (Rom. 10:5–13). But no one keeps the law perfectly (3:9–20, 27–30; 4:1–8). Moreover, salvation will never come through human law-keeping, for that would mean Christ died in vain (Gal. 2:21). And that is certainly not the case!

No one will be saved by the "righteousness that is based on the law," but instead only by the "word of faith" (Rom. 10:5, 8). What is this word of faith? A general belief in God? A confidence to ask God for wealth and possessions? Neither. Rather, it is this message: "If you confess with your mouth that Jesus is Lord and believe in your heart that God raised him from the dead, you will be saved" (v. 9). This message is for all human beings, regardless of location, color, or ethnicity, for "everyone who calls on the name of the Lord will be saved" (v. 13, citing Joel 2:32).

Through a series of rhetorical questions, Paul teaches that to be saved from their sins, people must hear and believe the gospel (Rom. 10:14–15). This too is in accord with the Old Testament, namely Isaiah (Rom. 10:15–16; citing Isa. 52:7; 53:1). Paul sums up the matter famously: "So faith comes from hearing, and hearing through the word of Christ" (Rom. 10:17). That is, the faith that saves from sin and judgment comes from hearing the gospel of Christ and believing in him.

But what about God's chosen people, Israel? Though most of the first Christians were Jewish, most Jews both in Paul's day (vv. 18, 21) and today have rejected Jesus as their Messiah. And the overwhelming majority of believers are Gentiles. This too, sadly, fulfills the Old Testament prediction that God would make the Jews jealous by doing a work of salvation among the Gentiles (vv. 19–20).

Paul's teaching here is in accord with Jesus's own words: "I am the way, and the truth, and the life. No one comes to the Father except through me" (John 14:6). It also corresponds to Peter's preaching: "There is salvation in no one else, for there is no other name under heaven given among men by which we must be saved" (Acts 4:12).

Have you heard this gospel? Have you believed? Then you have been caught up in the greatest triumph and the greatest love story the world has ever known.

Oh, the Depth of the Riches and Wisdom and Knowledge of God!

ROBERT A. PETERSON

ALTHOUGH MANY FIRST-CENTURY Jews rejected their Christ (their Messiah), God has not given up on them. There is a future for the descendants of Abraham and Sarah. Their salvation, as all salvation, will be based on God's grace, not human deeds. For if salvation were on the basis of deeds, "grace would no longer be grace" (Rom. 11:6).

In God's amazing plan, Israel's rejection of Christ has meant salvation for the Gentiles. Paul knows this well, for God commissioned him to be an apostle to the Gentiles. And remarkably, God chose to bring the gospel to the Gentiles in part to make Israel jealous so that they too would believe in Jesus.

Now, none of this should make Gentile Christians proud, as if they have earned God's favor. Not at all! Rather, they are wild olive branches grafted into the natural tree, the root of which is Israel (vv. 17–18). Gentile believers are to remember that the root supports them and not vice versa! If they do not faithfully pass on the gospel to their descendants, the knowledge of God among them, too, may be lost.

Indeed, all pride is excluded by God's wonderful grace. Instead, believers are to fear God, not with a paralyzing fear of his wrath but with a humble fear that refuses to take for granted either salvation or pleasing God. Paul concludes by reflecting on the profound way in which God has orchestrated history so that both Jews and Gentiles would be shown mercy through Christ (vv. 30–32).

What is the proper response to such a grand plan of salvation? Paul is our example, as he praises God: "Oh, the depth of the riches and wisdom and knowledge of God! How unsearchable are his judgments and how inscrutable his ways! . . . To him be glory forever. Amen" (vv. 33, 36). We too are privileged to praise God for his sovereign grace granted to us. In Christ, we have been granted all that we could ever hope for or desire. Our worst is behind us and the best is yet to come. What a wonder of grace that God would send his own Son to redeem lost and wayward rebels such as us. As we reflect on and enjoy this grace, let us pray for our friends and neighbors and, as God leads, prayerfully and kindly share the good news with them.

OCTOBER 23 · ROMANS 12:9–21

Because of That, . . . This

ELYSE FITZPATRICK

MARTIN LUTHER CALLED the book of Romans the "purest gospel,"[11] for in this book, as in no other, Paul outlines the entire gospel message: our need, Christ's fulfillment of it, the transformation the gospel brings, our ongoing war with indwelling sin, and God's great love for us despite our failure.

In this passage, Paul outlines some practical implications of God's saving mercy. Because we are saved "by the mercies of God" (Rom. 12:1), we are freed to live lives of love. Because we've been given such good news, we no longer have to fight to be loved, or live self-indulgently to try to make ourselves feel better.

This passage helps us understand what it looks like to live out a grateful response to the truth of the gospel. For instance, because we've been so radically loved and welcomed, we are freed from competing for the limelight and will instead seek to "outdo one another in showing honor" (v. 10). Our hearts are set aflame with zealous, fervent service to the Lord; now we have a motivation to serve that is much more profound than the bare command "You must serve others." Our slavish desire to be served is reversed by the love of the One who "came not to be served but to serve, and to give his life as a ransom for many" (Mark 10:45).

We are transformed from grumpy pessimists into hopeful optimists because we've been united to Christ in his resurrection, empowering us to "rejoice in hope" (Rom. 12:12). We can now "be patient in tribulation" (v. 12) because we know that nothing comes to us but through Jesus's nail-scarred hands. We can come to our Savior constantly—when we fail, when we succeed, when we're doubting and lost—and know that he loves to hear from us and continues to intercede for us. We can be radically generous and hospitable, because we know that in him we've been given everything we need (v. 13; Rom. 8:32; 1 Cor. 3:21).

Do you see how this good news enables us to "bless those who persecute" us? (Rom. 12:14). We don't curse those who mistreat us in an effort to protect or elevate ourselves—because Jesus became a curse for us by dying on a tree (Gal. 3:13). He teaches us to identify with all who rejoice and with all who weep (Rom. 12:15). We can live in harmony with one another because the cause of all our conflicts, the desires that wage war demanding their own way (James 4:1), have been silenced in the overwhelming forgiveness and righteousness of the cross.

And so, in light of "the mercies of God," we are free to present ourselves, with our desires and our relationships, to God "as a living sacrifice" in grateful response to all he's done.

OCTOBER 24 · ROMANS 13:1-7

God's Governing Authorities and You

GLORIA FURMAN

JESUS TAUGHT US TO "render to Caesar the things that are Caesar's, and to God the things that are God's" (Mark 12:17). The people marveled at Jesus in response to this teaching. We, today, may also marvel at this gospel-grounded, God-centered perspective on government. Paul is writing to those who are called to present their bodies "as a living sacrifice, holy and acceptable to God"; he assumes that through God's Spirit we're being transformed by the renewal of our minds (Rom. 12:1–3).

As our minds are renewed by God's Spirit, we are convinced that God is in control—which means that no one attains a place of power in government outside of the will of God (13:1). The ruler is "God's servant" (v. 4) who is appointed by God (v. 2). Whether such a leader is a Christian or not, his authority is delegated to him by God. It follows that those under the rule of God's appointed servants must submit to them as unto God.

God ordains human government as "an avenger who carries out God's wrath on the wrongdoer" (v. 4) for the good of his people (Gen. 1:27; Ps. 22:28). In the renewing of our minds we also understand that no human government can fully address all evil. Human wickedness is bound up in our sinful hearts and can be atoned for only by Jesus Christ. Jesus himself will deal with all evil, whether he dies for an individual's sins on the cross or punishes that person for his sins in eternity.

The questions of submission to an unjust government, usurped authority, or corrupt policy are not addressed directly in Romans 13. Paul is not declaring what to do in every situation where human government fails; he is addressing the origin of this authority. The Bible teaches clearly that we should seek God's approval first and foremost, and must never submit to a law that would incur God's righteous anger (Ex. 1:17, 20–21; Dan. 3:18; Acts 5:29). Paul's appeal to the conscience (Rom. 13:5) sets the limit of our obedience to human government. The law of God trumps every man-made law, so our loyal submission is ever, primarily, unto the Lord Jesus Christ.

It is easy to be skeptical toward human government. Perhaps we even sneer at the possibility that any good could come from it. But such attitudes are not becoming for the Christian, who respects God's authority in establishing government. The Christian humbly does "what is right" and submits as unto the Lord, paying all of what is owed—taxes, revenue, respect, and honor. In our law abiding we are commended by God himself, whose approval is our joy!

OCTOBER 25 · ROMANS 14:13–23

Let Love Rule

TRILLIA NEWBELL

SECONDARY PRACTICES CAN become primary issues when our hearts and minds are not nurtured by the grace of the gospel. We can be tempted to judge others whose convictions are different from our own, and to pressure them in a way that is out of accord with the way God treats us. Paul recognized this tendency, and he addressed the churches in Rome accordingly. Members of these churches had been quarreling about food (Rom. 14:2). The old covenant required that certain "unclean" food be avoided. But under the new covenant, all food became lawful (Col. 2:16–17). The problem was (and is!), old habits are hard to break, particularly habits based on religious tradition. Some members of the church in Rome simply couldn't bring themselves to eat food that had been prohibited for so long.

Instead of chastising these Christians or pressuring them to conform, however, Paul explains that each person should follow his conscience and be "fully convinced in his own mind" (Rom. 14:5). The important thing is that every member of the church treat one another with the same grace God has shown them.

Paul urged the Roman Christians to respond to differences of opinion *in love* by respecting their brothers' and sisters' convictions. He says, "For if your brother is grieved by what you eat, you are no longer walking in love. By what you eat, do not destroy the one for whom Christ died" (v. 15). The word "destroy" in this verse underscores the gravity of our actions. Our goal must always be to guard and strengthen the faith of our brothers and sisters in Christ.

Paul elsewhere teaches that we are to be humble and "count others more significant than [ourselves]" (Phil. 2:3). This is difficult, since we are naturally inclined to think of our own interests. But by God's grace, we can look to the interests of others. We do this by focusing our thoughts on Christ, "who, though he was in the form of God, did not count equality with God a thing to be grasped, but emptied himself" (Phil. 2:5–7).

Perhaps we don't have trouble with what others eat. But we may find ourselves bothered by our friend's choice of schools, use of alcohol, or decision either to work outside the home or to focus on homemaking full-time. We may wrestle with wanting others' walks with the Lord to mimic our own. When that's the case, we must look to Jesus, who, to the point of death, counted even those who would deny him, beat him, and curse him as being above himself. Let us learn from his example and be willing to die to ourselves for the sake of our brothers and sisters.

Gospel Surrender

JANI ORTLUND

AS PAUL NEARS the end of his letter to the Romans, he shows us what believing the gospel will look like in our lives together. The gospel lifts us from our natural self-focus. When we surrender to the gospel, we begin moderating the demands of self for the sake of unity.

If you are strong in a certain area, you have "an obligation to bear with the failings" (Rom. 15:1) of a weaker sister. You are to accommodate yourself to her sensitivities and burdens. Gospel-saturated women don't chafe under the inconveniences caused by a weaker Christian. We all disappoint each other, and Paul says that the gospel gives us a resource by which we can absorb these disappointments and instead extend grace by building one another up.

With Christ as our example, we are to please our neighbor, not ourselves. Christ had a purpose higher than himself. It so consumed him that he willingly suffered for it. When we belong to him, self just doesn't matter that much anymore (1 Cor. 10:24). To live this way will take the discipline and hard work of slogging it out day by day, putting others above ourselves. "The Scriptures" instruct us in this kind of life (Rom. 15:4). Remember that when Paul was writing, "the Scriptures" meant the Old Testament. Don't disdain the instruction found there. Reading the Old Testament will build your confidence that God himself is a God of grace, encouraging you to act the same way toward others.

The God of endurance and encouragement can bless us with unity. Paul asks God to give believers such unity that we sound like one voice—no discordant members out of key with other Christians (vv. 5–6). He wants our lives to be so peaceful together, so agreeable (12:16; 2 Cor. 13:11), that we harmonize as we all tune ourselves to the mind of Christ (Phil. 2:4–8). When self is demoted for the common good, we make beautiful music together!

With the example of Christ, the instruction of Scripture, and the encouragement of our heavenly Father, we can open wide our hearts to everyone who loves Jesus. We can welcome others among us, despite their flaws, because that is how Christ welcomes us (Rom. 15:7). Our unity is based on the gospel of grace; Jesus welcomes all believers on the same terms. We have no right as Jesus's sisters to impose conditions for fellowship which he doesn't require.

And this God of hope can fill frail, disheartened, pessimistic women with all joy and peace as we believe in him (v. 13). Gospel surrender yields God-sized joy, peace, and hope. Let's open our hearts to him and rejoice as he floods us with an overflowing hope through the power of the Holy Spirit.

The Wisdom of God

DAN DORIANI

IN 1 CORINTHIANS, Paul works to correct the pride and divisive spirit that characterized the church in Corinth. The Corinthians had formed antagonistic parties, and they justified their dissension by claiming that they followed one hero or another (1 Cor. 1:10–17). They had trouble separating themselves from the "gods" of human power and human wisdom, just as we do. A right understanding of the cross should terminate such nonsense.

Jesus was an enigma to Jews and Greeks alike. The Jews loved signs of power, but Jesus came in weakness. The Greeks loved wisdom (v. 22), but Jesus was unschooled in what *they* considered wisdom. Power and wisdom have always been revered, but they are not gracious gods. Take wisdom, for example. The god of human wisdom rewards only the educated elite. But these "wise" ones have never found God through their intellect. Instead, they fashion gods that resemble themselves (vv. 19–21; Rom. 1:21–23). Both wisdom and power are gods of human self-sufficiency.

The gospel is the opposite. It presents Jesus, slain in weakness, raised in power. He is a state criminal who, by his humiliating death, defeated death, the devil, and sin. This defies wisdom. "The cross is folly to those who are perishing," but it is the power of God for the saved (1 Cor. 1:18).

The gospel of salvation by faith in Jesus, crucified and risen, is "a stumbling block to Jews and folly to Gentiles" (v. 23).

To the Jew, a crucified Messiah was a contradiction. The Messiah, they thought, would be triumphant and blessed, but the crucified were cursed and humiliated. To the mighty Romans, a crucified man was evil and weak. To Greeks, the hope of resurrection was absurd, for they viewed the body as something to be left behind upon death. But "the foolishness of God is wiser than men" (v. 25), for the crucified Lord atones for our sin and the risen Lord gives us the richest hope.

The church reflects the gospel's inversion of worldly values. Few Corinthians were wise, powerful, or noble when God called them. He chose the foolish "to shame the wise" and the weak "to shame the strong" (vv. 26–27). In some places today, the elite are less religious, while in other places the educated and prosperous are attracted to the church. But in all places, the outcast and marginalized warm to the message of creation in the image of God and re-creation in the image of Christ. The only thing we contribute to our redemption is the sin that made it necessary. No one, however mighty, can "boast in the presence of God" (v. 29). The gospel levels humanity and exalts God.

OCTOBER 28 · 1 CORINTHIANS 2

Wisdom Does Not Come from the Web

TASHA D. CHAPMAN

WE LIVE IN an age of information overload. With the press of a button we can access more data than the world has ever had before. But are we wiser? Or are we more confused with possibilities, more opinionated with facts, and more disconnected from our world, from our Creator, and from each other? True wisdom would mean understanding who we are, why we exist, and what we should be doing, in light of creation and eternity. Facts without faith do not provide identity, meaning, or purpose.

In Paul's day, Corinth was also a place of information overload. As a thriving crossroads of trade routes, it boasted cultural and religious knowledge, with numerous temples to the gods, and places of learning and philosophical debate. But this "wisdom" created challenges and conflicts within the young church. Paul wrote this stern letter to correct their beliefs, ministry practices, and moral behavior in light of biblical principles. And he started by correcting their thinking about wisdom.

True wisdom involves godly living (1 Cor. 13:1–3, 8–10). It is very different from society's "wisdom" and is foolish to others since its focus is Jesus Christ (1:18, 30; 2:2; 3:18–23). Wisdom is a gift from the Holy Spirit, who helps us gain God's perspective and empowers us to act on it (2:12–13).

Though we gain information through media and the Internet, we do not gain wisdom. Nor does wisdom come from celebrities or motivational speakers. Yet we often follow the culture in wanting teachers and church leaders to be entertaining, witty, and attractive, as if those qualities would guarantee our learning. Thus, we need Paul's correction as much as the Corinthian believers did. We must ask:

Does my identity come more from magazines and others' opinions, or from prayerful consideration of what Scripture says is true of me (6:19–20; 12:14–27)?

Do my hopes and fears fluctuate with newscasts, or do I gain assurance from God's promises (1:7–9; 15:20–24)?

Do I imitate the lifestyles of neighbors and TV characters more than those of people in the Bible (4:14–17; 10:1–14; 15:33–34)?

Do I make sense of life more from novels and movies than I do from God's true story of creation, rebellion, redemption, and restoration (15:1–8, 20–26)?

Such questions point us back to Scripture and challenge our pride, so that our "faith might not rest in the wisdom of men but in the power of God" (2:5).

The Danger of a Little Leaven

CAROL CORNISH

IN THIS SECTION of his letter, Paul deals with a case of sexual immorality by a man who was part of the Corinthian church. The man's sin was so perverse that Paul says it would not be tolerated even by unbelievers; but shockingly, those within the church were not addressing it at all. They were acting as if they could simply overlook the sinful behavior—or worse, accept it.

The way that we conduct ourselves directly affects our brothers and sisters in Christ. By God's good design, the church functions as a body (1 Cor. 12:12–31). What one part of that body does has profound implications for the body as a whole. In addition, as those who bear the name of Christ, we are responsible before God to maintain a good reputation within our communities. Otherwise, our witness will be sullied and we will be no different from unbelievers. How will the unbeliever see a need for Christ if the people inside the church behave as immorally as those outside it?

The purity of our minds and bodies is a major concern in Scripture. We are responsible (in the power of the Holy Spirit) to keep ourselves pure and to encourage such purity in other Christians. We are called to be like Christ—to live such godly lives that others will be able to see a reflection, however slight, of the goodness and purity of Christ. We cannot live any way we please. Sin is serious business. It offends God and harms the sinner, the person(s) sinned against, the church, and the witness of the gospel.

Church discipline is sometimes necessary to protect the integrity and witness of the church. When this is the case, the goal is *always* the restoration and healing of the one sinning. We are called to expose sin (Eph. 5:11), but never for the purpose of shaming a beloved brother or sister, or out of a spirit of self-righteousness: "Rather, speaking the truth in love, we are to grow up in every way into him who is the head, into Christ, from whom the whole body, joined and held together by every joint with which it is equipped, when each part is working properly, makes the body grow so that it builds itself up in love" (Eph. 4:15–16).

If we want to know Christ more intimately and love him more deeply, our lives must be marked by purity. Jesus said, "Blessed are the pure in heart, for they shall see God" (Matt. 5:8). Though the meaning in the Beatitudes refers to an eternal seeing, it is also true that those who pursue purity have clearer spiritual sight now. The Lord can trust that they will not drag his Spirit into places and situations of defilement. Demonstrate Christ's love for you by living a pure life.

OCTOBER 30 · 1 CORINTHIANS 7:25–40

The Present Form of This World Is Passing Away

ROBERT A. PETERSON

IN THIS PASSAGE, Paul gives practical advice to unmarried and widowed Christians. His advice has sometimes been misunderstood. Paul writes "in view of the present distress" (1 Cor. 7:26). This is another way of referring to the "last days." John, as he writes toward the end of the first century, says, "It is the last hour" (1 John 2:18). What are the last days? They are the times between the first coming of Christ and his second coming.

Some say that when Paul writes, "The appointed time has grown very short" (1 Cor. 7:29), he thinks Christ will return within the Corinthians' lifetimes. This is mistaken, however, because he also urges readers to do various things that would be unnecessary if Christ were definitely coming soon. Rather, Paul wants us to live in light of Christ's return, which will occur at a time we do not know. Because Christ has risen, "the present form of this world is passing away" (v. 31), and believers should live accordingly. We must fulfill earthly responsibilities while we "seek the things that are above, where Christ is seated at the right hand of God" (Col. 3:1).

This includes matters pertaining to marriage, Paul's main topic here. This teaching too has been misunderstood. He does not speak against marriage or sexual relations within it. On the contrary, he warns marriage partners not to "deprive one another" of sexual union, except for a limited time for prayer, lest Satan tempt them (1 Cor. 7:5). Although Paul happily remains unmarried to better serve the Lord, he teaches that both marriage and singleness are gifts from God.

In light of the urgency of living in the last times, Paul acknowledges that remaining single allows "undivided devotion to the Lord" (v. 35). Married couples, on the other hand, must consider pleasing their partners as well as being concerned about the things of the Lord. Paul counsels couples with burning passions to marry and counsels those without such passions not to marry. Christians are free to marry or not. Paul chooses the latter option and recommends it but does not impose it on others. Church leaders must present singleness as a meaningful option for Christians; believers must be urged to consider singleness as a valid way of wholeheartedly serving the Lord.

Above all, remember that marriage is about the gospel. Christ our bridegroom has come, and he will come again to reclaim his bride—which includes both single and married believers. This is the true significance of marriage, as we live in a world whose present form is passing away.

Rights and Wrongs

CLAIRE SMITH

THE EARLY CHURCH father Tertullian tells us that observers of the church in the second and third century said of Christians, "See how they love one another." Apparently the Christians in those early times stood out from their society in this regard. But the comment might not have been made of the Corinthian church in Paul's day. Rather than outdoing each other in showing love and honor (Rom. 12:10), they tried to outdo each other in many far less consequential ways—whether it was competition in terms of so called "knowledge" (1 Corinthians 8), in freedom during worship (11:2–16), in abundance of food at the Lord's meal (11:17–34), or in spiritual gifts or power (12:4–30; 14:1–40).

What made them different from their culture was not how they loved each other, but what criteria they used to decide who was in the in-crowd and the out-crowd. The strong had little regard for the weak, and they were more concerned about their "rights" than about doing right. They were forgetting that the Lord had died for each person, and that they were each a treasured part of his body.

How far they had wandered from the way of Christ! He did not despise the weak—he was himself rejected and despised (Isaiah 53) and delighted to draw near to weak people. He did not exalt himself—"he humbled himself by becoming obedient to the point of death, even death on a cross" (Phil. 2:1–8). He did not insist on his rights and freedoms—he surrendered his rights and freedoms, out of love for the Father and for us. He went so far as *dying* for us. He was not strong or wise by human standards, but "Christ crucified" is the power and wisdom of God (1 Cor. 1:23–25).

The Corinthians had forgotten that strength or wisdom or power or reputation were not the highest prize. Love is. And so they were to seek the good of others, not their own good (10:24). This meant building up the faith of those with fragile faith, and not putting stumbling blocks in their way. With those who did not yet know Christ, it meant removing every offense and obstacle other than "the offense of the cross" (Gal. 5:11).

Paul lived like this. He would not eat meat if it would lead "weak" believers to sin against their conscience (1 Cor. 8:9–13). He lived as a Jew to win the Jews. He lived as one outside the law to win those outside the law. He became weak to win the weak. He became all things to all people, that by all means he might win some (9:22).

Paul was simply following Christ. And this is the great call on us today (11:1).

NOVEMBER 1 · 1 CORINTHIANS 10:23-33

Liberty and Love

JESSICA THOMPSON

THERE WAS MUCH confusion in the early church about eating food sacrificed to idols. Under the old covenant this would have been prohibited, but Peter's vision in Acts 10:9–33 showed that, in light of the coming of Christ, God was overturning the ceremonial laws of the Mosaic covenant.

This included the distinction between clean and unclean foods. Such ceremonial laws were not to get in the way of Jewish believers enjoying fellowship with Gentile believers.

Paul addresses the issue of food offered to idols in 1 Corinthians 8 and 10. In chapter 8, he discusses food eaten within the walls of a pagan temple, while in chapter 10 the setting is a private home. Chapter 8 focuses on believers' relationships with other believers, and chapter 10 on our relationship with unbelievers. His instructions differ according to the context, but the underlying principle is the same: our "rights" are never to become a stumbling block to others.

Paul's concern is that the Corinthians act toward others in a way that points them toward, rather than away from, Christ. Thus, while it may be "lawful" for believers to eat meat sacrificed to idols, it may not be "helpful" (1 Cor. 10:23). Christians are to love others in the way they were loved by Christ. "Let no one seek his own good, but the good of his neighbor" (v. 24).

The Corinthians are to respond based on the circumstances under which the food is offered to them. They are not to question their host concerning whether or not the food has been sacrificed to idols; rather, they are to simply eat (v. 27). However, if someone does inform them that the food has been sacrificed, they must not partake. Why? "For the sake of the one who informed you" (v. 28). The important thing is to protect the conscience of that individual. It is not a matter of whether or not the food is clean or unclean; it is a matter of loving others more than loving the liberty to eat whatever we want.

We should also take note that, in chapter 10, the believer is sharing a meal with an unbeliever. The early Christians were around unbelievers enough to be sharing meals with them. Likewise, it is important for us to form relationships with unbelievers, taking the time to really know and understand them so that we can live in a way that will "give no offense" (v. 32). Our aim as believers is to always advance the gospel, whether we eat or don't eat, drink or don't drink (v. 31). This is the aspiration of all interaction we have with unbelievers. We long "that they may be saved" (v. 33).

Body Life

DONNA THOENNES

SINCE PAUL'S ENCOUNTER with Jesus on the Damascus road, his days were consumed with spreading the gospel and encouraging believers in their faith. He was a dedicated evangelist and disciple maker who confronted any people, philosophies, or misunderstandings that hindered the gospel. Paul spent a year and a half in Corinth, founding and nurturing the church there. So when he learned of the divisiveness at the Lord's Supper caused by arrogant, powerful members, he knew they had failed to grasp his teaching.

From the beginning of his letter, Paul appeals to the Corinthians to "be united in the same mind and the same judgment" (1 Cor. 1:10), and he asks the insightful question, "Is Christ divided?" (1:13). The implication is clear: if Christ is not divided, the church should not be either, for it exists to reflect God's character.

God's sovereignty is on display here, as he foreordains the membership and spiritual gifts of each local church. Each member is there by God's design alone, not by human fabrication or maneuvering. If one member were missing, it would be something less than a body; imagine a sensory organ telling the external limb it has no need of it! Because God has arranged all indispensable parts, no one should dare think of another, "I have no need of you" (12:21).

Paul takes it one step further: Beyond simply recognizing that each part is vitally important for their church to function, the Corinthians should actively care for one another (v. 25). "If one member suffers, all suffer together; if one member is honored, all rejoice together" (v. 26). What a beautiful picture of a deeply caring relationship! We should orient our lives in a way that encourages this kind of body life. We are not to be silently envious when life goes well for another, nor silently gleeful when another faces a setback. We rejoice and suffer together.

While Paul is clearly calling the Corinthians to be unified, he is also calling them to rejoice in their diversity. Within a beautifully unified church there are various gifts and ministries. We must strongly resist the inclination to rank these gifts and ministries, assuming some are more honorable than others; all of God's gifts are to be embraced and appreciated.

Paul's ancient words speak right to our hearts. We can succumb to the temptation either to set ourselves apart (out of pride) or to blend in (out of fear). If we share Paul's passion to spread the gospel and disciple believers, we will humble ourselves, fight for unity, love diverse gifts, and thank God for his design. The health and witness of the church is at stake.

NOVEMBER 3 · 1 CORINTHIANS 13

All That Really Matters

DANE C. ORTLUND

FEW BIBLICAL PASSAGES rebuke and reorient our scale of Christian significance like 1 Corinthians 13. This is not merely a text that outlines what it means to get married—to be read at weddings. It is a text that outlines what it means to be a Christian, and as such it should be kept front and center in our lives as believers.

Sandwiched in between two chapters in which Paul deals with problems in the very gifted Corinthian church, having to do with tongues and prophecy, here Paul re-centers his readers. He reminds the Corinthians, and us, of heaven's scale of significance.

Paul says that supreme elegance with words (1 Cor. 13:1), superior knowledge and faith (v. 2), and even ultimate self-sacrifice (v. 3) are all worthless apart from love. This arrests us. For the apostle puts his finger on those very things that appear to carry great clout with God. If God isn't happy with our words, our knowledge and faith, and our sacrifice, what in the world *can* please him?

Impressive speech, knowledge, and sacrifice can all be exercised out of a fundamental absorption with self. Any of these things can be done to soothe our conscience, or to help us feel superior to other believers, or to solidify our sense of God's approval of us. Only love, real love, is "self-proof." For that is what love *is*—delighting to place another before ourselves. We all approach every relationship with one of two mindsets: either a your-life-for-mine mindset or a my-life-for-yours mindset. In these verses Paul is painting a picture of what a my-life-for-yours mindset looks like: it is patient and kind. It does not envy or boast. And so on. Love is glad to inconvenience itself for the sake of helping someone else. Love is the great and beautiful trade-off: my comfort for yours.

What in the world can fuel such self-denial? It feels like death, of course. Why would I give up energy, time, emotional resources, and everything else for another? I'm barely surviving as it is!

The answer is that there was One who walked the earth who spoke perfectly, who had prophetic powers and all knowledge and faith, and who even delivered up his body in self-sacrifice. But he did all these things in love. We follow a Savior who loves us despite our unloveliness. Only in reflection on this undeserved grace do our hearts settle into the joyous life of love that Paul outlines in this passage.

NOVEMBER 4 · 1 CORINTHIANS 15:50-58

Victory over Death

KERI FOLMAR

WHY DO CHRISTIANS sing at funerals? The world mourns without hope for their loved ones; but while Christians do mourn, we also rejoice in the certain hope of the loved one's glorious resurrection and ever-increasing joy in the presence of our Lord. We sing at funerals in celebration of Christ's victory over death, won at the cross and displayed at his resurrection.

The immortal Son of God took on flesh and blood and drained the venom from the sting of death. Jesus perfectly fulfilled the law and took the punishment for our sins. For the believer, there is no poison left in death. We may sleep, but we will awake and enter into eternal rest in the arms of our Savior.

When Jesus walked out of the grave in a new, invincible body, he was the first instance of the very kind of body we will one day have. He was the "firstfruits" of one great harvest (1 Cor. 15:20). In Jesus, the final resurrection of the dead has already begun!

One day we too will receive new bodies, unable to be corrupted, unable to be sick, unable to die. In this life we struggle daily with sin, "but we shall all be changed, in a moment" (vv. 51–52). No long, drawn-out metamorphoses: "in the twinkling of an eye" (v. 52). No more sin! No more "mourning, nor crying, nor pain anymore, for the former things have passed away" (Rev. 21:4). We will live this new life for eternity with our Lord. "Death is swallowed up in victory" (1 Cor. 15:54).

Beloved sisters, live now in light of eternity. "Be steadfast" (v. 58) in your suffering. Be "immovable" (v. 58) when tempted to sin. Serve your family. Bear witness in your workplace and neighborhood. Encourage others in your church. Be "always abounding in the work of the Lord" (v. 58), because it is never in vain.

This life is a vapor that quickly vanishes (James 4:14), but your labor in the Lord will bear fruit that lasts forever. Why not wear out these temporal, mortal bodies in service to the One who will raise us imperishable, without stain of sin, and give us bright white robes that display the good works we have done in Christ? As C. T. Studd wrote,

> Only one life, 'twill soon be past,
> Only what's done for Christ will last.
> And when I am dying, how happy I'll be,
> If the lamp of my life has been burned out for Thee.

NOVEMBER 5 • 2 CORINTHIANS 1

The Divine Paradox

ANN VOSKAMP

IT'S COMING FROM all sides, this pressure in a sinful world that just keeps falling upon us. You can feel it. The pressure of time, of bills, of work . . . of habitual sins . . . of life. A day can press you down to flattened discouragement. Discouragement is a hijacker: it presses you up against a wall, hijacks your purpose, steals your joy, and chokes your hope.

But there's air for your lungs: "Blessed be the God and Father of our Lord Jesus Christ, the Father of mercies and God of all comfort, who comforts us in all our affliction" (2 Cor. 1:3–4). You have more than a friend in your affliction, you have a Father, a Father of "mercy"—*oiktirmos* in Greek. It means compassion, pity, mercy—not merely a passing response, but a feeling from the heart. When your heart feels flattened, the heart of your Father feels mercy.

He knows what your "affliction" feels like. *Thlipsis* literally translates "a pressing, a pressure." Amid overwhelming pressure, God "comforts" us: *paraklēsis* literally means being "called to one's side to strengthen."

When you are stressed, you have a God who strengthens. When you are flattened, you have a God who fortifies. When you are crushed, you have a God who comforts.

The Holy Spirit is your Comforter and Strengthener. When you think you don't have any strength left, you can know that he never leaves you. Heaven's economic policy affects the bottom line of everything: when you suffer more, God gives more strength. And, you extend this grace to others under pressure (v. 4). Christ was crushed, and through this he comforts us; Christ suffered, and through this he strengthens us. We share in the sufferings of Christ (v. 5), and through our sufferings and afflictions and pressures, we comfort and strengthen others. The divine paradox is that God turns problems to praise. There are blessings in our burdens. Paul urges us to

1. Thank God for the pressure—because pressure down leads to strengthening up (vv. 3–4).
2. Thank God for the pressure—because pressure down leads to us strengthening others up (vv. 4–5).
3. Thank God for the pressure—because pressure down produces a diamond-quality character that a thousand celebrities and millionaires couldn't buy up (v. 6).
4. Thank God for the pressure—because pressure down pushes us from self-reliance up into the arms of God (vv. 8–9).
5. Thank God for the pressure—because pressure down leads to praises up (vv. 10–11).

In a fallen world, the pressures fall on us from every side. But we who belong to Christ are given heaven's perspective and can whisper thanks for the pressures, knowing these burdens nurture true praise.

NOVEMBER 6 · 2 CORINTHIANS 2:5-11

Community Forgiveness

TASHA D. CHAPMAN

BEFORE PAUL VISITS the church in Corinth a third time (2 Cor. 13:1), he sends this letter. He pleads for the believers to pursue God's ministry of reconciliation and seek the purity and unity of the church (5:11–21; 13:11). One specific way in which they need to do this concerns an individual who had come under church discipline and now needs to be restored to loving fellowship. As a wise pastor, Paul first reminds the church of his love for them (2:4). Then he both models forgiveness and instructs the church in how to forgive the offender.

Paul begins by discussing the impact of the offense. The church needs to acknowledge that the offender caused pain and grief to them all. Therefore, all must be involved in restoring that person to fellowship. This is a practical outworking of Paul's earlier instruction on the body of Christ. In the diversity and unity of the church, each member is needed for the body to function; and all suffer if one part suffers (1 Cor. 12:21–26).

We often err in this regard by leaving expressions of repentance and forgiveness to private meetings between the few individuals most injured. We might do so out of fear of conflict or out of concern for the offender, wrongly thinking this protects him. However, if the wrongdoing impacted multiple people and many know about it, then the process of restoration must involve all these same people. Otherwise, members of the body will continue to be divided in secret, leaving open the likelihood that grudges, suspicion, and further offenses will continue to grow out of the original conflict. Satan uses this to destroy communities (2 Cor. 2:11).

Paul does not mention the guilty person's name. He knows the letter will be passed to other churches in the area (1:1). Since they were not involved in the conflict, specifics could cause further harm. We need God's help not to gossip and thus spread division by discussing conflict details with those not involved.

Our fear of conflict is very costly to the church since it keeps us from the good and hard work of pursuing unity in Christ (2:7–8; Matt. 18:20; Phil. 2:1–11; 4:2–3). Christian discipleship requires us to correct and restore each other through the process of confession, repentance, forgiveness, and reconciliation (Eph. 4:32; Luke 11:4). Jesus empowers us to love and forgive because he loved and forgave us first, reconciling us to God (2 Cor. 5:17–21). Loving discipline is not purposefully hurtful or vengeful (2:6–8; 7:8–10; 13:10). Everyone involved will be blessed through the mutual healing that restores fellowship, unity, and love to the church.

NOVEMBER 7 · 2 CORINTHIANS 3

Letters of Recommendation

BETHANY L. JENKINS

LETTERS OF RECOMMENDATION were common in the early church because false teachers would travel around, teaching heresy and leading new believers astray. When Paul first arrived in Corinth, however, he did not come with a letter of recommendation, because at the time there were no Christians there. Thus, within a few years, the Corinthians began to wonder whether he was a self-appointed apostle. They began to question his authority.

Paul argued that if they wanted to know whether he was a true apostle, they did not need a letter of recommendation; they needed to look no further than at their own lives: "You yourselves are our letter of recommendation, written on our hearts, to be known and read by all" (2 Cor. 3:2). His apostolic accreditation was their transformed lives, which were evident to anyone. He himself had guided and shepherded them as they turned away from paganism, immorality, secularism, and idolatry.

No, they were not perfect. Paul knew that they had experienced problems with forming factions (1 Corinthians 1), making judgments (ch.

4), engaging in sexual immorality (ch. 5), bringing lawsuits against one another (ch. 6), and wounding one another's consciences (ch. 8), among other things. How did their failings not discredit his own ministry?

The answer is that their salvation was not in the law. The law could not save them; it could only slay them (2 Cor. 3:6). The Spirit, however, had brought them from "the ministry of condemnation" to "the ministry of righteousness" (v. 9). In Christ, the veil over their hearts was lifted and removed (v. 16). Thus, although they were not perfect, they were free. As Paul told them, "Now the Lord is the Spirit, and where the Spirit of the Lord is, there is freedom. And we all, with unveiled face, beholding the glory of the Lord, are being transformed into the same image from one degree of glory to another. For this comes from the Lord who is the Spirit" (vv. 17–18). In other words, they were in the messy process of sanctification.

As we consider the genuineness of our own faith, can we look at the lives of those around us and say that they are our letters of recommendation? Have they been so transformed by our ministry or other interactions with them that, although they are not perfect, their hearts testify to their being transformed "from one degree of glory to another"? Do they relate to God as slaves to an owner or as children to a father? Do their hearts increasingly desire to know God?

NOVEMBER 8 · 2 CORINTHIANS 4:7-18

Fragile but Functional

MICHELE BENNETT WALTON

WE LIVE OUT our daily lives amid people enslaved by the fear of death (Heb. 2:15). Separated from Christ, unredeemed humanity worships beauty, hopes in the here and now, and fears all that reeks of age and death. The messages bombard us, and the glances of others accuse us when we fail to sacrifice our time, energy, and money on these worldly altars. Secretly, we may find our own hearts caught up in the anxious pursuit of airbrushed beauty and vitamin-enriched health.

As Christians, we carry both life and death in our bodies each day. Whereas unredeemed man is dying in Adam (1 Cor. 15:22), we are both living and dying at the same time! What does this mean for us, for our physical bodies? Paul describes our bodies as "jars of clay"—frail, imperfect, and yet *useful* vessels. These are the vessels that God has ordained to carry the light of the gospel, which is a much higher calling than the pursuit of earthly beauty and success. So we understand what it means to carry life in our bodies.

Perhaps the more puzzling question is this one: What does it mean to carry death in our bodies? For Paul, the meaning is apparent; when Paul described himself as "afflicted," "perplexed," "persecuted," and "struck down," he was speaking quite literally. Chapter 11 documents these experiences. Throughout 2 Corinthians, we see how Paul's very person is the vessel God uses to show his character to people amid circumstances beyond human endurance (2 Cor. 1:9).

Many of us will never find ourselves facing the types of persecution that Paul faced. Yet we still have daily opportunities to show God's kindness, strength, and mercy in the face of what those around us fear. We are fragile but functional pieces of pottery, putting the death and victory of Christ on display before the world.

"So we do not lose heart" (4:16). This doesn't mean that we will stop noticing the wrinkles or be unconcerned about a diminishing 401(k), but it does mean that we can regard them as the transient things they are. We do not sell our souls for the sake of our bodies, for another little potion or another little jewel. What difference would it make today if you remembered that your body is a jar of clay? Ponder the "eternal weight of glory" awaiting you (v. 17).

Reconciled!

SUSAN HUNT

THIS PASSAGE IS packed with precious and profound realities of our relationship with the Lord God. It compels us to read it over and over, and then demands our wonder and worship.

The rebellion of our first parents separated us from God. This cosmic scandal rendered us helpless and hopeless. There was no way to work our way back to God. We could neither initiate nor accomplish reconciliation with him. Our fallen nature doomed us to live for ourselves. This shallow, self-centered existence was our destiny. The Good News is that God did what we could not do. By his sovereign initiative, the Father credited ("imputed") our sin to the sinless Son and credited the Son's righteousness to our account. This—what Martin Luther called "the happy exchange"[12]— is the only solution to our alienation from God. Here is the epicenter of it all: "in Christ God was reconciling the world to himself" (2 Cor. 5:19).

The peace treaty between God and us, signed in the blood of Christ, totally changed our position and our practice. We have a dazzling destiny because we have been reconciled to God. Christ, our Substitute, died for us; therefore, we have died to our rebellious nature. Our union with Christ liberates us from living for self and empowers us to live for his glory. We have a new heart that loves beyond our capacity to love (Eph. 3:17–19).

Gospel wonders never cease. The loveliness of our reconciled relationship to the Lord leaves us breathless, but to be entrusted with the message of reconciliation is also astonishing.

The call to the ministry of reconciliation (2 Cor. 5:18) would be extraordinary in any context, but it is especially so in the context of Paul's complicated relationship with the church in Corinth. It was a divided congregation. There was open rebellion against Paul, yet he pursued them because of two seemingly contradictory motives: fear (v. 11) and love (v. 14). These impulses, however, were perfectly compatible. Paul's knowledge of the holiness of God (v. 11) combined with his knowledge of Christ's love for him (v. 14) coalesced into a life controlled by God. There was only one way to describe this epic event. This was not a makeover: this was a new creation. The old was gone. The new had come. And it was all from God.

Like Paul, we have broken relationships that cause deep pain, but gratitude for our reconciliation to God impels us to push through the pain and reflect the grace, mercy, and forgiveness of God even to those who hurt us. As his ambassadors, it is our high calling to show and tell the glorious message of reconciliation.

NOVEMBER 10 · 2 CORINTHIANS 8:1-15 AND 9:6-15

Glorifying God in Giving and Receiving

W. BRIAN AUCKER

HOW WE MAKE or spend money are sensitive subjects. As the second major section in 2 Corinthians, these passages comprise perhaps the most extensive teaching in the Bible on giving. Paul urges the Corinthians to join with other Gentile believers to complete a collection or "act of grace" for the poor in Jerusalem (2 Cor. 8:6, 7, 19). The lessons of these chapters touch upon all resources granted to us by God, whether money, time, or talents.

Challenging life issues may tempt believers to cling to resources for self-preservation. But in giving to others we show that we have first given ourselves to the Lord. Through the example of giving in the Macedonian churches, Paul challenges the Corinthians to reveal their own love for God by giving. In giving more than expected, the Macedonian churches had expressed joy amid severe affliction and contributed in spite of their dire economic conditions.

Ultimate motivation for giving flows from the eternal Son of God, who abandoned the status and privilege of his heavenly dwelling to take on human flesh and give himself for his people. Confronted with sacrifice of this magnitude, one's individual contribution may appear trivial. Remove such thoughts! In light of the decisive sacrifice of Jesus Christ, Paul issues no command nor advocates reckless giving. Instead, enthusiasm, a joyful heart, and giving in proportion to one's means remain keys to faithful giving (8:10–12). All giving is done under our Lord's watchful eye, and he knows its value.

Paul's concluding instructions return to the importance of motivation over magnitude, since "each one must give as he has decided in his heart" (9:7). Neither resentment nor coercion should accompany acts of generosity. Generous giving and bounteous reaping come only by remembering God's extravagant provision, expressed with phrases like "all grace," "all sufficiency," "all things," "all times," "in every good work"—and all in one verse! Such abundant provision enables us to provide generously for others, resulting not in material gain but rather a "harvest of . . . righteousness" (9:10).

The Corinthians' generosity will produce thanksgiving to God. In "supplying the needs of the saints," the Gentile Corinthians confirm to the Jewish church in Jerusalem the genuineness of their Christian faith (9:12). Giving affords a concrete means to express our faith in the gospel (9:13). In response, when God provides for our needs through others, we pray for the giver and give thanks for Jesus Christ, the greatest of all gifts (9:15).

NOVEMBER 11 · 2 CORINTHIANS 11:1–15

Paul and the False Apostles

KRISTEN WETHERELL

GOD'S LIVING AND active word is profitable in many ways, and in Paul's confrontation of the Corinthian church we see an example of one such way: for reproof and correction (2 Tim. 3:16). The Spirit searches our hearts and graciously warns us by giving us a glimpse into some of the problems of the early church. Nothing is new under the sun, and we will be wise to learn from history, trusting that God's words are just as relevant for the church today as they were when Paul first wrote them.

Here Paul is calling out "false apostles," men who came to the church preaching in the name of Jesus but then led the church astray "from a sincere and pure devotion to Christ" (v. 3). These teachers also boasted in their own reputations and undermined Paul's. They did so in three ways.

First, they attacked Paul's position. In Corinth, someone's vocation was only as valuable as its compensation. Paul knew this, and so he refused to take the Corinthian church's money. To support himself, he worked as a tentmaker instead (Acts 18:1–3) and accepted money from other churches (2 Cor. 11:8). Because Paul preached in Corinth for free (v. 7), the other preachers argued that his ministry was less legitimate than theirs.

Second, the false apostles ridiculed Paul's lack of power. Much of Paul's preaching landed him in persecution's way and in jail—many of his Spirit-inspired letters were written behind bars. Rather than receiving suffering as a part of the Christian life, as Paul did, the super-apostles resisted it as an indicator of failure (see 11:16–33).

Third, they mocked Paul's personality. The false apostles were bold in voice and skilled in public speaking. But Paul was not, so they mocked him, describing his "bodily presence [as] weak, and his speech [as] of no account" (10:10). Even Paul admitted he was "unskilled in speaking [but] not so in knowledge" (11:6).

Paul's letter challenges our definition of greatness. Position, power, and personality do not necessarily equal faithfulness. "As the serpent deceived Eve by his cunning" (v. 3), so can the church be deceived by the pattern of this world. We must be on guard in at least two ways. First, we must beware worldly measures of success as we pursue faithfulness to Jesus and his gospel (v. 4), for the greatest among us will be his servants. Second, we must guard against influencers and leaders who come in Jesus's name but are in fact servants of Satan, "[disguising] themselves as servants of righteousness" (v. 15).

May we pursue a sincere and pure devotion to Jesus Christ and allow that to be our definition of greatness.

Strength in Weakness

KERI FOLMAR

WE THINK OF weakness and strength as opposites. To be strong is good and means to be without weakness. To be weak is bad and means to be without strength. Most of us want to be thought of as strong. We are concerned that people won't think highly enough of us if we show our weakness.

Paul was seemingly a strong man with a fruitful ministry. His visions of heaven strengthened him to endure much hardship and motivated his extraordinary labor for the gospel. He had seen the glories of where he was headed and could say, "To live is Christ, and to die is gain" (Phil. 1:21). But Paul did not boast in the details of his visions. He refused to boast in his strength, but boasted only in his weakness. Paul wanted people to think highly of Christ alone—to see his power.

Paul embraced suffering. His inability to rid himself of the "thorn" (whatever it was) or avoid difficult circumstances showcased God's power working in and through him. Paul preached the gospel, but God was doing the work of saving sinners and building churches. It was God who was strong.

Jesus's crucifixion was the ultimate display of strength through weakness. Being abused, mocked, and reviled required great strength. The Son of God "upholds the universe by the word of his power" (Heb. 1:3). It would have been a small thing to destroy his enemies, but he was strong enough to become weak for our sake, submitting even to death on a cross. His weakness satisfied the wrath of God, brought the glory of the resurrection, and resulted in ultimate power over sin and death.

The same power that raised Jesus from the dead (Eph. 1:20) works within us through "weaknesses, insults, hardships, persecutions, and calamities" to make us content for the sake of Christ (2 Cor. 12:10) and to conform us to his likeness (Rom. 8:29). God graciously sends thorns of adversity to chisel away our hope in the worldly things in which we find our satisfaction, comfort, and security, and to cause us to hope in him alone. Jesus is the lover of our souls who will satisfy our deepest longings. His immense power to satisfy and purify sinners is exalted when we are content in our weakness.

Christian sister, one day Paul's ineffable vision will be your life. You will rejoice as the strong, gentle hand of your Savior removes every thorn and wipes every tear away. For today, be strong by contenting yourself with weakness for the sake of Christ. Weakness and strength are not opposites but two sides of the same coin. When we are weak, then we are strong (2 Cor. 12:10).

By Faith Alone

SAM STORMS

THE BLESSINGS THAT come to us through faith in Jesus Christ are precious beyond words. To be forgiven of our sins, redeemed from spiritual bondage, reconciled to God, adopted into his family, and given a hope that cannot be shaken are of such value that we struggle to measure their worth. But the greatest gift of all is that we are justified by faith in Christ! How shall we fully grasp what it means to stand before a God of infinite holiness and purity and hear him declare, "Righteous!"

An unbeliever may envision life as a ledger book, on one side of which the person's religious and moral assets are listed. Here are listed the many good deeds, the financial sacrifices, the promises kept, and the performance of countless religious rituals. We hope these moral accomplishments outnumber the spiritual debts listed in the other column—everything we owe God but have failed to pay. Life becomes a tedious attempt to amass more assets than debts. But it is all to no avail.

When faith comes alive and we trust and treasure Christ above all else, God takes the blood of Jesus and wipes clean from the debit side of that ledger every deficit, debt, liability, sin, and failure. But he doesn't stop there. As we look across the page to the asset side of the ledger, we see but one word: Christ! His righteousness is our sole possession! He is our only credit! He is our only hope! All our confidence and trust are now in him alone.

Though our religious works be many, they are of no saving value. Paul had a righteousness that came from the law, but it gave him no confidence in God's presence. No matter how much we may obtain, we can never know if it is enough. Even if we succeed in observing some religious ritual or conform to some moral law, there is no guarantee that we will continue to do so into the future. And how would we even know whether the righteousness we think we have produced is precisely the righteousness God requires? It's hopeless! Our righteousness must come from a source beyond ourselves.

We must put our confidence in a righteousness that comes through "faith in Christ" (Gal. 2:16). We do not gain righteousness because of faith or on the basis of faith, as if faith were the God-approved substitute for good works. Faith is not an alternative way of earning God's favor. Faith is the very antithesis of merit. Faith is our confession that we are unable to do anything to win God's approval. Faith always looks away from itself and to its object, to that in which the soul has placed its trust and hope and confidence. Justifying faith looks to Christ alone.

NOVEMBER 14 · GALATIANS 3:15–29

Gospel Identity

KERI FOLMAR

MOST FIRST-CENTURY JEWISH leaders found their identity in their heritage and the law. Their father was Abraham, and as his children they were specially chosen and given God's law. As observers of the law, they believed they were right with God. We, too, often lapse into law-observance for our right standing before God. We become slaves to our idea of what a good Christian does or how a good Christian lives. But the law was never designed to make us right with God or satisfied with ourselves (Gal. 3:18).

The law was given to show us our sin, "so that the promise by faith in Jesus Christ might be given to those who believe" (v. 22). Repentance and faith in Christ break the chains of bondage to the law and sin and transform slaves into sons. Jesus, the true and final offspring of Abraham, the only Son of God, gave himself to deliver all who would believe on him, "for in Christ Jesus you are all sons of God, through faith" (v. 26).

Faith changes our identity. We who "were baptized into Christ have put on Christ" (v. 27). If you have put on Christ, he cannot be taken off. In Christ, you are adopted by the Father, heir to the promises of God (v. 29). You are not your nationality, your work, your gender, or the number of children you have. You are not what you do or what others think of you. You belong to Christ. He is your new identity.

This new identity changes everything. In Christ, God your Father views you as bearing the name and character of his beloved Son. You can rest secure in his arms of love and kindness as a beneficiary of his grace. And the benefits are many. The Father's love and acceptance remain on you and can never be taken away. You have the ever-increasing joy of knowing the God of the universe and spending eternity with him. You have the help of the Holy Spirit to put on Christ and live increasingly like him. You have the blessing of participation in the family of God (v. 28). And you have the privilege of being Christ's ambassador in the world, sharing his message of justification by faith.

The law does not give life (v. 21). The gospel gives you a new identity and life abundant. As the English revivalist John Berridge wrote three centuries ago,

> Run, John, and work, the law commands,
> yet finds me neither feet nor hands,
> But sweeter news the gospel brings,
> it bids me fly and lends me wings![13]

Works and Fruit

LAUREN CHANDLER

THROUGH CHRIST WE have been freed from our bondage to sin, our inability to serve anything else but our own kingdom and selfish desires. For those who trust in Christ's sufficient work on their behalf, there is no longer enslavement to the flesh. We have been set free! We have been given a new identity. Still, a battle rages. Will we be led by the Spirit or gratify the desires of the flesh? To submit to one is to reject the other.

Walking by the Spirit implies both direction and empowerment. The Spirit shows us when and where to take our next step, while also supplying the power to do so. Saint Augustine put this reality into a pleading prayer: "O Lord, command what you will, and give what you command."[14]

Scripture uses the term "walking" to indicate a pattern of living; it is ongoing, not once and for all. Moment by moment, we must decide whether to yield to the leading of the Spirit or the urgency of the flesh. Even in our walking, we are tempted to fall. Jesus, in Gethsemane, recognizes the reality that "the spirit indeed is willing, but the flesh is weak" (Matt. 26:41). In our spirit, we may desire to follow the leading of the Spirit, but we still feel the nagging of the flesh to fight for what we want, what we feel we deserve. It is in those moments that we lean into the Spirit to not only guide us but to give us the strength to obey. God gives both the command and the provision. All is of grace.

The works of the flesh are what most naturally flow from unregenerate human hearts. They reveal the focus of the heart. Sexual immorality, impurity, and sensuality show a view of other people, not as created in the image of God but rather as objects for indulging one's personal fantasies. Idolatry and sorcery expose one's desire to reach the spiritual realm without accepting Christ as the only way to God. Enmity, strife, jealousy, fits of anger, rivalries, dissensions, divisions, and envy reek of dissatisfaction with what God has graciously given. Drunkenness and orgies are abuses of what God has provided as good and enjoyable within the confines of his wisdom.

When we walk in the Spirit, abundant fruit is borne for the joy of the bearer as well as those around him or her. These attributes are sweet and satisfying, and they grow in increasing measure. Just as walking is a progressive process, so is fruit-bearing. Although the yield may seem small now, it is evidence that the Spirit is at work, guiding and providing.

From Death to Life

ERIKA ALLEN

WHEN ADAM AND EVE sinned in the garden, their relationship with God was radically and tragically altered. In an instant, they went from enjoying perfect fellowship with their Creator to being estranged from him. Because of Adam's sin, every person comes into the world with a sinful nature (Rom. 5:12).

Sin affects every aspect of who we are as human beings—our body, mind, and will are all tainted. The church calls this state of being "total depravity." It's tempting to think that we are born neutral, with the ability to choose between being "good" or "bad"—between following God or not. But the Bible says this isn't the case. Rather, our natural inclination is to sin (James 1:14–15). And we love that sin too much to turn from it by our own power: "no one seeks for God. . . . No one does good, not even one" (Rom. 3:11–12; see also John 6:44). Unable to come to God or even to desire to do so, we are born spiritually dead (Eph. 2:1) and are "by nature children of wrath" (v. 3).

Against this backdrop comes one of the most beautiful and remarkable phrases in all of Scripture: "but God . . ."

> But God, being rich in mercy, because of the great love with which he loved us, even when we were dead in our trespasses, made us alive together with Christ—by grace you have been saved. (vv. 4–5)

While we were still living "in the passions of our flesh, carrying out the desires of the body and the mind" (v. 3) and absolutely deserving of eternal punishment—God sought us out and "saved us, not because of works done by us in righteousness, but according to his own mercy, by the washing of regeneration and renewal of the Holy Spirit, whom he poured out on us richly through Jesus Christ our Savior" (Titus 3:5–6).

Because we were dead in our sins, God had to first bring us to life before we could come to Christ for forgiveness. When Paul says that God "made us alive," he refers to regeneration, the new birth that God gives us. It is this new life that enables us to come to Christ in faith. Thus, even faith itself is a gift from God. Our salvation is, from start to finish, all of grace (Eph. 2:5, 8–9). Though we have done nothing to deserve his mercy or love, God lavishes these things on us nonetheless. Let us rejoice, then, in "the immeasurable riches of his grace in kindness toward us in Christ Jesus" (v. 7)!

NOVEMBER 17 · EPHESIANS 4:17–32

Speaking as One Made New

ERIKA ALLEN

WORDS HURT. It is astonishing how long the effects of an unkind comment can endure. Often words spoken carelessly are as painful as a physical attack. Proverbs 12:18 compares such words to "sword thrusts."

The Bible has a great deal to say about the way we speak to one another, and it uses strong language. James 3:8 warns, "No human being can tame the tongue. It is a restless evil, full of deadly poison." The way we speak to other people is a powerful commentary on our walk with the Lord. If we are truly abiding in him, it will be reflected in our speech, because only through the power of the Holy Spirit can the tongue be tamed.

In Ephesians 4, believers are instructed to "put on the new self, created after the likeness of God in true righteousness and holiness" (Eph. 4:24). One of the ways we "put off" the old self (v. 22) is by refusing to speak in ways that do not reflect Christ. Paul writes, "Let no corrupting talk come out of your mouths, but only such as is good for building up, as fits the occasion, that it may give grace to those who hear" (v. 29).

The Greek word *sapros*, here translated "corrupting," is used elsewhere in the Bible to describe bad fruit (Luke 6:43) or bad fish (Matt. 13:48). It means *rotten*. Gossip, slander, coarse jokes, insults—all of these things have no place in the life of the church. Our speech should, without exception, have the effect of edifying and building up our fellow believers.

When one Christian speaks to another, the hearer should walk away a recipient of grace. Even when disagreements arise or rebuke is called for, the way we express ourselves verbally should have the ultimate effect of strengthening and encouraging our fellow believers' faith. Paul writes in his letter to the Colossians, "Let your speech always be gracious, seasoned with salt" (Col. 4:6). For we ourselves have been recipients of grace. God has spoken a gracious word to *us*, in the gospel (Eph. 4:32).

Make no mistake: obeying this command of Scripture doesn't come naturally to us. It requires daily submission to God. We must depend on him to guide our conversations. We must be sensitive to the Holy Spirit, knowing that he is grieved when we speak poorly to or against another individual whom he indwells (v. 30). We must "be quick to hear, slow to speak, slow to anger" (James 1:19). And we must be ever mindful of the fact that what comes out of our mouth is a reflection of what is in our heart (Matt. 12:34–37).

God has spoken a gracious word to us. We are called to speak gracious words to others.

NOVEMBER 18 · EPHESIANS 5:6–17

Godly Discernment

ERIKA ALLEN

A KEY THEME in Ephesians is the transformation that takes place in the lives of those who have been redeemed by Jesus. Having been reconciled to God through the blood of Christ, the sinful patterns that once characterized our lives give way to holiness in thought, word, and deed. In this chapter, Paul draws a sharp contrast between our former selves and who we now are in Christ. We have been transferred from darkness into light, and our behavior should reflect this dramatic transference (Eph. 5:8). In verses 15–17 Paul writes, "Look carefully then how you walk, not as unwise but as wise, making the best use of the time, because the days are evil. Therefore do not be foolish, but understand what the will of the Lord is."

"Making the best use of the time" involves being able to "discern what is pleasing to the Lord" (v. 10). The Bible provides principles for godly living; discernment is called for as we seek to apply these instructions. This application is what it means to "understand what the will of the Lord is" (v. 17).

How, then, does one gain this discernment? As Paul emphasizes in Philippians 4:8–9, our minds should be fixed on that which pleases the Lord: "Whatever is true, whatever is honorable, whatever is just, whatever is pure, whatever is lovely, whatever is commendable, if there is any excellence, if there is anything worthy of praise, think about these things." In order to grow in our knowledge of Christ, we must be constantly setting our eyes on and filling our minds with things that propel us toward holiness.

Great wisdom is called for, because as we seek the heart of God we are simultaneously bombarded by attitudes and mindsets that blatantly contradict his will. As Paul admits, "the days are evil" (Eph. 5:16). Discernment involves testing what the world says against the standard of God's word (Rom. 12:2).

Hebrews 5:14 describes spiritually mature individuals as those who "have their powers of discernment trained by constant practice to distinguish good from evil." Discernment is, in a sense, a spiritual discipline. We train our hearts and minds by studying and meditating on God's word, prayerfully listening for the Holy Spirit to reveal how we are to apply the truths of Scripture to our specific circumstances. And amid all our efforts to discern what pleases God is the glad confidence that, in the most ultimate sense, God is fully pleased with us already, on account of the gracious work of Christ on our behalf.

Exaltation through Humility

JEN WILKIN

THE HUMAN HEART craves exaltation. It longs incessantly for the highest place. And, mystery of mysteries, it believes itself worthy of that place! Apart from the redeeming work of Christ, we spend our days in an endless climb, hand over hand, always reaching for the next level of human glory, the surmounted aspirations of others forming the very rungs of our ascent.

Philippians 2:1–11 tells us that the path to exaltation is not a climb but a free fall. As Jesus proclaimed throughout his earthly ministry, the kingdom of heaven is a study in paradox—strength through weakness, wealth through poverty, freedom through slavery. Here, Paul speaks the poetry of the beautiful paradox of the incarnation: exaltation through humility; the sinless Son of God, taking on weak flesh and becoming sin, suffering to the point of death. Christ, by going to the lowest place, is exalted to the highest place.

In Deuteronomy 8, we are told three times (Deut. 8:2, 3, 16) that God led Israel into the wilderness for the express purpose of humbling them and testing them, "to do [them] good in the end" (v. 16). Christ, too, endured testing for thirty-three years, but to do *us* good in the end. Having been found worthy, he entered into his rest and was seated at the right hand of the Father. He will always be exalted higher than we are, because we can never go lower than he did. During our time of wilderness testing in this life, our humbling can never go to the depths that his did. Unlike him, we know sin in our innermost parts. Unlike his, our time in the wilderness is deserved.

Will you allow your wilderness time to do its needful work of humbling you? Or will you, in unbelief, spend these years trampling others to exalt yourself? Never are we more like Christ than when we humble ourselves in preferential love toward others, when we give them better than they deserve.

Do you crave fellowship with the One seated at the right hand of power? Humble yourself in his sight. Confess your weakness and rebellion.

Acknowledge your utter need of his ongoing, inexhaustible grace. Place the interests of others above your own. The wilderness is not your time for exaltation—that will come in due time (James 4:6–10). One blessed day, you will ascend the hill of the Lord. But for the believer, every song of ascents is preceded by a song of descent, a hymn of our free fall into grace. Offer this poem of paradox gladly, after the pattern of your Savior, to whom belongs the highest place.

NOVEMBER 20 · PHILIPPIANS 4:1–9

Calm Leadership amid Conflict

TASHA D. CHAPMAN

THE UNITY AND PEACE of the church is a primary concern of the apostle Paul as he instructs his beloved believers in Philippi to pursue Christian maturity (Phil. 1:3–8; 2:12–13). So, when two ministry leaders are in conflict, Paul considers it important enough to mention in the letter to the whole church. He commends the leaders as equals in gospel ministry with himself, invites another leader to help them, and reminds them of their secure salvation.

In these few words Paul models calm, godly leadership (see also 3:17). He does not take sides in the conflict. He does not write angry, fearful, judgmental, or blaming words. Instead, he instructs the Philippians from an eternal perspective on the grace of God. He expects obedience in resolving the conflict to be a response to what God has already done through Christ. He does not motivate them with fear or a need to win God's favor. Paul builds relational trust and respect with his personal affirmations, showing confidence in their ability to work it out. He does not micromanage or bully or threaten. He is genuinely concerned for the church and for the individuals, but he is not anxious.

Anxiety is like a disease; it easily spreads from a leader to all in a group, stealing joy and peace as it grows. Anxiety is our reaction to real and immediate threats, but it can also be our chosen response to daily conflicts and challenges. In our fast-paced, dog-eat-dog world, we can build chronic anxieties around imagined and distorted threats. What if we are late! What if they do not like the food! What if the kids disobey in front of the neighbors! What if I do not make the grade! What if the boss gets angry! What if I never get married! What if . . . ? This habit of anxious, insecure thinking leads to selfishness, defensiveness, and black-and-white thinking. And these reactions result in further conflicts. In our anxiety we alienate others, or try to control others, or allow others to manipulate us. Over time, both workaholism and immobilization result. Anxiety is a root of all kinds of chaos and sin.

Paul gives us a counter to anxiety. Though he is in prison, with his life threatened, Paul has joy and peace in the Lord (4:1). He directs the Philippians to pursue the same (3:1; 4:4). Because God is sovereign, holy, near, redeeming us in love, and coming again soon, we always have reason to rejoice in him, to trust him, to remember his past blessings, to thank him, to love others, to pursue unity with believers, to pray expectantly with confidence, and to feed our minds with godly contemplations (vv. 8–9).

NOVEMBER 21 • COLOSSIANS 1:15–23

The Supremacy of Christ

COLLEEN J. MCFADDEN

WHO IS JESUS CHRIST? We could spend hours meditating on the rich words Paul uses in Colossians 1:15–23 to describe our Lord and Savior. "He is the image of the invisible God" and "the firstborn of all creation" (Col. 1:15). He is the head of the church, "the beginning," and "the firstborn from the dead" (v. 18).

Similar to asking who Jesus is, we can learn more about him by asking, "What has Jesus done?" This passage tells us that he is responsible for all that exists: "all things were created through him and for him" (v. 16). It is also through him that "all things hold together" (v. 17). He has reconciled us to God (v. 20), and he has made us holy (v. 22). It is good and right to meditate on these eternal truths.

Put simply, Jesus, as firstborn of all creation, has created all things; and Jesus, as firstborn from the dead, has reconciled all things. The word "firstborn" does not mean that Jesus is a created being, having been created first in order to create others. Jesus has always existed, before time, as part of the triune Godhead. Nor does the term merely mean that he was the first to be resurrected from the dead. This is not a chronological term. Paul employs this term to emphasize the importance of Jesus's role as the one who has the highest honor. As the firstborn, Jesus is his Father's heir, indicating his superiority over all things, things in heaven and on earth (vv. 16, 20).

Jesus is not only supreme in his status as firstborn; he is also supreme by that which he has accomplished. He created *all things* (v. 16) and he will reconcile to himself *all things* (v. 20). When creation was complete, "it was very good" (Gen. 1:31). It couldn't be improved upon. But when Adam and Eve disobeyed God by eating the forbidden fruit, sin entered the world, and with it corruption. Reconciliation was required to restore peace between God and his creation. When Jesus died on his cross, his blood provided the perfect reconciliation (Col. 1:20).

But it does not end there! Jesus died and rose again. He is the firstborn to rise from the grave. His reconciliation covered our corruption and made us holy, blameless, and above reproach (v. 22). This is a far cry from being what we once were: alienated, hostile, and evil (v. 21). What a great hope! Paul tells us not to turn away from this true gospel, but to continue steadfastly in the faith (v. 23).

NOVEMBER 22 • COLOSSIANS 2:6–15

Only Christ

CLAIRE SMITH

A TREE IS ONLY as good as its roots, and a house is only as solid as its foundations. Similarly, a faith is only as good as the object of that faith—and there is none better than Christ, and, in the final analysis, none other than Christ.

This is the case because of *who Christ is*. He is fully God. He is not a smaller, lesser version of God, or a good man who became God. He is and has always been God. He is "the image of the invisible God" (Col. 1:15), the fullness of God in human flesh, and all rule and authority belong to him. There is none better than Christ.

This is also the case because of *what Christ has done* for those who trust in him. In his death on the cross, Christ cancelled the debt we owed to God for our sinful rebellion against his rule (2:14–15). He paid the debt we owed so that we can be forgiven. There is nothing more to be paid. We are no longer God's debtors. Through his death on the cross, Christ also defeated and humiliated every evil spiritual force, so there is nothing that can stand against him, and no power that can accuse us. Christ has done it all.

This is also the case because of *what God has done* for those who trust in Christ. We have been filled in Christ, so that we lack nothing spiritually. We have been circumcised in him, so that our connection with sinful humanity has been severed, and we now belong to Christ (vv. 11–13). Through faith, we have died with Christ, and God has made us alive in him and raised us with him, so that our spiritual home is in heaven, where Christ is seated (3:1–3). True spiritual blessings, both now and for all eternity, are found only in Christ.

Sadly, there will always be deceivers who will say that Christ is not the only way or that he is not enough. Their arguments will sound wise and sophisticated and plausible, and will win the approval of the watching world, but their origin is demonic. Believing these lies will rob us of Christ and all his benefits.

This is why we are to be like trees grounded and rooted in Christ, and like houses built firmly on this rock (Matt. 7:24–27; 1 Cor. 10:4). It is why we are to stay firmly on his path and not wander from his way (John 14:4–6). There is only one Christ to believe in, and he is the Christ of the Bible, the friend of sinners and the hope of the world.

Christ Is Your Life

ELYSE FITZPATRICK

HOW DOES THE world portray Christian women? At best, we're considered quintessential Stepford wives: doormats without a voice. At worst, we're painted as ignorant, repressed, angry, backwoods dolts. The world doesn't have a category for Christian women.

So what *are* Christian women like? Colossians 3:5–17 tells us: We are women who pursue purity, generosity, and worship. We are forbearing and honest. Our speech reflects hearts set aflame by the gracious love of our Savior. We shun bigotry in every form. We are meek and forgiving. We know inner peace, even when everything around us is coming apart. Most importantly, we are women who love. We love because we have been loved so well. Stepford wives? Hardly. The world has never understood women like this. It doesn't know what to do with us.

We are Mary the mother of Jesus, who put aside her reputation for the honor of suffering for God's plan. We are Elizabeth the mother of John, who found joy and heartbreak in her latter years. We are Mary Magdalene, who brought to Christ her troubled past and was welcomed. We are the immoral woman whose kisses the Holy One received, who found forgiveness through her tears (Luke 7:36–50). We are Mary the sister of Lazarus, whose profligate worship of her dear Friend brought down upon her the censure of a traitor and the thanks of God (John 12:1–8). We are Priscilla, who with her husband "risked their necks" for Paul, working hard so that she might teach the gospel to people like Apollos (Rom. 16:3–4). We are Phoebe, known for protecting the poor, who was entrusted to deliver the most important letter ever written (Rom. 16:1).

We are women who are truly alive, truly living in the light of our Savior's love. We are not fooled by this world or its slander of us. We know who we are. And Colossians 3:1–4 paints a beautiful portrait of our invincible identity. We have died to all the lies and allurements of the world because we live in the truth that Jesus has died in our place. We are risen with the resurrected One to a new life so full of love and welcome that we no longer need to fight to be loved. Although we work hard, we know our work is for the Lord, not for man (Col. 3:23). We don't have to worry about our reputation or what anyone thinks of us. Most importantly, we no longer worry about God's opinion of us, for we have been "hidden with Christ in God" (v. 3).

He smiles on us. And that smile is all we'll ever need, no matter what the world thinks. Who are we? We are his.

NOVEMBER 24 • 1 THESSALONIANS 4:13–18

Take Comfort; Jesus Is Coming!

DONNA THOENNES

THE THESSALONIANS had questions for Paul, questions that grieved them. Some of their fellow church members had died, and they were afraid that these loved ones would miss out on the blessings brought by the Lord's return. In this passage, Paul lovingly corrects their thinking regarding what will happen to those who are in Christ but have died. He wants to be certain that the Thessalonians do not "grieve [like those] who have no hope" (1 Thess. 4:13). Paul explains that Jesus will come again, and it will be majestic: he will come with the voice of an archangel and the sound of the trumpet (v. 16). Paul comforts them with the truth that those who have fallen asleep will be taken up with Jesus first, and then those alive at his coming will meet them in the air and be taken up together with him. Paul's final consolation is, "and so we will always be with the Lord" (v. 17). Do not fear, Thessalonians; the Lord will come, and you will dwell with him forever!

In verse 18, Paul reveals the significance of this issue. Just as he has encouraged them, the Thessalonians are to do the same for one another: "Therefore encourage one another with these words." The truth of Jesus's second coming has the power to reassure those who are worried or downcast. It was not solely Paul's responsibility to minister to the Thessalonians by teaching the truth. They had a responsibility to one another to embrace, deliver, and share these truths among themselves. Rather than wait for his letters or his return visit, they were to demonstrate their identity as competent ministers to one another. They were not to wait for the professional, but to build up the church by speaking the truth to one another.

We are challenged alongside the Thessalonians to encourage one another with the reminder of Jesus's second coming. We share the responsibility and opportunity to console others with the word of God. It is living and active and brings comfort and hope. Within the body of Christ, ways to encourage one another are numerous and diverse, but we must know the word in order to be able to minister with it. Although we are sometimes fooled into thinking we can provide meaningful encouragement with something other than the truth of God's word, anything else is a paltry substitute and always leaves us aching for something deeper and longer lasting.

Let us live in light of the second coming, encouraging our fellow saints with the truth of God's word as we watch and wait. There is hope even in death—Jesus will fulfill his promise to come for us, and we will always be with the Lord. All sadness will be undone.

NOVEMBER 25 · 1 THESSALONIANS 5:12–28

Living in Light of Our Immortality

BETHANY L. JENKINS

ALL OF US are going to die. And we know it; death is inescapable. An awareness of our own mortality is part of what it means to be human. It's not just that we are going to die; it's that *we know* we are going die. In our fallen state, this knowledge elicits a wide range of emotions and responses—and many of them involve, at least on some level, fear and anxiety.

The Thessalonians thought about death and immortality, too. The Greek worldview at this time in history included a very pessimistic view of death. Perhaps it's not surprising, then, that the Thessalonians responded with fear and apprehension when some members of their church died unexpectedly. Because they didn't understand that both the living and the dead would be saved at the second coming, they seemed to believe that these members, who died before Christ's return, would be lost forever. No doubt they were concerned about their own final salvation as well—what if they, too, died before Christ returned? Paul wrote this letter, therefore, to assure them that the dead would be resurrected to eternal life. The Thessalonians need not fear death, because Christ "died for us so that whether we are awake or asleep we might live with him" (1 Thess. 5:10).

Knowing that "God has not destined us for wrath, but to obtain salvation through our Lord Jesus Christ" (v. 9) spurs us on to holy living. We shouldn't fear death—nor should we live as though our time on earth doesn't matter. In his final remarks, Paul exhorted the Thessalonians to live in light of their glorious future. They were to "admonish the idle, encourage the fainthearted, help the weak," and "be patient with them all" (v. 14). Like the Thessalonians, we are summoned to strive for holiness as we await the coming of our Savior. Rather than feeling insecure or anxious, we too can have unwavering confidence in Christ—rejoicing "always," praying "without ceasing," and giving thanks "in all circumstances" (vv. 16–18).

We need not fear death, for whether we are alive or "asleep" when Christ returns, we will be with him always. "Now may the God of peace himself sanctify you completely, and may your whole spirit and soul and body be kept blameless at the coming of our Lord Jesus Christ" (v. 23).

NOVEMBER 26 • 2 THESSALONIANS 2:13–17

A Pastor's Heart

DONNA THOENNES

WHILE CONTEMPORARY CHRISTIANS might be accused of not thinking often enough of the Lord's return, the Thessalonians were thinking about it so much that it kept them from faithful daily living. Paul had written about the coming of the Lord in his first letter to the Thessalonians, but they had either misunderstood or ignored the letter and thus were deceived by errant teaching. They believed the Lord had already come, and so they were dismayed. In response, the good pastor warns them, equips them, and prays for them.

Paul warns the Thessalonians to not be "quickly shaken in mind" (2 Thess. 2:2), and he appears frustrated that they have forgotten what they were taught: "Do you not remember that when I was still with you I told you these things?" (v. 5). If they had remembered what he had taught them, they would not have been deceived! He graciously equips them with the details of the second coming, so they might withstand the deceptive message that someone was trying to teach them. Good news for the Thessalonians: they hadn't missed Jesus's second coming, and now they knew what to expect!

After Paul clarifies the facts surrounding Jesus's second coming, he encourages the Thessalonians: "But we ought always to give thanks to God for you" (v. 13). Though frustrated with their forgetfulness and vulnerability, he is thankful for them. He reminds them that God chose them so that they might share in Jesus's glory, and he ministers to them by telling them who they are in Christ (v. 14). There is such power in rehearsing for one another the blessings that are ours in Christ. We need to be reminded of our true identity, especially since it doesn't always match up with how we feel or behave.

Paul transitions seamlessly to prayer (vv. 16–17). He reminds the Thessalonians that God loves them. He invites them to remember their eternal comfort and hope, to be strong in the face of deception or persecution. God has given comfort and hope in the past; now Paul asks God to again comfort their hearts "and establish them in every good work and word." We need a holistic sanctification, of both belief and behavior, rooted in God's past work and future promise.

What an example Paul is for us! When we are disappointed with a sister who forgets what she has learned, departs from tradition, or allows herself to be deceived, we can respond with similar loving correction with the truth, gratitude to God for her, reminders of her identity in Christ, and prayer for comfort and hope.

Trusting God's Word

CLAIRE SMITH

SOME HAVE SAID that the Bible's teaching on men and women, and 1 Timothy 2:11–15 in particular, is unclear or no longer applies in the contemporary church. But that is not so. This text means what it says, that Christian men and women have some different ministries when they gather. Specifically, leading the church family, and regularly and authoritatively instructing them in God's word, are responsibilities for men, not women. But can we be sure this teaching is good for us?

Yes! We can be sure because it comes to us in God's authoritative word, which he has lovingly given us to tell us how to live and please him (2 Tim. 3:16; 2 Pet. 3:16).

We can be sure, too, because God is our Creator (Gen. 1:26–28; Psalm 139). He knows what is best for us, and from the very beginning he gave men and women different responsibilities, which are reflected in the order and way in which he made us (Gen. 2:4–25; 1 Tim. 2:13). These differences are for our good, even though they were frustrated in the fall (Genesis 3; 1 Tim. 2:14).

We can be sure because God is concerned for the welfare of all people. His word tells us to pray for all people, and to pray for the human leaders he provides to rule over us, so that all may benefit from a stable society (2:1–2; Rom. 13:1–7). Such prayers reflect his care for all people.

He is particularly concerned for the welfare of his people. We are his household, the church of the living God (1 Tim. 3:15). We belong to his family, and he dwells with us. This is why those charged with leading must lead and teach well, and live lives that advance and adorn the gospel (3:1–13; 4:16).

But the greatest reason for trusting and rejoicing in this teaching is found just a few verses earlier. It is that God wants all people to be saved (2:3–6). Our greatest need is salvation from the wrath of God, and God has met that need perfectly and exclusively in Christ Jesus. There is not one God for men and another for women, or one for Jews and another for Greeks (Gal. 3:26–28). There is only one God, and only one who can bridge the gap between sinners and God—Christ Jesus, who in great love handed himself over for our sakes (1 Tim. 2:5–6).

We can be sure that this same God—who loved his enemies (us) so generously—wants only what is best for all his children as we seek to serve him faithfully in his church (Rom. 5:8–10).

NOVEMBER 28 • 1 TIMOTHY 6:11–21

Nurturing an Active and Engaged Faith in God

KRISTYN GETTY

ONE OF THE battles of the Christian life is to know what to turn away from. Paul instructs Timothy to run from the cancerous hold of worldliness. He is also to guide others away from this and from trusting in the false security possessions try to offer. Timothy is to root out the weeds of "irreverent babble" (1 Tim. 6:20) in the community of believers under his care, talk that chokes the purity of the gospel and leads people away from the truth. Like him, we are to keep ourselves "unstained and free from reproach" until Christ's return (v. 14). We must run from anything that compromises the beauty and value of the gift we have been given in the gospel.

Another battle of the Christian life is to know what to pursue. Paul tells Timothy, "Fight the good fight of the faith. Take hold of the eternal life to which you were called and about which you made the good confession in the presence of many witnesses" (v. 12). The call to fight "the good fight of the faith" and to "take hold" of eternal life involves both fleeing from sin *and* vigorously pursuing those things that are pleasing to the Lord. How do we take hold of the life to which we have been called?

First of all, we recognize that we are taking hold of a life that has taken hold of us. It is God who gives life to all things. It is he who is holy, immortal, and able, through Christ, to make us alive in him though we were once dead in sin. Like Timothy, we are called to be faithful soldiers of Christ contending for this faith, trusting in his all-sufficient revelation of grace, and telling the truth as it has been carefully and clearly spoken by the apostles.

Second, we seek by grace to be sensitive to and faithfully respond to his Spirit, who is working in our lives to grow in us the fruit of righteousness, godliness, faith, love, steadfastness, and gentleness.

Third, we invest all our resources in the eternal priorities of his kingdom, shaping the affections of our hearts and showing the sincerity of our faith in our consistent commitment to give and to serve. These are the riches the gospel should yield in our lives.

All who trust in Christ have a "deposit" (v. 20) entrusted to them to guard. The challenge for each of us is to be aware of where this deposit (the gospel) is under attack—and then to actively protect and contend for it. May God give us grace to cherish and preserve the gospel by which we have been saved.

NOVEMBER 29 · 2 TIMOTHY 1:3–18

Enduring Unashamedly

TRILLIA NEWBELL

THE WRITER OF Hebrews encourages us to "run with endurance the race that is set before us" (Heb. 12:1). The journey of faith in Christ requires endurance and, at times, long-suffering. Fortunately, we have a "cloud of witnesses"—those who have gone before us—as our examples of enduring in the faith (Heb. 12:1).

Timothy also had great witnesses, who not only had gone before him but had invested in him. His grandmother, Lois, and his mother, Eunice, taught him about Jesus, as Paul reminds him twice (2 Tim. 1:5; 3:15). Timothy's faith will be tested, but Paul urges him not to be ashamed of the testimony of the Lord (1:8).

Timothy, and all of us, can endure because God himself dwells in us by his Spirit. We are born again, and therefore our old self has passed away

(2 Cor. 5:17). We can "fan into flame" (2 Tim. 1:6) the gift that God has given us. We can face suffering and run with endurance because God has given us a spirit of power and love and self-control (v. 7). This enables us to put away our fears.

Timothy needs this exhortation—as do we all—because not everyone *will* faithfully endure suffering. Phygelus and Hermogenes were among those who had abandoned Paul (v. 15). Though we don't know much about them, we can assume that they were ashamed of Paul (and possibly of the gospel itself) because Paul highlights one faithful friend, Onesiphorus, who was not ashamed of his chains (v. 16). Paul therefore encourages Timothy to share in suffering as a good solider (2:3).

We can all relate to the desire to give up. But as Paul reminds Timothy, we can guard the deposit entrusted to us because it was given to us by God. He saved us and called us to this holy calling, not because of anything we have done or could ever do, but because of his own good purpose and grace, which he predestined before time (1:9). Paul therefore is not ashamed of Jesus, "who abolished death and brought life and immortality to light through the gospel" (v. 10).

As we guard the deposit entrusted to us, we do so with eyes firmly fixed on Jesus, "the founder and perfecter of our faith, who for the joy that was set before him endured the cross, despising the shame, and is seated at the right hand of the throne of God" (Heb. 12:2). By his grace and in his strength, we can journey on in confidence.

NOVEMBER 30 · 2 TIMOTHY 2:14-26

A Vessel for Honorable Use

ROBERT A. PETERSON

PAUL INSTRUCTS HIS disciple Timothy while drawing contrasts between him and the false teachers. Much of Paul's instruction concerns speech. Timothy must remind his hearers "not to quarrel about words" or use "irreverent babble," the very things false teachers do. Such methods do not help but only hurt others, sometimes very seriously (2 Tim. 2:14, 17).

By contrast, Timothy is to avoid "foolish, ignorant controversies" that only "breed quarrels" (v. 23). Instead, he is to devote himself to the teaching of God's word, being tolerant in the face of opposition and seeking to correct false teaching gently, hoping God might give repentance to the opponents. We all benefit from having our speech exposed to the light of God's word. By God's grace may we "let no corrupting talk come out of [our] mouths, but only such as is good for building up, as fits the occasion, that it may give grace to those who hear" (Eph. 4:29).

Paul brings words of encouragement and challenge. First comes the encouragement: "The Lord knows those who are his" (2 Tim. 2:19). Faithful believers are strengthened by realizing that God knows his people personally and will distinguish the true from the false. We too can rest in God's control of the world and our lives. He is God; he is ours, and we are his!

Then comes the challenge: "Let everyone who names the name of the Lord depart from iniquity" (v. 19). Paul has just said that God's everlasting arms are underneath (see Deut. 33:27), supporting his church. Now he exhorts his readers to pursue holiness. They are not to use God's sovereignty as an excuse for laziness or license. Rather, they are to seek him with all their hearts as they separate themselves from the false teachers and their destructive doctrines. God wants his people to worship with like-minded believers in churches that honor his word, teach clearly the way of salvation, and promote vital spiritual life. Do you belong to such a fellowship of believers?

Paul directs Timothy (and all Christians) to "flee" and "pursue" (2 Tim. 2:22). We are to flee "youthful passions," impetuous impulses and actions that characterize youth. And we are to pursue "righteousness, faith, love, and peace, along with those who call on the Lord from a pure heart" (v. 22). Unlike the false teachers, by God's grace we are to cultivate virtues toward God—godliness and faithfulness—and toward our fellow human beings—compassion and harmony. May God give us grace to do so!

Teach and Live What Is Good

DONNA THOENNES

WHEN WE UNDERSTAND Paul's desire to leave behind a strong and healthy church, we might expect that his letter would emphasize evangelism or church growth strategies. Instead, he says that our trust in the Lord and love for one another are ultimately what will strengthen the church.

In Titus 2, Paul contrasts Titus with false teachers and gives him a huge task. He tells him to teach his church the behavior and character which "accords with sound doctrine" (Titus 2:1). It is striking, however, that this teaching is not a series of theological lessons. It is godliness. Paul weds Christian doctrine with practical Christian duty.

Titus is to teach older men, younger men, and slaves specific behaviors and character traits. Likewise, he is to teach older women to be reverent and avoid two specific moral failures: slander and addiction to wine. Older women, in turn, should teach younger women what is good: to love their families, "to be self-controlled, pure, working at home, kind, and submissive to their own husbands, that the word of God may not be reviled" (v. 5). Paul's comprehensive categories of "older" and "younger" women suggest that all women have a responsibility to other women—to remind one another of theological realities that give meaning to otherwise mundane days. It takes intentional effort (and often some discomfort) to buck age segregation in the church and have meaningful discipleship relationships between generations!

Paul reminds Titus of the high pastoral expectations on him, instructing him "in all respects to be a model of good works" (vv. 7–8). His teaching must be bolstered, confirmed, and made effectual by example, not in word only. As Titus models good works, he will avoid criticism from those who oppose him (v. 8).

Paul veered from his normal pattern in this short letter to Titus. Instead of giving the gospel truth first and then the behavioral implications, he starts with behavior and then moves to gospel truth. Starting with "for"

(2:11), he offers the theological foundation for his instructions: Jesus has come and is coming again. "For the grace of God has appeared" (v. 11), and we wait for "the appearing of the glory of our great God and Savior Jesus Christ" (v. 13). Paul challenges us to look in opposite directions at the same time: backward to when Jesus came in grace, bringing salvation; and forward to when he will come again in glory. This deliberate orientation is a daily discipline and makes us "zealous for good works" (v. 14). We will be motivated to live righteously, letting our behavior flow from our belief, as we are grateful for Jesus's first appearing and hopeful for his second.

DECEMBER 2 · PHILEMON

The Religious, the Rich, the Rebellious, and You

ELYSE FITZPATRICK

IN THE LITTLE book of Philemon we learn about the transforming power of the gospel as we're introduced to three different characters, all of whom have been radically transformed by the good news. The first person we meet is Paul, a man who once put all his trust in his own ability to fulfill all the law's demands (Phil. 3:4–6). In fact, he was so sure of the rightness of his religion that he made it a practice to track down and kill anyone who didn't see things his way. Meet Paul, the Pharisee, the religious.

The next character we're introduced to is Philemon. Philemon had been what we might call a self-made man. He had been wealthy and owned slaves who had no choice but to do his bidding. As a Roman citizen, he had justice on his side. He could exact justice on anyone who failed to obey his orders. And yet he had become a follower of Christ, embracing the truth that he was a sinner in need of a Savior. Before coming to Christ, he could have viewed any of his slaves as little more than chattel to be used and discarded. He was Philemon the rich.

A third character we meet is a man named Onesimus. Once the property of Philemon, he had run away. Onesimus knew that the sentence of death hung over him: he was a runaway slave and possibly also a thief to boot, and the hope that his life would end in anything but painful execution was beyond imagining. So he hid himself where all criminals hide: in the big city, in Rome. He was Onesimus the rebel.

Three very different people who at one time viewed their lives as completely their own were each destined to meet a fourth person. They would meet Someone who would change everything, Someone who knew everything about them and yet loved them. They met Jesus, the Redeemer, who loved the religious, the rich, and the rebellious.

Jesus the Redeemer transformed them all. Paul the religious became the world's greatest spokesman for grace. Philemon the rich became Philemon the brother of a runaway slave. And Onesimus the rebel became Onesimus the humble, the redeemed. It is thought that Onesimus became the first bishop of Ephesus, and eventually died a martyr's death for the faith. Yes, execution in Rome was his destiny—but not for the reasons he once thought.

It doesn't matter what category you find yourself in today. Religious, rich, rebellious, or any other: Jesus the Redeemer can transform your life so that you can know you are truly loved, welcomed, and more useful to the Redeemer than you ever thought possible.

DECEMBER 3 · HEBREWS 1

Jesus: The Incarnate, Final, and Exact Word

BETHANY L. JENKINS

THE AUTHOR OF Hebrews was writing to Palestinian Jewish Christians—that is, people who were nationalistically Jewish, linguistically Hebrew, and religiously Christian. They were living in a pluralistic society, where being a Christian meant that they were marginalized and persecuted. Although it was fairly safe to practice the Jewish religion, the Roman authorities did not allow an open embrace of the Christian faith. Thus, the believers wondered, "If God loves us, why is our life so hard?"

To answer this question, the writer of Hebrews turns our eyes to Jesus. In Christ, he says, God has given us his incarnate Word. He has spoken to us by a *person* so that we may know him in relationship. God did not merely give us information about himself; he gave us himself: "he has spoken to us by his Son" (Heb. 1:2).

Moreover, in Christ, God has given us his final word. The writer of Hebrews compares what came before Christ to what came *in* him: "Long ago, at many times and in many ways, God spoke to our fathers by the prophets, but in these last days he has spoken to us by his Son" (vv. 1–2). In other words, Jesus is better, fuller, and more excellent; he is even superior to the angels (vv. 4–14).

Finally, in Christ, God has given us his exact word. "He is the radiance of the glory of God and the exact imprint of his nature" (v. 3). In the Old Testament, there is a special fire that leads the children of Israel through the wilderness (Ex. 13:21), stops the Egyptian army (Ex. 14:24), and descends upon Mount Sinai (Ex. 19:18). This fire is a physical manifestation of the glory of God so that we can behold his beauty, transcendence, and holiness. As the "exact imprint of [God's] nature," therefore, Jesus Christ is that fire. He is the glory of God in the presence of his people.

Thus, fixing our eyes on Jesus, we return to the question: "If God loves us, then why is our life so hard?" Some of us may think that since Jesus went to the cross, we do not have to suffer. Yet Christ calls us to share in his sufferings if we want to share in his glory (Rom. 8:17). We can endure adversity knowing that the incarnate, final, and exact word of God was abandoned by him so that we might be embraced. As we go from weariness to rest, from estrangement to presence, and from isolation to community, may we fix our eyes on Jesus until he has brought us home.

Above but Not beyond Us

CLAIRE SMITH

MOST PEOPLE LIVE their lives striving to reach their full potential. Many people finish their lives realizing they never reached it. Fewer people realize that it was always beyond their reach. Fewer still know the reason. It is because of sin.

God created us with great dignity and promise. He generously placed us over his creation. Humanity was the pinnacle of all he had made, for we were made in his own image (Gen. 1:26–2:3). But despite this great honor, we sought to be greater still. We sought to be God (Gen. 3:5–6). We each rebelled against his loving rule and earned for ourselves the just penalty of death. But God did not abandon us.

He gave us his Son, Jesus, "who for a little while was made lower than the angels" (Heb. 2:9) but is now crowned with glory and honor—not because of his power but because of his willing humiliation and suffering (1:3–4).

God gave us a representative man, who became one of us so that he could die as we die, not because of rebellion against God but out of obedience to him. He chose to take on flesh and blood for us, and humbled himself out of obedience and love (2:9; Phil. 2:6–8).

God gave us a Savior, who suffered the penalty of death for us and was made perfect through that suffering. So there is no other way to be rescued from the coming wrath than by him (Heb. 2:10; 1 Thess. 1:10).

God gave us a merciful and faithful high priest to represent us before him, to offer an atoning sacrifice for our sins, to intercede for us before the throne of God, to mediate between God and humanity. His priesthood will never end (Heb. 5:9–10; 10:12).

God gave us a perfect sacrifice for sins, offered once for all, the greater Son of David, who cleansed and sanctified us by his own blood (Heb. 2:11; 7:27; 9:26; 10:10, 14; 13:12).

God gave us a victorious liberator, who through his own death destroyed the one who holds the power of death—the devil—so that we might be freed from our slavery to the fear of death. He defeated the last enemy that threatened us all (1 Cor. 15:57).

Last but not least, God gave us a brother—a majestic brother seated in heaven (Heb. 1:3), a brother who cares for us, who like us has been tempted but was without sin. When we are tempted in any way, he is able to provide everything we need so that we do not sin.

His name is Jesus, and he is not ashamed to call those who believe in him "brothers and sisters." What a Savior!

DECEMBER 5 · HEBREWS 4:14–5:10

Draw Near—Stay Near

SUSAN HUNT

THE WRITER CONTINUES his theme of perseverance by calling us to "hold fast" (Heb. 4:14) to our faith. He anchors this gospel imperative to the ministry of Jesus our great high priest, who understands our weakness so well that he made provision for our perseverance. We are given fellowship and encouragement (3:13) and the word of God (4:12–13). Now the writer reflects on the powerful provision of prayer.

The invitation to "draw near" would be shocking to these Hebrew believers who lived in the context of the Levitical priesthood. They knew that approaching God required a representative who would offer sacrifices and intercede for them. They knew that only the high priest had access to the Most Holy Place, and that only once a year. The writer knew they would have questions, so he built the case for this radical shift by referring to the Old Testament to show the superiority and sufficiency of Christ to be our high priest.

High priests were chosen from among men (5:1), emphasizing their identification with the travails of humanity. Jesus partook of our humanity (2:14–18), "yet without sin" (4:15). A high priest did not act for himself alone but represented God's people (5:1). Jesus, the perfect Son of God, was "not ashamed to call them brothers" (2:11–12). The high priest offered sacrifices for the people (5:1). Jesus offered his perfect life as the perfect sacrifice. When he hung on the cross, he bore the full weight of his people's sin. If one drop of God's wrath against sin fell on us, it would obliterate us. Jesus drank the cup dry (John 18:11), and the veil in the temple ripped open (Ex. 26:33; Matt. 27:51; Heb. 10:19–23); through Jesus we have access to God! A high priest was called and appointed by God (5:4–6). The writer quotes Psalm 2:7 and 110:4 to show the eternality of Jesus's call, which both precedes and supersedes the Mosaic priesthood.

Jesus entered our condition so completely that he learned experientially what it means to obey as a human. He died for our sin, yet he does not despise us for our sin. He prays for our victory over sin.

If Jesus is your high priest, you are invited to draw near to a throne of grace, not a throne of judgment. Your perseverance in staying near to Jesus is bound up with his priestly ministry. Your assurance that you will persevere is not grounded in self-confidence but in the Father's promise to accept the work of Jesus on your behalf. Jesus will persevere in praying for your perseverance, so hold tight, with confidence that he always holds you tightly in his love.

DECEMBER 6 · HEBREWS 6:13–20

The Great Promise Keeper

MARY A. KASSIAN

NOT LONG AFTER becoming Christians, the Jewish-born readers of this letter were exposed to severe persecution—imprisonment, confiscation of personal property, and public ridicule, all because they followed Christ (Heb. 10:32–36; 12:4). Since then, they had faltered in their faith (5:11–13). Despondent over an apparent delay in the Lord's return, and with more persecution ahead, they had begun to abandon hope. Many were tempted to renounce Jesus and go back to the security of Jewish religion, whose adherents were protected by Roman law.

The writer of Hebrews wanted to confirm that Jesus Christ was God's messianic high priest—the fulfillment of the entire Jewish sacrificial system—he who "is able to save to the uttermost those who draw near to God through him" (7:25). He urged his readers to "have the full assurance of hope until the end" and to imitate the great heroes of faith who had unflinchingly trusted God's promise (6:11–12). In verses 13 to 20, the wavering Jewish believers are asked to consider the example of their ancestor, Abraham. God had promised Abraham that he would make of him a great nation, and that all the nations of the earth would be blessed through him (Gen. 12:2–3; 18:18). But in Genesis 22:16–18, God confirmed this promise with an oath. That promise was, so to speak, doubly binding: God's word made it sure, but it was additionally confirmed by his oath.

Abraham had to wait twenty-five years for the birth of his promised heir, Isaac. But during those long years, he doggedly trusted the Lord. When God makes a promise, God keeps the promise! The writer of Hebrews compares the oath God made to Abraham with the oath he made about the Messiah: "The LORD has sworn and will not change his mind, 'You are a priest forever after the order of Melchizedek'" (Ps. 110:4). Although he doesn't directly quote that oath, he expects his Jewish readers to make the association and get the point: Jesus Christ is the fulfillment of God's oath to provide the Jews—and all the nations of the earth—with a great, eternal high priest. The fact that God followed through on his oath to Abraham was proof that he intended to follow through on his oath to provide a great high priest. Abraham's experience was "strong encouragement" for the Jewish believers "to hold fast to the hope set before" them (Heb. 6:18).

The same encouragement lands on us. The Lord has given us "his precious and very great promises" (2 Pet. 1:4), and he is the great Promise Keeper. When times get tough, we can anchor our hearts on the certainty that "all the promises of God find their Yes" in Jesus! (2 Cor. 1:20)

When New Is Better

BRIAN BORGMAN

PRIESTS, SACRIFICES, and covenants are not usually the terms we use when we think about our relationship with God. However, the Old Testament unfolds these themes in a way that shows us we can relate to God only through a covenant. We approach him only through a mediator or priest. Our sins can be dealt with only through sacrifice. More than any other New Testament book, Hebrews shows us how the truths of the Old Testament are fulfilled in Jesus Christ.

The writer of Hebrews labors to show the supremacy of Jesus's priesthood. He is a better priest than Aaron and his sons because he is God's Son, he belongs to a better priestly order, and he lives forever. The writer also demonstrates the supremacy of Jesus's sacrifice: Jesus's sacrifice is better than all the old covenant sacrifices, since it was once and for all and it permanently took away our sins. Alongside these two great themes of Jesus Christ's priestly ministry and his priestly sacrifice is the new covenant, in Hebrews 8.

The old covenant was a good covenant. Moses was a good mediator. But there was something fundamentally broken in the old covenant. Moses and all the priests were sinners, and they all eventually died. The sacrifices were animals. The law was written on stone. The old covenant could not be effective, let alone permanent. God built the flaws into the system to point to something better. The old covenant demonstrated the holiness of God and the sinfulness of man, but something was lacking. The old covenant could not change the heart or truly remove our sin.

Jesus Christ came into this world to establish a new covenant. This new covenant was promised in the Old Testament, and as promised, it is better than the old. Christ himself is the better mediator, serving in the better priesthood, having offered up the better sacrifice, and now we have a better covenant enacted on better promises. Those better promises are the permanent removal of our sin, the law of God written on our hearts, and a true knowledge of God mediated by Jesus through the Holy Spirit.

We do not relate to God on the basis of the rules and regulations of the old covenant. That covenant is now obsolete (Heb. 8:13). God accepts us solely on the basis of the finished work of Christ our high priest, and he has brought us into an unbreakable relationship with him through the new covenant. We are secure in his grace through the work of God's Son. Because of Christ, our sins are forgiven and God remembers them no more. The new covenant is better!

DECEMBER 8 · HEBREWS 9:11-28

Touching the Blood of Christ

JOSEPH P. MURPHY

SHEDDING OF BLOOD has always been necessary for forgiveness of sins. Under the old covenant, sacrifice was necessary to cleanse and purify everyone and everything, so that they could face a new day of life on earth with God and his people. Death was the consequence of mankind's original disobedience. For the disobedience to be forgiven, the consequence must take place. Under the Mosaic covenant, God provided that death through the sacrifices of animals in the place of his people. But such sacrifices were effective for only a limited time and scope, and therefore they had to be repeated continually, for as long as people sinned.

God's provision for redemption under the law was necessary. It served its purpose in this limited scope, and it did, and still does, remind God's people of the profound seriousness of sin. Yet its limitations appeared clearly when Jesus Christ "abolished death and brought life and immortality to light through the gospel" (2 Tim. 1:10).

With his coming as high priest, Christ also took on the role of Sacrifice for all of his people. He could then offer himself for the sins of any fallen human who comes to him. By his death, his blood purifies all who avail themselves of it. Christ's sinlessness means that his sacrifice is without any blemish, a perfect life poured out in his blood. Our Lord bore the consequence of all of our sin himself, granting us forgiveness without requiring payment of any kind. We can contemplate but never fully fathom the depth of God's love for us in absorbing that ultimate and very human consequence of death. The mystery of Christ's person, both fully divine and fully human, runs throughout this contemplation: "*how much more will the blood of Christ . . . purify our conscience*" (Heb. 9:14).

Christ's accomplishment has eternal significance. His blood cleanses us for eternity, once for all. The efficacy of his blood is in the actual presence of God, not in a temple made to represent that presence. Symbols have always been necessary, but the reality to which they point is Christ. Christ is sacrificed for us, but how are we then covered by his blood? His blood doesn't touch us physically, as with the sprinkled blood of sacrificed animals. God calls us through the gospel, and we receive the cleansing by placing belief and trust in Jesus, our high priest and sacrifice. Faith is the touch of the heart that connects us to Christ.

DECEMBER 9 • HEBREWS 10:1–18

The One Sacrifice That Perfects Us

CAROLYN MCCULLEY

WHENEVER TRAGEDY STRIKES, it is our common response to enact new laws, impose rules and fines, and institute regulations to make our lives safer. These are not bad impulses. Many such efforts will prevent future harm. But we all know laws do not ultimately change hearts. They exist to protect the community at large and to uphold common standards of behavior. Essentially, our laws are designed to protect us from one another.

But God's law is designed for something entirely different. Hebrews 10:1 says God's law not only upholds his standard of holiness. It also foreshadows "the good things to come." When we think about the law, most of us tend to define the concept in terms of restrictions and regulations, not as a model pointing us to perfection. When the Old Testament law required continuous animal sacrifices, it was a reminder that "it is impossible for the blood of bulls and goats to take away sins" (Heb. 10:4).

God's law both highlights our shortcomings and points to the only One who could make a sacrifice once and for all to provide full forgiveness of sins and, astoundingly, to perfect those who are being sanctified by this sacrifice (v. 14).

Imagine how the original readers of Hebrews must have felt to be assured that this ceaseless cycle of animal sacrifice could end! Jesus Christ was the fulfillment of the prophetic promise found in Psalm 40:7–8, which is quoted in part in this passage: "Behold, I have come; in the scroll of the book it is written of me: I delight to do your will, O my God; your law is within my heart." Because Jesus delighted to do the Father's will, we now can have the same attitude. For his perfect sacrifice enables the prophetic promise, found in Jeremiah 31:33–34, that God will write his law on the hearts of his people and forgive their sin.

This passage in Hebrews is an emancipation proclamation of the highest order! We who have been enslaved to sin's relentless hold are now free—free from the futility of endless sacrifices, free from the judgment for our sin, and free to delight in God's will. What had once seemed impossible to accomplish has now been done on our behalf! We are rescued, redeemed, and renovated—made ready to worship him who sat down at the right hand of God and rested because his single sacrifice for our sins was sufficient (Heb. 10:12).

Gathering the Stories of Living Faith

KRISTYN GETTY

RATHER THAN BEING a random collection of individual stories, the Bible links people across hundreds of years of ancient history, moving purposefully forward, gathering people in as it tells its big story. In this chapter we find examples of the life just described a few verses previously—someone holding onto an enduring faith that preserves the soul. Chapter 11 helps define this faith. It is a confidence in the "not yet" that has been promised to us. It is not a faith that is blind or without reason, but a faith that does not hold all the pieces yet. It is not simply about "having faith" but specifically trusting in something, in Someone, in the one true God.

While each life story shows the many different colors of a faith-filled life, these men and women shared several common characteristics. First, they demonstrated a settled allegiance to God and a desire to please him. God's calling and God's reward made all else pale in comparison. Second, although they did not see what was to come, they trusted and built their lives around the One who holds all together and fulfills his promises. Third, they were imperfect people who put their confidence in a perfect God to restore them and bring them home. Although flawed, these people are celebrated for their faith, and we can take comfort in this.

These stories "still speak" (Heb. 11:4) to us today, reminding us that to live a life of faith is to please God. We can daily accept and extend the grace made available to us at the cross. We can live in freedom, trusting in God's promises and submitting to his goodness as he finishes the work he started. We can believe his perfect purposes are at work even when we can't see or understand them. As strangers in this world, we will never truly feel at home here—but we do not lose heart. Instead, with every new morning, we drink in his mercy and steady our lives once more to keep going, eyes homeward. May our lives be added to this list of saints, together declaring triumphs of faith and testimonies of his grace until the day our faith is as sight and our songs of praise to our faithful God fill the courts of heaven.

DECEMBER 11 · HEBREWS 12:1–17

Where Do You Look in Times of Trouble?

ELYSE FITZPATRICK

WE ALL KNOW what trouble feels like. Whether it arises from persecution, from the struggle with our own sin or the sins of others against us, or simply from life lived in a world stained with tears, no one escapes suffering. Trouble is painful, and sometimes that pain is so intense that it is all we can see. Overwhelmed by our trouble, we become weary and think that perhaps we ought to just throw in the towel. Then, amid all that weariness and pain, we begin to wonder whether God has stopped loving us—and that thought brings the greatest pain. After all, if God really did love us, he wouldn't allow us to suffer like this, would he? We begin to think that maybe he's stopped loving us, or that he's angry and punishing us for some reason. And that is the darkest pit of all.

Hebrews was probably written to a group of Christians suffering for their faith. Over and over again, the writer bids his listeners to hang on to their hope and faith amid great trial (Heb. 3:6; 4:14; 6:18; 10:23). In this passage in chapter 12, the author directs us to look away from our trouble and the doubt it creates and to look up to "Jesus, the founder and perfecter of our faith" (12:2). We are to look to the One who is the very reason for our faith and who has already completed everything necessary for it. Because he's already done everything necessary for the Father to welcome us as his own, we may confidently believe that he continues to love us—even amid this trouble. He meant it when he said, "It is finished." God's anger and wrath toward believers is truly finished.

When we look to Jesus, what do we see? We see a Savior who knows by experience everything there is to know about suffering. Think of this: Jesus, the founder of our salvation, was made "perfect through suffering" (2:10). Jesus, the Sinless One, who never did anything needing correction, suffered on our behalf—throughout his entire life, and most particularly when he bore all of God's wrath for all of our sin on Calvary.

Whatever you're facing today, if you're a believer, you can be assured of this: You aren't being punished for sin. No, Jesus bore all of God's wrath for all of your sin (1 John 4:10). Your suffering may indeed be part of God's kind discipline, or he may be teaching you more about his ability to satisfy you, or more about how his love can sustain you in trouble. But one thing is certain: he hasn't stopped loving you. In fact, his discipline is proof of his love for you (Heb. 12:6–8). Look to your Savior. He knows and loves you.

Hearing and Doing

BETHANY L. JENKINS

JESUS TOLD ONE of the Pharisees, "I say to you, unless one is born again he cannot see the kingdom of God. . . . That which is born of the flesh is flesh, and that which is born of the Spirit is spirit" (John 3:3, 6). But if we have been born again by the Spirit, why do we still struggle with the things of the flesh?

Being born again does not mean that our problems are over. It simply means that we have the potential to live as liberated people. When we become Christians, God changes our relationship with the law. Instead of it being a means of slavery, it becomes a means of liberty. The word that gives us new birth now becomes the agency to grow our new faith. The result is freedom. How does that happen?

First, we must receive the word—that is, we must hear it, accept it, and believe it. James writes, "Let every person be quick to hear, slow to speak, slow to anger; for the anger of man does not produce the righteousness of God. Therefore put away all filthiness and rampant wickedness and receive with meekness the implanted word, which is able to save your souls" (James 1:19–21). What, if anything, does anger (vv. 19–20) have to do with meekness (v. 21)?

Anger is energy released to defend something, and therefore, it is not intrinsically wrong. Jesus, for example, gets justifiably angry at injustice and abuse. There is, however, an anger that is sinful. It is rooted in pride. This more common kind of anger flares up quickly, leads us to do things that we regret, and comes from our need to defend our own self-image. The opposite of this type of anger is meekness. In other words, James is saying, "Do not be angry; instead, be humble. Release your self-righteousness, which denies the gospel of grace, and be receptive."

Second, if we want to be liberated, not only must we receive the word; we must also obey it. James writes, "Be doers of the word, and not hearers only" (v. 22). Full freedom includes both negative freedom—freedom *from* interference or constraint; and positive freedom—freedom *for* excellence and vision. When we receive "the implanted word," we receive freedom *from* sin and *for* righteousness. The word is not fundamentally a list of things we can and cannot do. Instead, it is a message from heaven that gives us the joy of being able to live out our theology. We get to be the "doers," not the "don't-doers." Thus, the more we receive and obey the word, the more free we become.

DECEMBER 13 • JAMES 2:14–26

Faith and Works

SUSAN HUNT

JAMES IS A passionate pastor, wanting his people to live in light of the gospel they profess and not to let their situation determine their attitudes and actions. He is also a practical pastor, pulling no punches as he shows the connection between faith and works.

This relationship between faith and works is incredibly current. We face the same temptation to antinomianism—the belief that we can have Jesus as Savior but not as Lord—that Christians have always faced. James warns us against such deception.

James says, "a person is justified by works and not by faith alone" (James 2:24). Paul says we are "justified by faith apart from the works of the law" (Rom. 3:28). How can both be true? Actually, these statements are fully compatible. James and Paul even reference the same person as an example to prove their point. In Romans 4 Paul refers to Abraham (Gen. 15:6) to explain that justification is God's declaration that a sinner is righteous on the basis of the righteousness of Christ. James refers to an event thirty years later (Genesis 22) to show that Abraham's faith was "justified," or proved, when he was willing to offer his son in obedience to God's command. Paul refers to the legal justification of a person *by God*. James refers to the judicial justification of a person's faith *before the world*. Both point to the same thing—our need for a Savior to redeem us from sin and to empower us to do good works (Eph. 2:8–10; Phil. 2:12–13).

Faith and works are distinct but inseparable. As the Reformers explained, it is faith alone that justifies, but the faith that justifies is never alone. Justification is *by* grace alone *through* faith alone, but it is not a faith that *is* alone; it inevitably produces obedience. Faith without works is dead, and works without faith is dead (Rom. 14:23). Saving faith, through the regenerating work of the Holy Spirit, is alive. It grows. It loves. It serves. It trusts and obeys God's word. If it doesn't, it is dead. It is false. It never was saving faith. Saving faith never dies; false faith never lives. The Holy Spirit produces obedience in those the Father justifies on the basis of the work of Christ.

This glorious gospel compels us to prayerfully examine our affections, commitments, words, finances, marriages, friendships, leisure—everything—to ask if our lives demonstrate the faith we profess. If so, thank God; if not, "repent and turn to God, performing deeds in keeping with . . . repentance" (Acts 26:20). Then anticipate that he will do in and through us more than we can imagine "according to the power at work within us" (Eph. 3:20).

DECEMBER 14 · JAMES 3:1–12

Why Did I Say That?

ELYSE FITZPATRICK

WE ALL KNOW what it is like to walk away from a conversation and say to ourselves, "Why did I say *that*?" How many times have you wished that you could take back words spoken foolishly, or longed to have another opportunity to voice what you really meant? Me, too.

Every one of us resonates with James's assessment: "We all stumble in many ways. And if anyone does not stumble in what he says, he is a perfect man" (James 3:2). When James says that it is only the "perfect" man who doesn't sin in what he says, he really does mean "perfect." He means absolute sinless perfection. In other words, the only people who never sin in what they say are those who are already in heaven. That's why James plainly states, "no human being can tame the tongue" (v. 8). No matter how we try, we'll never completely tame this indwelling evil, this small member "set on fire by hell" (v. 6).

James's warning about the destructive power of speech comes in a context—a context of God's love for us even though we continue to fail. James gladly addresses as brothers and sisters those who fail in their habits of speech (vv. 9–10). If God's acceptance of us were predicated upon our conquering this sin, we would be in dire straits indeed. Yes, we will continue to sin and struggle to tame this "restless evil, full of deadly poison" (v. 8), and we will never in this life be completely successful in doing so. But we do have hope.

Our hope lies in the fact that all of our foolish, destructive, unbelieving words were assigned to our Savior's record on Calvary. He answered for every foolish word we have spoken. And then his Father punished him in our place. He poured out upon him his full wrath for all our sinful speech, so that we would have *his* record of saying only the words his Father had given him (John 12:49–50).

It is in this hope, then—the hope of forgiveness and welcome through the saving work of Christ—that we must begin again, every day, the effort to speak words that reflect the transformation that has truly taken place within us. When our mouths are full of boasting about Christ's work for us, we will no longer feel driven to "[boast] of great things" (James 3:5) about ourselves. When we rest in his forgiveness, we won't feel compelled to curse others who have sinned against us.

Will we continue to struggle? Sure. But a day is coming when every word we speak will be glorious because our hearts will be filled with praise for what he has done for us. Thank God!

The Prayer of Faith

TRILLIA NEWBELL

THE FALL OF humanity into sin wreaked havoc on all that God had made good and beautiful. Sin corrupts, erodes, and destroys. The older we grow, the more we experience the physical effects of the fall. It doesn't take great illness to know that we are slowly decaying. Aches and pains that we never felt in our prime years become sharply noticeable. Some of us will experience debilitating disease as well. James provides some guidance for what we should do when this happens: "Let him call for the elders of the church, and let them pray over him. . . . And the prayer of faith will save the one who is sick" (James 5:14–15).

The leadership in present-day churches is organized in various ways, but in the Bible, "elders" refers to pastors and overseers (Acts 20:17, 28; Titus 1:5, 7; 1 Pet. 5:1–2). James encourages the sick to call on the elders because they were known as wise and mature in the faith. Paul explains that an overseer must be a man who is above reproach (Titus 1:7). So we too call upon these men, not because they are replacements for God but because God has given them to us for such times as these—to serve and pray for us when our words are few.

James does not say that the sick person must exercise faith in order to be healed, yet he does say that "the prayer of faith will save the one who is sick," and his sins will be forgiven (James 5:15). James could be addressing our physical sickness or our soul sickness—our sin. We know that God does not always heal. Even now, many of us have ailments for which we have prayed for healing, with no apparent results. God is good and sovereign over all circumstances. The healing may be on earth or in heaven with a resurrected, glorified body, but it is cruel to tell the sick that they will be healed, right here and now, if they just have enough faith.

Perhaps what God desires for us most when we become ill, and what this passage seems to highlight, is that we humble ourselves and call out for help. James encourages the sick to call the elders, and reminds us, too, that we should confess our sins to one another (v. 16). God has given us the church as a gift. We do not have to suffer alone. We can humble ourselves and ask for help, confess sin, and allow others to carry us in faithful prayer. Ultimately, we know that we can "with confidence draw near to the throne of grace, that we may receive mercy and find grace to help in time of need" (Heb. 4:16).

DECEMBER 16 • 1 PETER 1:13-25

Called to Be Holy

MIKE BULLMORE

THE GROUND OF our right relationship with God (justification) is the finished work of Christ on our behalf, laid hold of by faith (Eph. 2:8–9). We are not made right with God or kept right with God by our good conduct. Nonetheless, how we conduct ourselves is also a hugely important component of the Christian life. We are urged repeatedly to "walk in a manner worthy of the Lord" (Col. 1:10). It is this concern with conduct that occupies the apostle Peter in this passage.

From its bold opening verse all the way through, we are called by this passage to a distinctive way of living in the world. It calls believers to be "holy in all your conduct" (1 Pet. 1:15). It calls us to "conduct yourselves with fear" (v. 17). It calls us to "love one another earnestly" in "obedience to the truth" (v. 22).

But even in his explicit attention to conduct, Peter consistently anchors his call for Christian conduct in theological truth. Specifically, he urges us in our conduct to carefully ponder, and then take our cues from, four preexisting, God-anchored realities.

First, Peter points us to the "grace that will be brought to [us] at the revelation of Jesus Christ" (v. 13). Though the fulfillment is yet to come, God has given us the promise of this future grace and he intends that promise to wield influence and to translate into prepared, courageous, and sober-minded conduct now.

Second, Peter reminds us of the very character of God. Rather than taking our cue from our "ignorant" (godless) desires, we are to directly model our conduct after God's holiness, which here speaks not just of his other-ness but also of his moral purity.

Third, and perhaps most poignantly, Peter calls us to a certain conduct based on the inestimable price of our redemption: "knowing that you were ransomed . . . with the precious blood of Christ" (vv. 18–19). Consider Christ's death on your behalf, Peter tells us, and let that amazing sacrifice shape how you live.

Fourth, Peter speaks of the very source of our life—namely, "since you have been born again, not of perishable seed but of imperishable, through the living and abiding word of God" (v. 23), you should act in a way that reflects this source of life. Both the quality ("imperishable"), and the content (truth), of God's word shapes our conduct. Ultimately, what we need to see is that God is not calling for our obedience in a vacuum but in light of the richness of his goodness to us in the gospel.

DECEMBER 17 • 1 PETER 3:1-7

Wives and Husbands

ROBERT A. PETERSON

THE CHRISTIAN FAITH involves much more than matters of doctrine relating to the church. The apostles wrote letters teaching things pertaining to God, humanity, Christ, salvation, and much more, showing believers how to love God and other people. Paul and Peter included in their letters instructions for parents, children, and spouses, teaching us how to apply the gospel to family life.

This is what we find in 1 Peter 3:1–7. Peter exhorts Christian wives to submit to their husbands, even if the husband does not know Christ. Why? So that "they may be won without a word by the conduct of their wives" (1 Pet. 3:1). Christian women are to live out the gospel before their unsaved husbands. Wives are to put more emphasis on character development than on hairstyles, jewelry, or clothes (vv. 2–4). If they honor God in this way, they will be spiritual daughters of their mothers in the faith of old, such as Sarah (vv. 5–6). And the wives' submission is to be out of fear not of man but of God, who saved them by his grace.

Although Peter, in this passage, devotes more words to women than he does to men, his few words to men here hit home with all Christian husbands. That is because of the way God created men and women. Wives want to be loved and understood by their husbands. So Paul commands Christian men to love their wives "as Christ loved the church" (Eph. 5:25). Peter commands Christian men, "Live with your wives in an understanding way, showing honor to the woman as the weaker vessel" (1 Pet. 3:7). What does it take for a husband to understand his wife? Considerable love and energy spent in listening to her words and heart. Most men are physically stronger than their wives. Peter enjoins them to use their greater strength to love and defend their wives, never to abuse them.

Why does Peter place such difficult demands on believing husbands? Because their wives are their fellow heirs of the saving grace of God that brings eternal life (v. 7). Christian husbands and wives are spiritual partners. In addition, Peter warns of adverse effects of Christian men failing to understand and honor their wives; they risk hindering their own prayer life (v. 7).

Marital relationships are very important to God. In the home, above all, believers are by God's grace to live out the gospel before their children and a watching world. We have been saved by such lavish grace. It is our great privilege to exhibit this grace within marriage.

Entrusting Our Souls to Our Faithful Creator

CAROL CORNISH

WE LIVE IN a fallen world. What does that mean? It means that everything and everyone in this world is affected by sin. So, why are we shocked when bad things happen? When we are surprised by suffering, it often indicates that we do not understand what God is doing in the world and in our lives. Christians do not escape suffering; rather, we are called to be salt and light until Christ returns. This side of eternity, it is God's will that we suffer various trials and thus follow in our Savior's footsteps.

Suffering reveals what we live for and where we put our trust. When we suffer, we tend to respond in one of three general ways: with a stoical attitude, with unchecked emotion, or with trust in God's loving kindness. Stoics deny their pain; nothing touches them or ruffles their feathers. Those who display out-of-control emotions deny the goodness, wisdom, and sovereignty of God. But Christians who endure tragedies and heartache and respond with trust in God honor him greatly.

When we suffer, we face increased temptation to doubt the value of suffering. We will increase our sorrow if we think we are being singled out by God for negative treatment. But God allows suffering into our lives precisely because he loves us and wants us to trust his judgment about what we need. God calls us as Christians to a high standard—to a life that glorifies him no matter what. And in Christ we have an example of One who loved and honored God perfectly. Christ suffered and then was glorified. United to Christ, we too suffer, and we too will be glorified. Suffering is to be expected. It produces good as it weans us from the things of this world and directs our minds to the things above (see Col. 3:1).

There is joy in suffering (for the sake of Christ) because suffering identifies us as God's people. We are his very own, we belong to him, and God is committed to our care and to the salvation of our souls. We endure to the end because our Father carries us on to the end. Don't be immobilized by suffering. The Lord has never let down one of his people. He is full of grace and power, and he will provide the strength we need to endure—even enabling us to do so with a deep joy. Those who suffer in God's way continue to serve his kingdom, for they know that is where their hope is, now and for eternity.

DECEMBER 19 · 2 PETER 3

Transformed by Hope

SAM STORMS

THIS FINAL CHAPTER of Peter's second letter has one overriding concern: *hope*. Whatever mockery the world may make of our confidence in the return of Christ, whatever delay we must patiently endure until we see him face-to-face, it is our rock-solid hope in his coming that sustains us at all times. The non-Christian world will insist that our faith is a fantasy, but Peter assures us that "the day of the Lord" *will* come (2 Pet. 3:10). This is the hope that inspires "lives of holiness and godliness" as we look for the appearing of our God and Savior.

To live without hope that God has a purpose for human history, a purpose for *our* personal history, would be senseless and, for most of us, impossible. To live without hope that there is a conscious eternity following physical death, that Jesus Christ is alive and will deliver his people from death and sin and destruction, that truth will be vindicated and all lies exposed, and that genuine justice will finally be done, is simply inconceivable.

Our hope in the second coming of Christ empowers and motivates us to tackle head-on the problems of the present. It is hope in the second coming of Christ that gives meaning and value to life in the present. It is hope in the second coming of Christ and his power to transform our bodies and to subject all things to himself that gives us a reason to patiently endure the scorn of those who deny that Jesus will ever come back.

We must ask ourselves: what is the supreme attraction of Christianity? Is it the transformation of our bodies? Is it walking on the streets of gold and being reunited with friends and family who have already died? Is it mingling with myriads of angelic beings and traveling at will throughout distant galaxies?

As glorious as such things may be, they pale in comparison with the preeminent desire of our hearts—seeing and being with Jesus Christ! What will make the new heavens heavenly and the new earth a far better home than our present one is that Jesus will be there for our everlasting joy and satisfaction!

DECEMBER 20 • 1 JOHN 2:1-8

Process Matters

MICHELE BENNETT WALTON

"A NEW COMMANDMENT I give to you, that you love one another: just as I have loved you, you also are to love one another" (John 13:34). When Jesus spoke these words prior to his crucifixion, the new command may have seemed less radical than it really was. But to those who heard it after his death and resurrection, the fullness of Christ's love was much more plain. It could now be seen that loving as he loved was a profound calling.

This command to love was on John's mind as he wrote the letter of 1 John. For though these Christ-followers were less than sixty years removed from the historical events of his death and resurrection—as well as being surrounded by apostolic witness and indwelt by the Holy Spirit—there were false teachers and new doctrines circulating in their midst.

First John can be difficult to read. Full of bold assertions and knowing confidence, it makes us uncomfortable. The almost relentless call to obedience can tempt us toward legalism or even provoke us to despair. But the end of this passage in chapter 2 gives us helpful context for understanding all of John's exhortations.

John explains in verse 8 that the validity of the command to love can be seen in Christ and also in us "because the darkness is passing away and the true light is already shining." The Greek verb translated *is passing* is passive, whereas the verb translated *is shining* is active. The picture it paints is of the active light imposing itself upon the passive darkness. But the plainest implication is apparent even in our English translation: both verbs are continuous, pointing to the fact that darkness and light are both "in process" on this earth.

Process matters if we are to think rightly about our sanctification. Our obedience will always be imperfect in this age, where both darkness and light are present. We will never love exactly as Christ has loved us. But the light is overtaking the darkness, and that process is at work in us because of Christ. God's word even explicitly promises us, "He who began a good work in you will bring it to completion at the day of Jesus Christ" (Phil. 1:6).

So John's exhortations can motivate heartfelt obedience without causing us to live in fear. For "if anyone does sin, we have an advocate with the Father, Jesus Christ the righteous" (1 John 2:1). Our salvation is not contingent—today or any day—on our own righteous performance but on the ongoing advocacy of Christ.

DECEMBER 21 · 1 JOHN 3:11–24

Obey the Call to Love, and Rest Assured

W. BRIAN AUCKER

IT IS NOT EASY to love amid the relational challenges confronting us in our family, work, or church setting. Love potentially withers further when confronted by some who deride expressions of biblical faith. What does God require of us? Various voices sing out answers, but the first letter of John presents a New Testament answer (see also Mic. 6:8). John beckons his "beloved" people to practice genuine obedience, love, and faith. These verses at the heart of the letter reiterate important themes. They also direct believers to embrace a life characterized by love (1 John 3:11–18) and provide them with practical expressions of assurance (vv. 19–24).

The summons to "love one another" grips us immediately, reflecting one of John's key themes. John contrasts two divergent destinies: death and life. On the one hand, Cain hated his brother's righteous deeds. This led to murder and "abiding in death" (see v. 14). On the other hand, by virtue of God's saving actions in Christ Jesus, God's people—once spiritually dead—are now alive (v. 14; Col. 1:13). Practically, this reflects another reverberating theme in 1 John: in Christ, the believer abides in God and God in the believer (1 John 3:24). This also corrects counterfeit definitions of love. Love is defined as the atoning, sin-forgiving, life-giving sacrifice of Jesus Christ on the cross (v. 16).

There are several consequences that follow. First, as Jesus prepared John, so John prepares us for opposition. Do not be shocked if hatred arises from the world (v. 13; John 15:19–20). Second, for the Christian, actions must complement words. Loving as Jesus loved involves practical expressions of love—first toward fellow Christians (1 John 3:16; 4:19), but also toward enemies (Matt. 5:43–48).

The command to love others with a God-imitating love shakes us to the core, yet John renders assurance. God knows both our hearts and the difficulties faced in carrying out his commandments (1 John 3:19–20). Those united to Christ by faith will bear fruit. This is why John associates commandment-keeping with abiding (v. 24). Our confidence in God's presence means that he hears our prayers, but answered prayer and obedience to his commands work in concert. To pray expecting the Lord to hear our concerns while maintaining a disregard for his commands or lack of concern for what pleases him is not confidence but self-deception (2:3–5). The two great biblical commandments are to love God and love neighbor. John summarizes these crucial commandments to us: trust in Jesus Christ; love one another (3:23; Luke 10:27).

Propitiation and God's Great Love

TRILLIA NEWBELL

THERE ARE TIMES when the work of Jesus can be mistakenly minimized to the baby in the manger. The baby is the sweet little Jesus who eventually did miracles and then died on a cross and rose again. The Christmas season, especially, has a way of bringing out these sentimental aspects of the faith. All of those statements are true: Jesus came in the form of a baby, performed miracles, died on a cross, and defeated death, rising on the third day. Yet the implications of what Christ did are staggering. Consider what John tells us in these verses.

Jesus is the propitiation for our sins (1 John 2:2). Propitiation is the turning away of wrath, and here it refers to Christ's sacrifice that bears God's wrath and turns it into favor. And Jesus did not die for friends or for those who loved him first (4:10, 19). No, as Paul says, we were not Jesus's friends—we were his enemies, and yet he still died for us (Rom. 5:10). Sin must be punished, and therefore God poured out his wrath on his only Son. In turn, he gives those who trust in his Son the righteousness of Christ. Undeserved favor and unearned righteousness is ours in Jesus.

Perhaps the single word "propitiation" sums up the fullest display of God's love for us: God's outpouring of wrath on Jesus so that we would not have to endure it; and his crediting of Jesus's righteousness to us. Jesus turns away God's wrath, and God's love brings assurance and casts out fear (1 John 4:18). His perfect love gives us access to him, and we no longer have to fear death; in other words, we don't have to fear God's judgment.

We know that Jesus's death was an act of love because, as 1 John 4:8 declares, "God is love." God is continually pouring himself out for the benefit of others. There is not one thing the Lord does for his people that is outside of the confines of his great love. His display of love in the gospel is the purest and truest love that exists in the universe. And in light of the way we have been loved, God summons us to love others. Loving others is the mark of the Christian: "whoever loves has been born of God and knows God" (v. 7). Love is the consequence of a heart transformed by the gospel.

On paper this might seem easy, but lived out it is difficult because of sin. Remembering that *all* (including we ourselves!) have sinned and fall short of the glory of God (Rom. 3:23) helps us relate to our neighbor with understanding and grace. We all need grace and love and forgiveness. Christ died so that we might live for him, and we die to our flesh as we learn to love others.

Our Sacred Center

JANI ORTLUND

MORE THAN FIFTY YEARS after Jesus's death and resurrection, the apostle John is writing to a local congregation with both joy and concern. He feels a fatherly care for them and encourages them to live in the love of God, walking in the truth that is found in Jesus Christ alone.

John reminds his readers—and us—that at the very foundation of our life together is our love for one another (2 John 5). And this love is not just a feeling. The way we demonstrate love is by walking according to his commandments in glad-hearted surrender (1 John 5:3).

John calls this way of living "walking in the truth" (2 John 4). Jesus is that truth, revealing to us the true God (John 1:14; 8:28–29; 18:37). He is not just one way to God. He is not even the best way to God. Jesus is the *only* way to God, and there is no reality with God for those who don't believe this (John 14:6). Jesus is our sacred center.

And so John cautions us all to be self-aware, to watch ourselves (2 John 8). Do we doubt either the full deity or the full humanity of Jesus? Do we embrace thoughts contrary to Scripture, presented to us by those who do not believe Christ is the only true way to God? If so, we are being deceived. We must not let doctrinal confusion threaten our spiritual integrity.

John goes on to warn us not to reach out beyond the teaching of Christ. God is not in such speculations (1 John 2:19, 23). This truth is the litmus test with which we must judge every teaching about how people come to God. You can't have God without Christ; when you abide in Christ's teaching, you have both the Father and the Son.

John also cautions about welcoming teachers who do not embrace true Christian doctrine. This is not a prohibition against inviting sinners into your home. Nor is it an encouragement to be isolated from unbelievers. Rather, it is a call to reject *false teachers* from your home, lest you appear to endorse their teaching. This warning becomes more compelling when we remember that the early churches were house churches.

John tells us to refuse even to *greet* a false teacher (2 John 10–11). Certainly this doesn't mean we must never even say "hello" to someone we disagree with in matters of faith. Rather, it means that we should not extend approval, assistance, or full fellowship to such people. We never want to lend support to someone who is working against the truth.

Christ is God. And all who come to God must come through him, and only through him. To weaken this truth undermines our faith and our future. Christ is our sacred center.

DECEMBER 24 · 3 JOHN 5–12

Imitate Good

CAROL CORNISH

ONE OF THE maxims of the New Testament is that our actions reveal the state of our hearts (our whole inner being). As a tree is known by its fruit, so "out of the abundance of the heart the mouth speaks" (Matt. 12:34). Diotrephes demonstrated the state of his heart by his wicked words and evil actions. His selfish ambition was causing dissension among the Christians in the local church. The apostle John writes to encourage faithful Gaius, who, in contrast to Diotrephes, is "walking in the truth" (3 John 3). Gaius is to continue to do so, despite the manipulative behavior of Diotrephes. John tells him, "Do not imitate evil but imitate good" (v. 11).

All humans are imitators. We are influenced by other people and tend to behave in ways similar to those we admire. Just as John cautioned Gaius against being swayed by Diotrephes, we need to exercise good judgment as we imitate others. Paul urged the Christians to whom he wrote to imitate the Lord and even himself as *he* imitated Christ (1 Cor. 4:16; 11:1; Eph. 5:1; 1 Thess. 1:6; 2:14; 2 Thess. 3:7, 9).

We ought to imitate the good we see in other Christians, and we ought to live lives worthy of being imitated. As our lives conform to the character of Jesus, we will manifest the Spirit indwelling us. In this letter, John commends Gaius for caring for the traveling teachers who visited the church. Similarly, we can support those who are sent by God to do this work.

As you study his word, ask God to give you the wisdom to know whom to imitate. Look around your church and your circle of Christian friends. Who is living such a godly life that you ought to imitate her actions? Pray also for the grace to live a life that others can emulate. Most importantly, study the Gospels, looking to imitate the life of Christ. Pay careful attention to the way Jesus interacts with people, to his words and his actions. What does he do? How does he respond to people? Why one way with this person and a different way with another?

What kind of fruit is being produced in your life? Remember that "the fruit of the Spirit is love, joy, peace, patience, kindness, goodness, faithfulness, gentleness, self-control" (Gal. 5:22–23). Can others see these qualities in you as you "keep in step with the Spirit" (Gal. 5:25)? Can they learn how to replicate godly attitudes and behavior from watching your life? Is the kingdom of God advancing because you imitate the King? Through it all, remember to look to Jesus; as John says, doing good is the mark of one who has "seen God" (3 John 11).

DECEMBER 25 · JUDE 17–25

Perseverance under Attack

KRISTYN GETTY

PROVERBS TELLS US that there are two voices calling out in the marketplace—the voice of wisdom and the voice of folly. All through the Christian life, both voices ring in our ears. Jude warns believers to be aware of these voices and the dangers of folly that can so easily pull them off course. Verse 17 is the turning point in this letter, as Jude describes how the life of a believer should look amid such noise.

First, Jude reminds his readers of the apostles' warnings about scoffers and ungodly people who aim to lead others away from the Lord (vv. 18–19). The early Christians lived in a time of great persecution. The gospel was under attack. Similarly, all over the world today the church is facing both subtle and blatant pressures to compromise in proclaiming the gospel.

Second, Jude asks believers to pay attention to their own spiritual walk. He uses action words such as "build," "pray," "keep," and "wait" to describe how to maintain the healthiness and fruitfulness of their faith. We need to treasure all the ways that help keep us close to the Lord. It's easy to wander and to label what should be called "sin" as "individual choices." Likewise, we are tempted to call selfishness "freedom." We can fool ourselves into calling darkness light. It's difficult to stay true to what we've been taught, to live disciplined lives, and to wait for what we cannot yet see.

Where in my life am I blurring the lines of truth? Such inward examination should not make us fearful. It is necessary as we seek to fix our eyes on Christ. We don't keep the course of steadfast faith accidentally. It's a costly path that requires diligence, repentance, and the Holy Spirit's sanctifying work.

Third, Jude encourages believers to reach out to those around them who are struggling, showing mercy to people with spiritual or physical needs. Christians are to care for those in doubt, pulling them from danger while holding strong to their own convictions. Sin is cunning. It creeps in and can ensnare anyone. It is destructive, and all of us are vulnerable.

Despite this sober warning, Jude concludes his letter with a glorious note of hope, a hymn of praise to God. We can fall in so many ways, yet the grace that first called us continues to cover us. God holds us in the palm of his hand. Nothing can separate us from his love as he enables us to hear his voice and persevere. He is the one who one day will present us blameless before himself, to his glory and praise.

DECEMBER 26 · REVELATION 2:1-7

Losing the Love You Had at First

LEE TANKERSLEY

IT IS OVERWHELMING to consider the priority that love has in the Scriptures. The two greatest commandments are focused on love (Matt. 22:37–39). Love is the first listed among the fruit of the Spirit. We are even told that if we "have all faith, so as to remove mountains, but have not love" (1 Cor.

13:2), we are nothing. It is no overstatement to say that all of our responsibilities before our Lord revolve around love.

This does not mean that love automatically accompanies all of our works as believers, however. In Christ's letter to the church in Ephesus, we are reminded that we can involve ourselves in many good works and commendable actions while neglecting this most crucial call to love. The Christians in Ephesus were not lacking in terms of diligent labor. They had worked hard and persevered in purity, were disciplined, and had stood strong against temptations to compromise biblical beliefs and practices, even when it cost them (Rev. 2:2–3). Yet amid all these commendable actions, the Lord tells them, "You have abandoned the love you had at first" (v. 4). Though they were laboring in a great number of good things, they had lost sight of the call to love.

Considering that it is possible even to give our bodies to be burned but not have love (1 Cor. 13:3), we must make sure that love for our Lord and neighbor is our utmost pursuit. Our Lord tells the church in Ephesus to "remember . . . from where you have fallen; repent, and do the works you did at first" (Rev. 2:5). If we recognize a lack of love in our lives, the solution is no different. Maybe there was a time when we rejoiced in the achievements of a brother or sister in Christ, but perhaps in light of our own personal struggles and frustrations as we strive to obey Christ, our rejoicing has recently given way to envy. The Lord calls us to remember that former time, repent of our lack of love, and return to loving as we once did.

Repenting and restoring love in our hearts requires, of course, that we fix our eyes on the gospel. Repentance is met with forgiveness and cleansing only because Jesus Christ lived, died, and was raised for our justification. And it is only as we set our eyes on the one who "loves us and has freed us from our sins by his blood" (1:5) that we are strengthened to love our Lord and our neighbor. We will love only as we remember that he first loved us (1 John 4:19).

Worthy Is the Lamb Who Was Slain

ROBERT A. PETERSON

IN HIS VISION, John weeps in frustration because no one could be found worthy to open the sealed scroll revealing God's purposes for history. However, one of the elders tells John to stop crying and announces that a worthy one has indeed been found: "the Lion of the tribe of Judah, the Root of David" (Rev. 5:5). The people of God have numerous enemies more powerful than they: sin, death, Satan, demons, and hell. Christ is the Lion from Judah, the mighty conqueror of our enemies. He overcame them in his death and resurrection (1:18). By God's grace, through faith, we enjoy the fruits of Jesus's victory: knowing God now, and sharing life with him and his people in the new earth forever!

Though John expects to see the Lion, instead he sees a "Lamb standing, as though it had been slain" (5:6). Paradoxically, the Lion *is* the Lamb! Christ is both our champion and the "Lamb of God, who takes away the sin of the world" (John 1:29). The Lamb slain, Revelation's most common symbol for Christ, speaks of Christ's giving himself in death as a sacrifice to redeem us from our sins. The seven horns and seven eyes symbolize that Christ is all-powerful and all-knowing. When the Lamb takes the scroll from God, a song of redemption breaks out in heaven: "Worthy are you to take the scroll and to open its seals, for you were slain, and by your blood you ransomed people for God" (Rev. 5:9).

God's ways are not ours. It is as the Lamb slaughtered that Christ is the Lion who defeats our foes! His death and resurrection qualify him to open the scroll and reveal the secret things of God. Christ's atonement is both effective and universal—in the biblical sense. It is effective because it purchases people for God from humankind. It is universal in the sense that it effectively redeems human beings from every ethnicity, language, locale, and political entity. Christ's blood—his violent death on the cross—delivers them and constitutes them a kingdom and priests to God. By grace they actually share in the Lamb's right as priest to approach

God's throne, as well as the Lamb's right as king to rule. Already they are priests in that they serve God. And they will reign in righteousness with Christ on the new earth.

What happens in John's vision when the new song is sung to Christ? An explosion of praise erupts among saints and countless angels! The Lamb's attributes are ascribed to him in worship by the heavenly host and redeemed human beings. Finally, both Father and Son are adored universally and forever (vv. 11–14). This is our future! Let us take heart and enjoy the great hope that is ours.

DECEMBER 28 · REVELATION 7:9-17

Worthy Is the Lamb

KATHLEEN CHAPELL

IT WAS EASTER MORNING, and as the director of our volunteer church choir, I was on pins and needles. I had planned ambitious music for worship that morning, maybe too ambitious: several choral anthems representing a variety of musical styles, all celebrating our Lord's resurrection. The biggest piece, the one beginning the entire service, was "Worthy Is the Lamb," from Handel's *Messiah*, followed by the Amen chorus from that glorious work.

It was time. The prelude was finished, and the pastor read those wonderful words: "He is risen!" The congregation responded: "He is risen, indeed—Hallelujah!" The massive organ chord sounded, and the choir began:

Worthy is the Lamb that was slain,
To receive power, and riches, and wisdom, and strength,
And honor, and glory, and blessing!

And soon the counterpoint:

Blessing and honor, glory and power, be unto him, be unto him!

I watched my singers worship as they sang. There was Hugh, singing with joyful tears in his eyes. Richard grinned as he caught my eye; we both knew how hard he had worked to learn this difficult music. Tricia's life had been turned upside down in the past months, and she sang with a grateful heart for the Lord's nearness. Helen, at eighty-nine, was still singing with a clear, strong voice, still intent on honoring her Lord. Madeleine sang with the energy of a young teen; she hadn't yet faced the trials of a lifetime, but she was eager to join in the worship of her Savior.

I think of these dear ones when I read this passage in Revelation. What a privilege to praise the Lord together on this earth! And what a glorious praise it will be when we join the saints of the ages, together with "a great multitude that no one could number, from every nation, from all tribes and peoples and languages, standing before the throne and before the Lamb" (Rev. 7:9), together at last and forever at the completion of God's salvation plan!

We need not understand all the amazing images and prophecies in the book of Revelation to recognize this certain message: Jesus Christ died for sinners—he died for *my* sin—he rose again, conquering sin and death, and, praise God, I will spend eternity with him! I will join this chorus of saints, washed clean by the blood of the Lamb, who are before the throne of God, who shall hunger no more, thirst no more, weep no more.

"Blessing and glory and wisdom and thanksgiving and honor and power and might be to our God forever and ever!" (v. 12). Amen, and amen!

DECEMBER 29 · REVELATION 12

By the Blood of the Lamb

ROBERT A. PETERSON

THIS CHAPTER SYMBOLICALLY presents a great conflict between a woman and a dragon. It has two episodes: the woman and the dragon; and Satan being thrown down to earth. Common to both episodes is the dragon, "that ancient serpent, who is called the devil and Satan" (Rev. 12:9). But who is the pregnant woman? She is Mother Israel, so identified because of her being "clothed with the sun, with the moon under her feet, and on her head a crown of twelve stars" (v. 1; compare Gen. 37:9). The twelve stars stand for the twelve tribes of Israel, God's covenant people (Rev. 7:4–8; 21:12).

The woman gives birth to the Messiah, "who is to rule all the nations with a rod of iron" (12:5); he is Christ, the newborn King. The dragon attempts to kill him at birth. But his attempt is foiled as Mother Israel's "child was caught up to God and to his throne" (v. 5). Concisely, John sums up Jesus's life and ascension, portraying him as born, taken up to God, and reigning with him. The woman flees the dragon's wrath into the wilderness, where God protects her.

The second episode features a war in heaven. Michael, a spiritual prince and archangel (Dan. 10:13, 21; 12:1; Jude 9), and his angels oppose the dragon and his angels (Rev. 12:7). The devil is defeated and cast out of heaven with his angels. At this a heavenly voice proclaims victory: "Now the salvation and the power and the kingdom of our God and the authority of his Christ have come" (12:10). Why? Because Satan can no longer accuse God's people in the court of heaven. This is not the final victory, for the dragon still wreaks havoc on earth. Nevertheless, according to verse 11, Christian martyrs overcome the dragon "by the blood of the Lamb" (Christ's atonement) "and by the word of their testimony" (their faithful witness).

In verses 13–17, the dragon pursues the woman (symbolizing God's people), but God rescues and protects her again. Satan continues his attacks, but to no avail, as God continues to deliver his saints. Each time the dragon meets defeat, he becomes more furious and mounts more attacks on the church.

Christians disagree concerning the interpretation of this passage's details, but its main lessons are clear. Satan and his demons are powerful and seek to destroy the church. But thanks be to God that the Lamb has overcome them through his death and resurrection! As a result, although Christians will suffer, some even as martyrs, God will prevail, and his people, "those who keep the commandments of God and hold to the testimony of Jesus" (v. 17), will enjoy him now and forever on the new earth. And to that we say, "Hallelujah!" (19:1, 6).

The End of History

MIKE BULLMORE

THERE IS A LONGING in all our hearts for things to be set right. From small injustices that have wounded us to tragedies that have affected communities to large-scale global wrongdoing and the subsequent human suffering—we long for wrongs to be dealt with and all to be made right in the world. God has promised to bring this about. The book of Revelation is the vivid depiction of how he will do so.

Revelation 15, with its scene of the arrival of angels and the opening of the heavenly sanctuary, marks a significant turning point in the unfolding of the drama. Verse 1 is an introductory summary of the scene. We know this because, even though the angels are named there, it isn't until verse 6 that the angels actually appear. Verse 1, in its summary, says that the scene that will follow represents the completion of God's judgment on mankind. With these angelically borne plagues, "the wrath of God is finished" (v. 1).

When we read those words, we should pause and recognize that something of enormous importance is represented here. What is introduced in this chapter, and carried out in the next, marks the end of a human history in which things have not been right, and the ushering in of a new age where the "former things" will have "passed away" and everything will be made "new"; God "will wipe away every tear" and "death shall be no more, neither shall there be mourning, nor crying, nor pain anymore" (21:4–5). Revelation 15 is a vision of the culmination of justice and a transition into a peace and righteousness of which there will be no end (Isaiah 9:7).

This is why there is a host gathered before God's throne, eager to sing out to him in celebratory worship (Rev. 15:2). They are ready to sing because, through this exercise of his just wrath, God is dealing conclusively with evil. And when they do sing out they say, "Just and true are your ways, O King of the nations!" (v. 3). And again, "All nations will come and worship you, for your righteous acts have been revealed" (v. 4).

It is very important that we see this exercise of judgment as the exercise of God's justice, truth, and righteousness. Ultimately, we need to see it as a manifestation of his glory (v. 8), before which we should all bow. Only then will we sing, as those who share in Christ's victory and as those whose deep longings for justice, righteousness, and true world peace have been fulfilled, "Great and amazing are your deeds, O Lord God the Almighty!" (v. 3).

DECEMBER 31 · REVELATION 21:1-8

A Happy Ending

CAROLYN ARENDS

WE SHOULD NOT confuse the use of vivid symbolism in the book of Revelation with the telling of a fairy tale. The visions given offer not an alternate universe but rather the most accurate possible insight into our own. Suffering is expected and intense, threats and temptations abound, and the stakes are always high. So, when we reach the gloriously happy ending that begins to unfold in chapter 21, we needn't assume we are encountering the cheap sentimentalism that compromises so many of our human tales. This is how the story *really* ends. "Write this down," God tells John, "for these words are trustworthy and true" (Rev. 21:5).

There will be, we are told, "a new heaven and a new earth" (v. 1). Where many believers once assumed this was a vision of God *replacing* the existing order, a growing number of biblical scholars now believe a more accurate interpretation is that God will *restore* and *renew* his creation. What is beyond debate is the assurance that in the new Jerusalem, God himself will dwell with his people (v. 3).

What will it be like to live there with God? We will enjoy a level of connection that can only be conveyed in the most intimate of metaphors—we will be Christ's bride (v. 2). God himself will wipe away every tear from our eyes, and "death shall be no more, neither shall there be mourning, nor crying, nor pain anymore, for the former things have passed away" (v. 4). The yearning and thirsting that so characterizes our current existence will finally be over—we will drink daily and deeply from "the spring of the water of life without payment" (v. 6).

There is a modern-day story about a missionary couple who discovered a massive snake in their home in the jungle. A local man with a machete came to the rescue and decapitated the snake. The trouble was, due to certain features of the reptilian nervous and circulatory systems, the snake did not yet realize it was dead. The missionaries had to wait outside all afternoon while the headless snake thrashed about destructively in their home.

It was several hours into their ordeal before the missionaries realized that their decapitated snake was a kind of picture of Satan and evil in this world. Jesus has already crushed the serpent's head (Gen. 3:15). "It is done!" God declares in Revelation 21:6. The snake just doesn't know it yet. And so, we live in a thrashing time. *But we know how the story ends.* We can endure, and, even better, we can participate in God's glorious, unstoppable mission. He is "making all things new" (Rev. 21:5).

Notes

1. John Calvin, *Commentary on Genesis*, comment on Genesis 24:52.
2. C. S. Lewis, "Is Theology Poetry?" in *The Weight of Glory and Other Addresses,* rev. ed. (New York: HarperOne, 1980), 140.
3. John Calvin, *Commentary on the Psalms*, comment on Psalm 104:31.
4. Laurie Klein, "I Love You, Lord," 1978, House of Mercy Music.
5. Source unknown, often attributed to Blaise Pascal (1623–1662).
6. John Calvin, *Commentary on Jeremiah*, comment on Jeremiah 7:5.
7. David Hume, *An Enquiry concerning Human Understanding*, L. A. Selby Bigge, ed. (Oxford: Clarendon, 1902), 114–116.
8. John Calvin, *Institutes of the Christian Religion*, I.11.8.
9. Charles Spurgeon, *Charles Haddon Spurgeon's Autobiography, Volume 1: The Early Years, 1834–1859* (paperback ed., independently published, 2017), 80.
10. Charles Wesley (1707–1788), "And Can It Be?," 1738.
11. Martin Luther, quoted from the first sentence of the "Introduction" to his "Preface to the Letter of Paul to the Romans." Available in various editions of his works.
12. Martin Luther, *Works of Martin Luther*, ed. Helmut T. Lehmann (Minneapolis: Fortress, 2002), 48:12–13.
13. John Berridge (1716–1793), cited in Charles H. Spurgeon, *The Salt-Cellars: Being a Collection of Proverbs, Together with Homely Notes Thereon* (London: Passmore and Alabaster, 1889), 200.
14. Augustine, *Confessions* X.29.40.

Index of Scripture References

(italic typeface denotes featured texts)

ESV Women's Study Bible

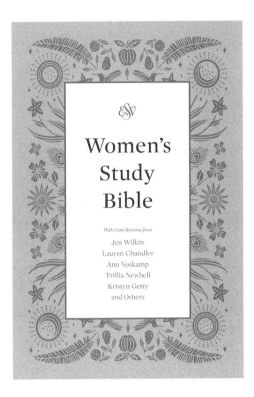

Designed to help women in all seasons of life pursue a deeper, transformational understanding of Scripture, the *ESV Women's Study Bible* was created for women who are serious about God's Word, want to learn more about what the Bible teaches, and want to apply Scripture's life-changing truth to everyday life.

For more information, visit **crossway.org**.